W9-BCC-136

DISCARD

Analysis of
Public Systems

The MIT Press
Cambridge, Massachusetts, and London, England

Analysis of Public Systems

Edited by

Alvin W. Drake
Ralph L. Keeney
Philip M. Morse

Copyright © 1972 by
The Massachusetts Institute of Technology

This book was designed by The MIT Press Design Department.
It was set in IBM Composer Century
by The Science Press Incorporated
printed on Mohawk Neotext Offset
by Halliday Lithograph Corporation
and bound in Interlaken AL1 395 Matte
by Halliday Lithograph Corporation
in the United States of America.

All rights reserved. No part of this book may be reproduced in any form or
by any means, electronic or mechanical, including photocopying, recording,
or by any information storage and retrieval system, without permission in
writing from the publisher.

Second printing, April 1974

Library of Congress Cataloging in Publication Data

Drake, Alvin W.
  Analysis of public systems.

  Includes bibliographies.
  1. Operations research—Addresses, essays, lectures. 2. Public administration
—Addresses, essays, lectures. 3. Municipal services—United States—Addresses,
essays, lectures. I. Keeney, Ralph L., 1944-   joint author. II. Morse,
Philip McCord, 1903-   joint author. III. Title.
JF1525.06D72   350'.000973   72-2075
ISBN 0-262-04038-7

Contents

Preface

This volume is presented in response to a need for a more up-to-date book on the application of formal modeling for the improvement of the delivery of public services. Because it is the work with which we are most familiar, chapters in this volume draw primarily upon the efforts of analysts at M.I.T. and at the New York City–Rand Institute.

Our first several chapters consist of perspectives on the interaction of analysis and the operation of public systems by professionals, each of whom has experienced a wide variety of applications from a particular point of view—a city budget official, the head of a large urban nonprofit research organization, a very experienced private consultant, and a representative of a large federal activity that works with many local government organizations.

Most of the volume consists of applications, ranging from preliminary formulations in relatively new areas of analysis to much more detailed aspects of particular systems. In general, our selection of topics favors fields of application that do not yet have their own highly developed methodologies and literatures.

Our own interests and activities in the analysis of public systems date back to research efforts begun by Drake and Morse at M.I.T. and to their 1966 M.I.T. Special Summer Program "Operations Research for Public Systems." A paperback book with that same title published by The M.I.T. Press reported on the presentations given during the first of five such annual programs. The 1970 program, offered by Keeney and Morse, emphasized present work and needs in the delivery of a particular set of public services and provided the initial stimulus for this volume.

Authors approached about participating in this volume displayed remarkable enthusiasm and cooperation, both in preparing their chapters and in improving the relationship among chapters. For compensation, authors received nothing more than copies of this book. Earnings from the volume will be used to support the Seminar and Visiting Scientist Programs of the M.I.T. Operations Research Center.

Our major debt, of course, is to our authors. Support for our own public systems work, some of which is presented in this volume, comes primarily from the Engineering Division of the National Science Foundation. The initial N.S.F. grant to the M.I.T. Operations Research Center, titled "Operational Methodology for Public Systems," constituted a pioneering effort for N.S.F. and for us. Results of that effort include widely disseminated research findings, the development of several new classroom subjects, and graduates with a new type of professional orientation.

The assistance of B. Katherine Swartz in preparing the final form of the volume has been invaluable. We are also particularly grateful to Ann LeMieux and Ginny Sherbs for their patience, kindness, and skill in typing so many versions of so many chapters.

Finally, in advance, we thank those kind readers who may send us their comments and corrections for future editions of this volume.

Alvin W. Drake
Ralph L. Keeney
Philip M. Morse

Operations Research Center
Massachusetts Institute of Technology
Cambridge, Massachusetts

Introduction

This book is focused on the use of quantitative, formal models as aids to decision makers faced with some types of public problems. The methods and models presented here are more closely associated with "operations research" than with other sets of words. These methods and models, of course, include only some of the systematic approaches useful for studying public systems. Some discussion of the underlying ideas for the use of formal models is included in this volume as part of Chapter 6.

There is far more experience and accomplishment in applying formal models and operations research to the military and private sectors than to the (nonmilitary) public sector. We are still limited by lack of experience, the difficulty of the problems, and by the restricted ability of public officials to direct and evaluate our modeling work. We hope this book will serve as one of many efforts at bridging this gap from both ends.

Probable Uses
This book is directed at students and professionals in technical areas and in public administration.

For a reader whose background is in analytic skills, we hope to introduce a relatively recent and rapidly growing type of work and something of the context in which it is performed. For public administrators and other management specialists, this book informs them of current work and assists them in developing their own perspectives on the role of formal models in the operation of public systems.

Several chapters involve little or no technical content. This is especially true for the first six chapters, which present overviews of the applicability, context, possible impact, and other aspects of public systems analysis. The remaining chapters, addressing particular problem areas, can be read to satisfy several types of interests. All of these chapters provide verbal accounts of the problems considered, the types of models employed, and the nature of results obtained. Several chapters include extensive lists of references. This book does not provide abstract presentation of mathematical techniques used in the analyses.

Some Background: Operations Research and Public Systems
The branch of applied science known as operations research arose when technical people began to ask why newly developed equip-

ment was not operating the way it had been designed to operate. In World War II, when it was crucial to get the most out of new equipment, this question was urgent enough to persuade a number of eminent scientists and engineers to try to find an answer.

Thus arose groups of technically trained personnel, employed in observing the behavior of operations, usually involving both people and equipment, and reporting their findings to the officer directing the operation. They came to provide an important link in the feedback control of the operation, helping ensure that the objectives of the operation were defined with care and pursued in a consistent manner.

After the war the techniques of data gathering and of theoretical analysis, which had been developed under pressure of the emergency, began to be applied by private firms. Wherever systems are so large or changes so rapid that the manager does not have time to learn by traditional empirical methods, these teams of analysts can help bring improvements in system design, operational efficiency, and effectiveness. Many industries now use such teams as part of the management and feedback control for their operations. Some have full-time teams, reporting directly to the top manager and having data-gathering contacts at all levels of management. Others utilize consulting teams from time to time to ensure the effectiveness of their operation.

Teams of analysts work best when in close contact with the top administrator; they can learn his criteria for operational success and can help him decide what policies can best achieve this result, without deleterious side effects. They do not, and cannot, supplant the manager; they are there to assist him in doing his managing as wisely as possible.

In the past few years, formal systematic analysis has begun to be applied more frequently to public services. To date, most of its impact has been at the lower echelons of management, where, *relatively*, the problems are not too complex, the data are easy to gather, and the models, whether adapted from other fields or newly created, are relatively simple. Only later, when these component parts of the "public system" are understood, can we hope for much improved predictions about the behavior of whole systems. A danger arises of which every analyst and every manager must be wary, the danger of excessive *suboptimization*. It may often occur that "optimizing" one part of the system is detrimental to the effectiveness of the system as a whole. For example, the fire chief's desire to have fire fighting apparatus almost always available at the instant of need, if achieved too well, reaches a point of diminishing returns and ceases to contribute positively to the need for adequate but economically sane expenditures on the full spectrum of municipal services. Such conflicting desires are typical of any complex operation and must be balanced at a higher echelon.

It follows that analysts must learn how each major part of a system behaves and they must refrain from advocating the suboptimization of one part before they learn what this will do to the system as a whole. Recent experiences in pest control and pollution prevention serve as examples of attacking too effectively only a few parts of complicated systems. Such cautions, of course, limit the rapid introduction of formal analysis into new fields and tend to discourage managers who desire quick advice. An analytic team must learn how to report on subsystems, while at the same time cautioning about possible side effects that need to be studied next.

The levels of systems and subsystems form an almost infinite progression. Nevertheless, we must try to study each major part, checking out models of its operation, before attempting to predict the behavior of larger, more complete systems.

This is the stage we have now reached in the study of public systems. Many teams are learning about and contributing to the operation of various aspects of the criminal justice system, fire departments, water resource systems, public transportation, health care systems, and so on. Such work began earlier in Europe than here, partially because several forms of centralized planning have been more acceptable there than here.

Results are now visible in certain problem areas. An overall impact will come about only as work is carried out on more parts of public systems so that, eventually, the knowledge can be assembled to predict the behavior of larger systems. Meanwhile, various elements can be improved in effectiveness, while possible side effects are being watched. Thus, it is important for public systems managers, at all levels, to become informed critics and consumers of formal analysis and, to some extent, actively participate in analyses of their parts of the system. Without close understanding and collaboration between managers and analysts, the possibilities for useful analysis of larger systems will remain remote.

Overview of the Book

We have tried to present reasonable coverage of the types of problems addressed to date. These range from large, vaguely defined issues (What is "clean" air? How do citizens talk to their governments?) to more defined concerns with the operation of particular systems (How does one propose and test operating rules for an urban fire department or for a regional blood bank?). Problems range also from strategic, one-of-a-kind policy or design decisions to the improvement of routine, continuing, operational services. Presently, most analytical contributions are found at the latter end of this range.

Studies can also be characterized by the types of systematic methods they employ, their place in the chain between planning and implementation, the level of governmental agency to which their products are addressed, and so forth. No book will do justice to all varieties of possible work. With emphasis on work we know well (primarily at M.I.T. and at the New York City–Rand Institute) and with some tendency to our common field (operations research), we have organized this volume in the following manner.

The first four chapters present perspectives from four authors who have had outstanding opportunities to participate in the interaction of public systems operations, management, and analysis. When much of the present analytic effort in New York City was developed, Frederick O'R. Hayes was the director of the New York City Bureau of the Budget, a position in which he served from 1965 to 1970. He writes as a city official, representative of the senior clients of studies, similar to many presented in this book. The New York City–Rand Institute, chartered as a nonprofit organization to apply "systems techniques" to some of New York City's major problems, was headed by Peter L. Szanton from its beginning in 1968 until 1971. He presents his insight on the operation of such an organization, along with a summary of some of the Institute's experiences. Martin L. Ernst, a vice president of Arthur D. Little, Inc., has had extensive experience in the analysis of public systems with a large, private consulting firm. He discusses views on the requirements for effective interaction between private consultants and public agencies. As chief of the Technical Analysis Division of the National Bureau of Standards, Edward Cushen has brought the analytic skills of his staff to the support of a very large number of city, county, regional, state, and federal

agencies. At the request of the editors, he reports some of his experiences, several years ago, with an innovative, experimental program with the governments of several medium-sized cities.

Chapters 5 and 6 are overviews and perspectives of a different
type, written by educators with experience in public systems analysis. Ralph L. Keeney and Howard Raiffa discuss the use of formal
analysis in the resolution of issues facing public agencies, with emphasis on the authors' professional specialty, decision analysis. As
a result of his involvement in a few of the projects reported in this
book, as well as some related experiences, Alvin W. Drake developed a particular concern with the ability of public agencies to
direct and to evaluate analytic work. He suggests some implications for the professional education of public officials and technical specialists.

Chapters 7 through 10 are concerned with the analysis of municipal emergency services. Edward H. Blum, head of the New York
City–Rand Institute Fire Project, discusses the general nature and
some details of a large, and particularly respected, effort in the
analysis of a public service. His chapter follows the project from
its formulation to the stage where many of its suggestions were accepted as policy changes in the operations of the New York City
Fire Department. Keith A. Stevenson has worked with emergency
ambulance services in several cities and he considers some of his
models and their implications. Richard C. Larson presents an example of a very brief, one-man study of a particular problem of
manpower assignment within one function of a police department.
This is followed by a chapter in which Jan M. Chaiken and Richard C. Larson assemble common aspects of many models for the
improved operation of urban emergency response units.

Chapters 11 through 14 consider particular aspects of public
services by means of relatively detailed formal models. John B.
Jennings begins by modeling a blood bank at a single hospital and
suggesting criteria for the evaluation of alternative policy decisions. He then develops a larger model to assist in the design and
evaluation of regional blood banking systems. Philip M. Morse
looks at library operations, showing, among other things, that the
data that organizations collect and the data that would most effectively support policy decisions may be quite different, although
the former can, through formal models, provide useful inferences
about the latter. Amedeo Odoni discusses a set of questions about

airport runway usage and models for the investigation of these questions. An introduction to modeling and analysis for some particular postal service operations is provided by Charles C. McBride.

Joseph Ferreira served as the initial quantitative analyst with the U.S. Department of Transportation Insurance Study. In Chapter 15 he presents two types of examples where quite mathematical formal models are critical to the understanding of policy issues in the field of automobile insurance, an area that is increasingly subject to public regulation at the state level.

Chapters 16 and 17 are concerned with aggregate, policy-related models for very large systems, and Chapter 18 studies the establishment of objectives for one such system. Alfred Blumstein directed and Richard C. Larson participated in the Science and Technology Task Force of the President's Commission on Law Enforcement and the Administration of Justice. They have continued their development of broad models that characterize the entire criminal justice system and their collaboration to suit their models to the operational, educational, and research needs of officials within that system. Their general model and a variety of its applications are presented in Chapter 16. David H. Marks has had considerable experience in the area of water resources, including a term of service with the Delaware River Basin Commission. He demonstrates formal models for bringing some structure to the discussion of programs for the protection of water quality. Howard M. Ellis and Ralph L. Keeney also discuss models associated with environmental quality. Their concern is with rational structures for developing realistic, operationally useful objectives for "clean air" programs.

Robert N. Grosse, looking back in Chapter 19 on his experiences as assistant secretary for planning and evaluation at the U.S. Department of Health, Education, and Welfare, begins with some comments on the introduction of simple formal models as planning tools at H.E.W. He then indicates, by example, some of the initial analyses performed on a variety of policy issues in the health field.

Chapter 20 is concerned with preliminary modeling and experimentation with systems to allow a government agency to be more conscious of public need and sentiment. The authors, John D. C. Little, Chandler H. Stevens, and Peter Tropp, have worked in this area with the governments of Puerto Rico and Massachusetts.

Our next two chapters represent very different types of modeling efforts in the field of education. Reginald W. Revans demonstrates the construction of formal models of classroom activity as a step in trying to understand the educational process that operates between teacher and students. From a very different point of view, Robert M. Oliver discusses the use of aggregate models for university planning and operations.

A recently completed study of a one-of-a-kind decision problem concludes the book. In Chapter 23 Richard de Neufville and Ralph L. Keeney present the analysis and results of a study to select a strategic policy for developing the airport facilities in the Mexico City metropolitan area. The analysis represented part of the basis for a presidential level decision.

Most of the chapters contain thorough references, both for related applications and for the mathematical techniques employed.

1 From Inside the System
Frederick O'R. Hayes

1.1 Introduction
The inauguration of John V. Lindsay as mayor of New York City began a period of reexamination and analysis of the programs and operations of the city government. The central vehicle for this reexamination and analysis was the Planning-Programming-Budgeting system (PPBS). PPBS provided a strong conceptual and managerial basis for a government-wide effort backed by the discipline of the budget and by the procedures for its preparation and administration.

At the beginning, the city had scant resources devoted to program or systems analysis. A small economic analysis staff in the Housing and Redevelopment Board and the Work Performance Staff in the Bureau of the Budget were the only significant, albeit limited, exceptions. Outside consultants had not been used for this purpose to any appreciable degree. The climate was, in fact, often hostile to the introduction of explicit analysis and to the use of outside experts.

An analytic capacity was built in the city in four basic areas:

1. *Bureau of the Budget.* New divisions were established for program planning and analysis and for budget and information systems, eventually with a total professional staff of nearly 40.

2. *Operating Agencies.* Parallel staffs were developed, with varying degrees of success, in the operating agencies. About 100 professionals are now so engaged.

3. *New York City–Rand Institute.* A new nonprofit corporation was established as a joint venture by the city and the Rand Corporation, currently with 50 to 60 professionals financed from $2 million annually in city contracts plus a $900,000 Ford Foundation grant as well as funds from the Department of Housing and Urban Development and the National Science Foundation.

4. *Consultant Contracts.* Effective arrangements were developed with several private consulting organizations, notably McKinsey and Company, MDC Systems, Inc., Kerr Associates, and Meridian Engineering. The nonprofit Vera Institute of Justice also played a major role. Approximately $5 million was invested annually in such contracts.

Even in a city with a budget approaching $8 billion, the increase in analytic resources was of sufficient magnitude to create an important impact upon the city.

The total effort embraced four different types of activity:

1. Program analysis and evaluation.
2. New program and project design and development.
3. Project management—the controlled implementation of new programs and projects.
4. Infrastructure design, especially the development of information systems.

The four types of activity are more often interrelated and overlapping than they are distinct and separate. The pragmatic phase of program analysis is the consideration of alternatives, and usually alternative approaches are conceived and developed as a basic part of the analysis process. Project management actually always entails the detailing and further articulation of new program design and frequently requires a return to, and a further extension of, the basic program analysis. Information system design often represents a modeling or analysis of program process.

A very substantial part of the program analysis has represented frankly opportunistic suboptimization. In many bits and pieces or components of large and complex program processes, the opportunities for improved program operation were visible to the unaided eye of the analyst. A comparison of the costs and benefits of the alternative against existing practice could be obtained through a relatively simple and limited analysis.

In other instances, pilot projects were designed and implemented to test new approaches. The pilot project is especially important where the attitudes of the participants are important to the success of the project. But the pilot project is also, in some ways, a substitute for the analytic modeling of complex program processes. For instance, most of the work of the Vera Institute [1] with the police and the courts has involved the use of pilot projects. And obviously the effect of paper and plastic bags on either overspill of garbage in the street or on collection productivity could scarcely be calculated without testing.

Some particular note should be made of project management, that is, process modeling and network scheduling. This approach was applied, relatively routinely, to the city's 2700 capital construction projects with the only novel element being the emphasis upon preconstruction activities. It was later extended to a wide range of new programs and activities to which the mayor attached a high priority. In both instances, it is yielding significant insights in the design of both program and administrative process and resultant proposals for improvement. Consultants, especially MDC Systems, Meridian, and Kerr Associates have played the major role in project management.

Only a small part of the total program research effort can properly be called operations research. In fact, only a small part involves the use of highly sophisticated analytic techniques. Most of the analysis of this character has been carried out by the New York City–Rand Institute and by other consultants, partially because of the special skills involved and partially because City staff were more effectively used in more immediate policy and program research and in formulating issues for consultant research. The extensive research program is summarized in Chapter 2 by Peter L. Szanton, and aspects of the Institute's efforts in the areas of police and fire operations are covered in separate chapters.

1.2 Experiences with Various Agencies

The program research effort worked well in some city agencies and departments and abysmally in others. The sine qua non was an administrator both interested in program analysis and able to attract the staff to do the job. The New York City–Rand Institute and the consultants provided a basis for a sizable expansion of effort over that possible with direct staff alone, but, in the main, they were useful only in those agencies with staff sufficiently competent in analysis to manage the consultant effort.

Program analysis and research live an uneasy coexistence with program operations. Operating officials are typically skeptical and often cynical and distrustful of analysis. Yet, the most effective program research depends upon close collaboration between operating managers and the researchers. This has been achieved to a surprising degree, sometimes by heavy participation of program operators from the very beginning, sometimes by a convincing demonstration of relevance.

The program research to date has had some marked limitations. First, significant efficiencies have often been effected in the production of proximate program outputs without any certain effect upon ultimate program objectives. For example, a score or more

analyses of component elements ot police operations were aimed
at increasing the proportion of police time spent "on the street."
This assumed that more police street hours would provide better
citizen protection against crime and increased apprehension of
criminals. But it is fair to say that we still do not know the relationship, if any, between police patrol and crime. We can have,
however, some confidence in the hypothesis that police do in fact
prevent crime; further observation and research will provide a
basis for more definitive conclusions.

It is not at all certain that we can view the problems of education with equal optimism. The successes of analysis at this stage
consist largely of the documentation of the failure of remedial
programs. The future, at this juncture, would appear to involve a
continued trial-and-error approach. The same is true to a very
large extent of all teaching programs from the university to manpower training. The complex world of health care has proved even
more difficult and less manageable.

One of the real frustrations has been the appalling growth rate of
virtually all of the problems to which municipal programs and services are directed. Crime, drug use, fire alarms, solid waste, automobile traffic, street litter, underprivileged children in the schools,
housing deterioration, illegitimate births, and female-headed families are all outrunning the programs designed to deal with them.
The continuing need to run twice as fast to stay in the same place
buries the successes from changes in the system and often obscures
their impact. Dollar savings, when achieved, have almost invariably
been reinvested in program or service expansion.

The research is best judged in terms of departmental programs
rather than individual projects. The best of these programs tend to
be relatively large, diverse, and of a continuing nature.

The fire department initiated its program of operations analysis
in January 1968. It is currently one of the most advanced among
city departments and virtually unique among municipal fire departments in the United States. The ingredients of success are a
small, technically competent staff under Assistant Commissioner
Paul Canick and the continuing support of a New York City–Rand
Institute team headed initially by Edward Blum.

The Institute's fire department research program is described by
Blum in Chapter 7. The program includes the single most ambitious project in the city's research program—a simulation model of

fire response. The research on the model produced highly significant and relevant interim outputs, including the design of an adaptive response policy in lieu of the standard dispatch of three pumpers and two ladders and an analysis of the impact of both additional companies and changes in response on high work-load companies. The Institute's work has also included a technological search effort that led to the use of "slippery water," a model of the Brooklyn dispatching operation which led to a redesign of that operation, and a study of a consolidated communication facility.

A new computerized dispatching and information system is in design on the basis of performance requirements developed with the aid of the Institute team, and many smaller but significant projects have been completed by city staff. A new and more economic apparatus replacement policy has been developed. A relatively simple analysis of fireboat requirements was the basis for reductions in the fleet with savings more than sufficient to cover the costs of the entire analytic program. More recently, a computer analysis has demonstrated (to the surprise of most of us) that increased peak-hour fire department staffing can be achieved within the rotating shifts required by state law.

In the Housing and Development Administration, program research involved a sizable agency staff under Assistant Administrator Arthur Spiegel as well as the extensive use of consultants including the New York City–Rand Institute, McKinsey and Company, Meridian Engineering, and others. The major output is an analysis of housing deterioration in New York, identifying the effects of rent control and of low-income tenancy, and estimating the increases in cash flow to landlords necessary for proper building maintenance [2]. This analysis was the basis for the first major modifications in rent control since its imposition nearly 30 years ago.

The Institute's work also includes a series of studies [3] covering most aspects of the economics of housing in New York—costs of construction and maintenance, the effect of subsidies and of tax exemption, the characteristics of occupants of subsidized housing, mortgage structure and investment return of various private housing, and evaluations of various specific city housing programs. Joan Ransohoff, of the Bureau of the Budget, and McKinsey and Company completed a major analysis [4] of the housing of the one-seventh of the City population dependent on welfare.

The impact of code enforcement programs on housing quality has been evaluated [5] and appropriate changes developed in program structure and emphasis. A structure has been devised for linking the extraordinarily large and complex site clearance programs under local and federal urban renewal with housing production capability under various federal, state and local programs. A problem building analysis model has been developed by the Institute and McKinsey to estimate both public costs and effect on owner economics of various assistance measures [6].

The Environmental Protection Administration (EPA) has responsibility for the collection and disposal of solid waste, sewage collection and treatment, water supply, and air pollution abatement. A series of studies [7] has been completed under Assistant Administrator Jerry Mechling with the aid of McKinsey and Company. A prototype analysis of air pollution control was done [8] by Carter Bales of McKinsey, identifying effect of control on on-site incineration including the most economic options for owners of buildings of various sizes, the probable impact upon solid waste collections, the estimated cost per household to cover landlord expenditures, and a sensitivity analysis for all factors involved. A parallel analysis was carried out for public buildings. A management information system has been designed to monitor the progress of compliance. Another study, reported by Ellis and Keeney in Chapter 18, was done with the cooperation of the EPA and represents a rather exploratory attempt to structure a particular air pollution problem.

The problems of waste collection and disposal and street cleaning have been given considerable attention by the EPA staff, McKinsey and Company, and the Bureau of the Budget staff. The approach has concentrated on subcomponents of the total system. The form of containerization has a significant effect upon productivity and street litter. Consequently, the use of paper and plastic bags was tested successfully with a 20 percent increase in productivity and reduced street spill; the city's health code is being amended to permit their use. An analysis of possible uses of large-scale detachable containers indicates savings of two-thirds or more in collection costs and this approach is now being extended as rapidly as possible. New larger collection trucks promised both a reduction in maintenance costs and a major increase in productivity by reducing trips to dump from a daily average of 2.5 to about 1.5; the entire fleet is being replaced on the basis of this analysis.

The 80,000 cars abandoned in the city annually are now being collected by scrap contractors at a net payment to the city, whereas collection by city tow trucks was costing nearly $50 per vehicle.

Optimum daily manpower requirements have been developed from a computer model designed by EPA in cooperation with the State University of New York at Stony Brook [9]; a proposal is now in collective bargaining for a revision in workday patterns to accord with the desired distribution.

The Urban Systems Laboratory at M.I.T. was engaged to analyze the effects of a $1 billion water tunnel project [10]. A computer model of the system was constructed to do this; the result was a significant reduction in tunnel size but a rejection of a proposed alternative for a pumping rather than a gravity flow system. The New York City-Rand Institute is developing a computer model of Jamaica Bay to explore the problem of sewage and effluent distribution in the bay with the expectation that the same technique can be used on the tidal estuaries around which the City is built [11].

The New York City-Rand Institute's work on police and criminal justice [12] covers some significant aspects of police performance: a distributional algorithm for allocating patrol cars, an evaluation of the effectiveness of police apprehension activities, an analysis of the effect of internal police disciplinary activities, an analysis of police recruitment and promotion, an evaluation of an experiment with increased staffing in a pilot precinct, and many other projects. The Institute's work with the department has been technically first rate, a genuine *succès d'estime*. But, unfortunately, a close relationship with departmental leadership never developed. The commissioner eventually terminated the contractual relationship.

The Vera Institute has also carried out substantial work for the police department and in the criminal justice area generally [1]. Vera has its own style and technique. Analysis proceeds quickly to pilot project design, collaboratively with the department. The pilot project is staffed and managed by departmental personnel to the maximum extent possible. After evaluation and debugging, successful pilot efforts are extended eventually to a department-

wide basis and Vera withdraws. The projects have included the
Manhattan bail reform and release on recognizance projects designed to reduce detention due to inability to supply bail, the
Bowery alcoholics project (now run by a separate nonprofit corporation) intended to substitute treatment for arrest of skid row
alcoholics, traffic and crime alert to eliminate unnecessary police
officer appearances in court; summons in lieu of arrest to eliminate the lengthy process of physical apprehension and booking for
lesser offenses; prearraignment to reduce that time for more serious cases; and the work release project to provide pretrial and presentence opportunities to shift delinquents to gainful employment.

These are the strongest of the agency research programs but
some disservice is done in not covering the less advanced efforts of
other departments and administrations. Some examples of work in
other areas should, however, be mentioned.

One is the allocation model built by Sally Streiter of the Bureau
of the Budget and further developed by McKinsey and Company
to test alternative distributions of education funds among community school districts [13]. Another is the estimating equation,
developed by Jon Weiner and David Gordon of the Bureau of the
Budget, predicting welfare case load solely on the basis of the real
benefit level [14]. Steve Savas of the City Administrator's Office
has produced a model to determine the optimum distribution of
city ambulances [15]. Gerald Hillman of McKinsey has done yeo-
man work in the construction of resident and commuter income
distributions and in the design of tax yield functions [16].

1.3 Some Lessons

Our experience has provided a number of important lessons in
research program design. The first, and most significant, is the importance of scale. We have been most effective in those agencies
that have moved rapidly to a relatively large-scale effort. The larger
program can be fairly comprehensive, embracing long-term as well
as short-term research and covering issues and projects arising from
operating officials as well as those identified by researchers. It can,
unlike small analysis efforts, make itself felt as a real factor in
agency decision making.

The second lesson is the value of pluralism. Complex combinations of direct staff and consultants produce numerous different
viewpoints and approaches, usually with real worth to the agency.

The housing research program is the best example, but it is true of all of the most advanced research efforts.

Third, continuity is also worthwhile. Despite staff turnover, the value to the city of both the direct staff members and consultants who understand the city's peculiar administrative and political topography is inestimable. Successful adaptation is replicable and the multiagency involvement of some consultants has proved especially valuable.

Last, the techniques of analysis vary widely, but the initial research agenda has involved, in the main, relatively simply analytic methods. This may change as the prospects for high-yield, low-cost analysis are exhausted and as new information systems begin to produce more of the data needed for formal model building.

References

1. See *Annual Report to the Criminal Justice Coordinating Council, July 1, 1970–June 30, 1971*, Vera Institute of Justice, New York City. See also, *The Manhattan Court Employment Project*, Criminal Justice Coordinating Council and Vera Institute of Justice, July 1970; *The Manhattan Court Employment Project of the Vera Institute of Justice*, Summary Report on Phase One: November 1, 1967 to October 3, 1969; *The Manhattan Bowery Project: In Lieu of Arrest Treatment for Homeless Alcoholics*, The Criminal Justice Coordinating Council of New York City and Vera Institute of Justice; *The Manhattan Summons Project*, The Criminal Justice Coordinating Council of New York City and Vera Institute of Justice; *Criminal Justice Coordinating Council: Two Year Report*, April 1969; *Toward Justice for the Poor: The Manhattan Bail Project*, Vera Foundation; *The Manhattan Bail Project: An Interim Report on the Use of Pre-Trial Parole*, C. E. Ares, A. Rankin, and H. Sturz, New York University Law Review, volume 38, no. 1, January 1963; *Pre-Trial Detention and Ultimate Freedom: A Statistical Study Foreword*, P. Wald, New York University Law Review, vol. 39, no. 4, June 1964; *The Effect of Pre-Trial Detention*, A. Rankin, New York University Law Review, vol. 39, no. 4, June 1964; *National Conference on Bail and Criminal Justice: Proceedings of May 27–29, 1964 and Interim Report May 1964–April 1965*, U.S. Department of Justice and the Vera Foundation, Inc.; *Experiments in the Criminal Justice System*, H. Sturz, Legal Aid Briefcase, February 1967; *Neighborhood Youth Division Program*, Vera Institute of Justice mimeo.

2. *Rental Housing in New York City: Volume 1. Confronting the Crisis*, edited by I.S. Lowry, RM-6190-NYC, New York City–Rand Institute, February 1970.

3. See *First Annual Report. The New York City–Rand Institute*, October 1970. See also, the following New York City–Rand Institute publications: *A Guide to Government Activities in New York City's Housing Markets*, D. J. Dreyfuss, J. Hendrickson, R-5673-NYC, November 1968; *Research on New York City's Housing Problems*, I. S. Lowry, P-4002, December 1968; *An Analysis of Alternative Measures of Tenant Benefits of Government Housing*

Programs with Illustrative Calculations from Public Housing, E. O. Olsen, J. R. Prescott, P-4129, November 1969; *Can Public Construction and Rehabilitation Increase the Quantity of Housing Service Consumed by Low-Income Familes?* E. O. Olsen, P-4256, December 1969; *The Effects of a Simple Rent Control Scheme in a Competitive Housing Market*, E. O. Olsen, P-4257, December 1969; *An Efficient Method of Improving the Housing of Low-Income Families*, E. O. Olsen, P-4258, December 1969; *A Methodology for Evaluating Housing Programs*, J. S. DeSalvo, P-4364, April 1970; *Effects of the Property Tax on Operating and Investment Decisions of Rental Property Owners*, J. S. DeSalvo, P-4437, August 1970; *The Landlord Reinvestment Model: A Computer Based Method of Evaluating the Financial Feasibility of Alternative Treatments for Problem Buildings*, C. P. Rydell, P-4477, October 1970; *Reforming Rent Control in New York City: The Role of Research in Policy Making*, I. S. Lowry, P-4570, November 1970; *Factors Affecting Maintenance and Operating Costs in Federal Public Housing Projects*, C. P. Rydell, R-634-NYC, December 1970; *Housing Code Enforcement in New York City*, M. B. Teitz, S. Rosenthal, R-648-NYC, May 1971; *Housing Assistance for Low-Income Urban Families: A Fresh Approach*, I. S. Lowry, P-4645, May 1971; *Rental Housing in New York City: Vol. II. The Demand for Shelter*, I. S. Lowry, J. R. DeSalvo, and W. B. Woodfill, R-649-NYC, July 1971.

4. *The Housing of Welfare Recipients: Opportunities for Improvement in New York City*, McKinsey and Company, 1969. Basic findings are included in *Rental Housing In New York City, Vol. II, The Demand For Shelter*, Lowry, et al., New York City–Rand Institute, June 1971.

5. *Housing Code Enforcement in New York City*, M. B. Teitz, S. Rosenthal, R-648-NYC, New York City–Rand Institute, May 1971.

6. *The Landlord Reinvestment Model: A Computer Based Method of Evaluating the Financial Feasibility of Alternative Treatments for Problem Buildings*, C. P. Rydell, P-4477, New York City–Rand Institute, October 1970. See also Chapter 8 in *Urban Analysis*, M. D. Kilbridge, R. P. O'Block, and P. V. Teplitz, New York, 1970, for an earlier version of the same approach.

7. Largely unpublished studies and drafts. Reports prepared by McKinsey and Company included the following: *Increasing Collection Productivity Through Selective Allocation and Improved Design of Trucks*, September 1970; *Improving Collection Productivity—The Project Team Manual*, November 1970; *Establishing Collection Productivity Targets, Volume I: Improving Management Information Reporting Within the Bureau of Cleaning and Collection*, December 1970; *Volume II, Exhibits: Improving Management Information Reporting within the Bureau of Cleaning and Collection*, January 1971.

8. *Air Pollution Issue Map*, McKinsey and Company, New York, 1968.

9. *Heuristics in Manpower Scheduling*, L. D. Bodin, A. C. Tucker, S. M. Altman, and E. J. Beltrami, Urban Science and Engineering, State University of New York at Stony Brook, USE Technical Report # 71-7.

10. *Systems Analysis of the Primary Water Distribution Network of New York City*, Urban Systems Laboratory, Massachusetts Institute of Technology, August 1969. See also R. de Neufville, "Cost-Effectiveness Analysis of Civil Engineering Systems: New York City's Primary Water Supply," *Operations Research*, vol. 18, no. 5, pp. 785-804, Sept.-Oct. 1970.

11. *A Water Simulation Model for Well-Mixed Estuaries and Coastal Seas:*

Vol. I. Principles of Computation, J. J. Leendertse, RM-6230-NYC, New York City–Rand Institute, February 1970; *A Water Quality Simulation Model for Well-Mixed Estuaries and Coastal Seas: Vol. II. Computation Procedures*, J. J. Leendertse, E. C. Gritton, R-708-NYC, New York City–Rand Institute, July 1971; *A Water Quality Simulation Model for Well-Mixed Estuaries and Coastal Seas: Vol. III. Jamaica Bay Simulations*, J. J. Leendertse, E. C. Gritton, R-709-NYC, New York City–Rand Institute, July 1971.

12. See the following New York City–Rand Institute publications: *Applying the Concepts of Program Budgeting to the New York City Police Department*, A. J. Tenzer, J. B. Benton, and C. Teng, RM-5846-NYC, June 1969; *An Analysis of the Apprehension Activities of the New York City Police Department*, P. W. Greenwood, R-529-NYC, September 1970; *Public Order Studies in New York City*, S. Wildhorn, P-4250, November 1969; *The Police Internal Administration of Justice in New York City*, B. Cohen, R-621-NYC, November 1970; *Designing for Security*, M. I. Liechenstein, P-4633, April 1971; *Minority Recruiting in the New York City Police Department*, I. C. Hunt, Jr., B. Cohen, R-702-NYC, May 1971; *Reducing Crime in Apartment Dwellings: A Methodology for Comparing Security Alternatives*, M. I. Liechenstein, P-4656, June 1971; *Improving Public Safety in Urban Apartment Dwellings: Security Concepts and Experimental Design for New York City Housing Authority Buildings*, W. Fairley, M. I. Liechenstein, and A. Westin, R-655-NYC, June, 1971; *Aids to Decisionmaking in Police Patrol*, J. S. Kakalik, S. Wildhorn, R-593-HUD/RC, February 1971; *Aids to Decisionmaking in Police Patrol: Survey Response*, J. S. Kakalik, S. Wildhorn, R-594-HUD/RC, February 1971; *Response of Emergency Units: The Effects of Barriers, Discrete Streets, and One-Way Streets*, R. Larson, R-675-NYC/HUD, April 1971; *Methods for Allocating Urban Emergency Units*, J. M. Chaiken, and R. C. Larson, R-680-HUD/NSF, May 1971; *The Flow of Defendants through the New York City Criminal Court in 1967*, J. B. Jennings, RM-6364-NYC, September 1970; *The Flow of Arrested Adult Defendants through the Manhattan Criminal Court in 1968 and 1969*, J. B. Jennings, R-638-NYC, January 1971; *Potential Uses of the Computer in Criminal Courts*, P. W. Greenwood, P-4581, February 1971; *Quantitative Models of Criminal Courts*, J. B. Jennings, P-4641, May 1971.

13. *Allocating Educational Funds to the Community School Districts*, McKinsey and Company, November 1970.

14. See "Income and Welfare in New York City," D. M. Gordon, in *The Public Interest*, no. 16, Summer 1969.

15. "Simulation and Cost-Effectiveness of New York's Emergency Ambulance Service," E. S. Savas, in *Management Science*, vol. 15, pp. B608–B628, 1969.

16. *The Development of a City Tax Program*, G. P. Hillman, McKinsey and Company, to be published.

2

Analysis and Urban Government

Peter L. Szanton

2.1 The Background

For almost four years New York City and the Rand Corporation have been engaged in an enterprise distinctive if not unique: the subjection of a wide variety of the City's problems to the scrutiny of independent analysts. This chapter is the attempt of a participant in that enterprise to describe the background of that effort and the novel arrangements made to institutionalize it, to outline the nature and effect of the analyses produced, and then to reflect on some of the lessons this effort has taught some of its participants.

As Chapter 1 makes clear, the Lindsay administration took office not only with a set of policy predispositions but also with an interest in rationalizing governmental operations. Regarding itself as having a mandate for reform and aware that New York's resources would prove steadily less adequate to its needs, the new administration determined both to secure greater financial assistance from the state and federal governments and to use available resources to greater effect. The latter effort centered on an attempt to develop effective planning, programming, and budgeting (PPB) systems in the City's operating agencies. The PPB systems required that decisions involving the allocation of resources were to be made only after the review of explicit statements of agency objectives, of at least crude analysis of alternative programs for meeting those objectives, and of detailed estimates of the relative costs and benefits of those programs. It was within this context that, late in 1967, Mayor Lindsay and Mr. Hayes asked the Rand Corporation whether it could assist in the analysis and reform of a number of city functions. At the same time the City was seeking similar support from universities and commercial consulting firms, and—most significantly—was greatly strengthening the internal analytic staffs in the Budget Bureau and in most of the major municipal departments.

For some years Rand had been interested in domestic issues; it had sponsored research in urban transportation, water supply, mental health, local government data requirements, and other nonmilitary, public problems. But is had been oriented primarily toward national security affairs and had never worked directly with a municipal government. Rand welcomed the chance to address a

variety of problems in a major city. So, for several months, small
groups of interested Rand researchers met with city officials to see
whether issues that concerned them seemed amenable to analysis
of a kind the Rand staff could perform. Outlines of studies to be
performed for four City agencies emerged from those meetings; in
January 1968 contracts were signed, Rand established a New York
office, and the work began.

The first four contracts were with the City agencies responsible
for police, fire protection, housing, and health. During 1968, work
began as well on problems of water pollution, correctional institutions, welfare, and the New York labor market. By the spring of
1969 a staff of 40 professionals was engaged in some 30 separate
studies in those areas, and it was clear that much of the research
under way would prove useful and important; some had already
done so.

But it was also clear, to the mayor's office and to us, that this
effort could become the basis for something more useful than a
barrage of single-shot studies. We thought that Rand's New York
office should become a new institution. It was to be independent
enough to be critical of City policies, insulated enough from the
City's daily operational concerns to work persistently on underlying problems, but close enough in its working relations with City
agencies to produce recommendations that were timely, realistic,
and usable. With luck, it would become a major center for urban
policy analysis, and a repository of detailed understanding about
the City. Unlike occasional special-purpose consultants, we would
work steadily with City agencies on a broad range of their problems; unlike university-based urban study groups, we would measure our success in terms of decisions affected rather than students
trained or reports produced.

By the summer of 1969 the legal framework for such an organization—the New York City–Rand Institute—had been established.
Essentially a joint venture of Rand and New York City, it was a
New York nonprofit corporation, staffed and administered by
Rand, subject to the oversight by a board of trustees chosen jointly
by Rand and New York City, and intended to work continuously
on issues of concern to New York. It was to be funded largely by
the City but partly also by foundations and federal agencies. Its
resources were its staff, which consisted by then of some 50 professionals of—I believe—remarkably high quality, drawn from a

wide range of academic disciplines and organized not by discipline but by area of substantive interest. Economics, mathematics, operations research, and engineering were the backgrounds that predominated, but the staff contained as well members trained in political science, biology, law, city planning, psychology, sociology, cost analysis, business administration, public health, a number of computer programmers, and a miscellany of other skills.

2.2 The Work
The work undertaken by the Institute has varied widely in technique, in purpose, in difficulty, in cost, and in result. In the first four years something over 120 separate studies have been undertaken. Some have attempted simply to establish basic information, like the analytic catalogue that described, in comparable terms, the very large number of housing programs in effect in New York. Some have been quick operational studies, performed by one analyst in a matter of days—such as the analysis of the number of telephone operators required to handle the shifting patterns of calls for police services discussed in Chapter 9 by Richard C. Larson. Others, like the extended analysis of the economic, social and demographic forces at work on the City's rental housing stock [8,9], have occupied six or seven researchers steadily for three years. Some have sought to apply new technology, as did the experiments that demonstrated that the addition in minute amounts of long-chain polymers to the water stream in a fire hose could greatly increase both the amount of water discharged and the distance the stream would travel in leaving the hose [1]. Some have extended the boundaries of an analytic skill, such as the simulation modeling of fire department operations described by Edward H. Blum in Chapter 7, and the work that produced a model able to specify in detail how, at numerous points in Jamaica Bay, water quality would be affected by alternative waste treatment facilities, under varying tidal conditions, temperatures, and potential changes in the configuration of the bay [5, 6, 7].

All of this work had one of three purposes: to increase the efficiency or effectiveness of a given municipal service, to revise a city policy, or to improve the process of city decision making.

Better Municipal Services
Our most common objective has been to help operating departments provide improved services within constrained budgets. We

have drawn such improvements from the redeployment of men
and equipment into patterns that more closely match variations in
demand, from information systems that bring together information on interdependent functions, from methods for more accurately assessing the consequences of alternative procedures, and—
occasionally—from the introduction of new technology. This is
work performed most readily by analysts whose training is in engineering, or operations research, or economics. It is work to which
quantitative, analytic tools are well adapted, and for which the
limitations of those techniques are least important. And it is work
worth doing. In a city that commits some $6 billion annually to
the provision of services, efficiency gains even of one-tenth of 1
percent can pay for a major research institute many times over.
Equally important, such gains increase disproportionately the
sums available in succeeding budgets for innovative and discretion-
ary uses. By fairly conservative calculation, the implemented results of Institute studies are now saving the City some $20 million
annually.

More Effective Policies
Less frequently, but with greater effect, the work has helped to
shape an agency's understanding of what had to be done. A good
example is provided by the housing research. The Institute's largest contribution here was not the battery of studies that helped
bring about a change in the housing and rent control laws. It was
the perception that underlay those studies: the major problem of
housing policy in New York was not the faster or cheaper provision of additional units of new construction but rather the maintenance of the City's existing housing stock. It was this stock that
would necessarily form the bulk of the City's housing inventory
over the next 30 or 40 years; but this stock was deteriorating and
being abandoned—the result of a speeding process of disinvestment
—at rates that would swamp any manageable program of new construction. This was by no means an insight unique to the Institute;
it had been urged both by some housing professionals and by affected interest groups. But in the light of the political and fiscal
problems of facing this situation, the historic emphasis of the
housing profession on building, the tendency of the public to
"keep score" on the administration in terms of the number of new
units constructed, and the incomplete and contradictory nature of

the data on deterioration, new construction remained the preoccu-
pation of the City government. The Institute's studies, together
with work done by others, presented first a picture of the deterioration process that was comprehensive, detailed, and authoritative
enough to compel attention; and then the design of a plausible, if
difficult, strategy for dealing with it.

Improving the Decision Process

The third objective is to improve the process by which policy is
routinely made. Some of our work addressed this task directly
by helping City agencies improve their planning, programming,
and budgeting functions; and to strengthen internal planning and
analytic staffs. And interestingly, the effect of these efforts has
been reinforced by others. Helpful analyses generate interest in
other analyses. Reliable data organized to illuminate a major problem stimulate demand for similar information on other issues. The
ability of a consultant's staff to provide a quick analysis of a new
proposal's probable effect generates a demand for internal staffs
of similar capabilities. And slowly new expectations and higher
standards emerge. It begins to seem routine that the effect of
public programs be reviewed, that alternative methods of achieving their purposes be considered, and that the relative merits of
those alternatives be measured with some care, against criteria
explicitly laid out.

Indeed, in some departments, this emerging new environment
may create a fundamentally changed view of management responsibility. Especially in those municipal services that, like fire and
police, have promoted only from within, and where everyone
within has begun at the lowest rank, the implicit traditional view
has been that a superior is someone who can do his subordinate's
job better than the subordinate. A chief of detectives must be a
master detective. A fire chief is expected to be a fire fighter of unusual skill. This is a tradition that serves well in emergencies but
poorly in the day-to-day operation of large organizations. In such
departments, analysts oriented toward improving the allocation of
managerial energy and departmental resources will find the going
difficult. But with luck, persistence, and departmental allies, they
may end by providing the perspectives and the tools—program-
matic budget formats, relevant new technologies, simulation models capable of testing the consequences of new modes of opera-

tion—which give the departments' managers both a changed view of their jobs and improved means for performing them.

2.3 Observations and Lessons
Let me now note the somewhat special environment in which we have worked in New York, and then attempt to elicit some lessons from that experience.

Special Circumstances
The Institute's experience in New York has taken place under circumstances unusual in both helpful and unhelpful ways. The New York environment was a favorable one in several respects. The effort had the strong and active support both of a mayor and of a budget director. It was performed for a City with a budget large enough—even when under strain—to be able to support sustained research. The client was a reform administration wanting to change the way municipal decisions were made, and anxious to improve the efficiency of City services and the effectiveness of City policy.

The effort was complicated, however, by two other characteristics of New York: the strength of its civil service tradition and the diffusion of its power. The government of New York is huge, employing some 400,000 people. Simply by force of numbers, therefore, government employees are a potent political force. The traditions of a career civil service are strong, moreover, and municipal unionism has grown highly militant. In such a city, the unions—especially those of the uniformed services—are suspicious of a body like the Institute on at least two grounds. They consider it likely to seek ways of reducing the work force; and they will regard its simple presence in the service of departmental management as weighing against the unions in the struggle to determine whether they or departmental officers will manage the departments. Some higher level civil servants, by contrast, view nongovernmental analysts less as a threat to the number of civil service jobs than as usurpers of tasks—attractive and important tasks—that might better have been left to analysts who were themselves civil servants.

The second complication, related to the first, is that although New York's government is in form that of a "strong mayor," power in fact is even more widely diffused than is usual in American cities. Municipal unions dispute changes that might elsewhere be unquestioned prerogatives of management; changed work rules for policemen or firemen may require action of the state government; actions within the City's power and not requiring the concurrence of one legislature—the city council—may need that of a second—the board of estimate; policy changes affecting a particular neighborhood or ethnic or racial group will normally find these groups alert, articulate, and determined to participate in the making—or blocking—of decisions that affect them; and business leadership is neither concerned nor powerful enough in local issues to provide the support for initiative that it does in other American cities. There is remarkably little of importance, in short, that the executive branch of the City government, having decided that it should be done, can count on being able to do.

As a citizen one may take pride in the degree to which government is thus made a participatory process. One may then view the major problem as that of equipping the various participants to enter the process on more equitable terms and with better information; I shall return to this point. But for the analyst accustomed to clients—especially in the federal government or the industrial world—whose abilities to put recommendations into practice are far less encumbered, such an environment may seem frustrating indeed.

Despite the idiosyncracies of New York, much of the Institute's experience does seem relevant to the general problem of improving policy making through research and analysis. The following reflections all seem to me of wider applicability.

The Conditions Required

The conditions required to produce research are familiar enough: researchers, adequate support, access to data, and time. Where the work is intended to be relevant to policy, an additional but equally obvious condition is imposed: researchers must address their work to issues policy can affect. But many research organizations, like the Institute and its New York clients, will wish to go further: to link analysis and policy making, and to produce work that will actually affect decision making. That objective imposes additional requirements:

Agency support

First, there must be support for the analytic effort from potential decision makers within the government. The support need not be wholehearted or entirely free of skepticism, but it must exist. Where it is absent, the analyst will find his access to data restricted, and the participation of city staffs in the study foreclosed. Perhaps most important, he will be unable—alone—to identify the kinds of analyses that might affect policy, or the schedule on which they must be produced in order to affect it.

A period of grace

Second, the analyst, if he is attacking problems of any scope or complexity, will need a period of grace. The tougher the issue, the longer the period required. Grace may be provided by personal relationships with the client, by the reputation of the analysts, by fiat from a mayor's office, or by extraordinarily good luck in solving quickly some other problem of concern to the agency. However derived, it will normally be necessary in order to sustain the effort during those opening months in which the presence of the analysts represents demands on the governmental agency—demands on time, attention, money, assistance in the acquisition and interpretation of data, and patience—which normally will far outweigh the assistance the analysts can then provide.

A manageable problem

Third, the problems attacked analytically should be within the power of the client—as well as the analyst—to deal with. The better and more conscientious the analyst, the more likely he is to be concerned with larger and more fundamental problems, and the more likely he is then to identify difficulties or to propose conclusions that the client, at least over the short run, has no substantial power to effect. A good example is the Institute's work for New York's Economic Development Administration (EDA), research that moved rapidly to an examination of the demographic forces at work in New York and to the economics of the labor market in the metropolitan area. These were issues of clearly fundamental importance to the mission of EDA, but they posed a challenge far beyond the capability of that agency, and indeed beyond that of the city government, to cope with. They consequently generated little interest and have had, as yet, no impact on policy.

Ripeness

Related to the last requirement is the problem of timing. There are rhythms of policy change, less predictable than the tides, but equally powerful. The more important the issue being addressed, the more necessary that it be not only a matter of concern to the governmental client, but in some larger sense ripe for resolution. The clearest example in our work has been the housing research. These were studies which, in addition to concluding that various administrative changes were necessary, proposed that a large-scale program of rent-assistance payments be instituted, and that rent controls should be revised to permit rents to rise until they covered the costs of adequate building maintenance. The latter two recommendations, and especially the last, involved great political difficulty. Roughly half the City's residents occupied rent controlled apartments. Controls had endured for more than a quarter of a century, and the recent tendency had been to extend them to previously uncontrolled housing. But the pace of building deterioration and abandonment in New York seemed to be accelerating, landlords and the banks continued to press for relief, and probably most important, the rent control regulations were due to expire at a fixed date in the near future. The issue, though painful, was timely. One result was that it was possible for the Housing and Development Administration to commission a large-scale analytic effort—involving various City staffs and a variety of consultants— two years in advance. Another was that an eager audience for the studies was assured.[1] But most important, it proved possible in fact to revise controls as we had proposed. (Rent assistance, involving budgetary demands beyond the City's current resources, was deferred.)

Making the Client a Consumer

Another way of putting the major problem of policy research is that it is far easier to make analysts effective at producing it, than it is to find City officials effective in using it. And since making the analytic work useful is a central concern of the analyst and far from the central concern of the policy maker, it follows that the analyst must take a special responsibility for helping the governmental client become an effective consumer. The analyst must en-

1. Indeed, overeager. *The New York Times* acquired an Institute analysis in draft and made it a front-page story. The city council, responsible for voting on the proposals to be submitted by the mayor but, under the terms of our contracts, having no right of access to the studies, grew annoyed. A group of councilmen brought suit against the Housing Administration to force the studies' release. The compromise offered was, in retrospect, a mistake: the publication of a summary of the studies. The summary was clear and forceful enough to be controversial but too slim to appear authoritative. It made us an easy target.

gage in his work in such a way as to enlarge the chances that it will be not only technically competent, timely, and realizable in its conclusions but also that it can be understood, relied upon, and put into effect by responsible officials. This requires continuous interaction with officials—with a minimum of jargon, a generous understanding of the particular bureaucratic, fiscal, and political constraints at work, and a persistent focus on the key question: "Then what should be done?" It also suggests that researchers be watchful for issues—such as "Do we really need all these records?" —that may look unexciting but genuinely concern lower and middle-level management and may be pregnant with much larger questions: "What information is actually needed for current purposes? What information would be needed for more effective management? What kinds of issues should management be addressing?" It also requires that researchers be aware that where an ambitious and lengthy research plan is developed it is important to produce intermediate results; often simple compilations of basic data will be useful.

And finally, where analytic work is intended to affect policy, officials and their staffs should be directly involved in the research itself. The Institute's work has been most successful where agency people themselves participated fully in the work—not merely pondering data, but checking assumptions, challenging hypotheses, proposing alternative lines of inquiry, and noting barriers to implementation. It is not always possible to find officials or staff members willing to involve themselves so deeply. But where this kind of joint effort does evolve, its benefits are enormous. The quality and relevance of the research are improved, officials develop stakes of their own in the success and utility of the studies; and, in the internal processes of the agencies, more analytic approaches to other issues develop.

External Support
It may also be worth observing that no city government—perhaps no government—should be counted on to bear the full costs of serious policy analysis. External funding from the federal government, foundations, individual donors, and so forth, is highly desirable; in some contexts it may be necessary. Substantial funds from sources independent of the principal client make it possible to begin work of importance which no city agency may be ready

to support; to augment the budgets for promising work inadequately funded; to make possible research on problems of a fundamental, methodological, or speculative nature; and, perhaps most important, to provide the fiscal safety net sometimes required for analysts willing to tell a government what it may not want to hear.

What Is "The City"?

One of the more difficult issues a policy analyst may face is that of his responsibility to persons and organizations other than his client. As the Institute's work began, we regarded ourselves loosely as working for "the City." In fact, however, we have worked only for the agencies of the executive branch of the city government. They and "the City" are not equivalent, and it is a nonequivalence that matters.

It matters for at least two reasons. Information is an element of power. Analysts working for one branch of a city government, where that branch can restrict to itself access to the results of the work, disturb the balance of power. Where the work addresses problems of little social importance, the disturbance will be correspondingly trivial. But the more important the subjects of the research, the more likely are the other branches—especially legislatures—to observe the imbalance, and to respond. The response will be one of two kinds. The legislature will seek either to provide itself with a corresponding analytic capability, or to strike such an instrument from the hands of the executive. The former course is clearly preferable not merely for the analysts who find themselves under attack but for the development of a more rational decision-making process. But it is also the harder and less likely. It has not occurred in New York City.

The second reason is that work such as the Institute's affects the balance of power as between government and the governed. More and more clearly our society is coming to regard interest groups—ethnic and racial associations, labor organizations, and neighborhood communities—as legitimate participants in local decision making. But these are groups with virtually no access to serious analytic support. I cannot say that our work has been much affected by this fact, but my own view is that it will be a problem of increasing social consequence. These interest groups, too, will resent the advantages of the executive branch and will regard them with diminishing tolerance. Over the long run then, the maintenance of serious urban policy research may well depend on the ability of our society to provide these groups, as well as governments, with the means of participating in public debate in a more informed and more rational way. And when we have found these means, I believe, we will find also that the quality and utility of the analyses performed for governments will improve. The spur of competition, the anticipation of counteranalyses, the expanded availability of data, all should press toward a competence, relevance, and comprehensiveness in policy analysis rarely seen today.

References

1. Blum, E. H., *Urban Fire Protection: Studies of the Operations of the New York City Fire Department*, R-681, New York City–Rand Institute, January 1971.

2. _____ , "The New York City Fire Project," Chapter 7, this volume.

3. Hayes, F. O'R., "From Inside the System," Chapter 1, this volume.

4. Larson, R. C., "Improving the Effectiveness of New York City's 911," Chapter 9, this volume.

5. Leendertse, J. J., *A Water Simulation Model for Well-Mixed Estuaries and Coastal Sea: Volume 1, Principles of Computation*, RM-6230, Rand Corporation, February 1970.

6. _____ , and Gritton, E. C., *A Water Simulation Model for Well-Mixed Estuaries and Coastal Sea: Volume 2, Computational Procedures*, R-708, New York City–Rand Institute, July 1971.

7. _____ , *A Water Simulation Model for Well-Mixed Estuaries and Coastal Sea: Volume 3, Jamaica Bay Simulation*, R-709, New York City–Rand Institute, July 1971.

8. Lowry, I. S., editor, *Rental Housing in New York City: Volume 1, Confronting the Crisis*, RM-6190-NYC, New York City–Rand Institute, February 1970.

9. _____ , J. DeSalvo, and B. Woodfill, *Rental Housing in New York City: Volume 2, The Demand for Shelter*, R-649-NYC, New York City–Rand Institute, June 1971.

3 Public Systems Analysis: A Consultant's View

Martin L. Ernst

3.1 Introduction

Among the many changes that took place during 1950–1970 was the extremely rapid spread in the use of consultants by industry and government. From a highly specialized activity amounting almost to a curiosity, consulting spread to become widely recognized and used. Early in this period, most consulting firms were both small and regional in nature; by the end, a number of them had become large concerns with offices throughout the world. These firms ranged from dedicated organizations, tied to a single purchaser of their services, through more diversified not-for-profit corporations, to very substantial, profit-seeking, management-oriented companies. The popularity of consulting as a profession steadily increased until, toward the end of the 1960s, it became one of the favorite choices of new graduates of the major business schools.

Growth in the size and popularity of the profession was paralleled by an increase in the range of its activities. Particularly in the late 1960s, as the magnitude of our social problems began to be felt by the educational and business communities, consulting organizations increasingly searched for a larger role in the solution of these problems. Having been accepted as effective contributors to the improvement of operations in business organizations and some government departments, consulting organizations sought to contribute similarly to resolving the many difficulties facing social organizations and public policy makers.

In this chapter, I should like to present a brief overview of consulting experience in the field of public policy, with particular emphasis on the application of formal modeling techniques to public systems. As will become clear, the formal modeling aspects of consulting cannot be discussed without reference to other aspects, because their effective application cannot take place in isolation; they form one of the tools of consulting but are best employed in the context of a broader client-consultant relationship.

Further, it must be noted that consulting is a highly personalized activity. Each organization, and even each senior consultant, tends to develop a distinctive style. The discussion presented here derives from my experience at Arthur D. Little, Inc., a large, broadly based profit-making organization that has worked more extensively with business and industry than with the public sector. Smaller and more specialized firms and not-for-profit organizations may view the situation somewhat differently. However, I believe the fundamentals concerning the relationships and environment necessary for effective work are relatively constant.

3.2 Early Consulting Studies and the Emergence of Operations Research

Although extensive involvement by consulting organizations in public problems is a recent development, consultants have done some work of this kind from almost the earliest days of the profession. As early as 1916, for example, Arthur D. Little, Inc., undertook an assignment for the Canadian Pacific Railroad to evaluate the economic growth potential of the province of Manitoba. The objective was to help the Canadian Pacific determine the rail network it should develop and the supporting investments it should seek, in order to encourage economic developments of benefit to both the province and the company.

Such early studies employed quantitative techniques, but useful formal models were not generally available. It is of interest to observe, however, that Arthur D. Little, Inc., is currently doing a very similar study for the Southeast Asia Development Bank; and in this case, one major component of the decision analysis involves the use of input/output models and sophisticated mathematical programming techniques.

The widespread use of formal models had to await both the availability of applicable techniques and the growth of consulting activity. Shortly after World War II, a number of participants in wartime operations engaged at least partly in the consulting process. Some of these organizations were established to service specific industries, such as the Airborne Instruments Laboratory, which was initially established to serve air transportation companies. Other organizations, such as the Rand Corporation and numerous smaller firms, got their start on military problems, but many of them attempted quite quickly to diversify into other public areas. The early attention of operations research to social problems is illustrated by the fact that the first Lanchester Prize of the Operations Research Society of America[1] was awarded to L. C.

1. The Lanchester Prize is awarded for the publication on operations research judged to be the best of the calendar year.

Edie for work concerned with traffic delays. Almost half of the first ten Lanchester awards dealt with problems of public interest; most of these studies were performed by internal research groups, but by the early 1960s members of a consulting firm had joined the list of winners.

Although progress was uneven, the middle 1960s saw a large number of organizations well equipped both with resources to perform social analyses and with staff deeply concerned about the problems and interested in applying analytical techniques to them.

3.3 Conditions Favoring Effective Consulting

Before we turn to the specific ways in which consultants use formal models to study public policy questions, it is useful to examine more broadly the conditions favorable for effective consulting work. In discussing these conditions, we are concerned only with consulting on organizational, policy, or operational matters; we exclude the furnishing of specialized expertise, the provision or straightforward manipulation of data, and other tasks that can be specified in great detail and do not require the consultants to understand fully the overall problems faced by their clients.

In the industrial world, where the marketplace has governed the extent and manner of use of consultants, the conditions described here tend to lead to effective work:

The client must feel a real need to solve the problem he brings to a consultant.

One might assume that this condition is always met, and in industry, with its cost consciousness and profit incentives, it normally is. However, even in industry, a surprising number of occasions arise in which the client's sense of need either is extremely transient or is specified in such broad terms that no reasonably defined consulting program can continue to maintain the client's interest over a time period adequate to perform acceptable work. In government activities, the massiveness of programs, combined with a variety of political and bureaucratic reasons for bringing in consultants, results far too often in the issuance of requests for proposals that do not serve to alleviate real and continuing client needs.

The client must possess a level of competence appropriate to the analyses performed on his behalf.

As a general rule if the client is unable thoroughly to comprehend and appreciate the work performed by a consultant, he will not be able to use it effectively. When a client is unable to handle modern quantitative techniques, his procedures, systems, and methods of reaching decisions may be quite primitive, but at least he understands and is not likely to misuse them. For such a client, a sophisticated modeling approach to operations or decision making will become either useless or dangerous once the consultant has retired from the scene. I think it can be stated almost unequivocally that consultants perform best when dealing with clients of high ability, who have chosen to employ them for reasons of economy, crossfertilization, speed of accomplishment, or any of a host of other reasons but who are quite capable of solving the same problem successfully by themselves if put to the test.

Work must be performed directly for those who will be making relevant decisions or for members of their immediate staff.
Except in occasional basic research jobs that consultants do, the usual objective of an assignment is the determination of some specific course of action. The recommended action rarely follows if those responsible for its consequences were not participants in determining the charter under which the consulting was done and in the ensuing relationship with the consultant. In ideal situations, the work and its implementation go hand in hand. Increasingly, the more successful consulting organizations find that their better clients do not regard a job as complete when the report is handed in but expect continuing assistance in carrying out the proposed program.

There must be a basis for organizational continuity in the activity being studied.
The requirement for continuity is closely related to the action and implementation aspects just discussed. Continuity is normally provided for by the structure of the client organization, although, in some instances, a consulting firm may provide continuing services over a long period of time. What is important here is that there are few meaningful "one-shot" jobs—jobs that can be implemented and ignored thereafter without monitoring and change. Needless to say, there are many individual decisions in which consultants may participate. Continuity is still supplied, however, through the consultants' contribution to the continuing decision-making process that goes on in the client organization. In a sense consultants perform an educational task here, and this is the continuing component that the client must pick up if the value is not to be lost.

The client assignment must be well defined, and its objectives must be clearly understood by all participants.
Lack of clear definition normally leads to a result that is divergent from expectations and this, in turn, leads to mutual dissatisfaction. The proper definition of objectives, however, requires not only that the consultant understand the immediate task, but that he be able to place it within the broader objectives and requirements of the organization he is serving. This broader definition provides the framework needed for the continuing interpretation of what the objectives mean and how they are best satisfied. Lacking such guideposts, the consultant can often meet the objectives in every technical sense but without the perspective that will make the results acceptable and useful to the client organization.
Contractual arrangements should be relatively simple and flexible, but without reducing requirements for performance on the part of consultants.
The steps necessary to complete a large study can seldom, if ever, be foreseen in detail; a proposal can at most provide a starting point. Most industrial contractors recognize this. The primary source of client control over performance is simply the fact that those authorizing the work can rapidly cancel the contract if dissatisfied and either recontract elsewhere or undertake the job with their own internal resources. The consultant is continually measured in terms of his ability to work toward the currently agreed-upon goals, with the knowledge that the contractor has little reluctance to terminate if his performance should start to falter.
The consultant staff must have a deep and personal interest in the work being performed and the client being served.
As in any professional activity, deep personal involvement is a key factor in getting the best out of people. One can "go through the motions" and do acceptable work but never a first-class job. Even when the analytical content is high, a large fraction of the analyst's efforts may be devoted not to the formal development of results but to explaining his results and working with those who must implement them. In my experience, the formal analysis must be complete and a draft report prepared by the time no more than 70 percent of available effort has been expended; the remaining effort will be more than fully employed in helping move the results through the process of implementation.

3.4 The Thorny Path to Working on Public Problems

I have spent a good deal of time discussing the environment that favors successful consulting, because I believe it furnishes some keys to understanding the weaknesses and strengths of past work on public problems and helps define the needs that must be met for effectiveness in the future. Consulting has unquestionably been successful in the industrial world and for the military departments. In terms of the foregoing environmental requirements, these two classes of organizations have much in common. Consulting for nondefense federal agencies and for state and municipal governments has not, to my mind, achieved an equivalent success—some of the reasons can be seen in terms of the requirements just described.

The range of national, state, and local government agencies currently tackling public problems—and thus constituting a market for consulting in matters of public policy—is so great that no general statements can apply to all of them. However, the following statements do apply to a significant fraction of the organizations:

1. Many of these organizations (for example, state and local units concerned with environmental control, community health, and education) have experienced recent and rapid growth; they have had limited experience in dealing with outside contractors and are still in the process of learning how to exercise effective control in this area.

2. Many major social units have a long heritage and a set of very strong traditions, as is the case for police departments, fire departments, and the U.S. Postal Service (formerly the Post Office); these traditions are difficult to alter except under strong outside pressures, such as those working on the military during World War II.

3. Many fields of social importance and public concern lack advanced education and training resources; this limits the speed with which modern technical methods can be understood, used effectively, and transferred from one activity, discipline, or geographical area to another. It also inhibits continuity in the development and application of new techniques.

4. In many important social areas, there are no government-run research facilities. In contrast, the Defense Department has always maintained a number of captive research establishments; these have provided personnel resources, both military and civilian, to

help evaluate, deal with, and utilize the work of outside contractors.

5. Many organizations suffer from limited funding continuity; too many "one-shot" jobs are performed, with little or no hope that further resources will be available to build on the first job and thereby make its results part of the ongoing activity of the unit involved.

6. Most work in social areas is tremendously fragmented and duplicative; the process of improving the way in which a task is handled may have to take place repeatedly in a vast number of organizations performing that task before its results will be widely felt.

7. The only reasonable excuse for current government contracting procedures is that no one has been able to devise a better method! The practice of seeking competitive proposals, each of which must effectively cost 2 to 5 percent of the contract price if of good quality, means that on any job with a significant number of competitors there is a net social loss that must be covered somewhere. The effort and commitment devoted to selecting "the best" proposal, and the many controls over funding authority, make it difficult to deal with situations where the winning consultant does not perform as well as anticipated.

8. Last, and undoubtedly most important, the whole goal-setting and decision structures of social agencies are strikingly different from those encountered in industry and the military, where objectives are few and simple and the authority structures relatively well-defined. Our major social agencies must continually balance many conflicting goals and objectives, often through very diffuse decision-making authority. In all organizations, politics are important; but in industry and most defense activities, the primary objectives are so widely accepted that they dominate the scene; if clear achievements toward those goals can be demonstrated, objections become difficult to maintain. In the world of social problems, the less certain (and often conflicting) objectives generate their own political constituencies, and demonstrably improved cost effectiveness is not necessarily enough to overcome opposition.

While there are many individual exceptions, these comments suggest that the environment provided by our public agencies often does not meet the conditions we have described as favoring effective consulting. As a result, consulting work on public questions has involved an uphill battle with a good deal of wastage and file cabinets loaded with unimplemented reports.

However, it would be overly pessimistic to conclude that there is no future in consulting for organizations like these. I believe that the prerequisites for successful work can be met in the public environment, and this chapter concludes by outlining the steps for meeting them. In addition, some of the troubles consultants and clients have had in this environment result simply from the lack of accumulated learning and experience on the part of both parties. Many important social agencies are simply in the process of learning how to handle consultants and outside contractors; we too easily forget the long and slow learning period experienced by industry and defense agencies. Similarly, neither the agencies nor their consultants have had as much time to learn how to deal with their problems as industry and defense organizations have had to deal with theirs—and the problems themselves are inherently more complicated. As more is learned, gradual progress toward concrete achievements should be expected.

The very diversity and fragmentation that at present limit transfer of knowledge and continuity of effort can be assets once we learn how to take advantage of them. The fact that so many independent organizations are striving to improve their performance provides a valuable opportunity for experimentation with a variety of approaches to any problem—an opportunity not likely to exist within a more monolithic structure.

3.5 Failures and Successes
It is not difficult to ascribe consulting failures to the lack of one or more of the conditions for successful consulting discussed earlier. In practice, most failures derive from a combination of factors rather than a single cause. The most common combination, to my mind, is the lack of clear and continuing need for the type of work contracted, together with failure to provide an adequate basis for continuity in the development and application of techniques. Two examples may illustrate this point.

First, during 1961–1963 we participated in the development of a large and relatively complex computer simulation of maritime shipping operations for the Maritime Administration. The product performed well in every technical sense, producing second-order effects that derived only very indirectly from input data but that quantitatively matched the same effects as they arose in the real world. Despite its technical success, however, I consider the project to have been a failure in terms of utility.

One element in this was that the level of complexity made it impractical for the Maritime Administration staff to maintain and exercise the computer model without either a significant expansion of internal resources or the availability of funds to contract for its maintenance outside. Thus, the level of sophistication was not a good match to the client's existing internal capabilities and would require special effort to ensure adequate maintenance and further development. While these difficulties might have been overcome, a more fundamental constraint arose because the main thrust of the MARAD program changed between the time the work was started and the time when it might have been employed. The simulation was designed to evaluate operations of ships significantly different from those previously built, but the later MARAD budget support, and its resulting plans, made a program to develop such ships infeasible. As a result, the simulation no longer represented the solution to a real and continuing need, and the basis for its support evaporated.

The second example involves a simulation we designed of the housing market in the city of San Francisco. Once again, the model performed well technically; it appeared to its builders to possess great interest and utility as a tool that could be developed further and used to test a wide range of hypotheses regarding the impact of possible government actions on the adequacy of housing for inhabitants of the city. Once again, however, its practical value was very limited.

Failure to utilize the model certainly derived in part from its complexity, the costs of developing data, and conducting and analyzing simulation runs. However, these difficulties were compounded by a change in the whole direction of urban redevelopment planning and by the fact that the work was essentially "one shot" in nature. The city did not receive continued funding support for model development and could not justify use of the model as a planning tool for the types of projects that eventually were practical for it to consider. Application to other cities would have required a strong program to develop improved analytical tools for urban planning, and no such central program existed.

The fate of the San Francisco model was closely paralleled by similar efforts of other consulting groups in the Pennsylvania–New Jersey area and in the city of Pittsburgh. In all cases, neither those in local authority nor those at the federal planning level had a feeling of real need, nor was there a long-term research plan that could serve to provide alternative support.

This combination of a change in the perceived needs of the client with a lack of mechanisms for developing continuity arises most commonly when we are analyzing large-scale problems about which there is no fundamental agreement as to how long-term solutions will be found. We do not know how to solve our urban housing problems, nor have we found an economical way for American shipping to survive successfully. As a result, those responsible for addressing these problems will keep trying alternative policies in an effort to find a solution, and with each change in direction, their perceived needs will alter. The same difficulty is at the heart of many other areas where good analyses have been performed but not effectively utilized; examples are mass transportation and elementary education. There are many needs in these areas to which consultants can contribute by the development of formal models but, particularly with large formal models, there is great risk that they will not be implemented as policies and approaches change in response to social and economic pressures.

Where the goals and the means are already better understood, large formal models have a better chance of use. For example, it has been many years since the U.S. Bureau of Public Roads first developed its network model. This model has been improved and applied in a wide variety of circumstances. It provides a tool of continued utility, simply because a family of users is available and well aware of its potentialities to meet their needs. It is being investigated currently, for instance, as a tool to study railroad routing and abandonment actions. Another example lies in the area of public health, where studies of epidemiology and models of the cost effectiveness of different procedures for detecting and treating diseases fill a steady need and are delivered to a relatively cohesive body with a professional interest in assuring the further development and continuity of such models.

Formal models have been most consistently successful when applied to smaller problems. Many examples are discussed in later chapters of this book. A key point is that we do know how to solve many classes of such problems and can demonstrate the fact. Thus we can

—Develop effective patterns for police car patrolling.
—Analyze the sources of delays in the criminal justice system and estimate requirements for reducing them.
—Simulate the factors leading to water pollution and analyze the effects of a variety of measures aimed at reducing pollution.
—Analyze the optimum location of fire stations.
—Evaluate alternative measures for collecting and disposing of solid waste.

Further, we can structure much larger and more complex situations in a manner that facilitates their study, even though effective and useful formal solutions may be beyond our capabilities.

When failures occur in such tasks, they usually result either from lack of adequate communications to ensure that lessons need not be learned over and over again, or from lack of sufficient understanding of the broader problem faced by a public agency to ensure that the analytical results are developed in a context recognized by the client as valid.

The latter factor is perhaps the more important. Public organizations, subject to social pressures and political constituencies, present a background with which the quantitative analyst is often ill prepared to cope. He can perform best when closely associated with personnel who are well attuned to the nonquantitative and political aspects of the problem arena. Except in very narrowly defined situations, therefore, the best formal analyses performed by our company represent only a component of the work; the successful implementation of such formal model results probably depends more on other, less quantitative, components than on the model's own merits.

3.6 Outlook for the Future

If I seem to have spent an inordinate amount of time on the difficulties and failures of past efforts to apply formal analysis to public systems, it is simply because I feel we learn more from these situations than we do from successes. At the personal level, I am quite optimistic concerning the role that we will play in the future. Recognition of the scale of our social problems is a fairly new development, and true commitment to their solution is even more recent.

Despite some of the problems inherent in work with public problems, past experience does suggest certain steps that will improve our ability to deal systematically with such problems. These steps can help to bring about the conditions necessary to successful consulting. More broadly, they are important to the future of research and policy guidance on public questions, regardless of whether the work is done by consultants or internally. The most important steps seem to me to be the following:

Development and improvement of educational resources, particularly for personnel in state and local governments.
Both industry and the military departments have for many years supported considerable postgraduate education for their personnel; state, local, and federal nonmilitary activities have supported very little in spite of great need. The development of curricula, institutes, and very possibly specialized colleges and other training facilities could do much to improve the competence of personnel at the front line of our social problems.

From the point of view of educational institutions, the complexity of the situation poses many problems. There is a need for graduates skilled in advanced techniques, but there is an even greater requirement for technical personnel who recognize the limits of their role and who can develop sensitivity, understanding, and a willingness to cooperate with others who are less well educated in a formal sense but whose experience will make the difference between success and failure.

Improved communications.
Improved communications, in the form of better specialized journals, broader publication of books, more seminars, and so forth, are likewise vital for improving competence, exchanging the findings of different programs, and helping to build continuity in the development of formal techniques.

New and improved research facilities.
Some of our socially oriented activities, such as those in the area of health, have major internal research establishments; but many other areas lack such facilities. As noted earlier, the availability of internal research capabilities contributes both to the supply of competent personnel and to continuity in technical developments, including mechanisms for absorbing and employing formal models.

This general requirement is becoming recognized both in universities and in government; one response, for example, has been the formation of specialized institutes devoted to issues such as urban problems. More effort is necessary in all areas but at least some moves are under way.

Longer term funding of research programs.
Longer term research programs are needed so that developments can build upon one another. Progress here can be expected as developments in the areas listed here generate pressure on major funding agencies to develop and maintain more cohesive and longer term programs.

Team building.
Finally, we need improvement in our ability to tackle problems with a suitable mix of quantitative analysts and those more aware of the total problem and more skilled at dealing with political realities, social pressures, incentive structures, and other factors that govern the practical utility of the analytic work. This is an area of major interest to many large consulting firms, because the ability to field skilled teams, incorporating such mixes, is one of the more valuable features of these organizations.

In the long run, the problem of proper team building may be the most critical factor in the successful application of formal models in public systems, because most of the other factors discussed earlier in this section will probably be taken care of over time. Team building, however, requires a depth of understanding and commitment that is perhaps more difficult to achieve as it requires that people with very different perspectives, background, and experience find first a means to establish sufficient contact to assure that all of the variegated skills can be made available and then a harmonious way of working together in spite of their many different characteristics. The proportion of a team that should be selected for technical qualifications can vary enormously from one assignment to another—from as little as 20 percent or so (below which the necessary quantum of participation is not achieved) to upwards of 80 percent of total participation. The nature of the job, the degree of political sensitivity, the eventual involvement and backing by public groups and officials, all influence the optimum mix. The most complex of sophisticated mathematical techniques may be involved in some cases while very practical but rudimentary analysis of data may be the appropriate input in another job.

Once these steps have established a basis for more effective work, the consultant role with respect to public policy can develop to parallel the role in industry: as an external check on internal competence, as a source of analyses less influenced by internal constraints or incentives than internal sources might be, as a means for overcoming problems of peak loads or lack of expertise in a subject, as a means for more rapid or economical progress toward a desired goal, and as a source of teams of personnel offering the particular combinations of capabilities needed. I believe we are making progress in the fundamentals necessary for effective application of formal techniques to public decisions; and if this is the case, consultants will almost surely play an increasingly important part in our attack on these problems.

4

Afterthoughts on Four Urban Systems Studies Performed with Small Cities

W. Edward Cushen

4.1 Introduction

In November 1967, the Department of Housing and Urban Development (HUD) sponsored a one-year experiment to determine how the systems approach might be productively used in solving some city problems. This chapter provides a short, very incomplete, narrative description of some of those studies, the circumstances of their operation, a subjective evaluation of their results, and a set of "lessons learned" for the future.

The concept of the experiment was to conduct two training courses in systems analysis for city managers and planners, one in November 1967 and the second a year later. In the intervening year, three to five cities would be helped in carrying out short systems studies that could be reported and evaluated at the second training session.

Participants in the exercise came from five groups:

1. The International City Management Association (ICMA), prime contractor, and professional society for city managers;
2. The American Society of Planning Officials (ASPO), a professional society for planners;
3. The Fels Institute of State and Local Government, a degree-granting graduate college in the University of Pennsylvania complex, from which many city managers have received their master's degrees;
4. The Technical Analysis Division (TAD) of the National Bureau of Standards, a two-year-old group of operations research, economics, human factors, and engineering specialists whose purpose is to assist agencies of government to use the systems approach; and
5. City managers, city planners, and city staff people from the cities forming the basis of the studies.

The one-week training courses in systems analysis were designed by John Parker and others associated with the Fels Institute, with some modifying suggestions from ICMA and TAD. Thirty attendees at the two courses were selected by ICMA and ASPO, with

Contribution of the National Bureau of Standards, not subject to copyright.

some emphasis given to cities whose managers and/or planners might have conditions more favorable to a successful experiment and with some small modifications in achieving a balance geographically and by city size. Manager-planner teams from four cities were invited.

The courses included play of a city game (Richard Duke's "Metropolis"); lectures on operations research (OR) techniques, systems concepts, data processing, and the planning-programming-budgeting (PPB) concept that was then just being introduced to civilian agencies; workshops in setting up a project; and a critique in search of ways to match up city needs with the analytic smörgasbord that had been displayed. Lectures were given by Fels and TAD people under the encouraging supervision of ICMA and ASPO.

At the conclusion of the first training session, a number of city managers volunteered their cities to serve as locales for the conduct of systems studies. The plan called for a conference to decide which study to undertake in each of the cities, and to develop a plan of action if it was decided to proceed. Typically, a study was to be a joint undertaking of several institutions. The city manager and/or planner was to serve as the primary user of the results of the study, and was expected to participate personally as much as his schedule would permit. TAD was to serve as technical coach to the city personnel, helping them design the project, monitoring progress, and advising whenever problem areas arose. A university or college in, or near to, the city was to be involved, and some commercial organization was to participate in the project. When the project was completed, an evaluation was to be made by all participants, and a final report provided to HUD. At the completion of the study, the city was to be in a position to initiate and use systems studies with relatively little continuing advice from those who had conducted the first study.

4.2 The Cities and Their Problems

Within a month after the completion of the training course, at least five cities had indicated a serious willingness to be among the experimental locales. A visitation team consisting of ICMA, Fels, ASPO, and TAD representatives traveled to the first four cities that volunteered: East Lansing (Michigan), Dayton (Ohio), Charlotte (North Carolina), and Poughkeepsie (New York). In each city, some preliminary thinking on the nature of their preferred systems study had been done, and discussed by phone and letter with ICMA, ASPO, Fels, and TAD prior to the visit.

The first visit to each city resulted in a rather explicit study design for each location, and this was accomplished without exception in the course of an evening's exploration, followed by a five- or six-hour planning session the following day. Each city staff had prepared well for the sessions: They had roughly identified what problem they wanted studied, they had selected a project that was reasonable in size for a 9-month study, and they assembled a large city representation to help in the discussions. One- or two-hour tours of each city were made at the beginning or midpoint of the project discussions.

East Lansing knew it would have to replace a central city fire station and suggested that the team undertake to determine how many fire stations the city needed and where they should be located. Dayton suggested one of several resource allocation studies that could mesh with another experiment being conducted there— Dayton was one of the 5-5-5 cities[1] in which the PPB system was being explored. Charlotte requested help in setting up a management information system. Poughkeepsie suggested an analytic comparison of ways to upgrade housing, concentrating on building code compliance.

Discussions of each city's proposed project resulted in some modifications, usually as a result of urging by the visitors.

4.3 Projects for East Lansing and Dayton
In East Lansing, the presence of the city planner permitted the study to be expanded to include several alternative future city environments rather than a single time slice analysis. The existence of rather extensive data on fire alarms in the city over the preceding 10 years provided a historical basis for comparison. Subsequent to the initial visit, Michigan State University was invited to participate, and their computer was used for production runs of the calculations.

In Dayton, resource allocation strategies for various programs were explored, largely in search of the particular set of programs that would have immediate visible results and that might help Day-

1. Five cities, five counties, and five states.

ton to bring about reinforcing benefits from the various federal
assistance programs in which it participated. Dayton was especially interested in working on a problem that would have immediate relevance in improving the lot of the inhabitants of West
Dayton, an area suffering from high unemployment and under-
employment, adverse health experience, and relatively high crime
rates. The Dayton planning discussions ranged more widely than
those in East Lansing. Dayton had hired an OR analyst for in-
house staff and had been participating in the 5-5-5 program for a
number of months. This prompted earlier discussions of whether
the linear programming approach to program selection might be
regarded as productive. At the end of the planning session, it was
decided to run a linear programming computation on the selection
among various job training programs available to the city, but with
some residual feeling that the project definition might require further modification. The city proposed that both university and
commercial resources could be readily built into the study itself.

4.4 Charlotte, a Broader View
The Charlotte discussions were particularly significant, in that representatives of neighborhood groups were present at the project
discussion in addition to members of the city staff. Charlotte had
already contracted with a commercial firm to prepare a management information system, and the TAD analysts urged that some
other project than the one proposed be undertaken. After about a
half-hour's discussion, it was determined that a facility location
problem be undertaken in the Model Cities area outside the city
center. That suggestion was initially less appealing than some other
alternatives, because facility location was already apparently a
good choice for East Lansing, and the team desired to have a
broader set of examples of the systems approach to illustrate. The
insistence by the neighborhood groups that this neighborhood facility location was important to them rapidly led to a new visual-
ization of the problem that catapulted this problem formulation
into a higher level of discourse. Basically, the fire station location
notion for East Lansing was a center-of-gravity calculation, with
weightings at the nodes for countable entities: number of people
whose lives were placed in jeopardy, frequency of fires, dollar
damage potentials, and fire spread probabilities. But in Charlotte,
there emerged a contrast between the perception of services ren-

dered by the administration and a perception of services received and acceptable to the target population. A problem statement whose purpose was to close a communication gap occurred nearly simultaneously to all persons present:

Calculate the optimal number and location of neighborhood facilities using traditional time, distance, and population measures. Calculate the optimal number and location of neighborhood facilities using perceived distances and perceived value of services received by the neighborhood populations. Compare the two answers to discover the extent to which improved usefulness of assistance programs might result if perceptions of the citizens formed the basis for choice of assistance programs.

From that point forward, a near-missionary zeal gripped most of the participants. The principal of the predominantly black high school offered to have a Model Cities Day, in which students and teachers could cover the neighborhood to check the adequacy of a two-year-old housing inventory to serve as a basis for sampling inhabitants, who then would be asked to participate in an in-depth interview in search of the needed "perceived distances and utility." The Community College offered to help. The local newspapers built the project into the total Model Cities plan that was announced in the local newspapers shortly afterward.[2]

Among the perceptions we hoped to measure were the following (all to be measured "actual" and "perceived"):

1. Accessibility time
2. Round trip time, including the service time
3. Availability of the service
4. Eligibility for service
5. Need for the service
6. Volume of service provided
7. Timeliness of service
8. Value of the service
9. Contribution to expanded opportunity
10. Threshold levels for noticeable value
11. Availability of a subsequent job

The study team itself had some misgivings about whether the

2. "400 Families to be Interviewed in Pilot HUD Project," *The Charlotte Observer*, April 24, 1968, followed by "$8 Million in U.S. Funds for Slums Headed Here," *The Charlotte News*, April 25, 1968.

project as stated was researchable, because there was little basis for believing that perceived distances could be treated analytically, much less perceived values. But the ardor of the Charlotte participants and my own stubbornness prevailed, and a study plan was created.

The model neighborhood area in Charlotte is really a collection of six neighborhoods whose collective geographical boundary resembles the shape of a butterfly. The area adjoins the city center, and is served by two bus lines moving toward the city center. It is traversed by a connecting link to Interstate Route 81. The neighborhoods include Greenville, Belmont, Villa Heights, and Wards 1, 3, and 4; and their racial and economic compositions are sufficiently distinct to make the boundaries a little more pronounced than might otherwise be expected. Neighborhood recreation facilities, located more or less in accord with traditional plant location theory, had not been patronized as had originally been hoped. This observation led to proposing the idea that plant location theory needed more realistic behavioral/psychological data inputs if the final facility locations were to be those that would be used. If locations are not used, the intended service is not delivered.

The full range of possible locations then could be

1. None, let model neighborhood residents use facilities already in existence, largely in the center city area.
2. One, somewhere in or near the model neighborhoods, possibly at the edge of the city center.
3. Two, one for each half of the butterfly-shaped area.
4. Three, four, or five, representing some compromise mixes to achieve better neighborhood accessibility.
5. Six, one for each of the model neighborhoods.

If perceptual distances from a projected user to the possible facility location could be obtained, then the calculations leading to the optimal location could be weighted by number of users, age of users, relative need of users, ability to pay for travel, and so forth, so that a variety of choices could be offered.

The range of possible services could include

1. Medical, including health education and medical examinations;
2. Educational, including training in homemaking, budgeting, household maintenance, and (where appropriate) African studies;
3. Counseling, including marriage, family, social;

4. Legal aid and advice, help in filling out forms;
5. Employment assistance;
6. Housing referrals;
7. Recreational facilities and training;
8. Financial advice, including loans, budgets, expenditures;
9. Day care and preschool training for youngsters;
10. Services intended to bring out the latent talents among individuals and groups in the neighborhood;
11. Creation of a unifying cultural point, for example, an African culture center, an experimental neighborhood-owned tufting mill, and so forth;
12. Provision of facilities, such as typing, sewing, shops;
13. A social facility, for example, for holding family reunions;
14. A chapel.

A short unstructured conference developed a list of 26 service possibilities, and more might have been generated.

Each of the foregoing services might be provided at a number of possible levels, ranging from a mere directory of available services in the city area, through a modest advisory service, to a full-fledged, staffed, and equipped service center.

Furthermore, it would be necessary to determine how much "clustering" of services would be required before the center might take on a real attraction to the neighborhood. A one-stop general service facility would possibly be better patronized and deliver services more efficiently and usefully than a scattered set of locations.

This, of course, meant that not only should accessibility as perceived by the user be measured, but also his perception of the value (utility) of the services offered.

4.5 Poughkeepsie

In Poughkeepsie, the project selected was the creation of a benefit-cost comparison of various strategies the city might use in bringing about building code compliance in the designated Model Cities neighborhood. A number of possible strategies appeared possible: strict code compliance with consequent shutdowns, low-cost loans to owners or occupants to improve the property, tax incentives, and so forth. Furthermore, there was some feeling that a "Jones effect" might be capitalized on. For example, if several houses were to be significantly improved, giving visible tokens of neighborhood improvement, the remainder of owners and occupants might be motivated to build a revitalized neighborhood. Neighborhood building inspectors agreed to help with data collection by providing some information beyond that needed to accomplish their task. The city social welfare workers agreed to estimate probable social effects of improved housing. City staff members agreed to estimate probable economic consequences of different improvement strategies. Thus a project was designed in which the unit of calculation was the individual house, and in which the analysis required comparing each of the different improvement strategies as it might be applied to each housing unit.

4.6 Going Ahead

Each of the study designs was reported to HUD in order to obtain its inputs and approvals. Useful suggestions were received for all cases except the Dayton one, in which the study design fell outside the definition of legally permissible ways to use the appropriation from which the study was funded. The question could have been resolved favorably if *facilities* had been involved; in the Dayton study plan, only *services* were in question. ICMA requested a reconsideration of the Dayton exclusion, and the studies in the other three cities were started.

The East Lansing study got off to an easy start. City personnel, with the city planner acting as a vigorous project leader, gathered data, refined the study plan, visualized new alternatives to be compared, speculated on ways to combine services, estimated the extent to which future demands for fire services might deviate from a mean value, and watched milestone accomplishment carefully. TAD was able to adapt a computer subroutine for least-path calculation that had been developed in its portion of the Northeast Corridor transportation study with relative ease and at little cost. TAD had project coaches in depth and visited the city regularly. The city manager was an active participant in project definition and the early stages of the study and was absent from the project only while computer program debugging and exploratory runs were in progress.

The Charlotte study was slower in making explicit that which had been agreed to in the project design stage. Although the tone and enthusiasm for the study continued, the necessity to develop a good questionnaire for a relatively new purpose required a large amount of design work by the TAD staff. Charlotte hired a professional sociologist for its staff, an event that was welcomed as a significant asset to the study. Independent university advice on the interview plan and purpose was obtained by Charlotte, and the pioneering nature of the intended work became still more apparent. Pressures for immediate action in the many Model Cities programs competed severely with the time needed to conduct the systems study, although the interview training program that had been scheduled was completed only slightly later than planned. Trial runs on the interviews were conducted, and the questionnaire design itself went through several iterations to replace academic phraseology with language that conveyed meaning to those interviewed. By the conclusion of the study, however, the questionnaires were modified to provide a badly needed socioeconomic profile, and the intended "perception" questions fell victim to the modified analytic plan.

The Poughkeepsie study was recycled through the design stage approximately a half-dozen times. City personnel in charge of, and those assigned to, the study were in constant demand for the solution of daily problems. The systems study was repeatedly placed in a "hold" status, and the city valiantly tried to keep the study moving by assigning replacement personnel, each of whom needed to be briefed on philosophy, concept, and status. Each new team revised the data collection sheets and the matrix format for analysis, at the same time that the neighborhood inspectors found the additional data items to be more cumbersome than anyone had expected.

The request for reconsideration of the Dayton study was denied. The advanced stage of progress on the East Lansing and Charlotte studies, as well as the difficulties with the Charlotte concept and the Poughkeepsie staffing, prompted a decision to hold the number of city studies to three, rather than adding a city halfway through the experiment. Dayton, meantime, had solved its manpower program selections in a more routine way, and the OR analyst had joined the city in a full-time capacity, giving an increasing amount of attention to the 5-5-5 study that was nearing completion.

4.7 Some Lessons

At this stage of the analysis, a number of hypotheses about "lessons learned" were beginning to emerge. They tended to concentrate in one of the following seven observations (most of which had been learned in World War II by the early operations analysts):

1. A "nuts and bolts" example is easy to understand, solve, and use. It has high chances of leading to tangible improvements, and will lead to still broader and more complicated analyses, which will also be easy to understand, solve, and use.
2. It is necessary to involve representatives of the user organization in the study and in a depth sufficient to guarantee constant attention from them.
3. Perhaps *even more* than in a typical federal organization, city staffs have less time to do analytic work than might be expected.
4. Problems related to social consequences and intended to improve the inner city quality of life have a degree of urgency that will not tolerate lengthy research investments. Conversely, a good systems solution to such problems appears to need just that research investment.
5. Communications gaps can be bridged if people with different objectives will jointly design a systems study. In those cases, there is less concern with the answers to the study that has been designed than there is a desire to capitalize on the communications opened up, so that other issues can be discussed.
6. There is little patience in cities with a long, large, expensive comprehensive systems study so common in the defense-aerospace community.
7. The team approach can work, but there are at least two hazards: the lack of an explicitly designated team leader with responsibility to deliver a result and the arrival of too many experts with conflicting advice.

4.8 Back to East Lansing
The East Lansing study proved, by nearly any criterion, to be the most successful of the studies undertaken. Although the technical details have been described elsewhere,[3] it will serve a useful purpose to summarize the concept of the analysis here.

---

3. Other reports describing the studies in greater detail, or from the points of view of city personnel involved have appeared: William E. Bseuden, "Systems Analysis for Urban Problem Solving," *Public Management*, 51, February 1969, pp. 14–15; G. Michael Conlisk, "Systems Analysis—How It Works in East Lansing," *Public Management*, 51, February, 1969, pp. 7–8; Louis C. Santone, "Application of Systems Analysis to Urban Problems," Municipal

East Lansing is a charming and quiet town with a population of
about 37,000. When the students from Michigan State University
are present, the population doubles. The city manager provides
fire protection service to the city, and, under contract, he also provides this service to the university. One of the fire stations is located on the school's campus. At the time of our project, one
problem confronting East Lansing was the fact that the city center
station was obsolete and would have to be replaced sooner or
later. The situation gave rise to the question: How many fire stations should East Lansing have and where should they be?

For the analysis, the city was represented as a series of nodes
and connecting links, where a city block represented the area serviced by one of the nodes and the streets that connected the inter-
sections then formed the connecting links.

The nodes which were possible candidates for fire station location were used as points of departure in finding the fastest path
from that location to any other point in the city. Thus we have a
network layout in which the elapsed travel time from intersection
to intersection represents what we shall call "impedance." If we
next assume that the fire engines will always take the fastest path,
we can then draw a frequency plot indicating the number of nodes
that can be reached by a fire engine in 30, 45, 60, and so forth,
seconds, assuming that the engines are available when needed. It
must be recognized that if any point is more than two minutes distant from a fire station, the fire protection is not considered adequate and the fire insurance rates on properties go up. In this
study, one analysis assumed that fire stations must be so situated
that all locations can be serviced within two minutes' travel time.
No matter how we juggled the variables, we could not reach all
nodes in the city in two minutes from a single fire station. We
then tried two station locations. Two fire stations would not do
it either. A satisfactory solution was obtained as long as we were
willing to allow for three fire stations in East Lansing.

Of course the problem did not end at this point. In this exercise,

Yearbook, 1969, International City Managers Association, pp. 225-232;
Louis C. Santone and Geoffrey Berlin, "Location of Fire Stations," in *Systems Analysis for Social Problems*, edited by Alfred Blumstein, Murray Kam-
rass, and Armand B. Weiss, Washington, D.C., Washington Operations Research Council, 1970, pp. 80-91; Alan J. Goldman, "Discussion," *Ibid.*,
pp. 92-103.

the city manager, planner, and fire commissioner assisted in the design of the project. At no stage of the development were they at a loss as to what problem was being solved, or how it was being solved. They were involved in the design of the project, in the acquisition of data, and the process of obtaining solutions with the aid of the Michigan State University computer. They understood the basic logic and the formulation of the analysis. This made it possible for them to think more creatively using a numerically described base case and take into consideration several dimensions that were left out in the first solution. For example, a densely populated area has a higher probability of fire than one that is sparsely populated. There is no point in treating a vacant lot similarly to a high-rise apartment. In a densely populated area more lives are in jeopardy and dollar damage caused by fire is also greater.

Success in obtaining good, plausible solutions from the analysis prompted the city officials to consider the long-range point of view. A time slice 12 years in the future was selected to symbolize possible ways the city might look. We considered probable population shifts, a possible deterioration of the downtown area with increased probability of fire, likely growth of high-rise apartments in the north of the city, and so forth. Given this new information, a three-station solution was the one that was again found to satisfy the required constraints.

Optimizing on the basis of the two-minute travel time was not enough. Every additional fire station involves land acquisition, building, staffing, and equipment. Cost comparisons of different ways of providing adequate levels of fire service then led to speculation about whether helicopters might replace some of the fire stations, whether fire prevention would be a better investment than fire fighting, or whether a better alarm system would be preferable.

When the nodes were weighted by population at those nodes, the preferred location for the center city fire station shifted five blocks away from the location implied by a flat map. When the nodes were weighted by frequency of fires, the shift was only two blocks. At this stage of the project, several research people associated with the fire underwriters became interested in the possibility of using the fire station locator to compare possible effects of changing criteria for rating cities.

East Lansing began to implement its suggested course of action, but this has been greatly complicated by recent legislation regarding the interaction of city and university services.

By the time the study was completed and reported at the November 1968 training course, interest among city managers was relatively high. A number of cities requested a run of the model under their circumstances. ICMA had for some months felt that models of this sort might be generalized for wide use and designed what has come to be called a "Technology Applications Program." One of the features of such a program would be the development of models, their test, and ultimate distribution to cities, along with technical advice on the use of the models. The fire station locator developed under this contract would probably be the first of a long series of such models. However, funding for adaptations to other cities was not available, and only occasional consulting could take place.

In the meantime, the Congress legislated the Fire Research and Safety Act of 1968 (PL 90-259). Conduct of research under this act is the responsibility of the Fire Research program of the Institute for Applied Technology at the National Bureau of Standards. The program director decided that a major contribution to fire service in the United States might be made if studies of an applied sort, similar to the fire station locator, were undertaken. Building on the East Lansing example, that program is now funding the development, application, and teaching of fire station locators, fire equipment calculators, shared service calculations, and community relations studies.

One of the impediments to rapid computations in the East Lansing case was the fact that districting of the city had to be done by hand, and the computation of optimal locations was therefore a series of volleys between the computer and the desk. When the East Lansing example was completed, TAD searched for a problem that could use the fire station locator but would allow the development of a computer-based redistricting program. (Such an example arose early in 1969, when the Montgomery County School Planning Board agreed to work with TAD to develop revised school district boundaries in an area now served by eight elementary schools in the Takoma Park vicinity of Maryland. The revised problem statement is; How many schools are needed in the immediate future, and where should the boundaries be? The components were the capacity of the schools, the number of teachers, the number of students, and the road network. Among the criteria used were the time it would take for the children to walk to school, how many children would have to walk three-quarters of a mile or more, or be bussed, in order to get to school, and also how to district in order to achieve better racial balance.)

4.9 Results in Charlotte and Poughkeepsie

The studies described in this chapter were initial learning experiences for all participants, and only in East Lansing did we achieve most of our goals from problem formulation to the beginnings of implementation to the development of methodologies of potential value to other cities. We, and our city clients, had much to learn about staffing, scope, and types of interaction conducive to productive studies.

In Charlotte, our main accomplishment was in bringing all parties together for problem formulation and in helping the city staff to obtain a more complete data base for their decisions. TAD lacked the personnel to follow through completely on a program as extensive as the Charlotte project, described earlier. The study did identify a rational need for six facilities rather than the one central facility that would probably have been built without the system study, and several of these facilities have been constructed.

The Poughkeepsie effort was an informative but not especially productive experience. Both TAD and the city staff underestimated the needs for substantial staffing with personnel who followed the project through from inception to implementation.

Incidentally, these study efforts, the training programs, and many other expenses all fit within a single ICMA contract for $80,000. I believe we have come a long way from these initial tries, both in the development of useful methodologies in particular problem areas and in understanding how to more effectively support the needs of busy city administrators. TAD, for example, presently is often capable of delivering assistance to cities willing to make reasonable investments of their own staff time, on problems similar to those described here, on contracts as small as $8,000 to $10,000.

4.10 A Related Experience

Our exposure to these city problems was followed very quickly by the appearance of a study conducted by the Federal Executive

Board in the city of Oakland, California. From an OR point of view, the problem statement might be stylized as follows:

What can be done to maximize the collective effectiveness of federal aid programs converging on a city?

Categorical grants and assistance programs from a variety of agencies (HUD, HEW, OEO, Labor, EDA, and others) had targeted on Oakland for a number of years. Still the indicators of city health were downward bound. It was apparent in the study that programs frequently conflicted with one another, or their timing was mismatched, or the state and local priorities precluded taking maximum value from the programs, or state and local matching resources were insufficient. Each of our simpler city studies had brushed against other programs, all intended to improve the inner city condition. The year was one in which civil disorders were prominent national concerns. Each of our city studies was a suboptimization, targeted on a city service. We were troubled by the need to include a larger horizon but were at a loss as to how to handle it. The Oakland example served an admirable additional purpose: It provided raw materials for creating the scenario for a management game. Because there was no funding for developing the game, the ensuing several pages simply suggest an outline of what might be done.

Any game requires three kinds of entities: the players, the things they exchange or use, and a set of rules.

In the Oakland game, players have been somewhat artificially limited to five:

1. A spokesman for the ghetto community,
2. An industrial player,
3. The city administration,
4. The county, and
5. Federal agencies with programs to improve the community.

These five players are abstractions. For example, there is probably no single representative of the ghetto community; there may be no single-minded industrial representative. The city administration is simplified to represent a unified image of mayor, council, city manager, and the administrative departments. County and state represent elected officials and members of legislative, executive, and judicial branches of government. The federal players represent the logical sum of departments and agencies such as HUD,

OEO, Labor, Commerce, HEW, Transportation, and so forth. Although the simplification is somewhat artificial, there is some implicit grouping of purposes in this representation. One of the lessons of the game could be that much could be gained from cooperation of the separate entities in achieving a common purpose.

One thing stands out from gathering the many decision-making entities into these five groups. Each has a different perception of urban need, a different perception of what is possible, and a partially frustrating awareness of the limitations on his flexibility.

The pieces in this game include a map of the city, a profile of its people and services, a budget, and a set of resources to be used. Since only the concept of the game has been developed, the specifics relating to these pieces are only suggested in the set of instructions given to the players.

The game rules are also undeveloped. Instructions to start the game have been prepared for each of the "players," who have been identified as "decision loci," since each player represents the position developed from the rebuttal and debate of the institutions gathered together. One such locus is included as an appendix to this chapter. An umpire manual would be needed to allow for calculation of results of decisions made, and to advance the scenario of the game.

Several initial plays of this game in classrooms, using simplified umpire calculations, have shown that there is a built-in deterioration of the urban situation in early time frames, and that there is a rapid student response in either taking unilateral drastic corrective action or a move to cooperative action.

Finally, we rediscovered something we had all learned in high school in classes that were then called "problems of democracy." The American government is, in reality, a system of governments, some 100,000 in all: state, local, national, and special units. If one wanted to do grand, strategic operations research in the delivery of services and freedoms to the American people, he would need to describe ways to improve the rules related to the delivery of those services as they pass through the various units of government. We experimented with a simple descriptive narrative and accompanying diagram to show how one type of project is delivered to the public, illustrating the steps taken and by whom.

4.11 An Afterword to an Afterthought

The purpose of this chapter has been to present an overview of one of the ways TAD began to learn about assisting cities with their problems, using realistic time frames and budgets. We could report on more convincing work performed since these very preliminary efforts, but (with suitable tooth pulling) I am glad to respond to our editors' request for a brief report on the experiment described here. It is anticipated that more complete reports on the three city projects will appear in a future issue of *Operations Research*.

Acknowledgments

An extremely large debt of gratitude is due to many people whose efforts caused these studies to have the results they did. Particular gratitude should go to John M. Patriarche, city manager of East Lansing and then president of the International City Managers Association; G. Michael Conlisk, East Lansing's planning director and project leader; William J. Veeder, city manager of Charlotte; Graham W. Watt, then city manager of Dayton; Theodore Maurer, then city manager of Poughkeepsie, Harold Weber, then city planner of Poughkeepsie; Louis C. Santone, deputy chief of TAD; Geoffrey Berlin, who with Santone provided the TAD analysis for the East Lansing project; June Cornog, who designed the original TAD questionnaire for the Charlotte project; Marcia Maltese, who adapted the fire station locator to the Montgomery County school example; Harold R. Millie, who assisted in starting the project; William Besuden, assistant director of ICMA; Robert Havlick, ICMA project manager; Leopold A. Goldschmidt, research director of ASPO; and John Parker, then with Fels Institute. The value judgments made about the studies should not be attributed to any of them but to the author. Comments that seem to be negative should not be regarded as critical of individuals or of cities but simply an attempt to summarize a situation as I saw it existing. Throughout the studies, I was deeply impressed by the professional skills of all we met, by their devotion to improving their cities, and by the cities themselves. Finally, I wish to thank Arnold Reisman and Al Drake for their sacrifices in transcribing, editing, and improving an earlier manuscript for this chapter. Drake's telephone bill, I suspect, establishes a new record for this kind of activity.

The four city project was funded under the Demonstration Cities and Metropolitan Development Act of 1966 (Public Law 89-754). Supplemental work on the school districtor, the management game, and intergovernmental relations was supported by funds appropriated to the National Bureau of Standards.

Appendix: An Example of a Decision Locus for the Oakland Game

Decision Locus: City Administration

You represent the city manager, mayor, council, and administrative structure of the city of Oakland.

Your city is a second-class neighbor to San Francisco and Berkeley. Industry is moving out; the racial balance is changing rapidly: whites are moving out at the rate of 11,000 per year, and nonwhites (largely Negroes) are moving in at a rate of 8,000 per year. Your city has a high rate of unemployment (6.4 percent citywide, and about three times that much in the ghetto target areas). The 25,000 unemployed men, 38,000 unemployed women, and 114,000 underemployed persons are restive, and you have had a number of riots. Your city is a port of entry for low-income households.

Your current city income for operating expenses is $42 million and your expenditures are $43 million. Your capital budget is approximately $11 million, not nearly enough to make the necessary maintenance improvements, let alone build a newer capital plant. Your tax rates are about as high as they can go for both industry and property bases. You have a 1 percent sales tax on most things except groceries, and 6 percent on tobacco. Your city debt is $43.3 million and rising slowly. Your city receives $3 million per year from the federal government and $3 million per year from the state of California. Because of matching fund requirements, you need to deflect some of your priorities to take advantage of federal antipoverty and economic development programs. Federal agencies believe you are receiving five times the amount of support your budget shows. Your pay rates for city employees are high ($8,200 to $8,800 for entering firemen and police), and you are an attractive city employer.

Your city shows a very apparent air of general deterioration; the exodus of industry and white middle-class families is reducing your tax base, and the demand for services is increasing. Three-quarters of the housing stock in the city was built before 1939, and 20 percent of the housing has been officially declared substandard. The city's capital plant is aging, and the expected subway was stalled because of an unanticipated increase in construction costs. Many streets are in poor condition, and a large part of the sewer system needs replacing. Many schools are inadequate; a recent estimate suggested that $75 million would be required to update the capital plant. You have repeatedly asked for a new school bond issue for the last ten years, and this has been repeatedly defeated at the polls. You do not have enough money to provide mainstream medical care for the poor, who underutilize the existing facilities. You have high disease rates among the poor. The welfare case load of 23,000 covers only about two-thirds of the families known to be eligible. Furthermore, about 80 percent of the 65,000 older people are eligible for welfare, and only one-fourth of them are covered.

One of the ghetto pressure points is the police force, which is only 3 percent Negro in staffing. The ghetto residents are calling for removal of the police from ghetto areas.

The federal government wants to help, but you find it difficult to accept all their offers because of the matching fund requirements. Common sense tells you previous investments have only begun to address the problem. Your problem: How to improve the city and provide the needed services?

5

A Critique of Formal Analysis in Public Decision Making

Ralph L. Keeney and Howard Raiffa

5.1 Introduction

It is almost a categorical truism that decision problems in the public domain are complex, much too complex. They almost universally involve multiple conflicting objectives, nebulous types of nonrepeatable uncertainties, costs and benefits accruing to various individuals, businesses, groups, and other organizations—some of these being unidentifiable at the time of the decision—and effects that linger over time and reverberate throughout the whole societal superstructure. It would be nice if somehow we could pour this whole mess into a giant computer system and program the superintellect to generate an "objectively correct" response. It just cannot be done! No matter how hard one squeezes the available objective data, it will not come close to providing answers for action. Indeed, such an "objective" analysis, where relevant data and information are processed, summarized, and exhibited for later action purposes by diverse types of decision makers, might fall so far short of providing guidelines for decision making that the output of the analysis may not pass the threshold of relevancy. It is our opinion that societal problems demand the consideration of subjective values and tradeoffs. The question, as we see it, is not whether subjective elements should be considered, but rather whether they should be articulated and incorporated into a formal, systematic analysis. The choice is between *formal analysis* and *informal synthesis*, and this metadilemma does not have an obvious solution.

In this chapter, we stick our collective necks out and offer some perspectives on the role and applicability of formal analysis in the making of public policy and in the operations of public systems. Our concern is partially with such methodology as operations research and systems analysis, but primarily we shall be interested in the growing body of techniques known as "decision analysis." In our minds, the distinction between decision analysis and the more traditional analytical techniques involves the degree to which the subjective attitudes of the decision makers are encoded into the formal analysis of problems. These subjective elements are introduced into decision-analytical frameworks through the use of judgmental or subjective probabilities and in the scaling of preferences and values by utilities. If one takes, as we do in this chapter, the prescriptive orientation, that purports to help the public decision maker choose an alternative course of action which optimizes some criterion, then we feel it is essential to incorporate his subjective attitudes and values into the analysis. Without these subjective inputs the domain of practical applicability of the methodological framework would be severely limited.

Now there is much more experience with the use of decision analysis in the private sector than in the public sector, but admittedly, this collected experience is still very meager. (See Brown [3].) Nevertheless, having acknowledged this paucity of relevant examples, some conclusions drawn from business applications may be tranferable to the public sector.

In the next section, we discuss the role of formal analysis in public decision making. Sections 5.3 and 5.4 concern, respectively, some of the characteristics of public problems that make them so complex and issues that must be considered when contemplating the use of decision analysis. The advantages of formalizing the decision making process are specified in Section 5.5, followed by sections addressing technical and nontechnical problems inhibiting the use of such analysis in the public domain. The paper concludes with a section on improving the climate for the application of formal analysis in public decision making.

5.2 The Role of Formal Analysis in Public Decision Making

Simply stated, the major role of formal analysis is "to promote good decision making." Formal analysis is meant to serve as an *aid* to the decision maker and not as a substitute for him. There is no attempt—nor would it be possible—to replace the judgment and resourcefulness of the public official.

Formal decision analysis helps the decision maker choose a good course of action by providing a rationale and methodological procedures for that choice. The analysis also can serve an advocacy role to facilitate the making or the implementation of a particular decision. As a process, it is intended to force hard thinking about the problem area: generation of alternatives, anticipation of future contingencies, examination of dynamic secondary effects, and so forth. Furthermore, a good analysis should illuminate controversy —to find out where basic differences exist, in values and uncertainties, to facilitate compromise, to increase the level of public debate and undercut rhetoric—in short, "to promote good decision making."

It is extremely difficult to do a good analysis on an initial attempt. Thus, first attempts must be considered somewhat exploratory in nature, and as such, the results are, to say the least, preliminary. However, if documented for scrutiny by others, these attempts serve well as a basis for comment and critical review, modification and improvement. In the process, procedures will be sharpened, standards of analysis improved, debate will become more focused, and hopefully decision makers will become more responsible to the common good.

There is a feeling that formal analysis is appropriate for repetitive operational decisions, such as, "Where should we send the sanitation trucks today?" or "What procedures should be used for operating airport runways in order to minimize travel delays?" But the feeling goes that analysis is nearly impossible for those one-of-a-kind, strategic decisions, such as: "Should we dispense methadone to heroin addicts?" or "Should we spend a billion dollars for research on nuclear breeder reactors?" No one claims it is easy to analyze complicated strategic problems, but we believe that many—not all!—of these strategic policy-type questions are amenable to systematic attack.

5.3 Characteristics of Many Public Decision Problems

In addition to their extreme complexity, a number of other properties tend to differentiate public problems from those in the private sector. For example, sometimes a problem is so ill defined that it is not clear who the primary decision makers really are. Furthermore, top-level public officials can resolve issues other than by fiat. They might turn it back to the concerned citizenry and ask for a formal referendum or stall a decision until the populace is allowed to speak through an acknowledged consensus.

Most public decisions affect various individuals and societal groups differently. Thus, there is a striving on the part of public officials to find an equitable solution. Imagine the case where the individuals in a society are divided as to whether they should make some improvement through a capital investment. One solution might be to make the investment and charge those people who pushed for this decision. But there is a complication: A majority of the citizens, for example, might be willing to pay for a new incinerator, but once it is constructed, all the citizenry, including those who did not support its construction, would benefit from the cleaner air. A good analysis would recognize both the fact that particular individuals were against construction and that they would eventually benefit in certain ways by its existence.

The marketplace itself can be considered as the decision maker incarnate for many societal, economic decisions. And even for those public problems that do not have a dynamic market mechanism, it may be possible to create such a market artificially. Alternatively, the public decision maker might choose on occasion not to dictate directly an outcome of a problem but to influence partially the dynamics leading to an outcome by manipulating the rules of the game. For example, legislation may be enacted that places constraints on the decision makers: "Commissioner, you simply can't build the new airport on that site, since it is a newly designated ecology preservation area."

Competition is a stimulus toward good decision making that rarely exists in public decision problems. In the private sector, if poor decisions are made by a firm, it will likely be eliminated by its competitors. By contrast, poor decision making in the public sector does not have such a nemesis. Here, the consequences of poor decisions are likely to be great amounts of wasted time, resources, and effort as well as a disillusioned public.

5.4 Issues of Concern in Public Decision Making

Essentially there are two types of analyses: those done for personal use, and those done to convince others. The personal analysis would likely incorporate very sensitive information, such as estimates of the future actions of political associates, a value placed on the life of an individual citizen, and value tradeoffs between the benefits to various identifiable groups. On the other hand, an advocacy document must be intentionally vague on such issues. Be that as it may, each of these analyses might have a common core of a good, relatively objective predecision analysis.

Certainly there is a moral obligation on the part of government officials to be open and honest, to share their real analyses with other government officials, agencies, and the concerned citizenry. But if this becomes the accepted norm, it could become increasingly impolitic to put down in black and white one's innermost

thoughts. When an analysis is put on display for general public review, one can hardly expect adversaries to give up without a fight.
They will scrutinize carefully the reasoning and seek out the soft
spots. This unfortunately means that it is very dangerous to base a
publicly announced decision on subjective feelings that are encoded into the formal analysis. Clearly, this is a major obstacle to
the use and disclosure of formal analyses in the public domain.

In practice, decisions are often judged to be good or bad depending on the eventual outcome. However, as we have mentioned, the
decision maker must choose an alternative course of action in the
face of uncertainty. One could choose an alternative that was
universally acclaimed by all those knowledgeable about the problem to be the best alternative, and then events could occur making
the chosen alternative the "wrong" decision. A good decision can
result in a bad outcome, and conversely. Because of the uncertainties and the fact that the decision maker is held accountable
for the eventual consequences of his decisions, there is a tendency
on the part of decision makers toward extreme risk aversion. The
personal rewards and adverse effects that the public official sees
for the "good" and "bad" decisions he makes are not necessarily
directly related to the good and bad effects his decisions can have
on the public. One bad decision can effectively erase the accumulated effects of many good ones.

A decision often has both short-run and long-run implications.
The public decision maker is essentially rewarded on the basis of
short-run outcomes: for example, what happens during the decision maker's tenure in office, and what happens before the next
election. To counteract this short-sightedness, the public officials
themselves and the mass media have an obligation to teach the
public to keep a balanced perspective of "immediate" and
"future" implications.

So far we have ignored the issue of how good analyses get done.
Who does them? Should it be outside consultants or an inside
group? Where in the organizational hierarchy is the analysis team
located? How does the introduction of an analytical team shake
up an existing bureaucracy? Enough has been written about
McNamara's introduction of planning, programming, and budgeting (PPB) into the Defense Department [7] that we shall only say:
the metadecision of whether or not to do formal analysis cannot
be divorced from the questions of organizational structure, of the

personal incentives for the people involved, and of the quality of the analysts. These and other relevant issues are addressed from different points of view in the chapters by Blum [2], Ernst [5], Hayes [6], and Szanton [8].

5.5 Advantages of Formalizing the Decision-Making Process

There are numerous pros and cons for formalizing the decision-making process, as opposed to managing informally the relevant information in one's mind, and neither strategy is clearly dominant. In this section, we shall mention some of the advantages of this formalization, and in the next two we cover many of the disadvantages.

Formal analysis stimulates insightful thinking about the interactions of various parts of the problem and the interrelationships between the problem and proposed alternatives. It forces an explicit consideration of the entire problem, and this process can be a catalyst for generating new alternatives to be considered and helps pinpoint where additional information is needed for decision-making purposes. This facilitates the gathering, compiling, and organizing of the data in a form useful to the decision maker. In addition, decision analysis can help promote more efficient interaction among group members working on a problem. Discussion can be raised above the level of just mentioning pros and cons of each alternative, and the substantive issues of balancing the pros and cons can be attacked.

Decision analysis provides a framework for decomposing a complicated problem into component parts so that various "experts" can simultaneously work on different aspects of it; then the methodology suggests a framework for systematically putting together these component analyses in a way that adds insight into the original problem. This is particularly significant in those cases where there are time constraints and no single person knows all the relevant information, but presumably various individuals have expertise on different aspects of importance. The public official can then delegate authority for the component parts of a problem to make clear to all concerned exactly who is responsible for what and to avoid potential conflicts of interest for individuals working on the problems.

A report on the results and implications of the study contains the rationale for choosing a particular course of action. Furthermore, it serves as a documented record of the work and provides the public official with an unambiguous interpretation of the assumptions made by his staff and others assisting him. In the process of producing such a report, the essence of disagreement between experts is often pinpointed, and hence one can attempt to uncover the reasons behind it. If such issues are made clear, it is less likely that the eventual decision will be made solely for the interest of some special group. In many cases, due to the care in preparation and the scrutinizing of the results, the likelihood that information is distorted would be lessened, and there should be fewer ambiguities and misunderstandings in reporting and interpreting the results.

A further advantage to the formal analysis of a decision problem is that it serves as a learning experience for the participants. By virtue of explicitly examining many of the difficult issues of a particular problem, their abilities to think systematically about complex aspects of public problems will likely improve. In addition, the mathematical reasoning, measurement techniques, and general approach to problem solving might be transferable to different areas of application.

5.6 Technical Problems Inhibiting the Use of Formal Analysis

Existing methodology and procedures are, in many cases, not developed far enough to model societal problems realistically. But let us be more specific.

There are not any systematic procedures for isolating problems. This is especially true in the public sector, where there is an intricate web of overlapping and interacting agencies. Solving one problem invariably creates other problems. We have all heard about the dangers of suboptimization—building a jetport in the Everglades may solve a transportation problem but it creates a conservation one.

Second, it is difficult to identify objectives and measures of effectiveness for a particular situation. One example of a systematic procedure for doing this is presented in conjunction with the air pollution control problem discussed in Ellis and Keeney [4].

Another difficulty involves specifying the possible consequences of the alternative courses of action. The costs and benefits accrue at various times in the future, and the individuals and groups that may be affected are sometimes not easily identified. It is extremely difficult to assess the judgmental probability distributions that describe the possible consequences when there are many measures of effectiveness. We need better techniques to acquire and incorporate subjective information into formal analyses. It is also important to quantify the value tradeoffs of the decision makers, that is, to get an indication of how much achievement of one objective is worth in terms of achievement of another objective. The preferences of affected individuals, which may be directly assessed or revealed through their actions, are important inputs to the decision-making process, too. Better and more reliable techniques and procedures are needed to obtain all the information just discussed.

Finally, we mention two problem areas particularly relevant to public decision making. The first concerns synthesizing the judgment and preferences of the individuals in a decision-making group in a reasonable and systematic manner in order to obtain what might be called the best course of action for the group. The second is: How can a decision maker rationally take into account the preferences of the individuals and groups who will be affected by a particular decision (but are not responsible for making the decision)? Much of the work on these problems has indicated theoretical limitations of intuitively appealing solutions. (For example, see Arrow [1].) The upshot is that they are even more complex than one would have initially thought.

To conclude this section, let us express our opinion that although there clearly needs to be a great amount of significant work done on the technical problems mentioned, we feel the techniques and procedures that are currently available are sufficiently developed to be an important aid to the decision maker. And no doubt, at least in this aspect, things will improve.

Some of the more important problems inhibiting the use of formal analyses in public decision making are discussed in the next section.

5.7 Nontechnical Problems Inhibiting the Use of Formal Analysis

Should a public official—say the head of an agency—spend funds for a formal analysis of his decision problem? Well, it depends in part on (1) whether he thinks the analysis could help determine his strategy, and on (2) whether he could use the analysis to implement this chosen strategy (for example, to help convince others).

Now if he does not understand the process he might not have any faith in the procedure; or, he might have faith, even if he does not understand the details, but he might not know enough to defend the analysis under cross-examination. Finally, he may fully understand the analysis, but he still might not be able to use this analysis because his audience is incapable of understanding the nuances of the formal argument. Such circumstances certainly inhibit the use of formal analyses.

We have all heard the admonition, "You can't put numbers on everything," or "Beware of quantifying the nonquantifiables." Certainly it is very difficult to articulate political issues, much less to quantify and measure them. But even if one could measure them, the public official would often be reluctant to do so. Such openness would not only leave him vulnerable to criticism but would eliminate much of his maneuverability.

Since the subjective components of a decision analysis are by nature more debatable than the objective components, adversaries concentrate on these aspects when attacking an analysis in an attempt to discredit the results. This has the effect that "hard" facts and data tend to outweigh "soft" subjective information in formal analyses. The consequence is that too much emphasis is placed on economics and efficiency and not enough on social and political implications.

One solution is to do two types of analyses: a private and a public one. But this proposed solution, as we indicated earlier, has severe societal penalities and goes to the heart of the public mistrust of its social institutions. We are on the horns of a dilemma. The public wants more attention paid to subjective considerations, wants more honesty and openness, but is not sophisticated enough to withstand the rhetoric of those advocates who stand ready to demolish any nonobjective arguments. Certainly this calls for the development of standardized procedures for quantifying that which is truly quantifiable, and we suspect that much more is quantifiable than the public realizes. After all, GNP is an awfully abstract concept that has taken on a tangible meaning of its own. Perhaps the public can also learn to internalize the meaning of other social indices of our quality of life.

Analysts can alter and subvert studies unbeknownst to naïve public officials. The analyst by specifying objectives and measures of effectiveness, by isolating the boundaries of the issues to be studied, by selecting the experts, by highlighting certain data, by suppressing findings, can mold the analysis in a manner favorable to his prior convictions. This probably does not happen very often on a conscious level, but we suspect this, to some extent, is omnipresent on a subconscious level. It is crucial that the public official not lose control to the analyst. This requires that the decision maker take an active part in the deliberations. Also to guard against biased studies and to raise the quality of the analyses, a public official could institute quality review or advocacy procedures requiring the analyst to "sell" his results to a reviewing board of experts not chosen by the analyst.

5.8 Conclusions

In our opinion, the theory of such disciplines as operations research, systems analysis, and in particular the methodology of decision analysis are now developed to the degree where they can be a significant aid to the public decision maker. It is important to accumulate critical experience with the use of those techniques on societal problems. And if this effort is to make any sense at all, it is imperative that public officials and members of their staffs begin to use formal analysis on projects of importance to them. The difficulty of such efforts, as well as their possible benefits, should not be underestimated. Often the total value of such analyses is not immediately apparent but rather accrues over time as successive analyses improve in quality and relevancy and as people learn how to interpret and implement such efforts better. We should not become disillusioned if initial attempts are somewhat feeble; the achievement of quality is an evolutionary process. Thus, we believe it is important to start doing, documenting, and critically reviewing these attempts with the spirit of learning. How can it be done better next time?

The climate for formal analysis of public decision problems needs to be improved. We must learn how to ameliorate our main nontechnical problem: lack of communication between the analytical specialists and the practically oriented decision maker. Methodologists must modify the analytical procedures to conform more with traditional methods of decision making in the public domain. They must be willing to dig in and work *with* the practitioners on their problems. Practitioners must experiment with more systematic procedures for decision making. They should be embarrassed to say, "Numbers and logic are a mystery to me." There is an obligation of both the methodologist and the practitioner to interact with each other. As a society we should produce more middle men—individuals who can comfortably walk on both sides of this chasm and who can facilitate communication between the two cultures.

Many of the technical difficulties inhibiting the use of decision analysis on public problems are beginning to be "solved." We feel, furthermore, that many of the nontechnical problems inhibiting such applications result from misunderstanding the procedures and misinterpreting the role and implications of formal analyses on the part of potential users, and not from any fundamental weaknesses in the theory. We authors, admittedly biased, believe the assumptions and methodological approach of decision analysis are sound and appealing. The fact is that we, methodologists, must continually improve our product and learn how to market it. The market potential is certainly there, and the potential societal benefits are enormous.

Acknowledgment

We thank Joseph Ferreira, Craig Kirkwood, and Katherine Swartz of M.I.T. for their constructive comments on draft versions of this chapter.

References

1. Arrow, K. J., *Social Choice and Individual Values*, Second Edition, Yale University Press, New Haven, Conn., 1963.

2. Blum, E. H., "The New York City Fire Project," Chapter 7, this volume.

3. Brown, R. V., "Do Managers Find Decision Theory Useful?" *Harvard Business Review*, May–June, 1970.

4. Ellis, H. M. and R. L. Keeney, "A Rational Approach for Government Decisions concerning Air Pollution," Chapter 18, this volume.

5. Ernst, M. L.. "Public Systems Analysis: A Consultant's View," Chapter 3, this volume.

6. Hayes, F. O'R., "From Inside the System," Chapter 1, this volume.

7. Mundel, D. S. and J. D. Steinbruner, "A Preliminary Evaluation of PPB," M.I.T. Center for International Studies, A/70-7, Sept., 1969.

8. Szanton, P. L., "Analysis and Urban Government," Chapter 2, this volume.

6 Quantitative Models in Public Administration: Some Educational Needs

Alvin W. Drake

The increasing use of formal models for the analysis and improvement of public systems has implications for several types of educational programs. When public officials and analysts have some common language and understanding of each other's orientation, formal models prove to be powerful tools for the definition and exploration of complex situations. A detailed explanation of how we arrived at the present state of such interaction would list many factors. As one item, consider how many college graduates today receive degrees in some form of business administration and how few receive at least an equivalent preparation for careers in public administration. This imbalance between the quantity and variety of people and skills prepared for the public, as opposed to the private, sector is but one of the reasons why we have so few people with understanding of what an urban or state government may be, what powers, responsibilities, and revenues are found at particular levels, and the processes by which public decisions eventually happen.

But these considerations are common knowledge. In this chapter, I am concerned with one part of the situation. My intention is to present some thoughts on how professional education in several fields could better prepare students for the application of more formal, quantitative models in the management of the public sector. I begin by discussing the concept of *formal models.* After a brief review of the personal background that leads me to my views, I offer a list of salient ways in which public problems differ from their private or military counterparts. This is followed by comments about some present modes of professional education, stated briefly enough to approach caricature. Hopefully, it will be adequate to fuel further discussion. In somewhat more detail, I offer conjectures on some types of academic experiences that might make public administration students more aware of the promise and pitfalls of using formal, quantitative models to assist in the resolution of public issues.

Much of my discussion considers what I suggest for the minimum academic experience with quantitative formal models for students who are preparing to become practicing public officials.

I refer to their field of study and practice as *public administration*. This term is also meant to apply, for our purposes, to neighboring fields such as public policy, policy analysis, urban studies and planning, government, and others. Although some of these students may develop into technical specialists or analysts, it is not they with whom I am primarily concerned here.

6.1 Formal Models

To me, a formal model is an *explicit abstraction* that represents the more significant features of an issue to be considered, identifies the variables of primary interest, proposes a structure through which the variables are related, and (usually) proposes measures of effectiveness for the comparison of alternative policies. The model may take on many forms, from a verbal, nonquantitative flow chart identifying, for example, the critical decision steps in how a state allocates its federal "Safe Streets Act" money, to a highly technical, quantitative, mathematical programming model for exploring the consequences of several policies for the management of regional water resources.

No formal model is a precise representation of reality. In considering public issues, we are most often concerned with approximate, highly aggregate models of but a few aspects of the problem at hand. Nevertheless, a formal model developed with some care will almost always be more useful than an implicit, less well defined model, stored in the mind of a single individual. "More useful" because the formal model:

1. Prominently displays its definition of the problem and its assumptions, making clear what aspects of a situation are and are not being taken into consideration.
2. Provides an explicit vehicle for discussion.
3. Often allows for empirical evaluation and improvement.
4. Encourages the application, when suitable, of highly developed forms of analysis.

At the very least, formal models might be said to provide powerful bookkeeping tools for processes individual decision makers would like to carry out in their minds. Some advantages and disadvantages of replacing more common, internal, "informal" models by formal bookkeeping tools will be discussed later in this chapter.

6.2 Some Personal Background

This section is provided to allow you to balance my comments
with the viewpoint from which I present them.

After an electrical engineering education and some years of
Army service, I joined the M.I.T. faculty in 1964 and developed
an interest in public systems applications of operations research.
My interests were assisted and encouraged by Philip Morse and
Gordon Brown, both of whom were ahead of their time in trying
to bring about some fundamental changes in orienting more of
M.I.T.'s academic and research efforts toward basic needs of the
public sector.

Working with graduate students at the Operations Research
Center, I first became involved with relatively technical aspects of
public systems, such as inventory control for blood banks, the dispatch and control of police and emergency ambulance vehicles,
and the scheduling of proposed advanced transportation systems.
Several chapters in this book report on dissertations performed
with my assistance. In fortunate cases, our students found opportunities to serve with activities such as the Science and Technology
Task Force of the President's Commission on Law Enforcement
and the Administration of Justice, the U. S. Department of Transportation's Insurance Study, and the New York City–Rand Institute. Work with state and local advisory panels, as well as a view of
other critical policy recommending agencies related to our technical efforts, necessarily broadened my interests. In particular, it be
came clear that our analyses were one very small step in the long,
and often incomplete, trip from formulation and analysis to implementation and evaluation.

As the urban crisis became so visible and got a name, several
changes occurred. The amount of analytic and technical work related to public problems rapidly increased. Student values shifted
and it was less necessary to seduce students out of mathematical
abstraction and high technology to turn their attention to more
applied concerns with problems of the public sector.

As I became involved with agencies and officials, there were
shifts in my own orientation. At the research level, I became interested in the systematic, but surely less technical, study of
broader issues. (How does a state allocate and spend its funding
from large federal programs? What functions of an urban police

department may be decentralized to respond productively to public interest in "community control?") Also, I began to learn about the limited tolerance that public officials, often highly educated within their own professions (usually law or public administration), had for the introduction of more formal analytic and management models. Similar problems, in the introduction of new models as management decision tools, and in the consideration of higher levels of technology, had, of course, been met with some success in the past in the defense and business communities.

To learn more about the penetration of modeling techniques into public administration, and to learn more about the context of the types of public problems that interest me, I spent a sabbatical year hosted by two of the new graduate programs in "public policy." I did what I could to visit other public administration programs at many schools, to learn about the profession of public administration and its literature, and to participate in related activities and conferences.

My primary concern that year was the place and style of formal quantitative models and methods in the public administration curriculum. I have also been thinking about how new public applications and interactions require changes in the culture and curricula of fields such as operations research, engineering, and management. As an operations research educator, I am concerned with all links in a chain that might eventually lead to more effective analysis in public agencies. This chain is relatively well developed in parts of the federal government; I am most interested in developments at more local levels of government.

6.3 What's Different About "Public" Systems?
My comments result in part from an estimate of differences between many issues in public management and those in other areas in which formal modeling is more firmly established. Some of these differences are

1. The clientele of a public issue, the most relevant administrators, and a relatively complete overview of the issue itself are harder to find. A firmer allocation of responsibility and accountability is found in the private and military sectors. Sometimes it appears that the survival of key public officials and their agencies hinges on the avoidance of such clear decompositions.
2. Measures of effectiveness for various public policy alternatives

are hard to specify and, usually, even harder to measure and evaluate. Constraints on available alternatives are fuzzy and, furthermore, local measures of economic and administrative efficiency may be but a small part of an appropriate set of criteria.
3. The problem itself, the available data, and the time available for analysis can often support only the most approximate, aggregate models and modes of analysis. The resulting formal bookkeeping is still likely to extend the thoroughness of the analysis that would be done only by implicit reasoning if formal models were not utilized. However, analyst and public administrator must keep in mind that, at best, the model captures only a significant fraction of reality.
4. Although particular types of public problems may require the development of new and resourceful methodologies for accomplishing difficult tasks, only in the rarest instances is there a similar need for the development of new analytic techniques or new technologies.
5. Satisfying technical solutions to quantitative models of situations will have to be modified for many good reasons. Collusion and competition among public agencies is probably more complex than the equivalent in the private sector. A model is incomplete in more ways than usual—for instance, initiation of action in one problem area often depends on compromises and arrangements with agencies primarily interested in entirely different areas. A quantitative modeler has to remember that his is only one part of a set of systematic approaches to a problem; the careful "political analysis" of an issue may be no less structured than his own approach.
6. State and local governments support almost no quantitative planning and development to prepare themselves for major future decisions. By the time a problem is subjected to analysis, most parties will already have taken strong positions, often based on quite different definitions of the situation and of their objectives.

6.4 Some Present Problems in Educating the Technical Specialist
Let me start by discussing difficulties from my side of the fence. To do so, I shall lump together education for engineering, science, operations research, and the more quantitative aspects of management science. Although only some students in these fields need ever be concerned professionally with work in the public sector,

one hopes that more of them and their skills will show up there. Some aspects of professional education in these fields that may limit seriously our students' abilities to work on public problems are:

1. We generate an unrealistic perspective by enormously emphasizing precise solutions to preformulated models. Our students become much better at getting from a model to its "solution" than they are at modeling (and even at tolerating) new, clearly important, but awfully fuzzy problems. In fact, I once heard a leading educator in operations research tell a distinguished assembly that he didn't see how our field and its schools could contribute to the resolution of public problems until mayors and their staffs are prepared to come to us with precisely formulated problems. He may still be waiting, and, if public administrators are equally flexible in their thinking, we can all quit now.

2. Partially as a result of a lavish and intense national defense program, our schools developed cultures that place the highest values on specialization for the development of more advanced techniques and technologies. Far lower values are placed on design, implementation, and problem formulation and resolution in broader areas. For the defense program, this wasn't too serious, because we also developed a large industry ready and able to translate new developments into implementation to meet at least the perceived needs of its clients. Defense expenditures were vast enough to support a highly specialized set of competences, leading to one's bringing *his* specialty, rather than a broad tool kit, to a problem. He worked at a considerable distance from "the problem" and, in many cases, he may never have known what it was. Our undergraduate programs became preparatory, quite abstract, and uncoupled from applications. The only professionals our students were likely to encounter were teachers and, alas, too often our values became the students' values. Our technical graduates probably assumed that other fields of knowledge and practice were structured the same way, leading to a graduate's tendency to work within his specialty, leaving other aspects of a problem, especially the less precise ones, to other specialists, whether or not they exist.

3. Up to the recent past, strong financial incentives were provided to encourage bright young people to choose technical fields. Technical education and research were financed on a scale never experi-

enced, for instance, by schools of public administration. Funding was adequate to provide a considerable degree of apprenticeship training inside the graduate schools.

What suggestions follow from such a list of comments? Most are obvious, but they require very significant changes of attitude from faculties whose professional and educational orientations have been formed over many years during the golden age of the defense program.

My highest priority item, for the types of schools discussed here, is that we at least provide our students with options that allow them to learn in lesser depth but about more things. We should provide the chance for students, while they are still in school, to apply broader knowledge to more important, fuzzier, and less antiseptic problems. For instance, I would like to bring more of our students to the point where, by systematic analysis, they would choose to attack problems in the delivery of public services at their most critical, rather than at their most technical, aspects. Before students develop individual technical specialties, whatever they may be, I'd like students to see more of subject material most suitable to the preliminary, aggregate modeling of larger systems such as applied economics, mathematical programming, decision analysis, and inference.

Our technical graduates may be among the very small part of the general population to whom it is natural to consider formal models to aid their understanding of complex issues. I'd like our students to be aware of the uniqueness of their approach, while, at the same time, acquiring enough experience at open-ended problems to realize that many issues simply can't have easily defined clienteles and satisfying "technical" solutions. As an example, Hardin's classic paper on the commons problem [2] is an excellent vehicle for discussion of the latter point.

These suggestions may appear to indicate limited aspirations, but they offer a large achievement beyond the present state of affairs in which we teach systematic modeling in so limited a context that, when confronted by *really* significant problems, our students are likely to throw away whatever systematic methods they may have experienced and tackle, on an emotional level, only the most visible appendages of public systems.

In this section, I have conjectured that much of the present system for the education of technical specialists may in fact limit their abilities to apply their knowledge to important public problems.

My own unhappy prediction is that the profession of public administration will more rapidly develop a capacity to "use" our skills than we will broaden ourselves and our students to apply these skills to significant problems. We are far more spoiled than our counterparts in public administration, and, in our educational programs, less flexible. We seem too likely to remain suppliers of overspecialized students whose outputs will be assembled at higher levels by people in other professions. As happened for some time in the industrial sector, modern management will not find many of our graduates playing some of the leadership roles to which they might contribute new and needed skills.

Were I a scientist, I might not be troubled by such a state of affairs. But as an engineer, representing a profession that developed almost exclusively by bringing knowledge from the sciences to problem solving in the world outside the university, I am disappointed to observe how slowly our curricula and our attitudes about professional accomplishment adjust to the pressing, relatively low technology problems of the public systems area. This appears in many ways, perhaps most painfully when technical educators talk about "solving" critical social problems rather than about training students to spend professional lifetimes attempting to understand and ameliorate the less attractive aspects of the human condition.

6.5 Formal Models in Education for Public Administration
Schools of public administration traditionally have not emphasized the use of formal models and quantitative techniques. Such schools operate almost exclusively at the graduate level, emphasizing the professional master's degree, and their students tend to come from the social sciences and liberal arts. In the past, curricula were relatively vocational in the sense that only limited abstraction was attempted and that models, when used, tended to be of the informal (not explicit) kind and were closely coupled to particular applications. Professionals and educators in public administration are quite wary of formal models, for many sound reasons and, also, for some less sound reasons.

Everybody agrees that the formal modeling of social and administrative processes is different in kind from the modeling of physical phenomena. Administrators are more than aware of the dangers of an analyst modeling well what is suitable for formal modeling by established techniques and being careless with other important aspects of the problem. But administrators are also skeptical of the modeling process because they are unsure of what it is, what it can and can't do, and because, of course, they themselves have had no chance to think about it outside the context of problems in which they are already embroiled.

As schools of public administration move more into the area of formal modeling, in a way similar to what happened to engineering schools about 20 years ago and to business schools about 10 years ago, all kinds of things are happening; although several of the largest schools have taken only preliminary steps in this direction. Traveling about the country, one can find students in public administration learning intricate computer languages, the simplex method for solving linear programming problems, elementary and intermediate calculus, matrix algebra, and just about any other quantitative topic you might suggest, including some of the most specialized imaginable statistical procedures. My feeling about such topics is that they are second order types of information for students who may spend only one or two subject semesters learning about formal models and quantitative methods. To overstate my view of current trends in some schools of public administration, I ask your indulgence for a brief digression in the following section.

6.6 Computer Programming Education at M.I.T., Circa 1954
Electronic computation was arriving to make possible calculations which formerly were tortuous or unthinkable. M.I.T. had a remarkable machine, named "Whirlwind," which performed computations at an astonishing rate. I knew a textile specialist who wanted to learn how to use the machine for computation related to her work.

Along with many other people with similar needs, she enrolled in our one-semester subject in computer programming. And what a subject it was, especially for a textile engineer. First she learned about resistors, capacitors, inductors, and diodes. Then she learned about vacuum tubes, active circuits, flip-flops, Miller integrators, core storage grids, and so forth. Those students who survived to the end of the semester learned, eventually, that if anyone were so culturally depraved as to merely wish to *use* Whirlwind, there were things called instructions which could be used to tell the machine what it is to do. Somehow, the resistors, capacitors, inductors, and all their friends would do their things without further attention.

I doubt that anyone questioned the nature of this subject in its day; one obviously had to "understand" computers and be able to design them before achieving the competence to be a user. Such subjects were originally taught, of course, by the people who developed the computers.

6.7 Objectives for a Quantitative Models Part of the Public Administration Curriculum

The point, of course, is a suspicion that today we are doing to public administration students what we were doing in 1954 to textile engineers who, as one aspect of their education, wanted to know how to use computers. In my view, many of the initial efforts at presenting quantitative models to public administration students are doing a great job on the almost irrelevant intermediate details. Time and effort might better be invested in helping students obtain a critical sense for formal modeling and for what it can and cannot do for them. Students who have suitable backgrounds and who desire to become analysts will still be able to do so, but the most critical educational tasks should be addressed first. The developers, applications specialists, and ultimate consumers of most techniques are almost always different people. I think it vital to accept this fact in presenting models and modeling to meet students' future needs.

As one approach to this topic, I shall suggest and comment upon some objectives and likely properties for a two-semester subject, "Formal Models and Quantitative Methods," for students for whom it may be their entire preparation in this area.

I consider the following to be an ambitious but feasible set of objectives for this part of the curriculum:

1. *To provide students with opportunities to develop their own perspectives on the uses, advantages, and potential dangers of formal modeling.* Formal modeling and quantitative procedures are not at all natural to most people. When applied to large problems, quantitative models are fought in some ways by social scientists

and in other ways by technical specialists. Social scientists may be
intolerant of a model's complexity, defensive about its use of unfamiliar concepts, or almost too aware of its creator's tendency to
grasp only the most quantitative aspects of a situation. They probably overestimate the sophistication of the implicit reasoning and
"internal expertise" used by an individual as the only alternative
to formal bookkeeping. Technical specialists, on the other hand,
tend to be uncomfortable with the imprecision of models of public issues, and they hasten to evaluate such models in terms of
all the considerations neglected by the model. I'd like to turn
some of their attention to concern with the selection and relation
of the few dominant variables, since I believe that this is almost
always more than an individual can achieve in the back of his
mind. I think we can offer our students a great deal by discussing
these matters in terms of actual cases, as well as in terms of particular techniques, doing what we can to have them form their perspectives based on information and experience.
2. *To help students develop an aware, unafraid, critical sense for
the modeling process and for performing plausibility tests on
models by checking their performance under simple conditions,
and so forth.* Public administration students are likely to be ex-
posed to models and formal modes of analysis, sane and insane,
many times during their professional lives. This will require considerable experience in discussing issues in terms of models, to the
point where students are prepared to fight bad models and their
results in terms of their weaknesses. Rejecting even bad advice on
the grounds of total disbelief in formal analysis seems to me an un-
promising approach.
3. *To familiarize students with a very fundamental set of formal
quantitative models, the concepts and assumptions they represent,
and the questions they investigate.* Here we are attempting to provide a closer familiarity and feeling for the most common components of the formal models tool kit. This is not equivalent to requiring that students learn the analytic techniques that allow a
person to proceed from each of these models to its consequences.
I believe that most or all students can quite easily acquire an understanding of common models in terms of the assumptions they
represent and the questions they investigate. It is usually the intermediate analytic details that require many unfamiliar prerequisites.
Several schools presently, I believe, get too entangled in trying to

deliver prerequisite knowledge and do not approach the point where the student sees its payoff. As one example of not taking on the intermediate analytic details, one could first introduce a set of models, spending considerable time on their assumptions and structure. Familiarity might then come from the use of interactive, real time computation to allow the students to "work" the models, making them less abstract, while avoiding almost all of the analytic overhead. Some of my associates tell me that I am professing cookbook education. They may be right. I think I am providing students of public administration with the most appropriate extension of their skills. (Recall Section 6.6.)

These objectives are overlapping and differ only moderately from each other. As a result of many visits and discussions, I conclude that most educators and professionals agree with this set of objectives. However, technical specialists, especially, argue that much more intermediate analytic technical detail is required to achieve these goals. And they are usually the people who teach the relevant subjects.

6.8 Some Properties of the Formal Models Part of a Public Administration Curriculum
It is not the purpose of this chapter to present detailed outlines for possible subjects. The relatively fine grain selection of material probably isn't particularly critical. But based on my experiences and biases, and backed by a dearth of supporting evidence, I shall present my conjectures about some properties of the formal quantitative models portion of a public administration curriculum. In the next section, I shall discuss in a rather general way some examples of what topics might be included as part of this minimum experience with modeling and quantitative methods.

I shall assume that from 20 to 30 percent of a student's time, over a two semester period, is to be used in the formal models and quantitative methods area. I think this is adequate for a minimum acceptable level of learning and exposure. I feel more strongly about the features listed here than I do about which models do or do not find their way into the syllabus. The following list of properties is based on my experience as a teacher and observer in such programs, as well as on some knowledge of how business schools adapted themselves, several years ago, to take advantage of electronic computation, the increased availability of useful quantitative models, and a broader variety of incoming students.

My list of properties for this part of the public administration curriculum is as follows:

1. No mathematics prerequisite beyond high school algebra.
2. May be taught with some efficiency to technical specialists alongside social scientists and admitted "math haters." (Aggregate modeling to support the understanding of public issues is a new topic for all these students, and they have much to learn from each other's views.)
3. Motivated primarily by discussion of applications and the applied literature, using a fair number of controversial studies. Nevertheless, it is vital that the subject include a careful abstraction and explanation of underlying models, making clear what they assume, what they explore, and, for future use, what they are called. If this abstraction is not performed with care, interpretation, and patience, the student is left with little knowledge he can use elsewhere. There is then the danger that he may be unsure of what features of a case under discussion are properties of the model and which are unique to the particular application. If this happens, the issues of modeling are probably lost along the way.
4. Contains almost no mathematical analytic details or procedures. Notions such as the area under a curve, the slope of a curve, the integral of a density over a volume, and so forth, have simple arithmetic interpretations and it is these interpretations we wish to convey. I believe these ideas are easily taught without attempting to teach calculus to students who do not already know it.
5. Takes considerable advantage of interactive computation in an "easy-to-learn" language for several purposes. The first time a student attempts to ask a computer to do anything, he gets an excellent experience in the need to provide an explicit and complete abstraction of the task at hand. The computer also allows students to become familiar with the notions mentioned in the previous item, without, for example, having to learn the analytic nature of those special cases where the operations may be performed symbolically. The student can also become comfortable with what he can and can't expect from computers and, from personal experience, come to understand the nature and limitations, for example, of simulation models.

6. The subject is a valuable experience but usually a poor prerequisite for preparing students for further study in formal analysis. Students may learn quite a bit about models and the modeling process, but they know almost no more calculus, linear algebra, and so on, than they did when they began the subject.

6.9 Some Indications of Possible Subject Content and Procedures
In my opinion, schools of public administration make an error when, as is often the case, they select a particular set of models (such as those from classical statistics or those from economics) and almost entirely neglect all other models. I prefer a wider, often less deep, experience with a variety of formal models and the types of reasoning they represent. This gives the student a better orientation for the professional experience he is likely to have as a consumer and critic of analyses of many types.

Discrete difference equations appear to me to be the most elementary, useful, and accessible mathematical models. They are easily worked, first by hand and then by computer. They describe the operation of dynamic processes over time and they allow one to become familiar with the concepts of system state and of process and control variables. Discrete difference equations allow one to track the behavior of important processes (such as disease control and population growth) for which, even with very simplified models, the mind alone cannot accurately relate policy alternatives to their consequences. Discrete difference equations rapidly bring a student into the difficult areas of assigning costs and measures of effectiveness to dynamic situations, including the usual conflicts between short and long term objectives. Much related literature is available that uses simple difference equations to represent major issues and to explore their policy alternatives. I especially like the use of Forrester's *Urban Dynamics* [1] here, because the work is important enough and controversial enough to have generated a considerable critical literature. Students can take advantage of that literature to consider how professionals of varied backgrounds discuss and evaluate modeling efforts.

Elementary mathematical programming models, but not their general solution techniques, seem to me to fit naturally into our fundamental set of models. Public applications are easily found, from work on school and congressional redistricting to many issues in economics and planning. The model is easily communicated, I believe, and it is not a large step, from a geometric picture solving a two-variable problem on the blackboard to the use of stored programs on an interactive computer system to work larger problems. Critical properties of the model and its solution, such as the interpretation of shadow prices, can be introduced without what I believe to be the almost wholly unproductive task of teaching these particular students the clerical details of the simplex method and the concepts of duality theory.

If such topics do not find their way into other parts of the curricula, the deterministic part of this subject would also present introductions and case readings to some less precise but equally useful types of formal quantitative modeling such as cost-benefit analysis and program budgeting. A good start on the latter topic may result if the line item budget of a nearby city or town is brought into the classroom for a discussion of its value and how one might wish to make it more useful. Program budgeting may be the ultimate case of considering the potential of simple formal bookkeeping to relate outputs to inputs.

Although I didn't list it separately, I expect students to become familiar and competent with electronic computation during this first, deterministic part of the subject. The overhead of this effort can be made minimal, especially at the start. I believe that interactive systems that allow time-share operation, with line-by-line diagnostics that effectively tutor the student whenever he presents an improper instruction, do wonders to increase the accessibility of the computer to the nontechnical student. It is true that such systems tend to be very inefficient ways of running large programs, but that wouldn't matter here. After the student feels comfortable and unintimidated by an "easy-to-talk-to" interactive system, it will be a simple matter to introduce him to a wider variety of systems for electronic computation.

Although the distinction between parts isn't too clear, I'd expect the probabilistic part of the subject to be about 50 percent of the class time. That part might begin with the elements of applied probability, with emphasis on the interpretation of fundamental concepts such as conditional probability, functions and expectations of functions of random variables, and the simplest notions of probabilistic processes.

My most central focus for the probabilistic models portion of the subject would be the interpretation and use of the fundamental model for the multistage problem in decision analysis. Students appear to accept this model as quite general and important. It provides a natural route for them to encounter the considerations of decision making in the face of uncertainty. Such considerations include the simple "laws" of rational decision making for an individual and the notions of utility theory, of the worth of potential experimental information, and the need not to confuse the assessment of uncertainty with the separate reasoning that goes into the assessment of the utility of possible consequences of the decision. This work leads quite naturally to a discussion of our limitations in being able to deal with group utility and the students' encounter with a simple, common situation that has no satisfactory technical resolution: the problem of decision making by groups of people.

The probabilistic part of the subject also, of course, considers matters of inference. Here I think it is especially important to trade in the time and effort usually spent on analytic procedures for time spent interpreting the types of questions asked, the structure of the models employed, and the types of results obtainable. I would want public administration students to know the logic behind significance and hypothesis testing, but I certainly would not risk burying them in analytic procedures for individual, specialized statistics. A student should become familiar with the questions asked and assumptions made by techniques that explore matters such as the analysis of variance and regression. For example, he should have enough experience with a few regression applications to take the results for what they are, and not for measures of causality. Once again, students who are equipped to do more in these areas may do so. Others are not being prepared to perform such analyses but to be aware, skeptical clients of such work.

Finally, the probabilistic section would include brief discussions of common phenomena and procedures, such as the elementary properties of congestion processes and the underlying ideas of dynamic programming for the solution of multistage decision processes. Previous simulation experience would be extended to the probabilistic case.

Several schools have programs that include subjects fairly close to the flavor and content of what I have described. Many more, however, have an almost entirely different approach: They attempt to be much more selective (and thorough), covering only a few of the topics suggested here, including their analytic structures. A considerable number of schools of public administration, including many of the schools with relatively large, established programs, have not yet made major steps toward increased acceptance of formal quantitative models. There is no shortage, at these schools, of faculty members who are sure that such material is not at all a fundamental entree on the menu of possible curricula for public administration.

At M.I.T., Joe Ferreira and I are in the early stages of the development of a subject of the type I have described. Initially, the subject will be directed primarily towards our graduate students with nontechnical backgrounds such as those in urban planning and political science. We expect the subject enrollment to include also students whose background and professional interests are more representative of those usually associated with M.I.T.

6.10 Summary

I have argued that developers, practitioners, and consumers of formal quantitative modeling work will most often be different sets of people. This chapter focused on needs for better preparation of practitioners and for providing more aware consumers.

I believe that present educational programs for engineers and other technical specialists contain many features that work against the ability of students to work in the area of public systems analysis. Most of the leading needs of this area cannot, at least at this time, support the high levels of abstraction, technology, and specialization that we impart to our students. This observation is commonplace. But professional education in technical fields, it seems to me, accommodates far too sluggishly our requirements for more breadth, more value on general problem formulation, and on the *implementation* of existing techniques and technology. Students in technical fields tend to be adept at the solution of classes of precise models but almost intolerant of modeling issues for less precise questions.

For students in the wide variety of fields I have referred to as public administration, an introduction to formal models and quantitative methods seems to me to be a vital part of their education. I think it is a major error to present the relevant topics much as they have been traditionally presented to the technical specialists. Trying to do so consumes far too much time on mathematical material prerequisite for particular solution techniques. If we are willing to address our efforts to the modeling process and to classes of models (the concepts and assumptions they represent, the questions they investigate, and the evaluation of applied modeling work), I think we can better suit the needs, interests, and aptitudes of most public administration students. The analytic methods required to get from most models to their solutions are, given the prerequisite overhead they involve, relatively peripheral to the first order needs of students in public administration. Objectives, likely properties, and a loose sketch of a formal modeling and quantitative methods program, involving about a quarter of one year's time in the public administration curriculum, have been suggested.

Interactive computation appears to be a promising vehicle for demonstrating modeling techniques as analysis and decision aids for public administrators. I believe it makes the models less abstract and enhances a student's understanding of the behavior of models, especially when the analytic solution techniques are neither within his grasp nor natural to his way of thinking. (An interesting application of this type of thinking to the needs of planners in the criminal justice system is discussed near the end of Chapter 16.)

I am more hopeful about present gaps being bridged from the administrative side than from the technical side. Even that development, I believe, requires the participation of technical specialists and other professionals willing and able to make severe departures from the cultures and educational traditions of their individual fields.

To whatever extent formal education does matter, I believe that no type of professional training is as crucial to our future well-being as is quality education for the administration of the public domain.

Acknowledgment

I am grateful for the hospitality and exchanges of ideas I encountered in my visits with educators and students in public administration from more than one dozen universities. I hope my hosts will find this overview useful, however severe and simplistic it may be. Especial gratitude is due to the primary hosts during my 1970–1971 sabbatical year, the Graduate Programs in Public Policy at Berkeley and Harvard. Thanks also to Richard Larson for his thoughtful comments on an earlier draft of this chapter.

References

1. Forrester, J., *Urban Dynamics*, M.I.T. Press, Cambridge, Mass., 1969.

2. Hardin, G., "The Tragedy of the Commons," *Science*, vol. 162, Dec. 13, 1968, pp. 1243–2148.

7

The New York City Fire Project

Edward H. Blum

7.1 Introduction

This chapter describes what is believed to be the largest concerted research project yet directed at urban fire protection. The work described is that of the New York City Fire Project, which has been and continues to be conducted jointly by the Fire Department of the City of New York (FDNY) and the New York City–Rand Institute.[1]

Supported by the FDNY, the project's research has been carried out by an interdisciplinary team: FDNY chiefs and other officials; engineers; an urban planner specializing in organizational behavior; applied mathematicians, including specialists in operations research, computer sciences, and statistics; economists; and a social psychologist. From the outset, a large part of the work has been done jointly by members from different disciplines, particularly when it has involved frontier research across disciplinary areas and the spectrum of activities that support implementation.

At the time of writing, the project had been underway roughly three and one-half years. In that time, its work had

1. Created new perspectives, methods, approaches, and results for the urban fire service.
2. Transformed these research products into operational information, insights, policies, and programs; helped put these into practice; and evaluated results.
3. Yielded, and continued to yield, gains in operating effectiveness conservatively valued at $10 to $20 million per year, annual returns more than ten times the investment.
4. Helped the FDNY develop new problem-solving traditions and capabilities and provide improved bases for its future policies and decisions.

The chapter aims to convey some of the style and substance of this work. For substance, we will focus in some detail on one area of the fire project's work: that concerned with effective use of fire

---

1. Earlier chapters by P. L. Szanton and F. O'R. Hayes outline the managerial and institutional settings of the New York City–Rand Institute and discuss the broad range of research that has been conducted. This chapter focuses on the largest of the New York City–Rand projects, the Fire Protection Project.

department manpower and equipment, and, in particular, with deployment or allocation of fire-fighting units. Within this focus, we shall set the context by describing briefly some points about urban fire departments and their operational problems. Then we will illustrate operational problems the research has addressed, describe some of the models developed to solve these problems and some major results that these models have yielded, and, note briefly what putting these results into practice has involved and what some practical experience has been.

7.2 Context

Our client and partner in this work is the Fire Department of the City of New York, which provides nearly all the fire protection, most of the alarm communications, and some nonmedical emergency services to the land and port of New York City. With roughly 14,500 uniformed men, 1,000 civilian employees, and 400 fire units, the FDNY is the world's largest paid fire department. Its organization and operations are much like those of its counterparts in other cities, but larger and more extensive.

New York City

When our joint research began in January 1968, the FDNY faced a number of serious problems. Some already were upsetting its operations and management and thus were widely recognized within the department, while others were manifested only as general undercurrents of concern to a sensitive few. Some were particular to New York City, while others were common to many big-city fire departments and even to the urban fire service in general.

Most conspicuously, as the work began, the fire department was operating under severely increasing strain. Fire alarm rates in New York City had tripled in the preceding decade and were continuing to skyrocket. The rapidly rising alarm rate imposed unprecedented demands on the department, demands that could not be met using then-standard management practices and fire-fighting technology. Communications channels were becoming clogged during peak periods, and routine paperwork was swamping key personnel. The command-and-control system functioned with aging equipment, which had worked well for a long time, but the number of incidents and the volume of information to be handled were growing much faster than the system's ability to cope with them. And as alarm rates continued to rise, strain in command-

and-control was increasingly accompanied by strained field operations.

Due to the rising alarm rates and alarm densities, by 1968 some fire-fighting units in high-incidence areas were responding more than 8,000 times a year and more than 20 times a night many nights of the year. These units were beginning to feel overworked, and the increasing workload was becoming a serious and potentially expensive issue in negotiations with the fire-fighting unions. Moreover, when several large fires erupted at the same time in one part of the city, it proved increasingly difficult to get enough units quickly to the later incidents, and dispatchers strained to maintain balanced coverage throughout the city in the face of the heavy localized demands for men and equipment.

At the same time, fire protection was becoming much more expensive. Between fiscal years 1957–1958 and 1968–1969, for example, the FDNY's total budgeted expenditures had risen from $99 million to more than $200 million, and were beginning to jump at 20 to 30 percent per year. The FDNY's budget had already exceeded the operating budget of the entire City of Boston. And straightforward budget projections assuming that then-current trends would continue were staggering.

The fire department had launched a number of energetic and thoughtful programs directed at these problems, but preliminary evaluation showed less favorable effects than anticipated. Traditional fire-prevention programs, developed for and apparently effective in industrial, commercial, and middle-class areas, seemed to be having little effect in the deteriorating slum areas where both existing incidence and growth in alarm rates were highest. In these high-alarm areas, there was a new community relations activity, which—though highly motivated—suffered from the same lack of basic understanding that plagued such activities everywhere. Multimillion dollar modifications of the command-and-control system had been proposed, but authorities questioned whether they could achieve what was needed. To relieve local concentrations of workload, a number of new units had been added—at a staffing and operating cost per unit of over $500,000 per year. But these had provided much less relief than expected, and several had become new high-running units themselves.

Often with considerable ingenuity, members of the fire department had proposed numerous other approaches to the department's problems. Given the tools then at hand in the fire profession, however, most competing theories seemed more or less equally plausible, depending perhaps on who had advocated them. Thus, policy debates often ran aground on vital but unanswerable questions, and all but conservative ideas tended to lose impetus.

Most of these problems were unique to New York City in degree rather than in kind; fire problems had simply come to a head first in New York. Indeed, a retrospective look at urban problems and innovations shows that New York City has frequently led in both —perhaps because its ills are writ large by the City's "size, scale, pluralism, dysfunctional city bureaucracies, and powerful civil service-labor movement coalition."[2] But New York was clearly far from alone.

Fire Department Problems

Fire alarm rates were rising rapidly in other big cities, too, and some cities outpaced New York. Reforms in command-and-control and fire-fighting technology and deployment were beginning to be seen as needed in several cities, although the shape of the reforms was still quite unclear. Municipal union strength was growing throughout the country, particularly in the East and Midwest. Service costs in many cities were rising faster than the revenues needed to pay them. And with the exception of a handful of big-city fire departments, the entire urban fire service received little effective support from industry, universities, or the federal government, and lacked an in-house research tradition.[3]

Let us look briefly at some of the common, underlying problems.[4]

The fire service mission is traditional and enduring: to prevent fires and to respond to those that do occur and put them out. Although most urban fire departments stress the preventive role, all are primarily organized to serve in crisis—to react promptly and

2. See Rogers [12], p. 60. Rogers refers not specifically to fire but to the factors that exacerbate socioeconomic problems in general.
3. The FDNY had been particularly innovative in certain areas. It had developed new equipment—such as the superpumper and the tower ladder—and installed the first fire department computer (an IBM 360/20, in 1967). But FDNY officials expressed the concern that even their innovating traditions and capabilities were fragile and unsustained.
4. A more comprehensive view can be found in Blum, [2]. It should be noted that not all of these problems are manifested in every city, and that many of them are less severe in New York than in other cities.

protect the community when parts of the physical or social order break down.

Men and Management

Perhaps more than any other municipal service, the fire service across the nation is linked by a sense of fraternity and tradition, the keystones of which are reliability, dedication, esprit, heroism, and self-sacrifice. This tradition underlies much of the fire service's effectiveness, particularly in the grueling and dangerous operations required to save lives and limit damage in serious fires. In the contemporary city, however, this tradition is gradually eroding and coming to seem anachronistic. Public adulation and even sympathy for the fire fighter has been waning, and in the larger cities demands on the fire service are increasingly becoming conspicuous symptoms of deeper social ills.

Fire fighters have become increasingly disturbed because their traditions and the values they represent appear to be disintegrating. Changing public attitudes, fragile relations with minority communities, and a trend toward bureaucratization have dimmed the luster of the job and shaken and transformed many firefighters' self-image.

This crisis in public- and self-identity has also afflicted fire-service management. Recruiting the most highly qualified men has become more difficult, and labor and community relations have become increasingly important concerns. Costs have been rising, but voter resistance to increased budgets and taxes has stiffened. And management itself has become more difficult and more complex, now that tradition no longer suffices to motivate and guide the skilled manpower on which the fire service depends.

Yet, nearly everywhere, some other traditions still dominate; for example, the only road to the top of larger fire departments is from within, and few training programs are available to teach management and organizational skills. Moreover, even among officers, the acculturation toward putting out fires is so decided that many of the best men prefer field command to top administrative or staff jobs.

Practices and Equipment

Despite the image of technology—of alarms, trucks, sirens, hoses, and ladders—fire service is still basically a *personal* service, provided in person at widely distributed, local sites by groups of men

having specialized interests, skills, and physical capabilities. Men
lay hoses and advance them. Men brave heat, flames, and toxic
gases to perform rescues. Men open up buildings to expose flames
to hose streams and to ventilate heat and smoke. And men command these operations at the scene. Facilities and equipment are
neither insignificant nor inexpensive, but the primary strength of a
fire department is in its manpower, and the preponderant expense
is still the annual recurring expenditure on personnel.

Indeed, in most urban fire departments, manpower costs amount
to more than 90 percent of the total budget. Increases in costs
have often followed increased demands for protection, which—
combined with the increasing strength of municipal labor unions—
have led to larger forces and to salaries, pensions, and fringe benefits that have outpaced the general price index. As a result, to supply, staff, and operate *one* big-city fire truck with its complement
of men—keeping the unit ready and running 24 hours a day, seven
days a week—now costs from $250,000 to $650,000 per year, depending on manning levels and salaries. In New York City, for example, a decision to add or remove four active fire units changes
the operating budget by roughly $2,500,000 per year.

Of the forces helping to retain this manpower-intensive character, one of the strongest is tradition, which remains influential
both within and without the fire service, despite its gradual ero-
sion. Even with the advent of motorized equipment and mobile
radio communications, for example, basic fire department practices seem to have changed little in the past half century. Practices
inherited from the past continue widely in traditional forms, and
most use manpower generously. Nearly everywhere except New
York, the insurance underwriters' "Standard Schedule for Grading
Cities and Towns" exerts a conservative influence and is increasingly viewed as an obstacle to effective management and innovation. On the other hand, tradition and most fire fighters' personal
inclinations call for risk taking and flexibility. These qualities are
increasingly discouraged by both formal fire department organization and increasing union pressures for work to be more highly
structured and defined.

In addition, as students of bureaucracy are quick to note, fire
departments are essentially line-operating agencies. Such agencies
are often ill-equipped in outlook, skills, and organization to under-

take novel or significant change.[5] They are usually especially ill-equipped to undertake efforts that involve more than minimal uncertainty and risk. The rewards for success within the organization, and its political setting, are usually small, and the price of failure disproportionately high [1].

In this setting, unfavorable external pressures have raised the barriers to major productivity change even higher.

To carry out its activities effectively, for example, the fire service depends heavily upon outside persons and agencies: those who formulate and administer the building codes, architects and building contractors, fire insurance companies (whose rating practices influence private fire protection, such as detectors, sprinklers, or brush clearance that property owners provide), telephone companies, private or auxiliary alarm services, and equipment manufacturers and suppliers. Within local government, the fire service depends upon many other agencies' programs: effective housing policies and programs, particularly those aimed at preventing deterioration and abandonment; effective trash collection, particularly in yards, halls, vacant lots, and other areas beyond the curbline; effective zoning; and effective leadership and social policies at all levels of government.

These persons, agencies, and activities lie beyond the fire service's direct domain and often are hard for it to affect. But when they perform poorly, they contribute to increasing the fire service's workload and impair its ability to carry out its mission.

These problems have been compounded in that the fire service has depended, and for the most part still depends, for information and new ideas largely on a few dedicated interest groups and professional associations, which are backed by limited financial resources and next to no research. Most of the research that has been done has either supported existing practices and products or treated subjects that, while important, are peripheral to the main interests and needs of the urban fire service—such as nuclear-blast fire problems, forest fires, and the chemistry of combustion.[6]

5. Though clearly not always so, as the significant changes introduced by the FDNY demonstrate. The other side of the coin is that fire departments also can be tightly organized, relatively monolithic organizations that may respond quickly to leadership in situations having commonly perceived outcomes and widely perceived goals.
6. Basic research on combustion chemistry might, of course, eventually lead to improved fire-fighting tools and tactics, as in the polymer area it has already led to improved fire-resistant and fire-retardant materials. But most

To some aspects of fire protection, technological change could contribute significantly, either by changing the basic nature of the service that the fire department must provide (for example, through less flammable bedding and furnishings or a comprehensive early fire detection and warning system) or by increasing the service capability per man. But technological changes in the fire-protective milieu have occurred slowly, even where suitable technology already exists, principally because market forces work against them. The changes add to costs, and there have been neither subsidies nor strong regulations to stimulate adoption.[7]

Fire-fighting technology has advanced, on the whole, even more slowly. Radio has just begun to replace voice and hand signals and messengers for tactical communications at the fire scene. Power tools have just begun to replace axes and crowbars in ventilating roofs and walls. Command-and-control is grounded in turn-of-the-century technology. New materials, new protective clothing, new fire detectors, new extinguishing agents, or materials to enhance water, have been introduced agonizingly slowly, in part because of the small and atomized fire service market and a fragmented and reluctant supply industry.

7.3 The Fire Project

Research Environment
Our research began, therefore, in an environment in which many were aware of the general need for change but unsure of the direction that change should take. Pressure for movement came both from within the fire department, from those who recognized the serious problems and wanted to do something about them, and from outside the department, mainly from the City Bureau of the Budget and other parts of the Office of the Mayor, which wanted to ensure that changes would be broadly beneficial.

---

urban fires are so diverse and heterogeneous, in their burning material as well as in their heat and mass transfer, that combustion experts now largely hold little hope for understanding them in detail. Indeed, the phenomenon of combustion itself is so complex that some leading researchers in the field have moved to other, seemingly more promising areas for research now that support for combustion work has been significantly reduced.

7. The major leverage over such technological changes exists at national rather than local levels because of the national scale of most of the relevant markets. Federal activity, such as that represented by the fledging flammable fabrics program, thus appears to be essential if the basic nature of urban fire protection is to change.

Strong pressure came also from the fire-fighting unions, whose positions defied clear definitions of in versus out. The unions had considerable political power, which had grown notably since the demise of the City's major political organizations. This power, together with increasing willingness to resort to political tactics, gave them a major role and a continuing impact on fire department policies. The issue from the time we began thus was not whether change should take place but what change and how.

As we were spared the burden of proving that real problems existed, so we were spared the burden of learning and overcoming research precedents. As noted earlier, there existed little prior research on major urban fire problems, and no analytical work on problems as complex as those in New York.[8] Together the fire project joint team thus had to create the perspectives, methods, approaches, and results of a new analytical field.

To have strong pressures for change and a nearly virgin research territory is an analyst's dream. But in applied research dreams must often meet a harsh reality. As soon as we were declared in the game, the pressures for change also became pressures on us for quick and "relevant" results that would take one of the several sides in a growing power struggle. We were called upon to become analysis's priests in an environment not notably kind to rationality. Maintaining independence and integrity, developing appropriate power relations, and staying abreast of key decisions timing became critical. It was clear, for example, that events could easily pass us by and relegate even the most skillful analyses to the massive archives of interesting but unused research.

To pioneer in the research area, it was important to develop a strong analytical basis—one good enough to yield new insights and ideas and rooted carefully enough in experience so that we, the fire department, and the public could have full confidence in its results. Building such a basis obviously required time. But simultaneously we were being pressed to provide immediate and short-term assistance, and it was clear that we might not have the chance to complete long-term research if in the short-term we did not do enough to pay our way.

8. Work on urban fire problems was under way, as we began, at the British Fire Research Station in Boreham Wood and at the British Home Office in London. Later, efforts began at the U.S. National Bureau of Standards, the Johns Hopkins Applied Physics Laboratory, and several university operations research, public affairs, business administration, and planning departments.

Making our way in this environment, we were helped enormously—as Fred Hayes and Peter Szanton have noted in earlier chapters—by being part of broader efforts underway within the New York City government to improve the quality of operations and decision making. Mayoral staff and the Bureau of the Budget were working to make analysis part of the budgetary process. And, both in line and staff positions, the fire department had begun—with strong mayoral support—to develop internal analytical interests and skills.

Although this broader analytical context, centered initially around PPB,[9] was valuable for many reasons, it is especially worth noting three:

1. It provided continuing evidence of top-level interest and support, and access for analysis to budgetary and political power that we alone could never initially have claimed;

2. It provided the basis for mutual learning among the different groups working on similar problems, and thus for "economies of scale" in developing information, insight, and new policy alternatives; and

3. It provided able people with a strong comparative advantage in handling relatively traditional immediate and very short-term issues, and thus freed the fire project at least partly for the relatively more technical and longer term work for which its skills and style were more appropriate.

The Research Program

Our charter was to help the fire department with a wide range of its important problems, focusing on those where the department, and the others working on fire problems, felt the greatest need for additional technical expertise. When we began, it appeared that the key to meeting many of the pressures on the fire department was to employ fire-fighting resources, particularly manpower, more effectively. Our research program was thus directed toward policy change in three basic areas:

—*Improved operations*—to ensure that men and equipment would be available where and when they were needed, in appropriate numbers and condition.

9. Planning-Programming-Budgeting, a management aid instituted in the New York City government by Mayor John V. Lindsay and Director of the Budget Frederick O'R. Hayes.

*—Improved technology—*to extend men's abilities and free them
to make the best use of their skills and judgment.
*—Improved management—*to develop and make the best use of
scarce resources and individual talents toward fire protection
goals.

Later in the research, the department asked us to broaden the
program, to explore means of improving the social and economic
milieu within which the fire department operates. We thus added
two more basic areas:

*—Reduced demands for fire department services—*to ameliorate
the social and physical origins of fires and other sources of fire
alarms.
*—Improved setting for fire protection—*to enhance the technical
and economic incentives for privately provided fire protection,
and to identify and stimulate desirable broader changes that may
be beneficial to overall fire protection.[10]

Within these broad areas, specific research emphases and subjects have evolved and changed with time. Our work on technology, for example, began by developing a feasible concept for
a comprehensive early fire detection and warning system, and by
initiating and catalyzing a fire-fighting breakthrough called "slippery" or "rapid" water.[11] Since late 1968 we have continued to
provide managerial and technical liaison for the "slippery water"
development program, to help ensure its success.

Our work on management has been broader. It began with PPB
and studies of command-and-control and specific studies of de-

10. For example, some measures to reduce the amounts of waste paper and
waste packaging materials generated, though aimed primarily at reducing
solid wastes, could also reduce the number and severity of trash-related fires;
day-care centers in poverty areas might also help reduce the number of child-
initiated fires and the number of child fire deaths.
11. "Slippery water," now often called "rapid water," is made by carefully
dissolving trace amounts of a special chemical—a long-chain polymer called
poly(ethylene oxide)—in water entering the fire pump. This solution permits
a fire department to increase the flow through a hose at a given pressure by
70 percent or more, and to more than double the reach of the stream. The
slippery water research and development program has had to overcome a
number of serious engineering difficulties, but with major commitment of
expertise and effort from the Union Carbide Corporation and the FDNY, it
has progressed rapidly and well. First-generation technology began field operations in the Fall of 1969; the advanced third-generation system began
use in New York in the fall of 1971.

partment components such as the fire marshal's investigation system. As our work on the communications system and fire-fighting deployment progressed, it evolved into the basis for an integrated management information and control system, for which we prepared the functional definition and have guided the development of detailed specifications. More recently, we have emphasized helping the department institutionalize the results thus far obtained—not only the specific results for current problems but also new policy processes designed to strengthen the bases for handling future problems.

Rather than lightly survey all of our work, I would like here to focus on one part of it—that dealing with the deployment of fire-fighting men and equipment.[12] This work is closely related in its impact to much of the rest of our research, as Figure 7.1 depicts. These figures show the principal stages in fire growth and fire department operations, with the corresponding important areas for research. We will center here on the research area numbered 11—analysis, modeling, policy and program synthesis for strategic deployment decisions. These are the decisions that must be made, both in planning and in the heat of operations, to provide and maintain the City's fire-fighting coverage, and to dispatch the appropriate units to respond to each alarm.

Research Style

In all the research areas, but especially in the work on deployment, our research style has been participative, multipronged, and interdisciplinary. Fire department and other City personnel have been involved in the work as closely and as intimately as possible, in very much a joint team. And in each area, often at the same time, the joint team has pursued several different approaches. Some involved helping the department with rather well-defined problems and issues, where our staff supplied an independent point of view and an assortment of tools and expertise to support the department's own activities. Some involved helping the department grapple with basic, ill-defined problems, where we were able to help clarify just what the underlying problems were and bring analytical expertise to bear on solving them. And some involved more traditional creative research—discovering things that had

12. A broader, albeit incomplete, survey of our work can be found in Blum [4].

**Stages in fire growth and
fire department operations:**

Ignition

Fire
growth

Spread

Detection of fire

Reporting to fire
department

Alarm identification
and processing

(A) → Status of men
and equipment

(B) → STRATEGIC DEPLOYMENT
DECISIONS

Dispatching

(C)

Important research areas:

1. Social origins of demands for services
2. Fire prevention regulations and activities
3. Materials technology
4. Building design and construction
5. Institutional setting for fire prevention

6. Early fire detection and warning systems

7. Voice reporting systems

8. Automatic status reporting
9. Communications and dispatching
    improvements
10. Management information and control
    system

11. Analysis, modelling, policy and program
    synthesis

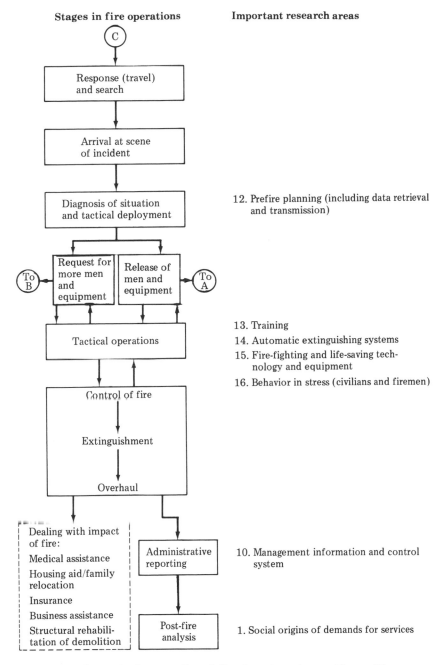

Stages in fire operations   **Important research areas**

Figure 7.1 Stages in fire growth and fire department operations with corresponding research areas.

not been noted before and bringing to the department and the fire profession new insights and capabilities.

The research itself has been staged in time and nested in organization. In this way, early results and learning experiences have helped to provide bases for the more advanced work to come, and the results from different parts of the work have fit together and proved mutually reinforcing. This research design also has facilitated carrying on short-term and long-range work in parallel, making easier the dual responsibility for helping the department with current crises and forthcoming decisions and preparing sound bases for the range of decisions the department seemed likely to face in the coming years. From the outset, we chose to center on issues that were clearly important and on which decisions would have to be made, and on areas where leverage existed, or could be created, for significant change.[13] This concrete focus, combined with the drive to develop a soundly based longer range perspective, has led to a number of major results.

From the beginning, strategic deployment has appeared to be nearly an ideal research area. The issues at stake were initially important and growing even more so, and it seemed clear that they would continue to matter over the next decade. The policies in use when we began work were encountering many difficulties, so that the potential gains from improvements appeared to be large. And many of the key problems appeared amenable to the techniques of analysis.

7.4 Deployment Research
Let us now look in more detail at some of the deployment research, beginning with basic problems and issues and some of the broader features of the deployment modeling, including measures of effectiveness. Then let us examine two specific deployment models—in particular, an analytical model that has yielded useful and unexpected results for fire-fighting units' dispatching assignments, and a policy-oriented simulation of strategic fire-fighting operations.

13. We have had our share of blind alleys and false starts (such as jumping early into the development of large optimization models that proved neither usable nor relevant, and spending time on special language-structures for simulating on-line dispatching decisions that turned out to be unnecessary.) The short-term and long-range work have at times conflicted more than they meshed, and our sense of priorities has not been infallible.

Basic Problems and Issues
Demand

As noted earlier, underlying many of New York City's fire deployment problems was a rapid rise in service demand. Between 1956 and 1970, for example, New York City fire alarm rates increased from 69,000 alarms per year to more than 240,000. The rate for every type of incident, from false alarm to structural fire, increased dramatically.[14] False alarms increased much more rapidly than any other type, so that by 1970 over 30 percent of all alarms were false alarms and less than 20 percent were for structural fires.

A strong concentration of alarms, both in space and in time, accentuates the effect of these increases. An area in the Brownsville section of Brooklyn, for example, frequently cited as one of the worst in the City, has for several years had an annual rate of over 10,000 alarms per square mile—more than 13 times the citywide average. Other areas in Brooklyn, parts of the Bronx, and areas in Manhattan also have alarm rates well above those typical of the rest of the City.

Similar variations occur with season and with time of day.[15] Most "nuisance" alarms,[16] for example, appear to vary with temperature, peaking notably during the summer, while structural fires (that is, fires in buildings) show a slight peak during the winter. The time-of-day peak is dramatic, as Figure 7.2 shows. Roughly 60 percent of all alarms arrive in the peak nine-hour period from roughly 3 P.M. to midnight. And the peak hourly alarm rate ranges from 5 to 15 times the low. There is thus often a thirty-fold variation in alarm rate between a mild winter morning and a hot summer evening.

Not only are the peak alarm rates often very high—often more than 30 alarms per hour in Brooklyn or the Bronx alone, for example—but the mixture of alarm types also varies considerably

14. By 1971, however, the number of fires of all types had begun to level out, and only false alarms and nonfire emergencies continued to increase rapidly.
15. We were most fortunate in analyzing detailed patterns of demand to have available from the FDNY, already in computer-compatible form, the records of all fire alarms in New York City in 1962, and from 1964 to the present. Cleaning up these records and making them readily usable took over six months of tedious work, but the file—with over one million alarm records—now provides a most valuable data base.
16. That is, false alarms, some nonfire emergency calls, and mischievous or malicious fires in rubbish or abandoned automobiles.

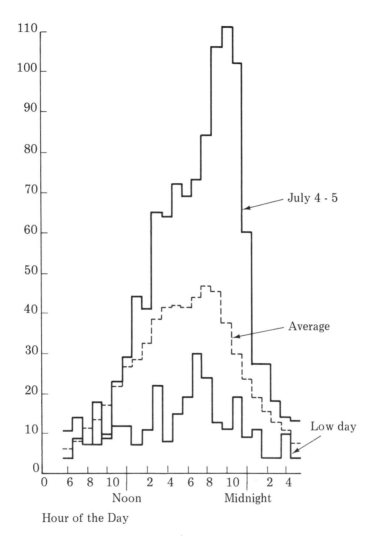

Figure 7.2 Hourly total alarms in New York City, 1968.

with area and time. By the late 1960s, traditional uniform deployment policies were thus doubly perplexed. Indeed, as our research began, perceptive observers had begun to note that deployment problems would be aggravated by attempts to retain traditional deployment policies in the face of nontraditional demands.

Traditional Deployment Policies

Nearly all paid fire departments, including the FDNY, had traditionally kept the same number of men and units on duty around the clock, even though demand in the afternoon-evening peak period is several times greater than demand during early morning hours. Similarly, most departments, including the FDNY, tried to maintain a uniform *standard response* of men and equipment to alarms in most areas at all times, although fire hazards and the likelihood that an initially indeterminate alarm will turn out to be a serious fire vary greatly with area and time of day.[17]

In the traditional deployment procedures, for an alarm at a given location, dispatchers consult an *alarm assignment* or *running* card to see which units to send. This card contains a list of the units closest to the site, ordered by proximity. In some cities, including New York, it also lists preplanned moveups or *relocations* to cover the area around the site should there be a large fire that draws many units away. These lists implicitly assume that only the one incident is active in the area at the time. In active periods, therefore, following the cards in areas with high alarm densities can quickly deplete coverage and lead to deployment problems that have to be settled by improvisation.

As the project's early analysis showed, therefore, the traditional system forced dispatchers to make ad hoc deployment decisions when the incoming flow of new alarms most pressed them for time. And, as the alarm rate rose, it led increasingly to responses containing fewer units than planned, to improvised relocations, to longer than normal response times, and to imbalanced workloads.

Deployment Issues

A number of serious issues had thus arisen in New York by the late 1960s. As alluded to earlier, these were mainly

—*Coverage and workload problems.* During peak alarm periods, some fire-fighting units in high-incidence areas were busy much of the time. The areas to which they were normally assigned were thus being left for extended periods with reduced coverage. And the increasing workload was stimulating union demands for more men and more fire-fighting units.

—*Response problems.* The department attempted to maintain its

17. In New York, this standard response comprised three engines (pumpers), two ladders (hook-and-ladder trucks), and one battalion chief—abbreviated as 3-and-2. As equipment became scarce, in peak periods, dispatchers found themselves unable to send 3-and-2 to each new alarm. They then often were forced to reduce the response, either to an intermediate size such as 2-and-2 or 2-and-1, or all the way to the minimum stipulated response, which was 1-and-1. In peak periods, the standard response thus could become only a nominal guideline.

historic standard response of three engines (pumpers) and two ladders to potentially serious telephoned alarms and to all alarms from street-corner alarm boxes, despite the serious coverage and work-load problems to which this policy contributed. Though only about two percent of all alarms really needed the full 3-and-2, many argued that to avoid undue risks in the absence of better information about the nature of incoming alarms it was better to send too many units much of the time than to be caught short when the full response was needed.

—*Nuisance alarm problems.* Nuisance alarms were viewed by the firemen as harassment and as resource diversions, which might dangerously delay getting needed units to serious events. Traditional educational and community relations programs seemed to be having little positive effect.[18] And the obvious approach of reducing response to high nuisance alarm areas foundered when tabulations showed that the areas with the most false alarms (excepting some parks) generally also had many residential fires, and had some of the City's most densely populated, hazardous buildings.

—*Relocation problems.* The alarm assignment card relocations were proving to suffer from serious problems: They inherently assumed that only one incident was active at a time in a rather wide area, and they triggered relocations only when major events occurred, although a number of minor incidents proved able to strip an area just as thoroughly.

—*Adjustment problems.* Rapidly shifting alarm patterns threatened to undermine the department's longer range decisions and commitments such as fire-house location and reconstruction. Suggestions had been made, for example, to remove fire-fighting units from areas that later became some of the most active in the City.[19] Similarly, the department anticipated major increases in alarm rates in several areas, but had been unable to get major resources

18. Indeed, some observers argued that the programs could well be making the nuisance alarm problem worse, by making more widely known among the city's youth the degree to which something so simple to commit as a false alarm was taken seriously by a major uniformed city department.
19. One set of such suggestions had been made by a group of local professors and students in the early 1950s. More than 15 years later, this study was continually cited to us as an example of why analysis and research was sure to be bad for the fire department. It proved a major obstacle that we had to overcome early in our work.

into the capital project pipeline before the problems became conspicuous.[20]

Deployment Modeling

In addressing these issues, we have created a wide variety of models to analyze and evaluate fire department deployment and suggest new policies. These models are directed, individually and together, toward the basic set of issues that underlies the list outlined earlier:

—How many units of each kind (engine, ladder, chief, and so forth) to have, and where to locate them;
—How many, and which, units to dispatch initially to incoming alarms;
—How and when to relocate or reposition available units;
—How to vary all three of the above policies with time and with changes in circumstances (such as alarm rates);
—The impact of reducing, or at least ameliorating, demands for fire department services;
—The impact of changing the resource commitment needed to handle the various types of incidents at the scene.

As the discussion in Chapter 10 by Jan M. Chaiken and Richard C. Larson indicates, there is no one model that, by itself, suffices to handle everything. Rather a variety of mutually reinforcing models is needed, each drawing on the most appropriate analytical tools to deal with particular sets of policy issues.

Models

Some of the models employ quite complex mathematical analysis to get at the heart of intricate deployment questions. Others rely more on the power of the computer to compile, generate, reshape, and analyze large volumes of information. And still others distill the results of complex analyses, or large numbers of computer

20. The adjustment problem was a major reason why one issue that was clearly *not* on any list was optimal fire station location—the one issue that had then received substantive operations research attention. City officials considered "optimal" locations irrelevant because (1) location decisions were made incrementally, and it always seemed clear at the time the general area in which each new station should go, (2) the main problem was site selection, and finding and obtaining good sites in the general area designated was often quite difficult, and thus dominated most other considerations, and (3) the uncertainties created by shifting alarm patterns more than washed out the short-term gains that any optimization algorithms seemed likely to bring.

runs, into easy-to-use "rules of thumb." What matters for each, however, is not the complexity or computer base of the model, but its quality—its insight, relevance and validity for the issues at hand. What has most interested both the fire department and the team have not been the models' details but what the models can yield, and how.[21]

Typical questions treated by the models include:

1. The number of units needed for responding and working in a region (and hence the minimum coverage and the likely need for relocation), depending on initial dispatch policies, alarm rates for different types of alarms, and the resource commitments (numbers of units, times) needed to serve the various types of incidents. This has been analyzed by means of a complex queuing model that predicts the frequency and duration of periods when more than n units will be needed.

2. How many units to dispatch initially to particular incidents, taking into account the probable severity of the incident, the number of available units, and likely future demands. This has been analyzed by means of an extended decision model, incorporating a complex Markov renewal submodel from which approximate solutions have been derived that yield practicable rules of thumb.

3. How many units are actually dispatched with a nominal standard response policy during peak periods. This has been analyzed by means of a queuing-type model in which the probability of sending the full response drops as the number of units available decreases.

4. How will the relative activity of units in an area be affected by additional units, full or part time, by changes in response policies, and/or by changes in alarm incidence and the times units are unavailable at alarms of given types. How much activity will the new units have? These have been analyzed by means of simple queuing-type models, essentially corollaries of the model noted in [3].

5. When gaps in coverage appear, which vacant houses should be covered, which units should be relocated into these houses, and when should the various relocations begin. Several different approaches have been employed, including integer programming and Markovian decision process formulations, dynamic covering algo-

21. Our models have been subjected to four broad tests: policy relevance, applicability, analytical or esthetic "taste," and operational validation.

rithms (using intuitive heuristics that work rapidly and well), and straightforward rules of thumb. These models attempt to account, in varying degrees, for the actual distribution of units at the time in question, anticipated new demands in relevant areas during the time period chosen for looking ahead, the periods for which units are expected to be unavailable at incidents already in progress, and special hazards and "costs" associated with the desired coverage and with the relocations themselves.

6. If suitable accommodations were available, where should new units—part time or full time—be placed to have the greatest effect on workloads? And, knowing specific locations where suitable space is actually available, what can one say about the effects of these locations on workloads, and the sensitivity to location of response times? These have been analyzed both through quite simple models (suitable for hand calculation or straightforward time-shared computing) based on elementary notions of location theory and through detailed computer models directed toward the question of response-time sensitivities.

7. Which units to send, given the number to be sent. This has been analyzed by means of a spatially distributed many-server queuing model.

Later we will discuss this last model in more detail, as we will the extensive deployment simulation, which analyzes, evaluates, and compares policies related to these questions and many others.

Application

The fire department has been intimately involved in developing, testing, and refining these models. And the department has used these models for a wide range of purposes. Both staff and line officials use them to see how various policies can and do perform, and why, and to see how to reshape and modify them to fit new circumstances. They have found that the models reveal key points of leverage, where actions will have their greatest effects, and thus enable the department to tighten the linkage between decisions and results. Used iteratively, prescriptive and simulation models have helped to create new policies and to distinguish worthwhile ideas from those that would be ineffectual or even potentially harmful. They have helped fire officials develop and gain acceptance for new programs and have provided bases with which to prepare for the future.

Criteria

Even though optimization has concerned much "public systems" literature, there are few optimization models in the earlier list. Of course, one of our main objectives is significantly improving the fire protection that the public gets for its money. But optimization in the usual sense does not apply to the problems and issues that have proved most important. Too many objectives matter for any one to be selected as paramount, and there is no operationally reasonable way of combining them all into a single index, especially where they conflict. Moreover, and perhaps more important, fire departments' prime responsibility is to provide emergency, contingency protection. They thus must perform at a high level under quite diverse conditions and circumstances, and the flexibility and adaptability required to do so usually must be gained at the expense of "optimality" in any narrow sense.

Space does not permit thorough discussion here of appropriate criteria and measures of effectiveness.[22] Let it suffice to note the following:

1. Traditional optimization often can be useful to explore selected dimensions of policy space and to develop the structure of potential new policy approaches. But optimal results should be carefully checked and shown to be robust with respect to relevant measures of effectiveness different from those used to derive them.
2. Average measures, such as average response time or expected work load, are valuable, especially in that they are often analytically tractable. In comparing operational policies, however, conditional averages (for example, average time until third arriving engine at incidents where three or more engines actually are used) and extreme or "tail" probabilities (for example, the probability that at least two of the three nominally closest engines would be available at least 50 percent of the time) are usually more appropriate and intuitively more acceptable.
3. Wherever possible, one should attempt to use measures of effectiveness that reflect the ultimate protection or lack of protection provided to the public—for example, preventable damage and loss of life. Unfortunately, neither the data nor the theoretical base needed to relate such measures to operational variables is

22. Blum [3] contains an extensive discussion of emergency service criteria and measures of effectiveness.

accurate or reliable enough to make the connection with reasonable confidence. We have attempted to bridge this gap with an interim measure, *avoidable damage*, evaluated through analysis of historical and technical data and through the use of subjective utilities [10]. But most of our work has had to rely on internal[23] measures of effectiveness, of which the most operationally useful include

—*Response time*—in particular, the vector of realized response times for all arriving units.
—*Coverage*—the geographical distribution of units relative to locations of potential demand (equivalent to latent or "virtual" response time).
—*Availability*—the ability of a particular unit or set of units to respond to alarms.
—*Escalation*—the growth of a fire or emergency to require more resources (and produce more "costs") than it would have if some reasonable alternative policy had been followed.[24]
—*Workload*—operational activity experienced by individual firemen and fire-fighting units.

Response Areas Model[25]

Let us now look in more detail at the model concerned with which units to send to particular alarms, given the units' locations and the number to be sent. Our approach to this important dispatch question is through the geographical districts, or *response areas*, that the units serve.

The analysis shows that *not* sending the closest units to selected locations can serve both to balance workload among units and to reduce average response time. In simple situations, it prescribes exactly which units go to which alarms if average response time is to be minimized. These prescriptions also tend to reduce the probabilities of very long response times.[26]

23. That is, inward looking, concerned specifically with what the fire department does rather than directly with the service it provides.
24. Escalation is a fire-oriented measure that looks at the times when an inadequate or poor policy causes an incident initially to get worse.
25. All material in this section leans heavily on (and in some instances is directly taken from) G. M. Carter, J. M. Chaiken, and E. J. Ignall [6].
26. In the model, the variable here called response time may be a general utility as well as response time, *per se*. Where one has a more general utility that varies monotonically with response time—such as that developed by Keeney [10], one may use it here throughout, without modifying the analysis.

We present here results for the case where the region under consideration is essentially served by only two units, and exactly one unit is dispatched to each alarm. This simplified case leads to qualitative conclusions that remain true for more complicated systems. Moreover, one can present the results for the two-unit case without elaborate assumptions and notation.

Findings for the n-unit case, though much more complex, have already been applied by the FDNY to modify selected response patterns during high-incidence periods. The modifications required are usually minor and are administrative in nature, so that the gains come essentially free.

The service discipline used in the two-units model follows a typical fire department pattern: Each unit responds to all calls for service inside its response area unless it happens to be busy servicing another call; in the latter case, the other unit will respond unless it is also busy. Thus we explicitly allow units to cross district boundaries.

This model differs from the typical approach to urban location-allocation problems in two important respects: (1) A unit serves its district only when it is available. The selection of a particular response area, therefore, determines not only the geographical arrangement of the points to be served from each location but also the probability of each unit's being busy. Both of these enter into the formulas for the objective functions. (2) We consider two types of objective functions at once. One measures the quality of service (for example, the response time), and the other measures the strains placed on the components of the system (for example, the workloads of the units).

Traditional Response Areas

Traditionally, to the question, "Which units should be dispatched to an incoming alarm?" the answer is simple: "Those closest to it." Nearly all fire departments and many other emergency services use this closest-unit policy. With it, the boundary between two adjacent response areas is simply the line equidistant from the home locations of the two units.[27]

Common sense dictates this policy. And the closest-unit division does yield minimum average response times when each unit covers

27. Modified by geographical eccentricities and barriers such as cliffs, mountains, water, bridges, limited-access roadways, parks, cemeteries, and so forth.

only its own response area or alarm rates are so low that the need for inter-area response arises rarely, if at all. When there are steep spatial gradients in alarm rate, however, this policy can lead to large variations in workload among neighboring units. It is clear that one can even out the workload by shrinking the response areas around hard-working units and expanding the others. But full workload equalization often leads to absurd results, with some areas receiving response times that are completely unacceptable. Traditional intuition thus leads one to expect that workload balance and response time are linked in a classic tradeoff, where improving one necessarily degrades the other.

Analytical Results

The model's analysis, however, contradicts this traditional intuition. It yields conditions under which other response area divisions *dominate* the closest-unit division, in that average response time is less *and* work distribution is more even. Though initially unexpected, this simultaneous improvement of two objectives has proved relatively easy to establish in intuitive terms.

For example, let us designate the lighter working unit as Unit 1 and the harder working unit as Unit 2. Relative to the closest-unit boundary, then, the boundary that yields minimum average response time lies nearer Unit 2, thus moving some alarms traditionally assigned to Unit 2 into the response area for Unit 1. This move has two main effects: (1) it transfers some of Unit 2's work to Unit 1, thus tending to even out workload; and (2) because of (1), it leaves Unit 2 free to handle the more frequent alarms that occur well away from the boundary in its response area, and thus reduces the need for the lighter running Unit 1 to make long responses to cover.

Because of the higher alarm rate near Unit 2, this reduction in long runs tends, up to a point, to offset the slight increase in response time to alarms moved to the Unit 1 side of the boundary. Where the spatial gradient in alarm rate is typical of that in the transition region between an active area and a light area, therefore, a slight shift in response areas reduces the probabilities of long response times and, up to a point, also reduces the average response time.

Mathematical Structure

Let us briefly note some of the model's mathematics. The original paper [6] should be consulted for details.

Our problem is to design response areas for two units serving a region B, with exactly one unit sent to each alarm. If R is any sub-region of B, we assume that alarms arrive in R according to a Poisson process with parameter $\lambda(R)$. We also assume that alarm arrivals in any two disjoint subregions are independent.

Now let A be the subregion chosen as the response area for Unit 1, and the remaining region, $B - A$, that for Unit 2. We can think of calls arriving from A as "Type 1 customers" for a queue, with rate $\lambda_1 = \lambda(A)$, and those arriving from $B - A$ as "Type 2 customers," with rate $\lambda_2 = \lambda(B) - \lambda(A)$. We then have a two-server queue with two kinds of customers, and the service discipline is as follows:

1. If a type j customer arrives when both servers are available, it is served by unit j, where $j = 1, 2$.
2. If a type j customer arrives when exactly one server is available, it is served by the available unit, $j = 1, 2$.
3. If a type j customer arrives when neither server is available, it is served from another location, outside the system under consideration.

For simplicity, we also assume

4. The service times for all customers are identically distributed with a finite average $1/\mu$, independent of the history or state of the system at arrival, the type of the customer, and the identity of the serving unit.
5. The system is in steady state.

Assumption 4 clearly neglects the effects of travel time as an integral component of total service time and as a contributor to possible escalation. Relaxing this assumption appears to offset slightly the gains that the model's results otherwise yield.

One can classify the states of this system in a number of different ways. For the purposes immediately at hand, we need only consider the states

AA = both units available
AB = unit 1 available, unit 2 busy servicing a call
BA = unit 1 busy servicing a call, unit 2 available
BB = both units busy

If the service times happen to be exponentially distributed, our system is a continuous-time Markov process, for which the equations of detailed balance in steady state are

$$\lambda P_{AA} = (P_{BA} + P_{AB}), \qquad\qquad (\lambda + \mu)P_{BA} = \lambda_1 P_{AA} + \mu P_{BB}$$
$$(\lambda + \mu)P_{AB} = \lambda_2 P_{AA} + \mu P_{BB}, \qquad\qquad 2\mu P_{BB} = \lambda(P_{BA} + P_{AB})$$

The solution, which has total probability 1, is

$$P_{AA} = 1/(1 + \rho + \rho^2/2)$$
$$P_{AB} = P_{AA}(\rho_2 + \rho^2/2)/(1 + \rho)$$
$$P_{BA} = P_{AA}(\rho_1 + \rho^2/2)(1 + \rho)$$
$$P_{BB} = P_{AA}\rho^2/2,$$

where $\rho = \lambda(B)/\mu$, $\rho_1 = \lambda_1/\mu$, and $\rho_2 = \lambda_2/\mu$. These values for the steady-state probabilities are actually valid for an arbitrary service-time distribution with mean $1/\mu$ [8].

We define the *workload* of unit j, W_j, to be the steady-state probability that j is servicing a call. Thus $W_1 = P_{BA} + P_{BB}$, and $W_2 = P_{AB} + P_{BB}$, so that

$$W_j = P_{AA}(\rho_j + \rho^2 + \rho^3/2)(1 + \rho), \qquad j = 1, 2.$$

The absolute difference in workload is thus

$$\Delta W = |W_1 - W_2| - P_{AA}|\mu_1 - \mu_2|/(1 + \mu),$$

which is proportional to the difference in total number of hours that each unit spends serving calls during a given time period.

The model assumes that each response is made from a unit's home location, with $t_j(\mathbf{x})$ denoting the mean time it takes unit j to travel $\mathbf{x}$ from its home location, using the fastest possible route. Let the average response time to all alarms, given that A is the response area of unit 1, be $\overline{T}(A)$.

Then, applying the P_{ij} derived earlier, lengthy but relatively straightforward analysis gives

$$\overline{T}(A) = \frac{P_{00}}{\lambda(B)} \int_A (t_1 - t_2 - s_0)\, d\lambda + \alpha,$$

where $s_0 \equiv \rho[T_1 - T_2]/(\rho + 1)$, T_j is the average response time if

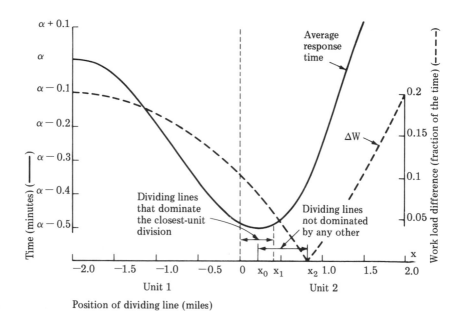

Figure 7.3   Example showing response time and workload balance versus position of dividing line.

all calls are answered from the location of unit j, and α is a complicated expression independent of the choice of response areas. As the form of this equation suggests (and as the cited paper proves in detail), the average response time $\overline{T}(A)$ may be minimized by selecting A, the response area for unit 1, to be the set $\{\mathbf{x} \in B: t_1(\mathbf{x}) - t_2(\mathbf{x}) < s_0\}$. Ordinarily there will be more than one choice for A that minimizes $\overline{T}(A)$, but the region commonly selected—all points closer to unit 1 than to unit 2—will not be one of them.

The concept of dominance arises from considering two important criteria at once: average response time and workload imbalance. Response area A for unit 1 is said to *dominate* response area A' if and only if $\overline{T}(A) \leqslant \overline{T}(A')$ and $\Delta W(A) \leqslant \Delta W(A')$, with at least one of the inequalities strict. Figure 7.3 illustrates the phenomenon of dominance in a simple example.[28] In this exam-

28. For this example, $1/\mu$ = 15 minutes, the response speeds v_1 = v_2 = 20 mph, the unit home locations are at $(-1,0)$ and $(1,0)$, the region is rectangular and stretches from $x = -2$ to $x = +2$ with an arbitrary height h, and

$$\lambda(A) = \frac{1}{2h} \int_A (x + 2)\, \mathrm{d}x\, \mathrm{d}y \qquad \lambda(B) = 4 \text{ incidents/hour.}$$

ple, most of the alarms are closer to unit 2 than to unit 1, and dividing lines as far as 0.8 miles from the midpoint are found to yield response areas dominating the usual choice.

Deployment Simulation

Our deployment simulation is the model most often used by the fire department, even though it is the most expensive to run and in many ways the most complex. Top department managers now use[29] the simulation as a routine policy and management tool to create and test proposed new policies, to check on the possible impact of changing circumstances, to review past conditions and programs, to see what data collection should be given the greatest emphasis and care, and to develop operational changes and modifications in detail. Together with the other models, on which it depends heavily for suggestions of what to try, insights and structure, the simulation has had a profound impact not only on fire department policies but also on aspects of its management style and ways of thinking.

It has given the department a powerful tool that is available to examine in detail ideas and prospective programs that could never have been given even reasonable scrutiny before. The energy and time required to obtain answers to important questions have greatly diminished, so much so that it is now quite feasible to make a number of iterative passes through a problem in a matter of days and have confidence in the results. Moreover, the model can analyze speculative questions as well as sober ones, making consideration of imaginative approaches reasonable and practical. Some members of the department have thus made extensive use of the simulation, often in highly creative ways.

Model Design

To achieve this wide acceptance and use has required both conscious and careful design of the model for policy use, rather than simply representation, and continual interaction between the fire department and analytical members of the joint team. From the outset, we developed the model for two main purposes:

1. *To offer insight into complex phenomena.* The simulation has been quite valuable, at all stages in its development, as an experi-

---

29. The simulation is still run by our technical staff. But as the model is fully documented and the department's in-house computer capabilities are enhanced, we expect it to be run increasingly by fire department personnel.

mental and learning tool. Accompanying the development of the various analytical models, it has led to insights that have opened the way for direct analysis, illuminated dimly perceived relations, and explicitly revealed the effects of complex interactions between variables and the higher-order consequences of suggested actions.

2. *To analyze, evaluate, and compare policy alternatives.* With considerable attention to experimental design and to verification, the simulation has provided a "policy laboratory," in the ways described earlier. A guiding question in developing this focus has been, "How can we best distinguish the difference between policies and reveal their performance in different problem situations."

Given this orientation and our close working relations with experienced chiefs, the model initially developed was rich in operational and policy detail, and lean and flexible overall. Directed specifically at the major deployment issues facing the department, it was—though lean—designed to accommodate additional breadth and detail as they seemed appropriate.

Initially, most of our effort went into representing operations and policies, and little into detailing geography and collecting exogenous data. There were two reasons for doing so: Too many other simulation efforts seemed to have spent a disproportionate share of their capital collecting data that later proved peripheral or unnecessary; moreover, the analytical models and early validations indicated that relatively simple geographical and data representations would suffice. Indeed, now that quite a rich texture has been added to the model in these areas, the major differences with the earlier results turn out to be of second-order importance.

The basic structure of the simulation follows the principal skeleton of Figure 7.1.[30] For the reasons noted above, fire-prevention activities, tactical operations (those carried out at the scene), and damage and losses have been represented only implicitly. But the model is set up to use explicit sub-models for these, should such additional features become feasible and desirable.

Experimental Design

In that the simulation was designed to be run often, and indeed has now been run thousands of times, much effort has gone into

30. See Carter and Ignall [5] for a description of the model as it stood in mid-to-late-1969.

experimental design. For example, major computing economies have been realized by using the simulation together with our many analytical models. The analytical results, often stimulated and/or confirmed by the simulation, have permitted us to trim whole dimensions from prospective simulation run patterns. Some equations and analytically derived curves have yielded insight and information that have significantly reduced the need for data to be collected laboriously in the simulation; others have explicated issues so well that whole sets of runs have simply become unnecessary. In addition, we have explicitly sought to distill and simplify simulation results into easy-to-use formulas and rules of thumb, both to keep the experimental design sparse and to make the results more comprehensible and useful.[31]

Some special techniques help reduce the numbers of runs that still must be made. One technique exploits the unique capability of a simulation to let alternative policies face exactly the same sequence of incidents. We prepare an incident tape with alarms sampled from the particular distributions of rates and patterns we wish to simulate. We then run all policies of interest against this tape, collecting comparative or "paired" statistics incident by incident. This technique clearly distinguishes the effects of different policies from the effects of changing circumstances, something quite difficult to do in the "real world." In statistical terms, it yields a variance roughly one-quarter that we would obtain running different policies against different samples of incidents and thus requires only one-fourth as many runs to compare policies at the same level of statistical confidence.

Another technique is designed to avoid the very large sample sizes (that is, number of simulated incidents per run) that would be needed directly to simulate relatively rare events, such as simultaneous large fires or fires that result in loss of life. This technique uses what we call *virtual measures of performance*, measures that reflect what would happen if an incremental (virtual) incident oc-

31. A rule of thumb that has proved quite useful, for example, is a modified form of the traditional formula relating expected travel distance to the inverse square-root of available facility density. This simple formula would not have been accepted as reliable or accurate enough for policy analysis without extensive testing and confirmation in the simulation. Now that it has been accepted, however, it has already obviated the need for many simulation runs and is expected to reduce greatly the number of runs that will be needed in the future. See Kolesar and Blum [11].

curred, given the state of the system at the time, but do not require that the incident actually occur. What we can do, for example, is interrupt the simulation at predetermined intervals and
sample the state of the system, for example, by recording the coverage or availability vector. Then, with the tape of state samples,
we compute the expected value of the measure for each state,
given the probabilities of alarms in the time period following the
sample, and compare these state measures statistically. When the
sampling and computation are carefully designed, it is possible to
reduce by an order of magnitude or more the total computing
required to compare the performance of alternative policies in
handling important but relatively rare events.[32]

Application

Let us note here briefly a few examples of simulation results that
have led to changes in fire department practice. Although the
model has since become almost a routine tool, it may be of interest to focus on its first major use—the 1969 contract negotiations
between the fire-fighting unions and the City of New York.

A major issue in the 1969 negotiations was workload. The
unions argued that a large number of units were overworked "as a
regular condition of employment." They demanded that the City
relieve this condition, preferably by pairing one new unit with
each "overworked" unit to split the workload. This proposal
would have meant adding from 40 to 75 new units, depending on
the level chosen to designate "overwork," at a cost of from $25 to
$45 million per year, not including the additional costs of salary
increases also being negotiated.

We first became involved in background discussions in January
1969, when we responded to a call for overnight assistance in formulating definitions of "workload" and "overwork." As we became more deeply involved, we began drawing on our then-fledg-
ling models and analyses to suggest and help devise new approaches to relieving workload and to help the department create
an array of possible programs. Certain basic questions recurred
often: What would be the effects of adding units in high-incidence
areas? What would be the effects of reducing the *standard response* from 3-and-2? If new units were added to an area, how
should they be deployed to be most effective? What would be the

32. In addition, the tape of state samples permits one to apply additional
measures of performance without having to replay the simulation.

effects of moving units at selected times of day? We began focusing our analytical work on these issues, and by the spring of 1969
we began obtaining usable answers.

Using the models, for example, quickly brought attention to the
important distinction between the nominal standard response and
the lower response that was actually able to be sent when high-
incidence areas became stripped during peak alarm periods. This
de facto reduced response was often lower than the new standard
response levels being considered. From this early analysis, therefore, it seemed quite possible that in high-incidence areas during
peak periods nominally reducing the response could, by retaining
better coverage, actually *increase* the response to many alarms.

More detailed analysis, using the simulation together with other
models, further showed that attempting to maintain a high standard response in these troubled areas vitiated much of the effect
of adding new units. With traditional deployment policies, the
new units would be pressed to fill out the *de facto* reduced response, rather than relieve currently hard-working units. Moreover,
much of the relief afforded the hard-working units would be absorbed by their responding to alarms they had been too busy to
cover. What relief there was would go disproportionately to lighter
working units, located on the periphery of the high-incidence area,
which would have to be called in to cover much less often. Response times in the high-incidence area would be improved, but
workload relief would be considerably less than anticipated.

Simply reducing the standard response, however, was also shown
by the simulation and other models to give less workload relief
than expected. If one reduced the standard from 3-and-2 to
2-and-2, for example, the engine that would be saved a response
would be the one (of the three) farthest from the alarm. Since the
high-incidence areas tended to be compact, the relief would again
go disproportionately to units around the periphery rather than
to the hardest working units in the center, especially since those
in the center were often too busy to respond when "third due,"
anyway. A more specifically tailored combination of policies was
clearly necessary.

Analysis and projections of fire incidence showed that alarm
rates (that is, numbers of alarms per unit of time) from roughly
3:00 P.M. to 1:00 A.M. were and would remain much higher than
the rates for any other times of the day. It also showed that in

high-incidence areas false alarms, rubbish fires, and other minor incidents are most frequent during these hours. These minor events do not require the men and equipment needed for structural fires.

Given these conditions, it seemed logical to consider an adaptive response—varying the number of men and equipment dispatched, depending on the likelihood of given types of alarms and hazards at various locations and times of day. To those who wondered how quickly the full standard response could reach a site if a street box alarm proved to be a serious fire, extensive simulation analysis showed that the best that could be expected actually happens: During peak periods, the adaptive response policy on the average got the full response to fires faster than the standard response could. The standard response often did not dispatch the full complement of equipment initially, and even when it did, it had so stripped the area that the third engine, say, had to come from much farther away.

For a wide spectrum of response policies and performance criteria, various models showed how many additional units would be needed (between 5 and 20, depending on the performance desired). They also showed clearly that important gains in protection and workload relief would be realized only with adaptive response policies and even then mainly during the peak hours. Both the fire department and the fire-fighting unions drew upon these results and used the simulation to evaluate dozens of specific bargaining proposals during the negotiations.

From the negotiations emerged a program of innovation, including an adaptive response policy and new fire-fighting units, called tactical control units (TCUs), that operate only during the hours of peak demand. The TCUs are activated at 2:30 P.M. and go off duty at 1:00 A.M.; they are dispatched in a way that ensures workload relief to neighboring units. Then, in helping make this new policy work, we assisted the department in improving the dispatching centers, choosing and designing the adaptive response areas, and selecting sites and dispatching policies for the TCUs and the new full-time units.

These deployment innovations have now been in practice, in varying degrees, for more than a year and a half. Evaluations indicate that the benefits for men and equipment have surpassed expectations. Tactical Control Units have provided the impact of full-time units, but at 40 percent of the cost. Adaptive response has consistently worked well, permitting equipment to arrive sooner with additional units available for immediate dispatch when needed. Fire officials have estimated that the increased effectiveness these innovations provide would have cost an additional $5 to $20 million per year if traditional policies had been maintained.

7.5 Implementation

Let us sketch briefly here a few points that have proved important in implementation.

From the outset, the project's *raison d'être* has been to help achieve policy change. Implementation has been an integral part of the research "guiding vision" and an explicit part of both overall and detailed strategies. From the beginning it has been apparent that shaping significant change in a traditional operating agency would require careful attention to substantive relevance and expertise, close client relations, and political power roles. Though analysts should nearly always stay out of direct politics, we did try to design our approach to give each of these the attention it needed.

As the preceding sections illustrate, our role, even in so relatively straightforward an enterprise as deployment analysis, has varied widely in character. At times we have unavoidably served as technicians; more often we have been experts, putting forth key ideas and playing a pivotal position. And, less often, we have been "activists," participating forcefully in the policy process to ensure appropriate follow-through and practice. In all these roles, we have strongly supported and been supported by the fire department's concerns. As my colleague Rae Archibald has argued,[33] achieving the expert role and occasionally playing the "activist" role are vital to getting ideas accepted and into practice.

More narrowly, in the research itself, we have tried to follow a few basic principles that may have wider applicability: building pillars for later research while learning; anticipating major problems and having tools and results ready for them; and making the most of opportunities afforded by crises and strong pressures for change. Models have been analyzed and designed for the real,

33. Private communication.

working environment, anticipating that results might not only be used as a basis for policy but also be put into practice in daily operations. Necessarily, therefore, the work has had to emphasize reliability, thorough validation and checking, attention to reality and detail, and full integrity and responsibility.

Although many results have already been put into operating practice, and a number of others are actively under consideration, much implementation effort yet lies ahead. We are working with the department on restructuring what has been termed meta-policy—the process by which policy is devised, examined, developed, approved, put into practice, and made to work. And the agenda for the near future emphasizes institutionalization: modifying the acculturation process; putting management and bugeting innovations into routine practice; continuing the development of new systems on which improved operations depend, such as the computer-based management information and control system now begin designed; and helping to make routine various new policies and new norms.

Support from the U.S. Department of Housing and Urban Development is helping us to extend and generalize our results to apply to a broad range of cities, and to disseminate them widely. Through this work, we hope to be able to have an impact on the intellectual framework (or *Gestalt*) of the fire profession and associated fields. Over the long run, we hope that our results might become a part of the way most municipal managers, fire chiefs, and associated professionals learn to see and think about urban fire protection, and thus achieve "institutionalization" on a lasting and broad scale.

Implementation has been greatly stimulated and enhanced by the structure and setting of the research, which have included

—A receptive agency, which recognized the relative obduracy of its problems and resolved to do something about them;
—Strong support at top and working levels, in a time of stress and strong pressures for change;
—A young, energetic staff interested in doing policy-oriented work to help the fire department;
—An effective joint research partnership between the agency and our research staff, conducted at a scale and over a period of time sufficient to do basic research as well as devise stopgap measures.

At the time of writing, the City of New York had invested a total of roughly $2 million in the work of the fire project and already received in return operating gains in effectiveness valued at nearly $20 million per year. Return on investment of a thousand percent per year, not common even in the private sector, would seem to attest well for work on public systems.

Acknowledgment

The research of the New York City Fire Project has been very much a joint enterprise, with important contributions at nearly every stage from Rae W. Archibald, Grace M. Carter, Jan M. Chaiken, Edward J. Ignall, Peter Kolesar, John E. Rolph, Carol E. Shanesy, Arthur J. Swersey, Warren E. Walker, and Robert K. Yin of the New York City–Rand Institute. In addition, specialized contributions have been made by Ronald D. Doctor, Colleen Dodd, Irving N. Fisher, Ralph L. Keeney, Shlomo Shinnar, Anne M. Stevenson, Richard Watson, and numerous reviewers and commentators. FDNY contributions have been too numerous to list here individually. I should like, however, to acknowledge especially the important support of Chief of Department, John T. O'Hagan, former Assistant Fire Commissioner Paul M. Canick, and the Program Officers assigned to the project—Deputy Chiefs Homer G. Bishop, Robert J. Brown, and Francis J. Ronan.

References

1. Archibald, R. W., and R. B. Hoffman, "Introducing Technological Change in a Bureaucratic Structure," New York City–Rand Institute, P-4025, 1969.

2. Blum, E. H., "Fire Service: Challenge to Modern Management," *Public Management*, 52, 11, 4–7, 1970.

3. ———, "Deployment of Municipal Emergency Services," New York City–Rand Institute, R-685, 1971.

4. ———, "Urban Fire Protection: Studies of the Operations of the New York City Fire Department," New York City-Rand Institute, R-681, January 1971.

5. Carter, G., and E. Ignall, "A Simulation Model of Fire Department Operations: Design and Preliminary Results," *IEEE Transactions on Systems Science & Cybernetics*, SSC-6, 1970.

6. Carter, G., J. M., Chaiken, and E. J. Ignall, "Response Areas for Two Emergency Units," New York City–Rand Institute, R-532-NYC/HUD, March 1971.

7. Chaiken, J. M., and R. C. Larson, "Methods for Allocating Urban Emergency Units," Chapter 10, this volume.

8. Chaiken, J. M., and E. J. Ignall, "An Extension of Erlang's Formulas Which Distinguishes Individual Servers," New York City–Rand Institute, R-567, March 1971; to appear in *J. Appl. Probability*.

9. Hayes, F. O'R., "From Inside the System," Chapter 1, this volume.

10. Keeney, R. L., "Preferences for the Response Times of Engines and Ladders to Fires," New York City-Rand Institute, 1972.

11. Kolesar, P., and E. H. Blum, "Square-Root Laws for Response Distances; Applications to Fire Service Deployment," New York City–Rand Institute, R-895, February 1972.

12. Rogers, D., *The Management of Big Cities*, Sage Publications, Beverley Hills, California, 1971.

13. Szanton, P. L., "Analysis and Urban Government," Chapter 2, this volume.

8

Emergency Ambulance Transportation

Keith A. Stevenson

8.1 Introduction[1]

While cities and towns in the United States have tightly organized police forces and fire departments with their relatively well paid members, the provision of emergency medical transportation has often been left to the consciences of civic-minded people. Consequently, the provision of emergency ambulance service across the country appears to be a disorganized and haphazard potpourri of people and interests. The list of organizations providing such a service includes morticians and small private operations that often struggle to stay in business, municipal police and fire departments that include ambulance services as an adjunct to their other work, small groups of volunteers, and such unlikely candidates as taxicab fleets and gasoline stations. Among many of these groups the quality of the care and transportation leaves much to be desired not necessarily because of obtuseness but often because of a lack of information, finance, and training.

The provision of emergency ambulance service shares a great deal in common with the police and fire services. All three involve the rapid response of a vehicle manned by specially trained personnel to a call for help that is unpredictable and that will require decisive, expert action at the scene. All three have experienced significant increases in the demand for the services they provide during the last decade, resulting in considerable strain on their resources. The emergency ambulance function has not received nearly the same kind of public support as have the police and fire services.

The emergency ambulance administrator, if he exists, operates with very limited resources. He has had great difficulty translating his very general mandate into specific numbers of vehicles, located at particular points in the community, and staffed by men who have been trained and equipped to handle the diverse situations they encounter. He has had even more difficulty convincing the

---

1. An emergency medical situation is one in which the patient will suffer severe discomfort, possibly permanent impairment of some of his faculties, or even death, if he does not receive expert medical treatment soon after the onset of his condition. It is in this sense that we concern ourselves here with *emergency* ambulance service, ignoring routine ambulance transfers such as those between hospital in-patient facilities and the patient's home.

public that his relatively high charges ($30 to $35 per trip) reflect the costs of generally having at least one ambulance available, and not any extortionary urges on his part. In this chapter we shall outline a procedure that can help the administrator to formulate specific proposals with regard to numbers of vehicles, to estimate costs and therefore to justify budget requests if the ambulances are operated as a municipal service, to evaluate alternative methods of providing the service, and to plan for the future in the face of changing demand patterns. Specifically, we isolate the transportation component of the total emergency ambulance service system and focus on the response time as a surrogate measure of system performance. The two elements of the response time are the time until an ambulance is dispatched after the reception of an emergency call, and the time the vehicle takes to travel to the scene. In this article, we shall concentrate on dispatch delay, and suggest that the interested reader consult other references for discussion of the important topic of emergency vehicle location [2,7,8,12]. In Section 8.3 we model the dispatch delay for an emergency ambulance system in which there is only a single source of ambulances. Ambulance services are generally provided in this fashion, and the model indicates that vehicle utilization is low, that marginal improvements in the level of services are expensive, and that the system is inflexible and that the resources of most communities are not being fully utilized. Then we expand the system to include secondary vehicles as a backup to the primary ambulances. Another model supports the notion that an improved, cheaper, more flexible service can be provided even with a generous policy of reimbursing the secondary ambulances (conceivably provided by local private ambulance companies).

Some Recent Trends
In the early sixties the rapid increase in accidents [1], the decline in the number of private physicians in general practice and the consequent increase in the use of hospital emergency wards [10] and the trend toward regional medical centers [12] focused attention on the emergency ambulance function, and specifically on the inadequacies of staffing, training, and equipment. The first response to the appeals for improved ambulance services came with the passage of state laws specifying minimum standards of operation for those engaged in the service. These covered the training

and licensing of ambulance personnel, the equipment carried on the ambulance and some features of the vehicle's design [12]. Unfortunately, the passage of high-minded legislation, while it may connote concern about a social problem, does not necessarily reflect complete understanding of the causes of the problem nor an intention to provide the means to overcome these. The legislation defining minimum standards of ambulance practice, while a necessary step in improving the quality of emergency care, did not provide the means for carrying out the improvements. Many small private companies operating their emergency services close to the economic margin simply declined to continue this aspect of their work when faced with the prospect of increased costs to meet higher standards. Even in some of our larger cities the emergency ambulance service is provided as it always was at standards that are now legally unacceptable because no money has been forthcoming to carry out improvements.

Organization of Emergency Ambulance Services
Emergency ambulance operations may be divided into three broad groups:

1. Private concerns: These are prominent in Southern and Western rural areas, often providing emergency service as an adjunct to more routine ambulance transfers. The very large proportion of morticians among this group seems to be declining, while nonmortician private companies are apparently expanding [5].
2. Volunteer groups: In small towns, rural areas, and even in some of the burgeoning suburbs, members of the community have banded together to provide a low cost service staffed entirely by volunteers.
3. Municipal services: In most of the larger cities (New York, Washington, D.C., Chicago, San Francisco, Boston, Baltimore) the emergency ambulance service is provided by one or another municipal agency, usually free of charge to the patient. The three agencies, one or more of which might be involved, are
a. Police: Station wagons and paddy wagons used for patrol duties are equipped with bandages, splints, oxygen tanks, and stretchers and respond to requests for emergency transportation received by the police dispatcher. Because the police vehicles are on continuous patrol throughout the area covered, the time taken to respond

to an emergency call is small. In addition, because the time between ambulance calls is spent on preventive patrol and on calls for police service, the cost associated with the ambulance function is low. Unfortunately, policemen generally receive only minimal training in first aid, and few police vehicles satisfy even the minimum standards on space and equipment set for ambulances.
b. Fire departments: Firemen receive more extensive training in first aid than policemen and most fire departments have rescue companies who treat the injured at fires. The rescue vehicles are designed to transport patients, and the fire department has undertaken to provide the nonfire emergency service in some cities. Most notable among these are Washington, D.C., Chicago, and Baltimore.
c. Hospitals: Contrary to popular belief, ambulances attached to municipal hospitals provide the emergency service in relatively few cities and towns. The best known of these services is in New York City where ambulances, located at a number of hospitals, are dispatched by the police communications center. The ambulance generally returns the patient to the hospital from which it was dispatched.

Some of the operational problems experienced by emergency ambulance services are similar to those facing the fire and police services: that is, the determination of the number, the location, and the relocation of emergency vehicles in response to spatially and temporally varying patterns of demand; the establishment of response strategies to deal with periods of heavy demand; the coordination of and communication with related services in the system. In addition, however, the ambulance service has had to operate with limited or no public funding, negligible career opportunities, and has therefore had great difficulty attracting qualified personnel, in maintaining and improving equipment, and in adapting itself to the new demands outlined in the previous section.

8.2 The Emergency Ambulance Service System
Emergency ambulance service is a part of the overall medical system. Its purpose is to deliver the victim of an emergency, in the best possible state given the circumstances of the emergency, to an appropriate medical care facility. This usually requires the rapid

transport of trained attendants and equipment to the scene of the emergency. It seldom requires very rapid transport of the patient to the nearest hospital. If the patient's condition has been stabilized at the scene, the advantage of delivering him to a hospital with facilities appropriate to the treatment of his injury or complaint will generally outweigh the disutility of a longer time spent in the ambulance.

We shall find it convenient for the purpose of analysis to divide the ambulance system into the three components identified by source[11] : communications, medical services and transportation.

The communications subsystem includes the means and methods by which information about the existence, location and nature of the emergency is transmitted through the emergency ambulance system. Figure 8.1 is a very simple representation of the system. At the center is the dispatcher who is first notified of the existence of the emergency by a citizen observer (usually by telephone), by the police (by radio), or by a telephone operator.

The dispatcher may attempt an assessment of the seriousness of the call, but in general concentrates on getting details on the nature and location of the emergency from the caller. Contact is then established with an ambulance, either verbally, if the vehicle and the dispatcher are at the same location, or by radio.

The most serious problem associated with the communications function is that of trying to judge the nature of a call for emergency service and to make some assessment of its priority. Because the responsibilities associated with misjudging the seriousness of a call and delaying ambulance dispatch are so great, the dispatcher

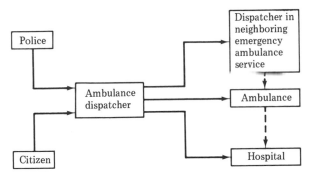

Figure 8.1   The communications subsystem.

makes little, if any, attempt to distinguish among calls. Most calls are treated as being of equal priority, which implies that any delays are imposed with equal chance on serious calls (where they may have dire consequences) and on nonserious calls (where there may be no effect at all).

The elements in the medical services subsystem are the most intangible of the three. The quality of these services provided by the emergency ambulance system is the criterion in terms of which this component of the whole system is often judged. Quality of service is an ultimately subjective measure, being a conglomerate of the training, experience and skill of the attendants, the equipment carried on the ambulance, the design of the vehicle, and the degree of access to appropriate expert medical care.

The important elements in the transportation subsystem are the ambulances, their number and location, and the location of the hospitals in the community. Other elements are the area of the region served, the availability of good roads, traffic conditions and other impediments to travel, such as rivers and mountains.

This chapter is devoted to the exploration of improved ambulance allocation procedures that would reduce the delays suffered by patients and the costs encountered by operators.

Measuring System Performance
Measures that are useful for indicating how well the system's objectives are being and can be achieved must be identified. From the general data published by emergency ambulance services about their operations, it is possible to derive a few informative statistics. Because of the way the data is collected, these statistics do not make reasonable measures of system performance. Instead, they are essentially descriptive and at best give insights into general operating procedures. The following is a list of the more useful of the statistics that can be easily obtained from the aggregated data of most emergency ambulance services:

1. The number of emergency calls per thousand population per annum.
2. The cost per patient transported.
3. The cost per resident per annum.
4. The cost per ambulance per annum.
5. The number of patients per ambulance per day.

Table 8.1   General Descriptive Statistics for Six Cities

City	Population (1000s)	No. of Ambulances	No. of Ambulance Runs per Annum (1000s)	No. of Ambulance Runs per 1000 Pop.	Cost of Service Per Annum ($1000s)	Cost per Patient ($)	Cost per Resident per Annum ($)	Cost per Ambulance per Annum ($1000s)	Patients per Ambulance per Day	Reference and Date of Data Source
New York (Hospital)	8,000	110	550	69	7,000	13	0.9	63.6	13.7	[4] 1966
San Francisco (Municipal)	952	16	17	18	1,100	65	1.2	69.0	2.9	[6] 1967
Baltimore (Fire)	939	14	42	43	915	21	1.0	65.0	8.2	[3] 1968
Boston (Police)	618	40	37	60	250	7	0.4	6.3	2.6	Boston Police Department 1968
Cambridge, Mass. (Fire and Police)	100	7	3.8	38	132	35	1.3	18.8	1.5	Author 1968
Petersburg, Virginia (Private)	38	2	1.2	32	43.8	37	1.2	20.0	1.6	[3] 1967

All of these give a general indication of current loads and costs and will provide guidelines for some of the more theoretical work. Item 5 is indicative of the very low utilization of ambulances in current operations. In Table 8.1 we provide examples of those statistics for six different cities, with very different characteristics and different types of emergency ambulance service [3,4,5,6, 10,12].

8.3 Analysis of Emergency Ambulance Transportation

The time sequence of events involving the emergency ambulance service that are initiated by an emergency is illustrated in Figure 8.2. Following the occurrence of an emergency, there is a delay until it is detected and contact is made with the ambulance dispatcher. If an ambulance is available it is dispatched almost immediately. Otherwise there is a time lag until a previously busy ambulance reports that it is free (dispatch delay). Once it has been dispatched the ambulance consumes time traveling to the scene of the emergency (travel delay). This time is a function of the relative locations of incident and ambulance, the local street patterns and traffic conditions. At the scene of the emergency the attendants render first aid in order to stabilize the patient's condition prior to transporting him to an emergency ward.

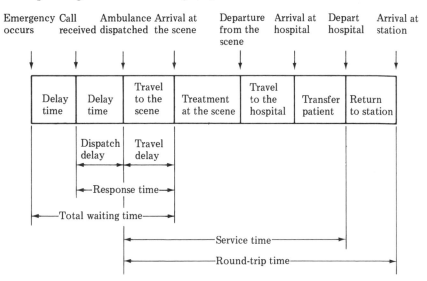

Figure 8.2 Sequence of events following an emergency.

The primary objective of the transportation subsystem is to respond as rapidly as possible to the demand for emergency service. Doctors have stressed the need for the arrival of medical aid as soon after the occurrence of the emergency as possible [9]. In this chapter we shall be primarily concerned with allocating ambulances in such a way as to keep the response time down to a reasonable level.

A secondary objective of the transportation subsystem is the reduction of the service time—the total time that an ambulance is occupied with one call. Reducing the service time increases the probability that an ambulance is available to respond immediately to an emergency call. This reduction can be achieved by reducing unnecessary delays in ambulance response and in the time spent traveling from the scene to a hospital.

The Single Ambulance Source Model

An initial effort at modeling the dispatch delay can be made by assuming that calls for the ambulance service are generated randomly in time. We can then describe the probability of k calls arriving in time T by the Poisson probability distribution

$$P(k,T) = \frac{(\lambda T)^k \, e^{-\lambda T}}{k!} , \qquad T > 0, \, k - 0,1,2, \ldots$$

where λ is the mean rate of call generation. For ambulance services this assumption appears to be reasonable over relatively short periods of time (a few hours). If N ambulances have been assigned to a region to respond to randomly arriving calls, any particular call will either encounter all N vehicles occupied on other calls or else there will be at least one vehicle available to respond immediately. If a number of calls arrive when no ambulances are free, a queue will form.

An ambulance is unavailable for the duration of a service time. By assuming (1) that this interval can be approximated by an exponentially distributed random variable with expected value $1/\mu$, and (2) that queues of patients waiting for ambulances are depleted on a first come, first served basis, we can construct a reasonable and mathematically tractable model of ambulance operations. These assumptions lead to an extensively studied N-server queuing model. The resulting probability Q_N that a call for service encounters a dispatch delay (that is, all N ambulances are already responding to calls) is [13]

$$Q_N = \frac{\rho^N}{N!} \left(\frac{N}{N - \rho} \right) \left[\sum_{i=0}^{N} \frac{\rho^i}{i!} + \left(\frac{\rho}{N - \rho} \right) \frac{\rho^N}{N!} \right]^{-1}, \tag{8.1}$$

where for convenience we have used ρ, defined as the *demand intensity*, with $\rho = \lambda/\mu$. Equation 8.1 is the well-known Erlang delay formula used in telephone traffic theory.

Both Q_N and its complement $1 - Q_N$ are measures of the system's performance, and we might describe the probability of not encountering a dispatch delay $1 - Q_N$ as the *service level*—the smaller Q_N, the higher the service level. In Figure 8.3 we indicate the number of ambulances needed to provide respectively (at least) a

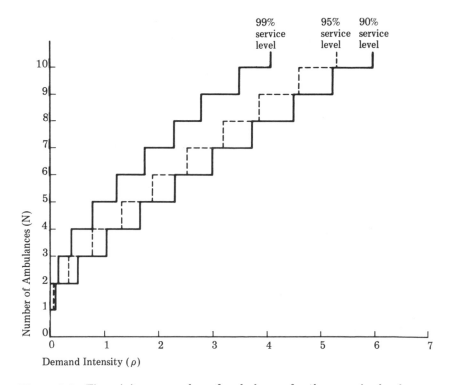

Figure 8.3 The minimum number of ambulances for three service levels.

99%, 95%, and a 90% level of service. With a mean call rate such that $\rho = 4$, we should require 8 vehicles at the 90% level, 9 ambulances at the 95% level and 10 ambulances at the 99% level of service. According to the desired level of service, ambulances may be allocated to each working shift on the basis of the anticipated demand intensity ρ for that shift.

Models such as this one have been proposed as an aid to administrators endeavoring to assign ambulances to working shifts. Armed with Figure 8.3 we can make a rough estimate of the number of ambulances required to provide an acceptable level of service during any working shift. It would appear, though, that this kind of model is most useful for the insights it provides into the system's operation. We can show quite easily that for small values of Q_N (that is, for high service levels) the utilization of the ambulances (the fraction of total time that the ambulances are busy) is approximately given by ρ/N. A quick inspection of Figure 8.3 shows that if the demand intensity ρ is small, then the utilization is very small (approximately 30%). This, of course, is the reason that small ambulance companies trying to provide a high level of service have encountered financial difficulties.

Figure 8.3 also suggests that to improve the system's operation at the margin is a costly proposition. We see that in order to improve service from the 95% to the 99% level requires an increase of about 20% in the number of ambulances. Since 80% of the cost of an emergency ambulance service is incurred in simply manning the vehicles [5], improving service to 4% of the patients requires a 16% increase in costs.

The Dual Ambulance Source Model

While the system described above is similar to many real-world systems, it is deficient in a number of respects:

1. The utilization of the ambulances is extremely low for reasonably high levels of service (low probabilities of delay).
2. It is extremely difficult to decide what constitutes an adequate level of service.
3. The system is inflexible. An unexpectedly low demand rate during a work shift results in idle crews, but no reduction in cost. An unexpectedly high demand rate, on the other hand, causes a drop in the level of service.
4. The system does not make use of all the ambulance facilities

available in most cities and large towns, namely private ambulance companies engaged in nonemergency work.

In this section we shall consider the introduction of a secondary source of ambulances. As before, we shall have a primary purveyor of ambulance service, perhaps provided by the municipal government, but in addition we shall provide support vehicles from another source. These secondary ambulances respond only when all the primary ambulances are unavailable. Their existence removes the need to provide enough primary vehicles to respond immediately to, say, 95% or 99% of all calls, thereby increasing the utilization of the primaries. The most important potential sources of secondary ambulances are the private ambulance companies engaged in the routine transportation of hospital patients. Police station wagons and fire rescue wagons (currently used as *primary* ambulances in some communities) could both be adapted for use as secondary vehicles. Finally, in an organized group of neighboring communities, the secondary ambulances for each community could be the available primary ambulances in the other communities.

Introducing a secondary ambulances seems to produce a significant cost saving, even when a very generous policy of reimbursing the secondary operators is followed. It is reasonable to postulate that each primary ambulance entails a fixed cost for the duration of the shift to which it is assigned. Secondary ambulances on the other hand are reimbursed only for calls that they actually undertake. By making the rate at which they are reimbursed an attractive one, private ambulance companies can be persuaded to join the emergency services.

We can model the system described here in very much the same way as we modeled the saturation delay in Section 8.3. Let us assume that in the time period under consideration calls for the emergency ambulance service arrive randomly in time at a constant average rate, λ calls per hour. We further assume that the time to service any call is drawn from the general probability distribution with finite mean $1/\mu$ hours. Finally we assume that there are two sources of ambulances: a primary source with N manned vehicles and a secondary source with an unspecified number of vehicles. The primary ambulances respond to requests for emergency aid whenever a primary vehicle is available. The secondary ambulances respond only when requested to do so because no primary vehicle is free.

The major difference between this system and the one described previously is that queues never form.[2] Analogous to Q_N, we define P_N as the probability that all N primary ambulances are busy. Over a long period of time T, the primary ambulances are simultaneously busy for a total time $P_N T$. All calls arriving in this time are answered by the secondary vehicles. We would expect there to be $\lambda P_N T$ such calls. Since the system we have described may have only $N + 1$ separate states, it is relatively easy to show that

$$P_N = \frac{\rho^N / N!}{\sum_{i=0}^{N} \rho^i / i!}, \qquad \text{where } \rho = \frac{\lambda}{\mu}.$$

Using this model, we see that ambulances may be allocated so that expected cost is minimized. During any working shift, the cost associated with the N primary ambulances is fixed, while the cost associated with the secondary ambulances is proportional to the number of calls answered. If relatively few primary vehicles are allocated to the shift, there will be a large number of calls answered by the more expensive secondary vehicles. If, on the other hand, too many primary vehicles are allocated they will stand idle for much of the shift. By assuming that the secondaries are paid at a rate per unit time, that is r times that for the primaries ($r > 1$), we can show that the expected cost of the system is

$$C = k (N + r\rho P_N), \qquad \text{where } k = \text{constant.} \tag{8.2}$$

Equation 8.2 has been graphed in Figure 8.4 as a function of ρ with the number of primary ambulances N as a parameter. We have arbitrarily set $r = 5$. The curves representing Equation 8.2 combine to produce a minimum cost envelope, so that at each value of ρ it is possible to specify the number of primary ambulances that result in the minimum expected cost. An administrator of an emergency ambulance service, having some idea of the parameters λ and μ at different times of the day, and knowing the

2. The configurations of primary and secondary vehicles resulting from this model ensure that the probability of there being no secondary vehicles available is negligibly small.

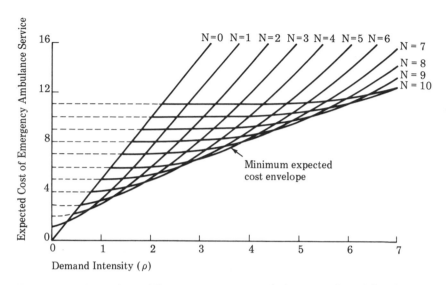

Figure 8.4   Cost of providing an emergency ambulance service with primary and secondary service. ($r = 5$) (N = Number of primary ambulances).

rate at which secondary ambulances would be reimbursed, can allocate the requisite number of primary ambulances to each working shift so as to minimize expected costs.

Advantages of the Dual-Source System
There appear to be a number of advantages to the system proposed in the previous section which have not been fully exploited in any community to date.

1. In general it appears that the dual-source system offers much greater flexibility than the single-source system discussed previously. Reasonably wide fluctuations in the demand rate may be accommodated without causing patients serious delays. Conversely the consequences of an erroneous prediction in the expected demand in a shift would be less serious than in a single-service system.

2. Even more important than flexibility may be the absolute reduction in costs that results from answering marginal calls with a secondary ambulance. In Figure 8.5 we compare the costs of providing three levels of single-source service with the dual-source service in which $r = 5$. It appears that by paying a secondary source

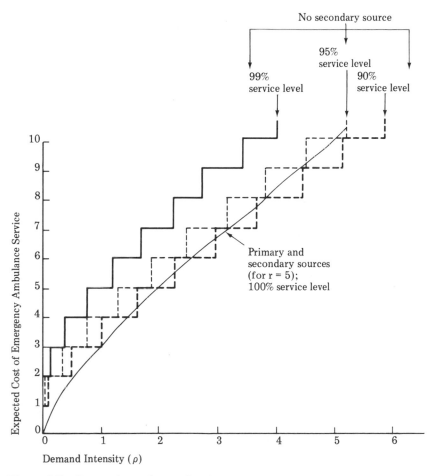

Figure 8.5   Comparison of costs for dual and single source models.

approximately twice as much per call[3] as the primary source we
can provide a service with no dispatch delay at about the same
cost as a single source operating at a 90% service level. The cost
reduction is most significant for small demand intensity ρ.
3. A final consideration is that the existence of a secondary source
of ambulances allows the dispatcher some discretion in the vehicle
he chooses to dispatch in response to a call. For example, at a

3. For the optimal configurations depicted in Figure 8.4, the secondary to
primary cost *per call* ratio can be shown to approximately equal 2.

point at which very few primary vehicles are free, the dispatcher has the option of sending a secondary ambulance to a call that he perceives as nonurgent and of keeping primary vehicles in reserve for urgent calls. Alternatively, if there is an available secondary ambulance in the neighborhood of an incident, while the nearest primary vehicle is a considerable distance away, then dispatching the secondary rather than the primary vehicle would reduce the time the patient waits for the ambulance's arrival.

8.4 Conclusion

In the previous section we developed and discussed a model of a particular type of emergency ambulance operation. The model is primarily an aid to decision making and would be used by administrators for

1. Allocating primary ambulances to the daily working shifts, and updating these allocations as demand changes.
2. Calculating budget requirements for the future operation of the service, and making decisions about the purchase of new equipment.
3. Changing the primary operation in response to changes in the fees required by secondary operators.

The primary-secondary system appears to have the following advantages (revealed in part by the model) over the single-source service:

1. A reduced cost at a higher level of service.
2. Much greater flexibility, resulting in lower costs when demand drops within a working shift, and the maintenance of the level of service when demand rises.
3. The specially large cost reduction over single-source operations when demand is low, that is, for small services.

The modeling procedures outlined in this chapter are useful from the administrator's point of view, offering both general insights into the system's operation (for example, the low utilization of ambulances; the high cost of answering the marginal call) which help to explain in part the problems encountered by all ambulance operators; and also fairly specific results (for example, the superiority of a dual-source ambulance system; methods for allocating ambulances to a city or town). Although emergency ambulance services have made significant improvements in the design and equipment of the vehicles used, and also in attendant training programs, to the author's knowledge little use is made of analytical models to influence policy. Because emergency ambulance services share many of the features of police and fire services, they will benefit from research currently under way in these areas, notably in terms of vehicle location and relocation. There remains the need, though, to explore other cost-reduction strategies so that all communities may provide an ambulance service capable of immediate response at a reasonable price. Some possibilities involve matching the pattern of vehicle assignment more closely to the demand, assessing priorities on calls and delaying response to low-priority calls when necessary, and combining ambulance services regionally to realize the maximum utilization of vehicles.

Related Work
Systematic analyses of emergency ambulance services first appeared in 1967 with an article by Manegold et al. [9] in which they isolated some of the elements of the emergency medical system. Their article specifically stressed the delay between the emergency incident and the arrival of an ambulance as crucial. In 1968 Savas [11] completed a detailed simulation study of ambulance location in a Brooklyn hospital district, demonstrating that by locating ambulances so as to reflect the spatial demand pattern, average response times and average service times could be considerably reduced. In the same year, Dunlap and Associates [5] published the results of a nationwide survey of emergency ambulance services, discussing problems faced by operators and indicating how simple modeling could aid in allocating ambulances to areas. Subsequently, Volz [14] described a simulation method for locating ambulances in rural areas. In addition to literature dealing specifically with ambulances, the interested reader should turn to some of the work done on police patrol operations [7] and urban service systems in general [8]. Chapter 10 by Chaiken and Larson [2] in this volume contains a good synthesis of relevant work and discusses some previously unpublished studies.

References

1. *Accidental Death and Disability: The Neglected Disease of Modern Society*, National Academy of Sciences and the National Research Council, September, 1966.

2. Chaiken, J. M., and R. C. Larson, "Methods for Allocating Urban Emergency Units," Chapter 10, this volume.

3. Cooper et al., *Description and Analysis of Eighteen Proven Emergency Ambulance Service Systems*, National Association of Counties Research Foundation, prepared for the U.S. Department of Transportation, 1968.

4. Dimendberg, D. C., *An Analysis of the Emergency Ambulance Service of the Department of Hospitals for August, 1966*, Department of Hospitals, City of New York, November 1967.

5. Dunlap and Associates, Inc., *Economics of Highway Emergency Ambulance Services*, prepared for the U.S. Department of Transportation, July 1968.

6. King, B. G., and E. D. Sox, "An Emergency Medical Service System—Analysis of Workload," *Public Health Reports*, vol. 82, no. 11, November 1967.

7. Larson, R., *Models for the Allocation of Urban Police Patrol Forces*, Technical Report No. 44, M.I.T. Operations Research Center, Cambridge, Mass., November 1969.

8. Larson, R., and K. Stevenson, "On Insensitivities in Urban Redistricting and Facility Location," R-533, New York City–Rand Institute, 1971.

9. Manegold et al., "An Overview of Emergency Medical Services," *Journal of the American Medical Association*, Vol. 200, No. 4, April 1967.

10. *Pocket Data Book: U.S.A. 1969*, Bureau of the Census, U.S. Department of Commerce.

11. Savas, E. S., "Simulation and Cost-Effectiveness Analysis of New York's Emergency Ambulance Service," *Management Science*, vol. 15, no. 608, 1969.

12. Stevenson, K., *Operational Aspects of Emergency Ambulance Services*, Technical Report No. 61, M.I.T. Operations Research Center, Cambridge, Mass., May 1971.

13. Syski, R., *Introduction to Congestion Theory in Telephone Systems*, Oliver and Boyd, London, 1960.

14. Volz, R. A., "Optimum Ambulance Location in Semi-Rural Areas," paper presented at the 38th National Meeting of O.R.S.A., October 1970.

9 Improving the Effectiveness of New York City's 911

Richard C. Larson

9.1 Introduction

This chapter summarizes the results of a one-month operational study of police emergency telephone operations in the central communications room of the New York City Police Department. It is somewhat more detailed than other chapters in this book. The study presented here represents approximately one man-month of effort and serves as an example of elementary quantitative modeling to improve an ongoing operation.

On July 1, 1968, a new consolidated communications system was officially inaugurated, in which all emergency telephone calls from the public were dialed in with a three-digit number 911 and channeled to a new central communication room (CCR) in downtown Manhattan. For those calls requiring police service, an incident ticket was filled out and forwarded to an appropriate dispatcher who sent a nearby available police patrol car to the scene of the reported incident. This central system replaced an earlier version that comprised seven dispersed dispatch centers. The purpose of the new system was to provide more effective and equitable police service throughout the city, in terms of quickly answering emergency calls and dispatching the appropriate police vehicles. It also facilitated the analysis of city-wide patterns of demand for police service and the police responsiveness to that demand. The 1968 system was considered an interim system providing the necessary phase-in time for a semi-automated dispatching system SPRINT (Special Police Radio Inquiry Network). With its real-time computer capability, SPRINT was planned to help dispatch patrol cars, interrogate records rapidly, analyze data, and eventually assist in more timely reallocations of the patrol force.[1]

The opening of the new CCR brought about a relative flood of incoming calls, with the callers either requesting police service or merely satisfying a curiosity as to whether the new system actually worked. This increased level of demand exacerbated those problems usually associated with the opening of a new facility (such as training personnel and adapting operations to unexpected situations). Complaints by citizens and operating personnel alike indi-

1. The SPRINT system was first activated in the Bronx in October 1969.

cated a need to reexamine operations and derive recommendations for improvements. After several preliminary probes by members of the New York City Police Department, a study team (headed by Lieutenant Hugo Masini and Lieutenant James Carvino) from the department's planning bureau was assigned to perform a management survey and analysis of the CCR. Results were to include implementation of recommended changes of CCR operations (with the concurrence of the CCR supervisory personnel), short-term training of various CCR personnel, and a final report to the commissioner, with recommendations concerning CCR operations. Particularly important were overall recommendations regarding the number and type of people assigned to answer the emergency telephone calls.

Before they began their work (in August 1968), the study team approached the author and other members and consultants of the RAND Corporation in New York (now the New York City–Rand Institute) to see if we would be interested in participating in the short-term effort and, if so, what our contribution might be. Our role was agreed to be one of assisting some of the more analytical aspects of the study, perhaps suggesting ways to assign manpower, while the planning bureau staff would focus heavily on overall organization, administration, and training of personnel.

This chapter summarizes the results of the subsequent one-month joint study effort, in which the author worked side-by-side with Lieutenants Masini and Carvino in Department Headquarters and other RAND employees assisted in data collection.

9.2 Description of Operations
Central to the new CCR operations was the Bell System Automatic Call Distribution (ACD) system. This system handles calls received over the department's 3-digit emergency telephone number 911 and calls transferred from the department's Centrex system. As implemented in CCR, the ACD had 48 operator positions: 24 "primary" positions and 24 "secondary" positions. For convenience, we label the primary positions consecutively from 1 to 24 and the secondary positions from 25 to 48.

We now trace a received call through the system.[2] Assume that a caller dials the police emergency number 911. His call is routed via

2. This system description applies to operations prior to implementation of the SPRINT system.

one of several trunk lines from the telephone switching center serving the area of the city from which the call originates to the CCR. The incoming call either (1) joins[3] a first-come, first-served queue at CCR[4] or (2) is assigned to an idle emergency operator (or "turret operator.") If option (2) applies (that is there is at least one idle turret operator), the ACD first attempts to assign an operator from the primary board; if this is possible and if operator i ($1 \leqslant i \leqslant 24$) was assigned to the last call, the ACD interrogates each position from ($i + 1$) to 24, then back to 1, 2, and so forth, until the *first available* primary board operator is found. If all primary board operators are busy, then a similar interrogation procedure is followed for the secondary operators. Thus, received calls can overflow directly into the secondary positions provided at least one secondary board operator is free. If option 1 applies, the waiting calls are assigned to operators as they become available. If the backlog in queue exceeds 30 seconds, bells ring rather loudly to indicate to all personnel that the system is in a state of severe congestion.

When a call is assigned to an operator, first the borough from which the call is originating is announced by tape recording to the operator, then the caller is on the line. The operator says, "Police emergency, may I help you?" From the conversation that ensues, the operator assesses the priority of the call, and if a police dispatch is judged to be necessary, he records the address and type of the incident. Also requested by the operator are the caller's name and telephone number. If a primary board operator does not think that a dispatch is necessary or if he judges that the call needs the attention of an experienced patrolman to handle it properly, the caller is told to hold the line, and the primary board operator switches the call to the secondary board. This type of switched call is referred to as a *transfer*. There may be a queue of transferred calls awaiting secondary board servicing; in such a case, this queue is handled in an approximate first-come, first-served manner, with waiting calls being assigned to secondary board operators as they become available. If there are queues before the primary board *and* before the secondary board (that is, if incoming calls

3. The probability of receiving a busy signal is very small, there being a queue capacity (in addition to those being serviced) of about 40.
4. The queue is very nearly first-come, first-served; the Bell System advertises that "stored calls are released. . . in approximately the order received." (Bell System ACD 60 Automatic Call Distributor.)

and transferred calls are waiting for service), then the ACD will not overflow incoming calls to the secondary until the queue of transferred calls is empty.

After a call that requires dispatch of a patrol car has been terminated, the turret operator completes the incident ticket containing the type and address of incident, name and phone number of the caller (if given), and other relevant information. This card is placed on a conveyor belt that routes the card to the appropriate dispatch area.

A dispatch area contains several display boards, manned by a number of dispatchers. Each display board contains status information for each patrol car within a division. (There are 18 divisions throughout the city.) The incident ticket, once it is routed to the appropriate dispatcher, either joins a queue of other waiting incident tickets or is handled immediately by the dispatcher. A queue of tickets might form in front of the dispatcher for either (or both) of two reasons: (1) There are so many tickets routed to the dispatcher in such a short period of time that he simply cannot handle them as rapidly as they arrive, and so they back up; (2) There are not patrol units available for dispatch near the region of the incident. (The *region near the incident* may correspond to a precinct for an ordinary call or to a division for a high priority call.) This second type of dispatch delay often dominates the sum of the response delays of the entire police emergency response system during critical busy periods (for example, a Friday or Saturday night). If there is a queue of incident tickets, the dispatcher assigns to cars as they become available the *most important* incidents first; this choice is subjective in nature. If no queue exists and if at least one patrol car is available for dispatch, the dispatcher attempts to assign the car judged nearest to the scene of the reported incident. If response time is critical, the dispatcher can ask for volunteers to respond or he can ask for the position of several nearby cars. (This assignment of the nearest car would be facilitated by an automatic car locator system). Once contacted, if the patrolman in the car confirms the dispatch, the card is time-stamped and placed in a tray which uniquely corresponds to the dispatched car. The pressure of the card closes a switch in the bottom of the tray which changes the car's status from "available for dispatch" to "servicing a call."

When the car has completed servicing the call, the patrolman so notifies the dispatcher by radio. He removes the incident card from the tray, updates the status, and stamps the time of final disposition on the card. The card is then ready for statistical tabulation and filing.

Many aspects of CCR operations have not been described by tracing this nominal call through the system. Particularly, we have not described:

1. Ambulance dispatch,
2. Safety and emergency division radio and operators,
3. City-wide radio frequency use,
4. Follow-up histories and notifications,
5. Fire alarm procedures,
6. Information requests (for example, automobile license plate numbers) from the field,
7. Emergency operations.

This short-term study emphasized normal operations—particularly those that are relevant to the turret operators.[5]

9.3 Data Ordinarily Collected

Data descriptive of telephone calls received and handled were recorded sometimes hourly and sometimes on a tour basis from so-called *peg count registers* installed by the phone company. The bank of peg count registers indicated the following:

—The cumulative number of calls handled at each position ($1 \leq i \leq 48$) since the last setting to zero;

—The cumulative numbers of calls incurring delays in excess of 15 seconds and in excess of 30 seconds.

—The cumulative number of callers who hung up before obtaining a turret operator.

—The cumulative number of overflows into secondary received from each borough.

There was also a totalizer register which indicated the total number of calls received in the ACD system since the last zero setting.

Each hour, the ACD supervisor (a sergeant) read the totalizer

5. As discussed in Section 9.13, analyses of the other components of the police emergency response system are given by Larson [2,3]. An interesting history of the communications division of the New York City Police Department is found in [7].

and the number of 15- and 30-second delays, abandoned calls, overflows into the secondary, Spanish calls,[6] calls received by borough, and calls received via Centrex and turret lines. These readings were not always entirely accurate, whether from register misreadings or because the readings were not always performed on the hour. Greater accuracy could have been achieved either by reading the registers photographically (as proposed by CCR personnel) or, preferably, by using some electronic sampling device.

Also, the ACD supervisor each hour recorded the total number of turret operator positions ($1 \leqslant i \leqslant 48$) manned during that hour. Unfortunately, this number was not broken down by secondary and primary positions.

For evaluation of individual operators, it was necessary to monitor the calls actually processed by the operator, perhaps by using the 24-hour tapes, each of which contains all telephone conversations and radio dispatches for a 24-hour period. For better evaluation of overall system operation, it would have been preferable to have additional data describing transferred calls waiting in queue before the secondary board.

9.4 Turret Operators
The turret operators at the time of the study were either uniformed patrolmen (sworn personnel) or police trainees (civilians). The trainees cost the department less than half as much per year (about $4,500) as patrolmen (about $11,000).

With the opening of the new CCR, it was felt that trainees could be assigned to the primary positions (1–24) with patrolmen in the secondary positions (25–48). This decision came from the belief that processing emergency calls is fairly straightforward, with only the address and type of incident needing to be recorded. It was felt that little police experience was needed to perform this often perfunctory task. If the trainee, upon questioning the caller, felt that the call either was not an emergency or required a trained officer to handle it, the trainee would transfer the call to the secondary board. From the secondary, a uniformed officer would be able to judge whether a car should be dispatched or, if the call was obviously not an emergency, he would be able to provide the police-related information that the trainee might not know. Thus,

6. A small number (usually four or less) of the secondary positions were reserved for Spanish-speaking operators.

in the system studied, most operators assigned to the primary positions were trainees, while virtually all those assigned to the secondary positions were patrolmen.

9.5 Two Major Problems

There were two major concerns about the system operation, once implemented: (1) Not enough people were assigned to the turret operator positions, and (2) too many calls were being handled as emergencies, thereby generating an unusually large number of patrol car dispatches.

The Number of Turret Operators

At any time during July and August, only about 20 to 30 of the 48 turret operator positions were occupied. This number fluctuated by time of day but not adequately to reflect the varying rate of calls received per hour. Because of an apparent shortage of men to fill the positions during the peak or overload periods, often over 30 percent of the calls received during a Friday or Saturday night were delayed 30 seconds or more before being answered. Usually over 50 percent of the received calls during these periods were delayed 15 seconds or more. And similar delays were not uncommon during normal hours. Delays of this magnitude must be considered serious, especially since a call's priority is unknown until it is answered by a turret operator; an "officer-in-trouble" call receives the same delay as one requesting information.

Some periods of the week consistently incurred large delays; other periods consistently incurred virtually no delays, there being almost always at least one turret operator immediately available for an incoming call. This imbalance indicated the need for scheduling that anticipated the hourly level of incoming calls.

The Number of Calls Requiring Radio Motorized Patrol (RMP) Dispatch

The number of calls received per day and the number of radio runs (dispatches) per day are plotted in Figure 9.1 for a period in July and August. (Certain days in July were omitted for lack of available data.) We may observe several heuristic properties of this plot:

1. The number of calls received has a 7-day periodic component. The local maxima on August 3, 10, and 17 all occur on Saturdays.

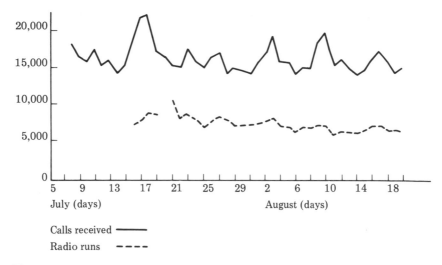

Calls received ▬▬▬
Radio runs   ▬ ▬ ▬ ▬

Figure 9.1   Number of calls received and radio runs per day.

2. The number of dispatches per day varies less than the number of calls received per day. This indicates either that a greater fraction of lower priority calls are received during busy days or, more likely, that the dispatch priorities of the system are adaptive and that cars are not dispatched for some of the marginal calls during busy days.

3. The large peak in calls received during July 16, 17, and 18 was apparently caused by the abnormally hot weather during those days.

4. The average number of calls received per day is about 15,000. The average number of radio runs per day is about 7,000 or 8,000. That is, about one-half of the calls cause patrol cars to be dispatched. This fraction decreased gradually over this two-month period, from about 56 percent during July 21 through 24, to about 46 percent during August 1 through 4, to about 43 percent during August 17 through 20.

There were two likely causes for the fraction of calls requiring a dispatch to be decreasing. First, the department had specifically decided *not* to dispatch patrol cars to certain types of low-priority calls (for example, reports of open fire hydrants). Second, the civilian trainees, in learning their job, were beginning to be able to screen out nonemergency calls.

Unfortunately, there were no data from the old borough dispatch system comparable to those plotted in Figure 9.1. Consequently, for the fraction of calls screened (that is, those not requiring dispatch), we could not compare the fraction before with the fraction after the new CCR began operation. The CCR personnel estimated, however, that about half of the calls received in the old system were screened out before a patrol car was dispatched. If this figure is accurate to within 20 percent (that is, if the true percentage screened was somewhere between 40 and 60 percent), then it was not clear that the use of trainees as turret operators had increased the fraction of calls for which an RMP unit was dispatched. Moreover, the steady decrease in this percentage suggested that trainees can learn screening procedures; however, no studies had been attempted to see if legitimate emergency calls had been screened out incorrectly.

9.6 Current Manpower Assignment Levels and Operating Characteristics

The fact that call-answering delays consistently occurred during some periods and not during others led us to investigate more thoroughly the problem of scheduling turret operators. Similar to patrol and other personnel, turret operators were deployed on a three-tour basis, Tour 1 being from midnight to 8 A.M., Tour 2 from 8 A.M. to 4 P.M., and Tour 3 from 4 P.M. to midnight. In addition, a very small number of volunteers worked from 6 P.M. to 2 A.M. During the time of the study, each operator was allowed a one-hour meal break and two half-hour rest breaks per eight-hour tour. On the average, therefore, *four* men were required to fully staff *three* positions at all times during a tour. The scheduling of the breaks allows considerable flexibility in determining the hourly level of manning within each tour. During the time of the study, *breaks were scheduled uniformly* throughout the tour for Tours 2 and 3 so that the manning level would be about constant throughout the tour. During Tour 1, breaks were scheduled uniformly from 3 A.M. to 7 A.M., effectively doubling the rate of breaks during this period, with no breaks given during the other four hours.

Figures 9.2 through 9.5 show for August 10 through August 13, consecutively, the following as a function of time of day:

—Number of calls received per hour;

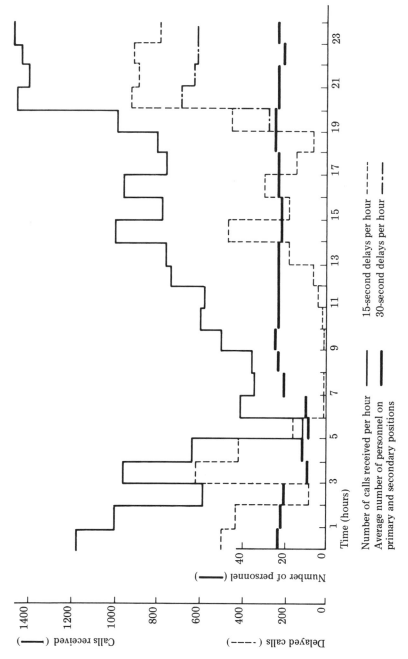

Figure 9.2 Distribution of calls, delays, and manning levels (Sat., Aug. 10).

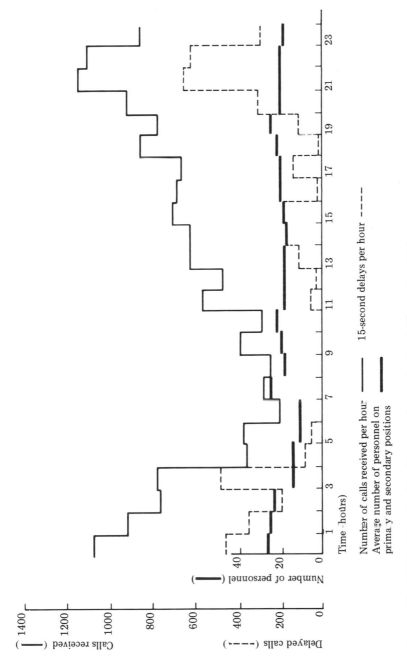

Figure 9.3   Distribution of calls, delays, and manning levels (Sun., Aug. 11).

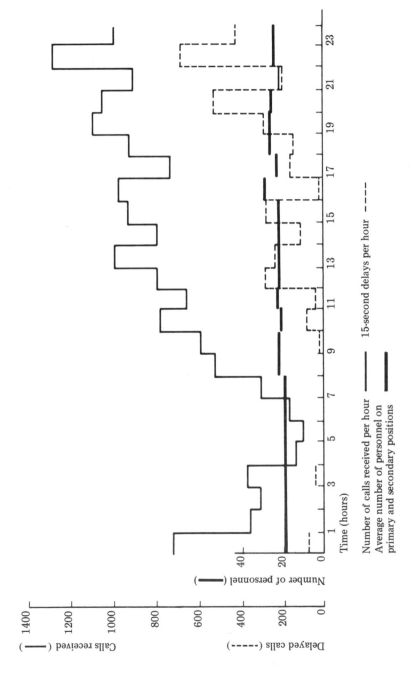

Figure 9.4   Distribution of calls, delays, and manning levels (Mon., Aug. 12).

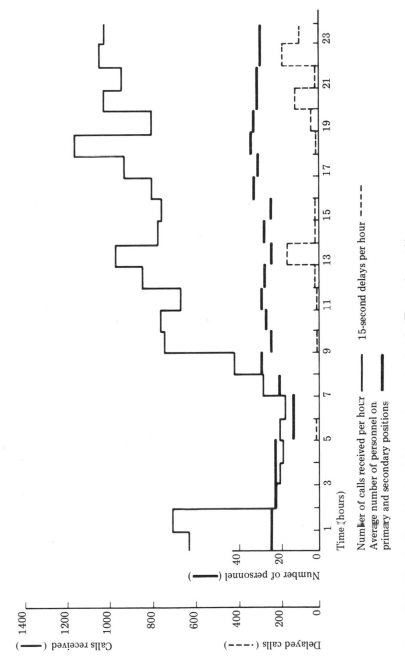

Figure 9.5   Distribution of calls, delays, and manning levels (Tues., Aug. 13).

—Number of 15-second delays recorded per hour;
—Number of turret operator positions manned each hour.

For a few hours, in addition, the numbers of 30-second delays and of abandoned calls are shown.

Let us examine in detail the figures for Saturday, August 10, in order to interpret these plots. Starting at midnight, the peak load of Friday night is just starting to taper off. The number of calls per hour decreases steadily from 1,180 to 580. Then, between 3 A.M. and 4 A.M. the number jumps to 960, then declines. Between 5 A.M. and 6 A.M. what must have been a recording error shows more calls recorded as being delayed at least 15 seconds than were actually answered. Such an error is not unlikely, considering the large number of registers that the supervising sergeant must read each hour. From 6 A.M., the rate of incoming calls gradually and steadily builds to a noontime plateau of about 800 calls per hour. With two exceptions, this plateau is maintained until 7 P.M., at which time the rate of calls jumps to 1,000 per hour. There is then one more jump at 8 P.M. to a constant Saturday evening plateau of about 1,450 calls per hour. The variation in the number of calls received per hour is quite large, ranging from about 200 calls per hour just before dawn to over 1,400 calls per hour during the evening hours.

The number of 15-second delays follows a pattern similar, but not identical, to that of the number of calls received. For instance, 500 calls are delayed 15 seconds or more from midnight to 1 A.M. This figure gradually drops until the unexpected burst of calls occurs between 3 A.M. and 4 A.M., during which time 600 calls are delayed 15 seconds or more. Virtually no delays are recorded between 6 A.M. and noon. During the afternoon, about one-quarter of the calls are delayed 15 seconds or more. Once the Saturday evening plateau is reached, the number of delayed calls increases drastically. *From 8 P.M. to midnight, about 60 percent of all calls are delayed 15 seconds or more and about 30 percent of all calls are delayed 30 seconds or more.*

The number of turret operator positions occupied each hour is not adjusted to the variation of input load with time of day. The only exception is between 3 A.M. and 7 A.M., when the number of occupied turret positions (about ten) is significantly less than at other times. *From 7 A.M. until midnight, however, the number of turret operators is virtually constant throughout the day, whereas the number of calls received each hour increases by a factor of about 4.3.*

Other charts show how generally true are these observations about turret operator deployment.

9.7 Decisions in Turret Operator Scheduling
Several types of allocation decisions must be considered in scheduling turret operators.

1. The total number of turret operators to be assigned to CCR;
2. The number of operators to be assigned to each tour;
3. The number of operators assigned per hour within a tour to the primary board and to the secondary board, given a fixed assignment of personnel for that tour;
4. For each of the previous decisions, the proper mix of uniformed patrolmen and civilian trainees.

If a change of operating procedures were allowed, alternatives such as overlapping tours should also be considered.

The present study considered only problems 1, 2, and 3. It did not distinguish between primary and secondary board operators. At the time of the study, the choice between primary and secondary board operators was made by the supervising sergeant. He often changed the assignment between boards either when the system was inordinately backlogged on the primary board or when congestion had been eliminated. This flexibility in real-time assignment between the two boards was encouraged. It would have been desirable, however, to provide the sergeant with information about both queues, secondary as well as primary. In the system studied, despite the fact that calls can be delayed for several minutes in the secondary queue, there was no information available concerning this queue.

9.8 Data Collected for Study
A sample of over 200 calls were monitored that were received on the primary lines during several different Friday and Saturday evenings in July and August. Tape recordings of the actual conversations were listened to, and for each type of call the following were recorded:

1. The duration of the telephone conversation time (to within five seconds of the actual time),

2. The general type of call,

3. Whether or not the call was transferred to the secondary.

A plot of the distribution of the telephone conversation time is given in Figure 9.6. The time is the conversation time per call of the primary board only and excludes possible secondary board conversation time and incident ticket completion time (after termination of the call). The mean time per call on the primary line was found to be 43.5 seconds for this sample.

By estimating the gap time between termination of one call and the answering of another during overload periods (when the queue is nonempty), we estimated the average time to complete an incident ticket (after termination of the call) to be about 15 seconds.

Workload data and other limited evidence indicated that mean conversation time on the secondary board was about 116 seconds. About 25 percent of the calls monitored were transferred to the secondary board.

To use a queuing model as a guide for manpower allocation levels, it is necessary to estimate the total average time spent by either primary board operators or secondary board operators, or

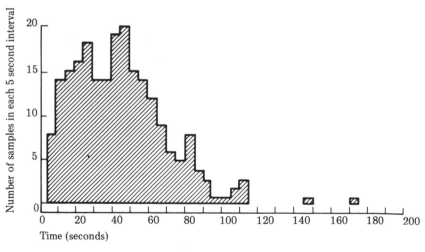

Sample size: 223
59 transfers
Mean: 43.5 seconds

Figure 9.6   Telephone conversation time of primary board operator.

both, per call received. This time includes not only telephone conversation but also incident ticket completion time during which the operator cannot process other calls. This total average time spent per call (TC) is computed as follows:

TC = (average primary board conversation time)
+ (fraction of calls transferred) × (average secondary board conversation time) + (fraction of calls requiring radio runs) × (average incident ticket completion time per call).

Using estimates of the data required by the equation, we get for an estimate of TC,

$$TC = 43.5 + \frac{1}{4} (116) + \frac{1}{2} (15)$$

$$= 80 \text{ seconds per call.}$$

9.9 A Turret Operator Allocation Procedure

After preliminary examination of the operating characteristics of the CCR, it was felt that a systematic, easily implemented method should be devised for better allocation of turret operators.

It was decided that the derived method should be directly relatable to policy decisions concerning system operation by requiring as input some prespecified level of service. With the present formulation, the service level specification is as follows: *Specify T and P*, so that sufficiently many turret operators will be assigned in order that the fraction of calls delayed *T* or more time units will be *P* or less.

The method would also include as input a prediction of the average number of calls to be received each hour. Successful application of the method would be limited by the accuracy of this prediction.

For the present study, it was felt that the method should satisfy three major objectives:

1. It should be simple, for ready implementation.

2. It should take into account the widely fluctuating input rate of calls.

3. It should incorporate the property of multi-server queues that

the same service level can be maintained for increasing input call rates with proportionately fewer servers.[7]

We did not feel that a detailed model, perhaps a computer simulation model, would be necessary to achieve large improvements in system operating characteristics. Also, the possibility of a simulation model was precluded at the time of the study due to lack of data describing the queue before the secondary board and due to time constraints on the study.

The simplest method which could have been proposed would be to assign operators in direct proportion to the anticipated input call rates. This method was rejected because its use would have implied an imbalance of system operation over time. Since the utilization factor (the fraction of time that a server is busy) would have been approximately constant over time using this method, calls received during relatively busy hours would incur much smaller delays on the average than calls received during hours of relatively light demand. In other words, an "equal workload" assignment of personnel would have overallocated during busy hours relative to the allocation during nonbusy hours.

Instead, we adapted the simple queuing model[8] $M/M/R$ to devise the allocation method. This model assumes that calls arrive in a Poisson manner, that the service time distribution is negative exponential, that there are R servers with identical characteristics and that the service discipline is first-come, first-served. In the actual system, the Poisson input assumption is a good one,[9] and the service distribution is approximately first-come, first-served, but the other two assumptions are clearly not met. First, in the CCR there are two classes of servers in tandem—primary board operators followed by secondary board operators—and the effective service time is not exponentially distributed. Yet, if we appropriately define the mean service time per call, application of the $M/M/R$ model should achieve the three stated objectives and its use should provide an improvement over a straight equal workload assignment.

Some resulting allocations, as given by the model, are graphically shown in Figures 9.7 and 9.8. Time is measured in *service*

7. That is, in a multiserver queuing system, the utilization factor or the fraction of time each server (turret operator) is busy, can be made to increase with increasing input rates, while maintaining the same level of service.
8. See any introductory text on queuing, for instance, Saaty [6].
9. See, for example, Larson [4], Appendix A.

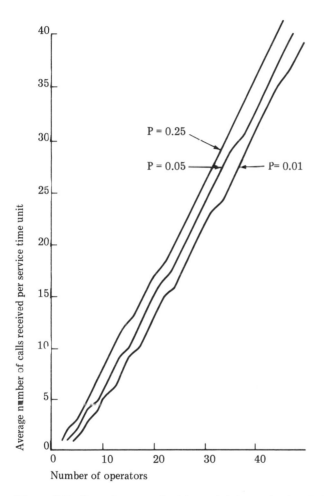

Figure 9.7   Operators required to maintain service levels for $T = 0.25$.

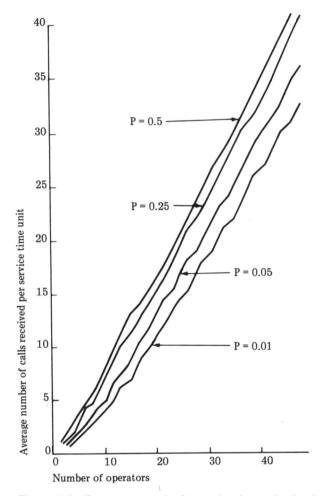

Figure 9.8   Operators required to maintain service levels for $T = 0$.

time units so that, for instance, if the average service time per call is 80 seconds, then 160 seconds would be two service time units. On the vertical axis in each figure is the average number of calls received per service time unit. For instance, if 20 calls are received, on the average, each minute and if the average service time is 80 seconds, then [20 · 80/60] ≈ 26.67 calls are received, on the average, each service time unit. The horizontal axis specifies the number of turret operators needed.

To use the graphs, both service level quantities need to be specified by police administrators: (1) A time T, such that if a call is delayed T service time units or more, the delay is considered inordinately long; (2) A probability P, such that the probability that a call will be delayed T or more service time units will be P or less. Once T and P are specified, one needs an estimate of R, the average number of calls received per service time unit; this estimate is computed from data describing past system operation.

We use the graphs as follows: Given an estimate of R and given T and P, we select the appropriate table according to the value of T; we then find the corresponding value of R on the vertical axis; we cross horizontally from this point until we intersect the plotted curve corresponding to the specified value of P. From this point of intersection, we go straight down to the horizontal axis to obtain the number of turret operators required. The number that we read off is the minimum number required to guarantee that, on the average, the fraction of calls which will be delayed T or more service time units will be P or less.

Example: Suppose we wish to operate at a level such that the fraction of calls which are delayed at least 0.25 service time units is 0.05 or less. Suppose also that for a given hour of operation during the week (say, 4 P.M. to 5 P.M. on Fridays) we estimate that 840 calls will be received. Suppose that the average service time per call is 80 seconds. Then,

R = (no. calls per minute) (no. minutes per service time unit)

$$= \frac{(840)}{(60)} \frac{(80)}{(60)}$$

= 18.67 calls per service time unit

Since $T = 0.25$, we consult Figure 9.7. We cross from the vertical axis at $R = 18.67$ and intersect the curve corresponding to $P =$

0.05. Then, going down to the horizontal axis to read off the number of operators required, we see that about 24 or 25 operators are required to maintain the specified service level.

This procedure can then be repeated to give the number of operators required for each hour throughout the week.

9.10 Applying the Method to Scheduling Manpower

Using NYPD data collected from July 29 through August 25, 1968, we illustrate our method to determine the number of turret operators required each hour, each day of the week, in order to satisfy a given service level criterion. We emphasize that critical to this method is an accurate estimate of the average number of calls received each hour during a week. Since the sampling period here includes only four weeks, there are only four sample values from which to estimate the average number of calls received during each hour. (Since the study, the department has continually collected these data to provide for effective allocations.)

We decided to derive allocations for each of two service levels. For the first service level, called the "relaxed service level criterion," we set $T = 0.25$ and $P = 0.05$ and estimated TC to be eighty seconds. Applying the method with the "relaxed" criterion, given the model assumptions and the estimated work loads, we arrive at an hour-by-hour allocation of turret operators such that *no more than 5 percent of the received calls are delayed* $0.25(80) = 20$ *seconds or more.* The second service level, called the "stringent service level criterion," was specified by $T = 0.00$ and $P = 0.01$.

A rescheduling to satisfy even the relaxed criterion would result in improved performance. For instance, during the month of the sample (with turret operators scheduled, typically, as shown in Figures 9.2 through 9.5), *about 17 percent of the received calls were delayed 15 seconds or more.*

The results of this application of the method are demonstrated in Tables 9.1 and 9.2, each corresponding to one day of the week. The columns in each table contain the following information (from left to right):

1. Hour of the day in military time.
2. Estimated average number of calls received during each hour.
3. Estimated average number of calls received during each service time unit.

Table 9.1   Day of the Week: Tuesday

Service level criterion:

(1) T = 0.025   Assume
     P = 0.05   TC = 80 seconds

(2) T = 0.00
     P = 0.01

Hour of Day (Military time)	Estimated Av. No. Calls Per Hour	Estimated Av. No. Calls Per Service Time Unit	Current Av. Allocation	Recommended Av. Allocation		Difference	
			Criterion:	1	2	1	2
0-1	650	14.5	23	20	25	-3	+2
1-2	450	10	22	15	19	-7	-3
2-3	350	8	22	12	16	-10	-6
3-4	250	5.5	17	10	13	-7	-4
4-5	200	4.5	17	8	9	-9	-8
5-6	180	4	13	7	8	-6	-5
6-7	180	4	13	7	8	-6	-5
7-8	250	5.5	20	10	13	-10	-7
8-9	450	10	24	15	19	-9	-5
9-10	650	14.5	24	20	25	-4	+1
10-11	650	14.5	23	20	25	-3	+2
11-12	550	12	23	17	22	6	-1
12-13	700	15.5	21	21	27	0	+6
13-14	800	18	20	24	29	+4	+9
14-15	700	15.5	22	21	27	-1	+5
15-16	800	18	22	24	29	+2	+7
16-17	850	19	28	25	31	-3	+3
17-18	850	19	26	25	31	-1	+5
18-19	850	19	30	25	31	-5	+1
19-20	850	19	30	25	31	-5	+1
20-21	900	20	28	26	32	-2	+4
21-22	900	20	28	26	32	-2	+4
22-23	1100	24.5	28	31	38	+3	+10
23-24	850	19	28	25	31	-3	+3
						-93	+19

Table 9.2 Day of the Week: Saturday

Service level criterion:

(1) T = 0.25   Assume
    P = 0.05   TC = 80 seconds

(2) T = 0.00
    P = 0.01

Hour of Day (Military time)	Estimated Av. No. Calls Per Hour	Estimated Av. No. Calls Per Service Time Unit	Current Av. Allocation	Recommended Av. Allocation		Difference	
			Criterion:	1	2	1	2
0–1	1300	29	24	35	43	+11	+19
1–2	1000	22	23	28	35	+5	+12
2–3	700	15.5	23	21	27	−2	+4
3–4	800	18	11	24	29	+13	+18
4–5	500	11	12	16	20	+4	+8
5–6	300	6.5	12	11	14	−1	+2
6–7	300	6.5	12	11	14	−1	+2
7–8	300	6.5	24	11	14	−13	−10
8–9	500	11	21	16	20	−5	−1
9–10	500	11	20	16	20	−4	0
10–11	600	13.5	20	19	24	−1	+4
11–12	600	13.5	20	19	24	−1	+4
12–13	800	18	20	24	29	+4	+9
13–14	700	15.5	21	21	27	+0	+6
14–15	1000	22	21	28	35	+7	+14
15–16	800	18	21	24	29	+3	+8
16–17	900	20	27	26	32	−1	+5
17–18	800	18	27	24	29	−3	+2
18–19	800	18	29	24	29	−5	0
19–20	900	20	28	26	32	−2	+4
20–21	1200	26.5	29	33	40	+4	+11
21–22	1300	29	29	35	43	+6	+14
22–23	1300	29	28	35	43	+7	+15
23–24	1300	29	28	35	43	+7	+15
						+32	+165

4. The average allocation of turret operators during each hour, the average being taken over the four-week study period.
5. The average allocation of turret operators specified by the model to meet the service level criterion, $T = 0.25, P = 0.05$.
6. The average allocation of turret operators specified by the model to meet the service level criterion, $T = 0.00$ and $P = 0.01$.
7. The difference between the model-derived allocation and the actual allocation of turret operators for $T = 0.25$ and $P = 0.05$. A + means more operators are needed during a particular hour; a – means less operators are required.
8. Same as 7, except that $T = 0.00$ and $P = 0.01$.

Examining these results, it becomes apparent that the hourly allocation of operators clearly did not fluctuate sufficiently to meet fluctuating demands for service. For instance, even for the stringent service level criterion of $T = 0$ and $P = 0.01$, the system was unnecessarily *overmanned between 7 A.M. and 9 A.M. every day of the week.* Using the same criterion, the system was relatively *undermanned from 8 P.M. to 11 P.M. every day of the week.* (The relaxed criterion of $T = 0.25$ and $P = 0.05$ indicates that the system is undermanned 13 of the 21 hours in the week that fall between 8 P.M. and 11 P.M.) Another time period which is often undermanned is the early afternoon hours before 4 P.M. Except for Saturdays and Sundays, the early morning hours are usually significantly overstaffed, even accounting for the fact that all rest breaks are delayed until the period from 3 A.M. to 7 A.M.

Further examination of the results indicates that the patterns of the demand for service throughout the day are not too dissimilar for the weekdays—Monday, Tuesday, Wednesday, and Thursday. In fact, a "typical" weekday workload pattern seems to exist between the hours of 6 P.M. on Sunday and 6 P.M. on Friday. The distinct weekend increases in demand start early Friday evening and continue through early Sunday morning.

The natural question which arises when using the model-derived allocations is, "What are the implications of the model-derived method to the overall assignment of manpower; for instance, should more men be added as operators, and if so, how many?" The answer to this question is not unique, but depends, of course, on the service level desired. A rank ordering of the days of the week, the ordering done by the number of operator man-hours which must be added per day to satisfy each of the two service level criteria, is seen in Table 9.3.

The rank ordering is the same for each of the service level criteria, but the overall implication about manpower levels are not. For each of the criteria, *Saturday and Sunday appear to be undermanned* and *Thursday and Wednesday appear to be overmanned.* For the other three days, the stringent criterion indicates an *underallocation* of manpower, while the relaxed criterion indicates an overallocation. Application of the stringent criterion throughout the week would imply that an additional 381 man-hours would be required at the turret operator positions. This is equivalent to about 63 additional man-tours (at six working hours per tour) or about 12.5 additional men, optimistically assuming five tours per week per man; on the other hand, the application of the relaxed criterion throughout the week would imply that 460 man-hours currently allocated could be eliminated. This is equivalent to an elimination of about 77 man-tours or a reduction in the number of men assigned, assuming five tours per week per man, of about 15 men. It is clear that with the present allocation of men to the turret operator positions, *a rescheduling of their assignments to anticipate fluctuating levels of demands for service would allow the system to operate at a service level somewhere between the so-called relaxed and stringent service levels.* Given all of the model assumptions and parameter estimates, the method suggests that the rescheduling should cause a reduction in 15-second delays by a factor of at least two and possibly as great as five.

Implementation of the method illustrated here required a separate method of tour scheduling which, given the derived demand for personnel, would be used to specify the starting hours of tours

Table 9.3   Rank ordering of days of week

Currently Underallocated		
According to the relaxed service level criterion	⎧ 1. Saturday ⎩ 2. Sunday	Currently Underallocated
	⎧ 3. Monday 4. Friday	According to the stringent service level criterion
Currently Overallocated	5. Tuesday	
According to the relaxed service level criterion	6. Thursday ⎩ 7. Wednesday	Currently Overallocated
		According to the stringent service level criterion

(allowing more than three, in general) and the total number of men to assign to each tour. Guidelines for constructing tour schedules are provided by Heller [1].

9.11 Implementation

The results of the study were presented in a formal briefing before the police commissioner and other interested personnel of the NYPD. Lieutenants Masini and Carvino were present at the briefing to indicate how the quantitative aspects of the study fit into their more comprehensive management survey. Their final report to the commissioner included a major section on the scheduling of turret operators, using the techniques and results of this chapter.

Within one month after the briefing, the recommendations of the study were implemented essentially in their entirety. The number of tours over a 24-hour period was increased from three to seven, with the number of operators assigned to each tour selected so that the total number manning the phones each hour was approximately equal to that recommended by analysis. Simultaneously, improved estimates of demand rates and service times were obtained as further data were collected and analyzed, thereby suggesting slight modifications in the recommended numbers to allocate. Each day, on the main bulletin board in CCR, the 24-hour profile of the previous day's operations was posted, including plots of calls received per hour, number of 15-second delays per hour, number of 30-second delays per hour, and number of phones manned each hour. This display provided very visible evidence of any severe congestion on the previous day, and supervisors came to pride themselves on having a minimum number of "bells" on their shifts of duty. (Recall that bells ring rather loudly whenever the in-queue backlog exceeds 30 seconds.) Most of the supervisory personnel appeared quite pleased with the new scheduling and all agreed that delays were reduced considerably. At the time of this writing, the implemented scheduling system is still in operation, with the SPRINT computer system providing very detailed statistics upon which to base future demand predictions. The department is considering the purchase of a special purpose small computer to monitor continuously the ACD system and to provide very timely recommendations for improved allocations of turret operators, using methods similar to those in this chapter.

9.12 Further Required Work

While developing the rescheduling described in this chapter, at
least two other questions requiring attention came to light. First,
further work was required in examining the properties of the secondary queue. At the time of the study there was limited evidence
to suggest that a fatigued primary board turret operator who is
given a call by the ACD immediately after completing a previous
call may simply switch the call directly into the secondary queue.
Although there were no data available to determine the extent of
this practice, the possibility of this happening was acknowledged
by operating personnel during the course of the study. This could
explain why a few citizens who dialed 911 *after* the rescheduling
of turret operators still experienced inordinately long delays until
they heard an operator's voice. (Recently, the ACD has been re-
structured to eliminate the secondary queue.)

Second, using the $M/M/R$ queuing model to infer values of the
average service time TC at various times of the day, we found that
TC actually fluctuates with the workload. During periods of
heavy work load, the mean time spent per call appears to be less
than that during nonsaturation periods. For instance, during one
hour in which 800 calls were received, 22 operators were assigned,
and about 25 percent of the calls were delayed at least 15 seconds,
the queue model suggests that TC is about 85 seconds per call. On
the other hand, during another hour in which 1,400 calls were received, 24 operators were assigned, and about 50 percent of the
calls were delayed at least 15 seconds; the queue model implies
that TC is about 54 seconds per call. This reduction in service time
could imply that operators are spending less time attempting to
screen calls and thus increasing the fraction for which a radio run
is required. If this is the case (a question requiring further study),
the saturation problem in the field would just be compounded,
due to a disproportionately large number of requests for radio
runs. For instance, a more desirable operating policy during saturation periods might be to increase the time spent per call on the
telephone in order to screen calls more finely, thus reducing the
number of patrol man hours required to service calls in the field.
The use of a constant average service time in the allocation
method of Section 9.10 at least partially reflected the desire of
CCR administrators to have sufficiently many operators on hand
so that heavy workloads would not necessitate abbreviated conver-

sations. If a policy were to be implemented in which heavy workloads brought about longer conversations for improved screening,
the allocation method would have to be modified to include this
change.

9.13 Relationship to Other Studies

The study described in this chapter represented approximately one
man-month of professional effort, obviously focusing on one very
particular aspect of operation of the police emergency response
system. Analyses of the remainder of the NYPD emergency response system are contained in Larson [3], and Larson [2]. The
first of these presented a method for allocating police patrol
cars to precincts by time of day (and day of week) in order to
achieve a set of stated objectives; application of the method to the
NYPD played a role in efforts of the mayor and police commissioner to implement a fourth tour (or fourth "platoon"), which
now operates from 6:00 P.M. to 2:00 A.M. The second study focused on dispatching delays, patrol car travel times and travel distances, service times at the scene, other time-consuming activities
of patrol cars, and the fine-grain spatial deployment of patrol cars.
Several inadequacies in operating procedures were found, and
many of these have subsequently been corrected by the department.

An analysis of the emergency response system of the Boston Police Department is given in Larson [4]. Among other findings, this
study concluded that the dispatcher's position was a system congestion point and recommended addition of a second dispatcher.
This recommendation was implemented shortly following the
study.

A complete list of other studies and reports known to the author
related to the police emergency response system (and the patrol
force in particular) is given in an annotated bibliography in Larson
[5]. That reference also develops a number of analytical and simulation models for studying a range of operational problems associated with the police emergency response system focusing on the
patrol force.

There are basically two directions in which to expand and generalize the class of operational models discussed in this chapter
and used in the above-mentioned studies. The first considers other
aspects of the criminal justice system, embedding the police sys-

tem in the larger system which also includes prosecution, courts, corrections, and the possible feedback of offenders back into the system following release. This approach is illustrated in Chapter 16 in which A. Blumstein and the author construct aggregate models of the criminal justice system for one state. The second direction of generalization steers toward other types of spatially distributed urban service systems and attempts to identify similarities and differences in system structure and decision alternatives in urban fire departments, emergency ambulance services, taxicab fleets, and emergency repair services, as well as police patrol forces. Efforts in this direction are described by J. Chaiken and the author in Chapter 10.

References

1. Heller, N., "Proportional Rotating Schedules," Ph.D. thesis, University of Pennsylvania, 1969.

2. Larson, R. C., "Measuring the Response Patterns of New York City Police Patrol Cars," New York City–Rand Institute, R-673-NYC/HUD, 1971.

3. _____ , *Models for the Allocation of Urban Police Patrol Forces*, Technical Report No. 44, M.I.T. Operations Research Center, Cambridge, Mass., 1969.

4. _____ , *Operational Study of the Police Response System*, Technical Report No. 26, M.I.T. Operations Research Center, Cambridge, Mass., 1967.

5. _____ , *Urban Police Patrol Analysis*, M.I.T. Press, Cambridge, Mass., 1972.

6. Saaty, T., *Elements of Queueing Theory*, McGraw-Hill Book Co., New York, 1961.

7. *SPRING 3100*, "The Communications Division," July–August 1968, (available from New York City Police Department), pp. 2-18.

10

Methods for Allocating Urban Emergency Units

Jan M. Chaiken and Richard C. Larson

10.1 Introduction

Urban police and fire departments, emergency ambulance services, and similar urban emergency service systems comprise an important class of governmental service agencies that until recently has not benefited from systematic analyses of operational problems. These systems operate in a complicated environment that includes temporally and spatially varying demand patterns, both explicit and implicit administrative, legal, and political constraints, and, often, ill-defined mixtures of objectives.

Our purpose in this chapter is to review those operational problems of these agencies that are related to the deployment of their vehicles and to report current progress on mathematical modeling approaches to these problems. The discussion focuses on the methods that are available, the extent of improvement that can be expected as a result of quantitative study, and the types of solutions that can be obtained. References are given so that the interested reader can pursue details which are not given here. Several of the problems discussed (for example, determining how many units to have on duty) are common to many urban service systems we are considering, while others (for example, allocation of preventive patrol effort) are experienced by only one agency.

Although we shall not focus on the mathematical details of any of the methods, we hope to be sufficiently precise to bring out the following points:

—The performance of emergency service systems is often affected in counterintuitive ways by changes in procedures or deployment.
—Popular operational "rules of thumb" often yield levels of performance which can be substantially improved by more formal methods.
—Simple changes in administrative procedure can often produce more significant improvements than expensive hardware systems or increases in manpower.
—The current state of research is sufficiently advanced in several areas so that many cities' emergency service systems could experi-

ence significant improvement simply by applying what is currently known.

—Additional research is needed in a number of areas.

10.2 Description of an Urban Emergency Service System

The class of urban service systems we are considering is characterized by the following properties:

—Incidents occur throughout the city which give rise to requests or calls for service (for example, fire alarms, crime victim assists); the times and places of occurrence of these calls cannot be specifically predicted in advance.

—In response to each call, one or more emergency service units (vehicles) are dispatched to the scene of the incident.

—The rapidity with which the units arrive at the scene has some bearing on the actual or perceived quality of the service.

Examples of such emergency service units include fire engines and ladder trucks, police patrol cars and scooters, ambulances, emergency repair trucks for gas, electric and water services, and tow trucks.

Although all urban emergency service systems share the characteristics listed here, they may differ in certain significant details.

—Some emergency units are ordinarily found at *fixed locations* at time of dispatch. Others such as police patrol cars are *mobile*. This distinction is important for both administrative and analytical purposes. For instance, in principle it is possible to vary the location, size and shape of police patrol sectors at will, whereas the response areas of fire units must be designed in relation to the (fixed) locations of the fire stations. Also, the dispatch strategy for *mobile* units can often be improved by a variety of location-estimation techniques which are not needed if units are positioned at known locations. For instance, a police dispatcher could improve decisions by querying the cars as to their locations[1] or using information from an automatic car locator system. The distinction between mobile and fixed-location units begins to break down during periods of high demand. At such times the units may be dispatched directly from one incident to the next, or they may be

---

1. Congested Radio frequencies often prohibit this type of location procedure.

dispatched while en route from a previous incident to their home location.[2] Under such conditions, the system's operation is not very sensitive to the distribution of initial locations, either fixed or mobile.

—Emergency services differ in the urgency of the calls they receive and in their ability to discriminate among types of calls in advance. For example, false alarms of fire are not at all urgent, but it is difficult to know which alarms are false.[3] On the other hand, a telephone call to the police reporting a past burglary can be identified as not requiring the immediate response of a patrol car.[4] In near saturation conditions the ability of an emergency service to distinguish the priorities of its calls critically affects operations. If a call can be identified as not urgent, the dispatcher may decide not to send any units, or he may hold the call in queue to await the availability of a unit near the scene; he may even place a call in queue when some units are still available, thereby protecting his ability to dispatch units to future high-priority incidents. However, if each call must be assumed urgent, then none can be delayed in queue. Then, when many units are unavailable, the dispatcher must either send fewer units to each incident, dispatch units from greater distances, or preempt units from missions on which they are presently engaged.

—For some emergency services the time the units spend between servicing calls is used for another important activity. For example, it is widely believed that routine patrol by police cars acts as a deterrent to certain types of crime [33,66]. If police cars spent nearly all of their time handling calls for service the preventive patrol function would suffer. Such an important secondary function is not present in all emergency service systems and should be distinguished from routine internal functions: rest, meals and training for the men, maintenance of equipment, and preparing written reports. For units that do have an important secondary

2. This pattern is also common for emergency repair services, in which the driver may contact the dispatcher at the end of one service to determine where he should go next.

3. Some cities maintain records of false alarm rates for each fire alarm box and adjust their initial response. These typically vary from 20 to 90 percent false.

4. Some requests for service are generated by field personnel, as when a fire chief signals a second alarm at a fire, or a patrolman calls for assistance over his radio. Such calls can be immediately identified as reliable and of high priority.

function, questions involving the dispatch of units cannot be answered exclusively in terms of the effectiveness of response to emergencies. For example, it may be desirable to place some calls to the police in queue simply to preserve the deterrent patrol. A fire dispatcher would rarely have occasion to make such a decision, since the available fire units are almost never engaged in any activity which could be judged more important than responding to an alarm.

10.3 Factors Influencing the Selection of an Allocation Policy

The *allocation* (or *deployment*) *policy* of an urban emergency service system determines the following properties of the system:

1. The total number of units of each type on duty at any one time. This may differ by time of day, or day of the week, or season of the year.
2. The number of men assigned to each unit.
3. The location or patrol area of each unit.
4. The priority attached to different types of calls, and the circumstances under which calls are queued.
5. How many units of each type are dispatched to each reported incident.
6. The particular units which are dispatched.
7. The circumstances under which the assigned locations of units are changed. (This operation is variously called *relocation, move-up, redeployment, repositioning* or *reinforcement.*)
8. When relocations are required:
a. The number of units that are relocated,
b. Which particular units are relocated, and
c. What their new locations are.

We are concerned here with methods that can be used to select or improve allocation policies. But it should be noted that many operational aspects of an emergency service system which are *not* part of the allocation policy may have a major influence on the quality of service provided. Among the most important are:

—The assignments given to particular individuals,
—The procedures followed at the scene of an incident, and
—Support functions: maintenance, supply, training, and administration.

Because cities differ widely in their properties and in the demands they place on their emergency services, it is clearly impractical to try to specify a single "optimal" allocation policy which can apply to all locales. Nor does "optimal" have much meaning in systems with ill-defined objectives and hidden constraints. But the theory underlying the allocation of emergency units is now sufficiently well developed that we can identify most of the quantitative factors that should be taken into account:

—The nature of the geographical area to be used,
—Population density and land use patterns,
—Time and space distribution of calls for service,
—Number of units of each type required to service calls,
—Travel speeds,
—Service times at incidents.

All of these factors will have some impact on the performance that can be expected from any particular allocation policy.

But the most fundamental difficulty arises in trying to measure performance. How do we know when an allocation policy is good? Which ones are better than others? These questions can only partially be answered in quantitative terms, and other factors specific to the type of service system being considered play an important role.

In the sections that follow, examples of various quantitative methods will be discussed and analyzed. Insights and interpretations derived from these methods will be discussed, and an attempt will be made to indicate how these insights may usefully guide an administrator's thinking about allocation policies.

There are basically two ways in which an agency administrator can use these methods. The first and most common application entails the examination and selection of improved methods for assigning a *predetermined* total number of men. Even in cases where there is a possibility of hiring additional personnel, it is important to determine what level of performance can be achieved with existing manpower. The cost of even a single additional emergency unit is usually large enough to justify whatever analysis may be required to bring about the same performance level without the added unit.[5]

5. Typically, somewhat over 5 man-years are required to fill a single post, around the clock, throughout the year. Thus, the direct manpower costs of

The second application, which has been recommended in planning and administration tests [33,67], is to use quantitative methods for determining the overall number of men required to meet some prespecified objectives. Because personnel costs often constitute as much as 90 to 98 percent of the budget of an emergency service, this use of quantitative methods to derive an allocation policy is virtually equivalent to determining the budget level of the service. However, this happens only on rare occasions. More typically, the administrator of an emergency service in a major city is faced with a total budget (or authorized strength) which he cannot change very much in one year.

A challenge in future years will be to implement both uses of these methods, with current systems performing effectively under a given budget level and required future budget levels evaluated from analyses of predicted demands and models of operation.

10.4 Determining the Number of Units to Have on Duty in Each Area

Methods Based on Geography and Land Use
Decisions regarding the total number and locations of a city's fixed facilities (for example, fire houses and police precinct stations) have usually been made solely on the basis of geography and land use patterns. This reliance on geographical factors has been reinforced by geographical standards and regulations which apply to many cities. For example, the Standard Grading Schedule of the American Insurance Association [2] is used in nearly all U.S. cities (except New York) to establish fire insurance rates. As a rule, cities will attempt to meet as many standards in the schedule as possible, so as not to have a lower rating than necessary. But for cities with a population over 200,000, the only criteria provided by the schedule for the number of fire engines and ladders to be located in each part of the city are based exclusively on geography and land use. For certain "high-value districts" the schedule requires every point to be no further than one mile from an engine company and no further than 1.25 miles from a ladder company. Moreover, within 1.5 miles of any point there must be at least 3

---

operating a two-man patrol car in New York are approximately $120,000 per year, and a single fire engine may cost over $500,000 per year.

engine companies, and within 2 miles at least 2 ladders. These standards may vary slightly from area to area, but for each type of area, the same kind of geographical standard applies.

The main deficiency of geographical standards is that they are meant to be substitutes for standards involving the time between receipt of a call for service and the arrival of emergency units. But this response time depends on many factors aside from geographical ones: the delays incurred in dispatching the units, the speed at which the units can travel, and the probability that particular units will be available. (It is little comfort to know that a fire house is within a mile of your home if the units located at that house would very likely be busy at the time you had a fire.)

Thus, as a general rule, it is not possible to determine whether an adequate number of units are located in each geographical area solely by inspecting a map of the city which shows the home location of each unit.

Another Traditional Approach: Work Load or Hazard Formulas
Instead of relying on a single factor such as geography, so-called workload or hazard formulas combine in a subjective manner virtually *all* factors that might be thought relevant for allocating units. They give an appearance of accuracy because of the large number of factors included.

Perhaps the most well-known such formula was developed for police use by Wilson in the late 1930s [65,66,67]. Wilson combined indicators of activity (such as number of arrests, number of calls for service of particular types, number of doors and windows to be checked) with other factors (such as number of street miles, number of licensed premises, and number of crimes) to arrive at a "hazard score" for each area. An area's score is computed by taking a weighted sum of the fractions of each of the factors associated with the area. The weights are subjective indicators of relative importance. In applying the formula, the total number of men (or patrol cars) are to be distributed among the areas in direct proportion to their hazard scores.

This procedure often produces unsatisfactory allocations that may have to be "juggled" by hand computations to arrive at a "reasonable" allocation. For instance, the 5 or 10 percent weighting often given to calls for service is not nearly adequate to avoid lengthy queue delays in certain areas during periods of high demand. The inherently linear form of a hazard formula precludes description of the highly nonlinear and complex interactions among system components that are often observed in practice. Such a formula also attempts a simple deterministic depiction of a system in which many of the variables are probabilistic. In addition, since factors such as arrests are more likely in sufficiently staffed areas, hazard formulas may have the perverse effect of indicating a need for additional personnel in areas that are already relatively overallocated. But the major difficulty arises in trying to determine how to improve the selection of the subjective weightings, a problem for which there seem to be no underlying principles or guidelines.

Wilson should be credited with introducing hand-calculable quantitative methods into a policy area that previously had depended on "command judgment" alone. But increased implementation of digital computers and recent developments in the theory of allocating emergency units have made reliance on a hazard formula unnecessary.

Modeling Methods
The approach emphasized in this chapter relies on constructing and analyzing mathematical models of operations. From a modeling viewpoint urban emergency service systems have two distinctive features: (1) probabilistic demands and service requirements over time and (2) probabilistic distribution of incidents and response units over the space of the city. The first gives rise to congestion when too much service is demanded in too short a time period. It is natural to examine such phenomena using queuing theory, a branch of operations research concerned with the performance of service systems where customers, ships, telephone calls, and so on, may have to wait "in line" until they receive the desired service. The second feature, corresponding to the system's spatial characteristics, gives rise to travel time distributions, patrol patterns, and so on. To the extent that space and time considerations can be separated, it is convenient to examine the spatially dependent properties of the system using essentially geometrical considerations. Then, in using these models in an allocation algorithm or other complicated decision application, we can incorporate the several criteria of each of the separate models, including

both queuing and spatial properties of operation. These topics are discussed further in the following paragraphs.

Queuing Models

In applying queuing theory to urban emergency service systems, the "customers" are the calls requiring dispatch of a vehicle. The consequences of having to place such a call in queue may be quite serious. Indeed, it is characteristic of emergency systems that a person's life or well-being may well depend on the immediate dispatch of a unit.

Thus, a primary objective of all urban emergency systems is to reduce to a low level the possibility that an urgent call will have to be placed in queue for more than a few seconds.

The probabilistic nature of the arrival times and service times of calls is such that one can never guarantee that *every* call will result in the immediate dispatch of a unit.[6] Thus, the objective of a queuing analysis is to assume that the *probability* of an important call encountering a queue is below some specified threshold (such as 1 in 50) or that the *average time to wait in queue* is below some specified limit (such as 1 minute).

To take a simple hypothetical example, we might imagine a city in which each police patrol car is assigned a geographical response area ("sector" or "beat") in such a way that no other car responds into his area. Then, whenever a given patrol car were busy, all calls from his sector would have to be placed in queue. Such an arrangement constitutes a "single-server queuing system," and, given reasonable assumptions, standard textbooks provide formulas that give good estimates of the probability that a call will experience a queue or the average time it will wait in queue [49,51]. One could use these formulas to determine the required number of patrol units as follows: A threshold would be selected for the maximum value of the probability of a queue (or average waiting time) to be permitted in any sector; then the sectors would be selected small enough to assure that the threshold is not exceeded. The total number of sectors designed in this way would then determine how many units are needed.

Although this example is instructive, we are fortunate that no urban emergency service system actually operates in this fashion.

6. Except if the number of emergency vehicles is infinite—or, as a practical approximation, is much too large for the budgets of most cities.

At fixed manning levels, other arrangements lead to fewer delays; or, at fixed performance levels, other arrangements require fewer total response units.

The simplest generalization of this model that has been usefully applied to real emergency services is the following: There is a fixed number N of vehicles, either located at one place (for example, a hospital) or distributed throughout a region, and each call requires the dispatch of one vehicle. A call is placed in queue only when all N vehicles are busy servicing prior calls. All calls are assumed to be identical in terms of their importance and service time distribution. With certain additional assumptions, the formulas describing this queuing system are easily derived [51].

Stevenson in Chapter 8 has applied this model to determining how large the number N of ambulances in a region must be (depending on the arrival rate of calls) to assure that only 1 in 100 (or 1 in 20, or 1 in 10) callers must wait for the dispatch of an ambulance. Given an estimate of the call arrival rate during each time period, an administrator can select a desired threshold probability and determine how many ambulances to have on duty for each time period.

The results of Stevenson's calculations have a property which is common to nearly all realistic queuing models: the number of units needed increases with the call rate, but not in direct proportion to the call rate. Thus, a doubling of the call rate would produce a requirement for fewer than twice as many service units. This observation constitutes an additional argument against using call-for-service rates in a linear fashion in workload formulas.

The same model has been used in St. Louis for the allocation of police patrol cars [48]. The city is divided into nine patrol districts, and a call is assumed to enter a queue whenever all the cars in its district are busy. For each four-hour time period, the police department estimates, using the N-server queuing model, how many cars will be needed so that at most 15 percent of each district's calls will experience a queuing delay.[7]

The next step in complexity of queuing models occurs when various call types have different priorities. As an example, Cobham

7. The results of this queuing calculation are not the *sole* basis on which cars are assigned to districts, since St. Louis also has a "preventive patrol" force that does not respond to calls, unless they have a very high priority. However, the use of queuing theory is an essential component of the allocation policy of the St. Louis Police Department.

[20] developed a model which assumes that higher priority calls are served first but retains the assumptions that one unit responds to each call and that all service times have the same simplified distribution. Although in most police departments calls are not explicitly assigned priorities according to specified rules, Larson has found this model useful as an approximation to current performance of police dispatchers and as a tool for analysis of the potential benefits of more precise priority schemes [43]. It has the advantage that it places emphasis on reducing the delays that are associated with important calls.

Greater realism could be introduced into this model by (1) permitting each priority level to have different service time distributions, or (2) allowing the service time to vary with the number of units busy.[8] But the effort required to design such models cannot be justified unless allocation decisions are found to be sensitive to the current model's assumptions and unless a comparable effort is devoted to collecting the analyzing service-time data.

One refinement of the multiserver queuing model has been found practical, and indeed necessary, for predicting the number of units busy at operations of a fire department. Fire dispatchers typically send *several* units to each alarm, while the previous models assume that one unit is sent to each incident. In addition, fire units responding to a particular call do not all complete service at the same time since each may have distinct duties to perform.[9]

Chaiken [17] has developed a quite general queuing model which allows for these features of fire operations. In particular, in this model

—Different types of alarms may require different numbers of units of various kinds;

8. The dependence of service times on the number of busy units is characteristic of most urban emergency systems, but it is difficult to measure quantitatively. One cause of the variation, which can be estimated at least roughly [44], is the increase in average travel time which occurs when distant units must be dispatched to calls. More important, however, is the fact that an incident may escalate when units do not arrive promptly; a small fire may become much larger and require a longer time to extinguish, or a reported marital dispute may result in serious assault before a patrol car arrives. Available data are rarely adequate to model these phenomena [34].

9. Some units may leave the fire scene when the fire is under control, while others will remain until extinguishment, and still others will continue to work after extinguishment on some duties known as "overhaul."

—The units may arrive singly, or in groups, and they may depart in similar fashion; and

—The length of time the units are busy at the incident depends on the type of incident.

This model assumes that queues are never permitted to develop. Instead, whenever units are required in one region of the city, it is assumed they will be dispatched from there or from another region, if necessary. In applying this model, one does not try to assure that the probability of encountering a queue is small. Instead, one requires that the probability of needing to dispatch units from a distant region be small. The computations required for this model, as well as the other queuing models discussed, are readily carried out on a computer.

Applying the model in New York City [16], one finds that at low alarm rates (such as occur in the early hours of the morning), the numbers of units needed to meet the requirements of the queuing model are well *below* the numbers needed to meet simple geographical requirements;[10] therefore the geographical factors predominate. However, in some parts of the city at times of high alarm rate the queuing model implies a need for more units than would be suggested by geography alone.

The same model could be utilized for analyzing operations in other emergency services which dispatch two or more units to certain types of incidents.

Travel Time Models

Although the typical travel times of four to ten minutes may be dominated by queuing delays during periods of saturation, travel time may comprise the greatest fraction of total response time during normal operating periods [45]. Thus, models are required which relate properties of travel time to the number of units on duty, geographical characteristics, arrival rates of calls, and service times at incidents. In periods of relatively light or moderate demand, the travel time models can replace traditional geographical factors in determining the number of units to have on duty, provided the units are spatially dispersed throughout the region.[11] In

10. See Section 10.4.
11. If the units are located at one facility, such as the "base case" for ambulances reported by Savas [56], then the travel time from the facility to incidents in the region does not depend on the number of units located at the facility, but only on geographical factors describing the region.

developing such models one has to take into account the probabilities of particular combinations of units being available, the dispatching rules, and other details of the system's operation.

The level of detail of such models depends, of course, on their
intended uses. On the one hand, for detailed implementations on
complicated urban environments, one may have to resort to em-
perical travel time distributions and tabulate different distributions under various weather and traffic conditions. Hogg [31]
used empirically measured travel times to select from a number of
potential sites for fire houses the set of sites which yielded minimal average travel time.

On the other hand, if only approximate results are required to
assist one's intuition by indicating first-order interrelationships,
simple analytical models may be more useful than detailed (and
expensive to obtain) empirical relationships. Several geometrically
oriented models show that expected *travel distance* is inversely
proportional to the square root of the number of available units
per square mile, with the proportionality constant dependent on
the spatial distribution pattern of the units. If units are *randomly*
located in a homogeneous region, with an average of r units per
square mile, one model [43, p. 323] shows that the average (right-
angle) travel distance for the closest unit is approximately $0.63/$
$\sqrt{r}$). If the units are not randomly located but instead are located
in such a way as to minimize average travel distance [46], the constant 0.63 is replaced by 0.47. Kolcsar and Blum [40] have found
similar results for the average travel distance of the second-arriving
unit when two are dispatched. The models also provide estimates
of the probability that travel distance will exceed any specified
threshold. Such models of travel distance can be used to compute
travel times once the effective travel speed is known as a function
of travel distance and other factors.

If the travel time models are tied to the queuing methods described above, the resulting model can be applied to determining
how many units to have on duty. The queuing model is used to determine the probability that n units will be busy, given N total
units on duty and other characteristics of the system. Larson [43,
p. 328] follows this approach to estimate average travel time, assuming each available unit is randomly positioned. It is similarly
possible to calculate the expected travel time under the assumption that the available units are moved, if necessary, so as to occupy the locations which give minimum travel time.

Kolesar and Blum [40] have studied the numerical output from these models, as well as data derived from experiments and from more complex models; they have concluded that a reasonable approximation in cases where unavailabilities are not too severe is to assume that the average travel time $\overline{T}$ is related to the *average* number of units available per square mile r by the following relationship:

$$\overline{T} = \frac{a}{r^b},$$

where a and b are readily measured empirical constants that depend on the particular region under study. Similar formulas apply to indicators of travel time other than the mean.

Such a result leads to the following method for determining how many units to have on duty in each region:

—Determine the empirical constants relating the selected indicator of travel time to the average number of units available per square mile, using data collected in the region.
—Estimate the arrival rates for calls in the region.
—Assuming N total units are on duty throughout the region, use queuing methods to calculate the *average* number of units available per square mile, and use this number to calculate the indicator of travel time.
—Select N so that the indicator of travel time and perhaps some indicator of queuing delay do not exceed specified thresholds.

Such calculation provides sensible allocations for all regions, whether they experience high call rates or not.

Methods Using Several Criteria

The simple analytical models described above may not, by themselves, be sufficient to determine the number of units needed. First, for services which engage in important activities other than response to calls, criteria relating to these activities have to be taken into account.[12] Second, and more fundamentally, easily quantifiable criteria (probability of encountering a queue, average travel time) do not often have a clear relationship to the true performance of the system. For instance, one would like to know the

12. For a general discussion of criteria which are appropriate for police patrol, see the report of Kakalik and Wildhorn [36].

actual benefits which accrue by decreasing response time. Such benefits might be lives saved, stolen goods recovered, property damage averted, and so on. Although preliminary research along these lines has been performed [34, 11, 27], the currently available empirical information is not an adequate foundation for an administrator's use in selecting allocation policies.

Thus, at present, one is forced to use available performance measures such as response times. A careful and realistic use of such measures can provide reliable proxies for more fundamental measures, as have been discussed by Carter and Ignall [12].

Given such a necessary reliance on performance measures, an administrator would usually want to employ several simultaneously to arrive at reasonable allocations. In addition to queuing and travel times, he could incorporate factors pertaining to other activities (for example, preventive patrol) and to administrative matters (for example, workloads).

Two criteria, travel time and response workload, are analyzed in Carter and Ignall's queuing model for determining the extent to which an added fire unit provides relief to overworked units in its area. It would be natural to assume that when units are added to a command, the *number* of responses made by each of its units would decrease, and this may be one of the secondary benefits of adding units which is particularly interesting to an agency administrator. However, since a full response to fires ordinarily requires several units, their model shows that adding a new unit will increase the chances of a full rather than partial response, thereby increasing the total number of responses of units in the area. Thus, if it is desired to reduce the workloads of units in addition to improving the response time, a greater number of units may be needed than is suggested by simpler models.

Larson [43] has developed a dynamic programming algorithm for allocation of police patrol cars to commands (for example, precincts) that can incorporate a wide variety of criteria. These can include (1) some measure of travel time; (2) the frequency with which cars pass arbitrary points while patrolling; (3) administrative restrictions on the smallest number of units which can be assigned to a command. For each criterion a patrol administrator specifies a desired threshold, or "policy objective," which may vary with command. For instance, for a particular command it may be decided that the average travel time should not exceed four minutes. Then, the algorithm supplies the command with enough patrol units so that this objective and all other policy objectives (constraints) are satisfied. Once the objectives are met, the queuing delay is treated as a variable to be minimized using whatever additional patrol units are available.

With limited police resources, of course, it is possible that a specific set of policy objectives is unobtainable. If so, the algorithm indicates the additional number of patrol units required to meet the stated objectives. To allocate the currently available number of units, the algorithm then requires a more modest set of objectives.

Compared to the allocations derived from a hazard formula, the algorithm-derived allocations appear to reflect more fully the operating characteristics of the system. For instance, in one large city the results suggest that during periods of relative congestion (for example, Friday and Saturday evenings), average queuing delay can be decreased significantly by diminishing resources in residential commands with relatively light demands and increasing resources in nonresidential commands which are heavily loaded. Such a redeployment of resources does not significantly degrade performance in residential commands since sufficiently many patrol units are retained to satisfy all policy constraints. Yet, average queuing delays in heavy work load areas can be reduced often from 30 minutes to less than two or three minutes.

Although such a finding may not be surprising, the calculation of this reallocation would be extremely tedious without the assistance of a computer algorithm that can compute the effects of each alternative and quickly discard "bad" ones. And, without models of patrol activity, it would not be possible to predict whether each alternative allocation satisfies the policy constraints and reduces the delay at the dispatcher's position in the best possible way.

In general, the quality of the allocations that an administrator can expect from any of the models described here depends on how much effort he is willing to have his staff devote to the application. An analyst who is not a member of the concerned agency cannot make an appropriate determination of what constitutes an "excessively long" delay before the arrival of a unit, or how much preventive patrol will be considered adequate, or what level of work load is "too great."

In the case of fire departments, where the various units dispatched to a single incident may arrive at different times, the analyst is not even in a position to know which arrival patterns are "better" than others. However, the field chiefs, who are completely familiar with their department's operating procedures at a fire, can provide valuable information. Through asking a series of questions such as "Would you prefer two fire engines arriving 1.5 minutes after an alarm, or one arriving at the 1-minute mark and one at the 2-minute mark?" it is possible to derive a chief's utility function for arrival times. Work in progress by Keeney [37] to develop such utility functions should make it possible to select the allocation of units so as to maximize a chief's utility of the resulting patterns of arrival times.

In regard to any of these methods for determining how many units to have on duty, it should be noted that there may be some difficulty in assigning individuals to shifts or tours of duty which best "fit" the desired assignments. Legal and administrative constraints can make this problem quite difficult. A heuristic approach is discussed by Edie [24]. A more general approach using a computer algorithm has recently been reported by Heller [29].

10.5 Design of Response Areas

A problem commonly shared by all spatially distributed urban systems is the design of response areas (districts or sectors or beats) that indicate where a particular patrol unit, fire engine, or ambulance is to have primary responsibility. In designing these administrative areas, agency administrators have stated several diverse (often conflicting) objectives:

—Minimization of response time;
 Equalization of workload;
—Demographic homogeneity of each area;
—Administrative convenience.

No single mathematical technique for design of districts is likely to take into account all the relevant factors. Yet, even some of the more simple, recently developed models have provided more insight into the problem than was previously available with ad hoc "rules of thumb" and, in fact, have shown several such rules to be invalid in most cases.

Single Sector Models

Traditionally, police planners have been instructed to design patrol sectors as squares, circles, or as straight lines along particular streets. The idea behind square or circular sectors is to keep at a minimum the time required for the patrol unit to travel to the scene of a reported incident in its sector. For instance, Wilson states that ". . . a square beat (sector) permits a maximum quadrilateral area with a minimum distance between any two possible points within it"[13] [67, p. 228].

One factor not considered in this statement is that, with mobile patrol units, travel speeds may depend on direction of travel; in such a situation, it will be desirable to design the sector so that the longer sector dimension corresponds to the direction with higher travel speeds. Using quantitative techniques, it is possible to predict the travel time characteristics of any proposed sector design and thereby determine which designs actually do minimize some indicator of travel time.

As an example, consider an urban region in which the streets form a mutually perpendicular grid (for example, as occurs in central Manhattan and certain other cities), running, say, east–west and north–south. Then, a shortest route of travel for the assigned patrol unit requires the unit to traverse the total east–west distance, plus the total north–south distance, between the unit's initial position and the position of the incident.[14] Given some simplifying assumptions, Larson has shown that average intrasector travel time is minimized by designing the sector so that the average time required to travel east–west *equals* the average north–south travel time. Since it is not unusual to find regions (such as in Manhattan) where the north–south speed is about four times as great as the east–west speed, this implies that the sectors should also be four times as long in their north–south direction. In this case, such a sector design can be expected to reduce average intrasector travel time by approximately 20% over that obtained by the rule-of-thumb design—square or circular sectors.

13. More precisely: among all quadrilaterals of a given area, the one with the smallest maximum distance between two points is a square.
14. Several interesting applications of this "right-angle distance metric" and other metrics have been discussed in [26] and [57].

Some of these ideas have already been applied by Bottoms, Nilsson, and Olson in the city of Chicago [7]. They have constructed a new sector plan of the city using rectangular sectors designed so that the average intrasector travel time never exceeds approximately three minutes.

Certain complications to travel involving one-way streets or obstacles such as railroad tracks would increase average travel time. Larson has computed the mean extra distance traveled due to these complications [45]. Although the results indicate a general insensitivity to most complications, certain responses involving one-way streets require three or more additional minutes for the unit to reach the scene.

Similar principles apply when drawing boundaries between the response areas of units which have fixed locations. If all the calls in a district are to be served by units from the fixed facility in that district, then the dividing lines must consist of points which are an equal travel *time* from two facilities, rather than an equal travel *distance* [46].

Influence of Intersector Cooperation

When an incident is reported from a response area whose units are busy, most emergency service systems will dispatch an available unit nearby in another response area. Such an arrangement is nearly mandated by queuing considerations, but it introduces subtle complications into the design of response areas. In the case of mobile units, it even raises questions about the need for restricting response areas of the units to be nonoverlapping. These consequences of intersector cooperation are discussed here.

Police Patrol: "Flying."

Police administrators are often heard to argue in favor of assigning patrol units to nonoverlapping sectors in order to establish a "sector identity" on the part of the patrol officer. This identity, which derives from patrolling and from citizen contacts made while responding to calls for service, is supposed to cause the officer to feel responsible for public order in his sector. However, given nonoverlapping sectors, one can show by a simple probabilistic argument [44] that the fraction of dispatches that cause units to travel outside their own sectors is usually equal to or greater than the fraction of time that units in that area are unavailable for dispatch. Thus, if patrol units are "busy" 40 percent of the time (a typical value), then at least 40 percent of all dispatch assignments cause the assigned patrol unit to leave its "own" patrol sector. In turn, at least 40 percent of all citizen contact occurring while responding to calls-for-service takes place in sectors other than the patrol units' "own" sectors.

The predicted amount of intersector dispatches (called *flying* in some police departments) has been substantially verified both by our own work [44] and by the reports of others [47]. These data showed that the amount of intersector dispatching is never significantly less than the percentage of time unavailable, and it may be significantly more. Intersector dispatches ranged from 37 to 57 percent of the total.

The extent of flying brings into question not only the philosophy behind nonoverlapping sectors but also a widely popular statistical procedure for computing workloads of police patrol cars. Usually a sector is associated with a "work load" that is proportional to the number of calls for service generated from within the sector. Thus, for instance, sector A would have a "work load" three times as great as sector B if sector A generated three times as many calls for service as sector B. And, it would usually be assumed that a patrol unit assigned to sector A would work three times as "hard" as a unit assigned to sector B. But considering the extent of flying, we know that the latter assumption is false and, in fact, the car assigned to sector B may be dispatched to calls in sector A sufficiently often so that both may work about equally "hard." Thus, to keep track of the workload of a patrol unit one must record the dispatch assignments of each unit and not the rate of calls for service from individual sectors.

There is one additional property of nonoverlapping sector systems that we should mention. It involves the "randomness" of preventive patrol. With nonoverlapping sectors, preventive patrol coverage in a sector is reduced to zero whenever the corresponding patrol unit is busy. Anyone, including potential criminals, can monitor a patrol unit's activity in some manner (for example, visual observation, listening to the police radio) and determine when a particular car is not patrolling. Then, since units are assigned to nonoverlapping sectors, a crime can be committed with near zero probability that the patrol unit will pass during the commission of the crime.

Given the undesirable features of a nonoverlapping sector system, how can an administrator revise and improve operations?

First, if the sector concept is to be retained, the large fraction of calls which are *low priority*[15] (that is, they do not require rapid response) can be "stacked" and handled by the car assigned to the sector of the call when that car becomes available. This procedure reduces the amount of flying and enhances "sector identity."

Second, the sector concept can be modified so that patrol units are assigned to overlapping areas (or sectors). This procedure enlarges the area with which each patrol officer should develop an "identity." In addition, it increases the "randomness" of patrol, a desirable outcome which is not achieved simply by stacking on nonoverlapping sectors.

Clearly, the number of possible combinations of alternatives is very large. Fortunately, quantitative methods using mathematical models of operations can structure one's thinking about these alternatives and, in fact, can predict the extent of improvement to be gained by a particular combination [43], [45].

Response Districts for Fire Units.

A fire unit's primary response district consists of all points to which it would be dispatched if an alarm were generated there, even if all other units were available. In the event of unavailabilities, the unit may also respond to alarms elsewhere. Fire departments have traditionally designed districts so that the dispatched units are the ones *closest* to the fire. This means that all points on the dividing line between two districts are equally close to some pair of companies.

With the modification of interpreting "closest" in the sense of "shortest travel time," one might expect this procedure to minimize overall response time. However intuitively reasonable this rule of thumb may appear, a recent analytical study by Carter, Chaiken, and Ignall [14] has shown that "equal travel time" dividing lines are usually *not optimal* and that overall average travel time is minimized by following a policy that often requires a unit other than the closest (in time) unit to be assigned to a particular fire.

The philosophy underlying this result is one that often appears in systems with unpredictable demands in the near future—it may be preferable to incur an immediate cost (for example, travel time)

15. For instance, even for those calls which are related to crimes, typically 75 percent are "nonemergency" and thus do not require rapid response. [62, p. 91]

that is slightly greater than the minimum possible immediate cost so that the system (for example, the collection of all fire apparatus) is left in a state which best anticipates future demands. That is, assigning, say, the second closest unit to the most recent fire may result in favorable positioning of units for the *next* reported fire, thus minimizing overall response time. Assignment of the closest unit to the first fire might have required an unusually large amount of time to respond to the next reported fire.

Carter, Chaiken, and Ignall have also shown that the boundaries which minimize overall average response times will, in many cases, also reduce work load imbalance (where workload imbalance is defined to be the difference in the fraction of time worked by the busiest unit and by the least busy unit). Thus, implementation of their derived procedures results in two types of gains—response time reduction and work load imbalance reduction.

Their boundary structuring procedures have been worked out in detail for the case of two cooperating units; current research is being directed at extending the results to systems with many cooperating units. The qualitative features of the results have already been used to arrive at preferable dividing lines in New York City Fire Department operations—and these results are currently being implemented.

10.6 Locating Units and Facilities
Closely related to problems of response area design are problems of location, including

—Which site to select for an additional facility;
—When consolidating two or more existing facilities into one new facility, where to place the new facility;
—*Prepositioning*, or where to locate units at the start of a tour;[16]
—*Repositioning*, or how, and under what circumstances, to change the locations of units during a tour to correct for unavailabilities as they develop.

Although there is an extensive literature on the subject of "facility location," most of it is presented in economic terms and ignores probabilistic aspects of operations. ReVelle, Marks, and Liebman [53] have recently reviewed a variety of applications of

16. "Tour" refers to the period of time during which a specific group of men will be working.

location theory to public sector problems, but none has yet been applied to the allocation of urban emergency units.

The work of Larson and Stevenson [46] is the beginning of a theory of facility location specifically designed for emergency services. Although further research is needed to eliminate some of their simplifying assumptions, this work tends to show that the optimal location of a new facility is rather insensitive to the precise location of existing facilities.

A considerably large body of analytical work has been completed, or is under way, concerning the *repositioning* of units during the course of a tour. Two examples are discussed here.

Local Repositioning: Police Patrol Cars
Consider a simple case with two patrol sectors, where the two sectors are adjacent squares with one common edge. Assume that each of the two units patrols its sector randomly, and that demands are distributed uniformly over the entire region. Each unit responds in its own sector, unless it happens to be available to respond to a call in the other sector when the other unit is unavailable.[17] A question of interest is, "At an instant when exactly one of the units becomes busy, is there any advantage in repositioning the remaining available unit? If so, how should this be accomplished?"

Whenever one unit becomes *unavailable*, consider the following three alternatives for the free unit:

Alternative 1: The free unit continues to patrol its own sector (that is, no repositioning).
Alternative 2: Assign the free unit to patrol both sectors uniformly (that is, "uniform repositioning").
Alternative 3: Station the free unit on the center of the boundary line between the two sectors (that is, "fixed point repositioning").

It is straightforward to show [43, p. 351] that Alternatives 1 and 2 have the same average travel distance.[18] And the distance for Alternative 3 is three-fourths as large.

Thus, in an average travel distance sense, uniform patrol repositioning (Alternative 2) offers no advantage over no repositioning

17. In this simple example we assume that calls arriving when both units are busy are handled by units outside the two-sector region.
18. Similar results hold if response *time* rather than response *distance* is used.

(Alternative 1). On the other hand, fixed point repositioning offers a 25 percent reduction in average response distance when compared to Alternatives 1 and 2. Similar results hold [43, p. 353] for regions of four cooperating sectors and for more complicated examples.

The results suggest that any local repositioning (among nearby sectors) is advantageous in a travel distance sense only if patrol is concentrated near the boundaries of the appropriate sectors. In practice, strict fixed-point repositioning may not be advisable because of lost preventive patrol coverage; still, if the free unit must remain patrolling, a large part of the travel distance reduction can be retained provided the patrol occurs near the appropriate sector boundaries. In fact, we have heard patrolmen remark that on an informal basis two units will occasionally agree to "cover" both sectors when the other unit is unavailable; this "covering" usually takes the form of concentrated patrol near the common sector boundary. To gain travel distance reductions when such covering occurs, it is necessary that the dispatcher be aware of the identity of the cooperating units so that he can assign the covering unit to a call in the busy unit's sector.

Global Repositioning: Relocation of Fire Units

By "global repositioning," we mean the reassignment of one or more available units to areas which may be a considerable distance from the areas to which they are currently assigned. For many years urban fire departments have relocated available units when a number of units in one area become busy fighting a large fire. Indeed, these relocations are preplanned, so that when a second (or higher) alarm is sounded, specified units respond to the fire while other units simultaneously move into certain fire houses which have been vacated by units at the fire. Such large-scale repositioning is not as widely used in other urban service systems, although situations continually arise (for example, police precinct-level congestion) in which repositioning of forces would reduce travel times and dispatch delays or provide some preventive patrol.[19]

19. The absence of global repositioning as a standard technique in police patrol operation may be explained by the fact that an accumulation of small incidents, rather than a single large incident, is most often the cause of whatever unavailabilities exist. Even fire departments are not likely to provide relocation guidelines for dispatchers to use in cases when several small fires produce as many vacant fire houses as a large fire might.

The following factors are important in determining whether to make a relocation:

—How long is the expected duration of the existing unavailability?
—How many units will have to relocate to accomplish the desired final locations?
—How long will it take for the units to travel to their new locations?
—Is the magnitude of the expected improvement in performance large enough to warrant the effort required to move units?
—Is there a good reason to believe that the units to be moved will be needed at their present locations in the near future?

Work still in progress at the New York City–Rand Institute is designed to produce an algorithm that will operate in a computer assisted dispatch system and will recommend relocations both for large fires and for unavailabilities which occur through an accumulation of smaller fires.

Several approaches have been tried. Swersey [61] developed an integer programming model to determine which fire houses should be empty and which should be full. His objective was basically to minimize the average travel time to incidents, taking into account the average time that busy units would remain busy. In addition, his procedure provided a penalty for each unit relocated. Once a solution to this model has been found, a standard assignment problem can be solved to recommend which units should move to which empty houses. Unfortunately, it was not possible to solve Swersey's model rapidly enough, using either branch-and-bound or approximate heuristic techniques [63], to make it an appropriate tool for real-time applications.[20]

The relocation method which is now planned for implementation has been developed by Kolesar and Walker [39] based on a suggestion of Chaiken. Instead of focusing on average travel time, which is not sensitive to many states of the system, this method utilizes ideas of "coverage." A point is said to be "covered" if at least one available engine company (or ladder company) is within T minutes of the location. If one or more neighborhoods are expected to be uncovered for an undesirable amount of time, a heuristic algorithm first determines which vacant houses to fill, then

20. The model can, however, be used to solve the simpler problem of determining where to preposition n units (fewer than the number of houses) in order to minimize expected response time when all n units are available.

which available units to relocate to the vacant houses. While this algorithm is not "optimal" in any sense, it appears to compute very reasonable relocations using a comparatively small amount of computer time.

10.7 Crime Preventive Patrol

Although other urban service agencies have certain patrolling activities (for example, fire departments "patrol" areas looking for fire hazards), the patrolling function is most important in urban police operations. A patrol unit is said to be performing "crime preventive patrol" when passing through an assigned area, with the officers checking for crime hazards (for example, open doors and windows) and attempting to intercept any crimes in progress. By removing opportunities for crime, preventive patrol activity is supposed to *prevent* crime. By posing the threat of apprehension, preventive patrol is supposed to *deter* individuals from committing crimes.

Most mathematical studies of police preventive patrol have occurred in the past several years, although some earlier work in "search theory" is also relevant to the problem. The term "random patrol" was introduced into police literature in 1960 by Smith [58] who stressed the need for unpredictable patrol patterns. Blumstein and Larson [5] developed a simple analytical model for spatially homogeneous random patrol in order to estimate the probability that police would pass a crime in progress. Elliott [25] quoted one of Koopman's [41] search theory results and attempted also to compute probabilities of space-time coincidence of crime and patrol. Recently, Rosenshine [54] analyzed certain problems that arise from the fact that the topology of streets may prohibit certain desired patrol patterns. Bottoms, Nilsson, and Olson [7] have applied some of these ideas to operational problems in the Chicago Police Department.

To illustrate one simple model, consider the problem of estimating the probability that a patrolling unit will intercept a crime while in progress. For a crime of short duration T_c that occurs on street segment i, one can argue that a reasonable upper bound estimate of the probability of space-time coincidence of crime and patrol is

$$P_c = se_i P_p T_c / L,$$

where s = speed of patrolling vehicle; e_i = a number between 0 and 1 reflecting the relative patrol coverage of segment i; P_p = fraction of total time spent patrolling[21], and L = a weighted sum of the segment lengths in the patrol sector, the weights being the e_i.

Even this simple formula provides certain insights. It illustrates that crime-intercept probability is directly proportional to coverage e_i, fraction of time spent patrolling P_p, duration of the crime T_c, patrol speed s,[22] and inversely proportional to a weighted sum of segment lengths L. The interaction of the response and patrol activities is also apparent: During periods of heavy call-for-service demand (that is, when P_p is small), crime intercept probability is small. A potential tradeoff exists between the amount of screening and/or delaying of calls for service, reflected in the value of P_p, and the likelihood of intercepting a crime in progress.

In applications of this formula one typically finds intercept probabilities below 1 in 100. Such low detection probabilities bring to question whether the threat of apprehension provided by preventive patrol is actually great enough to deter crime.

Any effective allocation of effort must reflect the relative likelihoods of crimes occurring at various times and places. Even raising the intercept probability from 0.01 to 0.02, say, could result in a doubling of on-scene apprehensions. By structuring a model of preventive patrol operation one finds that the allocation of preventive patrol effort is mathematically similar to an allocation of search effort problem studied by Koopman [41]. Application of Koopman's search theory ideas to allocating relative patrol effort e_i to maximize detection probabilities yields the following properties:

1. On street segments with sufficiently low crime rates, no preventive patrol effort should be allocated.
2. On segments which should receive preventive patrol effort, the effort should grow slower than linearly with crime rate.

This behavior again illustrates the inadequacy of linear hazard

21. The remainder of the time is spent answering calls and performing other duties.
22. This might be bothersome if one considers s to be a controllable parameter. But usually s is in the range of 5–15 mph and cannot be readjusted at will.

formulas which imply that preventive patrol coverage should be *directly proportional* to frequency of crime occurrence. Although much more refinement of Koopman's techniques is required before they can be implemented by police, we would expect the qualitative features of his solution to hold.

10.8 Simulation Models for Evaluating Proposed Changes in Allocation Procedures

An agency administrator is typically faced with a number of proposed changes in his allocation policy at one time. For example, the results of the models described in previous sections may suggest that he should add units at certain times of day, select new locations for some units, change response areas or patrol patterns, and modify the procedures for relocating units. In addition, certain technological innovations such as automatic car locator systems may have been proposed to accomplish some of the same objectives. Before making a choice among the alternatives, the administrator will want to have a realistic comparison of the benefits which can be expected from each approach.

For a thorough evaluation of such a comprehensive change in allocation procedures, one generally has to turn to much more complex and detailed models than the ones already discussed. Large-scale simulation models are typically used for this purpose. They can provide information about the effect of a proposed policy change on a wide range of variables: response times to particular types of calls, workload of units, queuing delays, availability of units, etc. Such simulation studies have been undertaken by Savas [56] to investigate the reduction of travel times which could be achieved by spatially repositioning ambulances, by Swersey [60] to analyze the operations of the dispatch centers of the New York City Fire Department, by Carter and Ignall [12] to compare a wide range of combinations of fire department allocation policies, by Larson [43] in a study of the allocation of police patrol and the potential benefits of utilizing a car locator system, and by Adams and Barnard [1] to study the value of an automated dispatch system for the San Jose Police Department. Recent work on efficient computer coding of geographical data [8, 35] has been of some assistance in designing such simulation models of urban emergency service systems.

A common feature of these studies has been the finding that

rather simple and inexpensive administrative innovations can often make a contribution to system performance which is equivalent to that of much more expensive hardware or increases in manpower. Swersey's study [60] provides such an example. In this case, the fire dispatching office in Brooklyn was experiencing an increase in alarm rates and consequent delays prior to dispatch of units which were beginning to be of some concern to the department. The simulation showed that computerized methods for recording, storing, or retrieving location information about alarms would not solve the essential difficulty, which had to do with the fact that a single man had final responsibility for every dispatch decision. Swersey's suggestion for dividing this responsibility, a basically administrative change which has been implemented, provided substantially decreased delays during peak-alarm hours.

Similarly, Larson's simulation [43] has demonstrated that the absence of an explicit priority structure for calls to police departments produces unnecessary delays for urgent and moderately important calls. Most departments have been reluctant to implement such a structure, stating that their policy is to provide rapid service to all citizens. However, some departments [21, 22] have begun to implement priority structures based on quantitative information derived from such models.

In addition, the Larson simulation was used to study the best use of automatic vehicle locator systems in police departments. The technology of such systems is well developed [38, 55], and recently field tests and operational installations have been reported [10,19,23,30,32,68]. Each system provides a central dispatcher with estimates of the positions of all service units (for example, buses, patrol cars, taxicabs) and with other status information (for example, current speed and direction, current type of activity).

In the Larson study [43, p. 289] analysis showed that superimposing an automatic vehicle locator system on a patrol force assigned to nonoverlapping sectors causes an average travel time reduction in the order of 10 to 20 percent, the exact value depending on the fraction of time each car is busy, number of sectors in a command, spatial distribution of calls, and so on. Analysis also showed that a system with fully overlapping sectors utilizing car position information has approximately the same travel time characteristics as current nonoverlapping sector systems without car position information. Thus, if there are reasons to want overlapping sectors, even to the extent of having no sectors at all, there would be little or no degradation in travel time characteristics of the overlapping sector system, compared to current systems, provided high resolution car position information is available. Apparently, the prepositioning advantages gained by assigning cars to mutually exclusive sectors are recovered by knowing exact car positions in a system with no deliberate spatial prepositioning.[23] (As mentioned in Section 10.5, arguments based on "regional identity" and "randomness of patrol" seem to favor some type of overlapping sector plan.)

This analysis is an example of an instance in which applying technology to a system "operating as usual" may not fully utilize the new technological capabilities.

10.9 Summary and Conclusions

Many of the allocation problems experienced by emergency service agencies, whether police departments, fire departments or ambulance services, are not unique to any particular agency nor are they confined only to the largest cities. Typically an increasing rate of calls for service over a period of years creates a situation in which a substantial fraction of callers with urgent emergencies must wait "too long" for the arrival of a unit. Moreover, the agency's field personnel may be spending so much of their time responding to calls that they are unable to pay adequate attention to other important duties or they may feel overworked.

Hiring a large number of additional personnel and providing them with new units, stations, and other equipment can almost always resolve the problems, but this solution may be neither feasible nor necessary to determine the best course of action. An agency administrator should consider a variety of alternatives, using quantitative methods to estimate the potential benefits of any combination of them.

As a first step, the arrival patterns of calls by time and place should be analyzed with attention paid to the number of calls that do not require immediate service. This may lead to plans for queuing or rejecting the calls of lowest priority, in which case callers should be informed as to whether a unit will be dispatched.

23. These statements are subject to the assumptions of the models used, the most critical of which is the assumption that the cars patrol independently of each other.

Next, the number of units actually needed to serve the remaining calls and perform other essential functions should be determined in accordance with the methods of Section 10.4. This analysis may reveal opportunities for improving service by moving units from one region to another or changing the hours of day at which units operate. On the other hand, the results may show that the desired level of performance cannot be achieved without adding units, in which case the administrator will have a good estimate of the actual number of men needed.

Next, the locations or "patrol areas" and dispatching rules for the units should be scrutinized to isolate opportunities to reduce delays further and balance workloads using the methods described in Sections 10.5 and 10.6. In addition, plans should be made to reposition units as the need becomes apparent. Since no static plan for locating the units can produce the best allocations under all circumstances, police departments should also consider the extent to which preventive patrol can be enhanced by designing overlapping sectors and by providing the patrolmen with guidelines for their patrol patterns.

Finally, when one has identified a number of promising allocation policies, each involving detailed changes in several components of the current policy, simulation models can be used to examine the consequences of each policy, thereby providing a mechanism for policy selection.

Although in many instances we do not yet know how to make the link between true measures of performance of emergency systems and the quantities which can be studied using analytical models, it is now apparent that many models are sufficiently developed to be of substantial assistance to agency administrators when carefully used. Many of the research goals for allocation of police patrol forces proposed in 1968 in a study for the Department of Justice [6, p. 168] are being approached, if not achieved. Wide interest is now apparent, as illustrated by reported applications of quantitative techniques in police departments in Boston [42], New York [64], St. Louis [48], Chicago [18], Cleveland [28], Tucson [3], Phoenix [15], and Great Britain [9]. The whole subject of the allocation of fire units has been developed in the past two or three years and has given an entirely new complexion to fire research. We expect that in the next few years, the models will improve in their sophistication and utility, and that agency administrators will make increasing use of quantitative models as their virtues become apparent.

Acknowledgments

We wish to thank our colleagues at the New York City–Rand Institute, many of whom are mentioned in the Reference section, and members of the Boston Police Department and the New York City Police and Fire Departments for their assistance to us during our discussions of the topics in this chapter. This work was supported in part at the New York City–Rand Institute by the U.S. Department of Housing and Urban Development and the National Science Foundation and in part at the M.I.T. Operations Research Center by the National Science Foundation.

References

1. Adams, R., and S. Barnard, "Simulation of Police Field Forces for Decision-Making in Resource Allocation," in *Law Enforcement Science and Technology III*, Port City Press, 1970.

2. American Insurance Association, *Standard Schedule for Grading Cities and Towns of the United States with Reference to their Fire Defenses and Physical Conditions*, 1956.

3. Bergstrom, K., "The Fluid Patrol System," in *Traffic Police Administration Training Program*, Traffic Institute, Northwestern University, 1966.

4. Blum, E., "The Deployment of Municipal Emergency Services: Overview and Summary of Results," New York City–Rand Institute, 1971.

5. Blumstein, A., and R. Larson, "A Systems Approach to the Study of Crime and Criminal Justice," in *Operations Research for Public Systems*, P. M. Morse and L. W. Bacon (eds.), M.I.T. Press, Cambridge, Massachusetts, 1967.

6. Blumstein, A., et al., "A National Program of Research, Development, Test, and Evaluation on Law Enforcement and Criminal Justice," Institute for Defense Analyses, Arlington, Virginia, 1968.

7. Bottoms, A., E. Nilsson, and D. Olson, in "Third Quarterly Progress Report, Operations Research Task Force," Chicago Police Department, 1968.

8. Brownstein, S. H., "Some Concepts and Techniques for Constructing and Using a Geographically-Oriented Urban Data Base," in *Socioecon. Plan. Sci.*, Vol. 1, 1968, pp. 309–325.

9. Bryant, J. W., M. L. Chambers, and D. Falcon, "Patrol Effectiveness and Patrol Deployment," in *Report on Home Office Project in Lancaster Division of Lancashire Constabulary*, University of Lancaster, Department of Operational Research, 1968.

10. Business Week, "Electronic Eye on Auto Fleets," January 17, 1970.

11. Capaul, J., N. Heller, and E. Meisenheimer, "A Stochastic Model for Allocating Police Patrol Units to Districts which Reflects Each District's Rates

of Injury, Property Loss, and Fear," paper presented at the 38th National Meeting of O.R.S.A., 1970.

12. Carter, G., and E. Ignall, "A Simulation Model of Fire Department Operations: Design and Preliminary Results," in *IEEE Transactions on Systems Science and Cybernetics*, SSC-6, 1970, pp. 282-293.

13. ____, "Predicting the Actual Number of Fire-Fighting Units Dispatched," New York City-Rand Institute, unpublished.

14. Carter, G., J. Chaiken, and E. Ignall, "Response Areas for Two Emergency Units," R-532, New York City-Rand Institute, 1971.

15. Casey, P., "Determining Police Patrol Car Requirements by Computer Simulation," M. S. thesis, Arizona State University, 1968.

16. Chaiken, J., "Estimating Numbers of Fire Engines Needed in New York City Fire Divisions, R-508, New York City-Rand Institute, 1971.

17. ____ , "Number of Emergency Units Busy at Alarms which Require Multiple Servers," R-531, New York City-Rand Institute, 1971.

18. Chicago Police Department, Operations Research Task Force, *Quarterly Progress Reports*, 1968, 1969, (A. Bottoms, Project Director).

19. Chicago Transit Authority, *Progress Reports*, Chicago, Illinois, 1969, 1970.

20. Cobham, A., "Priority Assignment in Waiting Line Problems," *Operations Res.*, Vol. 2, pp. 70-76, 1954.

21. *Crime Control Digest*, Detroit Police Department, September 11, 1968.

22. *Crime Control Digest*, St. Louis Police Department, January 14, 1969.

23. Distler, R., "An Active Infrared System for Vehicle Tracking and Ranging," in *Law Enforcement Science and Technology I, Proceedings of the First National Symposium on Law Enforcement Science and Technology*, Thompson Book, 1967.

24. Edie, L. C., "Traffic Delays at Toll Booths," *Operations Res.*, Vol 2, 1954, pp. 107-138.

25. Elliott, J., "Random Patrol," in *Law Enforcement Science and Technology II, Proceedings of the Second National Symposium on Law Enforcement Science and Technology*, Port City Press, 1969.

26. Fairthorne, D., "The Distances Between Pairs of Points in Towns of Simple Geometrical Shapes," *Proceedings of the Second International Symposium on the Theory of Traffic Flow*, London, 1963, published by OECD, 1965.

27. Fisher, I., and J. Midler, "Analyzing Municipal Fire Protection: Theoretical Framework," R-599, New York City-Rand Institute, 1971.

28. Gass, S., "On the Division of Police Districts into Patrol Beats," *Proceedings of the 1968 ACM National Conference*.

29. Heller, N., "Proportional Rotating Schedules," Ph.D. thesis, University of Pennsylvania, 1969.

30. Heubrocker, H., "Feasibility of Radar Beacon Techniques for Patrol Vehicle Tracking and Position Display," in *Law Enforcement Science and Technology I, Proceedings of the First National Symposium on Law Enforcement Science and Technology*, Thompson Book, 1967.

31. Hogg, J. M., "The Siting of Fire Stations," *Opl. Res. Q.*, Vol. 19, 1968, pp. 275-287.

32. Institute for Public Administration and Teknekron, "An Analytic and Experimental Evaluation of Alternative Methods for Automatic Vehicle Monitoring," 1968.

33. International City Managers' Association, *Municipal Police Administration*, fifth ed., 1961.

34. Isaacs, H., "A Study of Communications, Crimes, and Arrests in a Metropolitan Police Department," in *Task Force Report: Science and Technology, A Report to the President's Commission on Law Enforcement and Administration of Justice*, U.S. Government Printing Office, Washington, D. C., 1967.

35. Jacobsen, J., "Geographic Retrieval Techniques," International Business Machines, Gaithersburg, Maryland, 1968.

36. Kakalik, J., and S. Wildhorn, "Aids to Decision-Making in Police Patrol," R-507, Rand Corporation, 1971.

37. Keeney, R., "Preferences for the Response Times of Engines and Ladders to Fires," New York City–Rand Institute, unpublished.

38. Knickel, E., "Electronics Equipment Associated with the Police Car," in *Task Force Report: Science and Technology, A Report to the President's Commission on Law Enforcement and Administration of Justice*, U.S. Government Printing Office, Washington, D. C., 1967 (Appendix E).

39. Kolesar, P., and W. Walker, "A Relocation Algorithm for the MICS," New York City–Rand Institute, unpublished.

40. Kolesar, P., and E. Blum, "Square Root Laws for Response Distances: Applications to Fire Service Deployment," R-895, New York City–Rand Institute (to appear).

41. Koopman, B., "The Theory of Search III, The Optimum Distribution of Searching Effort," *Operations Res.*, Vol. 5, 1957, pp. 613-626.

42. Larson, R., "Hourly Allocation of Complaint Clerks, Dispatchers, and Radio-Dispatchable Patrol Personnel," *Proceedings of Second National Symposium on Law Enforcement Science and Technology*, Port City Press, 1968.

43. _____ , *Models for the Allocation of Urban Police Patrol Forces*, Technical Report No. 44, M.I.T. Operations Research Center, Cambridge, Mass., 1969.

44. _____ , "Measuring the Response Patterns of New York City Police Patrol Cars," R-673, New York City–Rand Institute, 1971.

45. _____ , *Urban Police Patrol Analysis*, M.I.T. Press, Cambridge, Mass., 1972.

46. Larson, R., and K. Stevenson, "On Insensitivities in Urban Redistricting and Facility Location," R-533, New York City–Rand Institute, 1971.

47. McCormack, R. J., Jr., and J. L. Moen, "San Francisco's Mission Police District: A Study of Resource Allocation," Center for Planning and Development Research, Institute of Urban and Regional Development, University of California, Berkeley, 1968.

48. McEwen, T., Project Director, "Allocation of Patrol Manpower Resources in the Saint Louis Police Department," Vols, I, II, 1966.

49. Morse, P. M., *Queues, Inventories, and Maintenance*, John Wiley, New York, 1958.

50. Parzen, E., *Stochastic Processes*, Holden-Day, San Francisco, 1962.

51. Prabhu, N., *Queues and Inventories, A Study of Their Basic Stochastic Processes*, John Wiley, New York, 1965.

52. The President's Commission on Law Enforcement and Administration of Justice, *The Challenge of Crime in a Free Society*, U.S. Government Printing Office, Washington, D. C., 1967.

53. ReVelle, C., D. Marks, and J. Liebman, "An Analysis of Private and Public Sector Location Models," *Management Science: Theory*, Vol. 16, 1970, pp. 692-707.

54. Rosenshine, M., "Contributions to a Theory of Patrol Scheduling," *Opl. Res. Q.*, Vol. 21, 1970, pp. 99-106.

55. Rypinski, C., "Police Message, Status and Location Reporting System, ' in *Law Enforcement Science and Technology III*, Port City Press, 1970.

56. Savas, E. S., "Simulation and Cost-Effectiveness Analysis of New York's Emergency Ambulance Service," *Management Science*, Vol. 15, No. 608, 1969.

57. Smeed, R. J., and G. O. Jeffcoate, "Traffic Flow during the Journey to Work in the Central Area of a Town which has a Rectangular Grid for its Road System," *Proceedings of the Second International Symposium on the Theory of Traffic Flow*, London, 1963, published by OECD, 1965.

58. Smith, R. D., "Random Patrol," Field Service Division of the International Association of Chiefs of Police, Washington, D. C., 1970

59. Stevenson, K., "Operational Aspects of Emergency Ambulance Services," Chapter 8, this volume.

60. Swersey, A., "Dispatching, Deployment, and Relocation of Fire Engines," *37th National Meeting of Operations Research Society of America*, Washington, D. C., 1970.

61. _____ , "A Mathematical Formulation of the Fire Engine Relocation Problem," New York City-Rand Institute, unpublished.

62. *Task Force Report: Science and Technology. A Report to the President's Commission on Law Enforcement and Administration of Justice*, U.S. Government Printing Office, Washington, D.C., 1967.

63. Walker, W., and S. Shinnar, "Approaches to the Solution of the Fire Engine Relocation Problem," New York City-Rand Institute, unpublished.

64. Wildhorn, S., "Public Order Studies in New York City," P-4250, Rand Corporation, 1969.

65. Wilson, O. W., "Distribution of the Police Patrol Force," Publication 74, Public Administration Service, Chicago, Illinois, 1941.

66. _____ , *Police Planning*, 2nd ed., Charles C. Thomas, Springfield, Illinois, 1958.

67. _____ , *Police Administration*, 2nd ed., New York, McGraw-Hill Book Co., 1963.

68. Zauderer, J., "Field Testing of an Automatic Vehicle Monitoring System," in *Law Enforcement Science and Technology III*, IIT Research Institute, Port City Press, 1970.

11 Blood Bank Inventory Control

John B. Jennings

11.1 The Problem and the Approach

One of the important medical resources of any community is its system of blood banking facilities. It is through such systems that blood is collected from human donors at one time and place, processed, stored, and ultimately provided for transfusion to hospital patients at some other time and place. Human blood—either whole or divided into derivatives—is a critical component in the treatment of many health problems, including such diverse ones as those involving surgery, anemia, severe burns, and leukemia. Today, more than five million pints are transfused in the United States annually.

In most areas, blood banks are organized into loose regional systems, each composed of anywhere from 20 to 200 hospital blood banks located in some geographically or politically defined area (for example, a city, a portion of a state). While the hospitals in such a system generally acquire a portion of their blood supply from one or more common central blood banks and one or more donor services, the hospitals typically interact with each other only infrequently in times of emergency. In most cases these systems have developed without the aid of central coordination and presently face a variety of problems that result from ineffective and inefficient modes of operation. Three of the most common and pressing problems are the following:

—A chronically short supply at the same time that as much as 15% to 25% of the available supply is lost through outdating.[1] This condition results both from a maldistribution of blood among blood banks and from a system-wide deficient supply.
—Susceptibility to sudden "stockouts" resulting from unpredicted large demands at one or more hospitals.
—High operating costs—in particular, large expediting costs and outdating losses.

To set these problems in proper perspective, consider the overall objectives of blood banking facilities:

1. Minimize the delay in meeting physicians' requests for blood. This objective represents the attempt to fulfill the blood bank's

1. The shelf life of whole blood is limited by law to 21 days in most areas.

reason for existence: to provide blood for transfusion to hospital patients. The importance of delay lies in several areas: physical injury to the patient, the cost to the patient of a prolonged hospital stay (at rates often exceeding $100 per day), and the opportunity cost to the public of congested hospitals.

2. Maximize the quality of the blood supplied. Clearly, blood must not be simply supplied, it must be supplied in a form that will be medically safe and effective.

3. Minimize the burden of transfusion therapy on the patient and the public. While this objective must be considered to be secondary, compared to the adequacy and safety of the blood supply, it is nevertheless, an important one. Two indices of this burden are the following: the cost of operating blood banking facilities and the number of pints (also called units) required by a bank in satisfying a given level of demand. Clearly, both patient and public have competing uses for the available funds. Wasted blood not only adds to cost but represents an unnecessary inconvenience to donors and past recipients of blood, who are generally required to replace all blood used, sometimes on a two-for-one basis.

While a blood bank is a medical facility, one of its central functions is the inventory function: the procurement, storage, and dispensing of blood. The relevance of inventory control to the problems and objectives discussed earlier should be clear. While a simple increase in the amount of blood collected would alleviate (but never eliminate) the problems of chronic shortages and sudden stockouts, it would do little to correct the problems of maldistribution and would compound the waste associated with outdating. An improvement of the *control* of blood inventories, on the other hand, affords the possibility of a balanced approach to all three problems. Far from being competing approaches, however, an increase in the total supply and improved inventory control should go hand in hand.

The control of blood inventories is a very complex problem for several reasons:

1. Both supply and demand are probabilistic.

2. Approximately 50 percent of all bloods requested by physicians, crossmatched,[2] and reserved are eventually found not

2. Crossmatching entails making sure that blood available for transfusion is fully compatible with the blood of the potential recipient.

to be required for the patient in question and are returned to the "unassigned" inventory.

3. Blood is perishable, the present legal lifetime being 21 days in most areas.

4. The control of the inventories at all interacting banks should be coordinated.

Because of these complexities, past work in the field of inventory theory has limited applicability. Most attempts to deal with the blood inventory problem have consisted on the one hand of rules of thumb found in practice to provide adequate service [3, 9], and on the other hand of analyses and simulations of highly simplified models of a single hospital blood bank [2, 7, 8]. A good review of these studies is given in Elston [1]. The only previous attempt to consider the interaction of hospital blood banks [10] concentrated on the collection policies of the central blood bank and suffered from an oversimplification of the hospital models.

In this chapter, we shall briefly investigate the potential benefits of improved control of inventories of whole blood, as well as the associated costs. The vehicle for this investigation will be a mathematical model of a system of blood banks, which is analyzed with the aid of computer simulation. The policies to be examined range from the specification of the ordering level for a particular blood type at a single hospital to the establishment of a system for the coordinated transfer of blood among hospitals.

The results of this investigation include a framework and the tools for the analysis of operational blood banking systems, as well as some useful insights regarding the nature of attractive inventory control policies. Further research must now be directed at adapting these results to specific groups of blood banks, developing policies which reflect the peculiarities of the actual mix of a given set of hospitals, designing the supporting transportation and information systems, and implementing the changes on an experimental and then permanent basis.

Before proceeding to the analysis, we must derive, from the three broad blood banking objectives cited earlier, a set of goals specifically related to the inventory function.

In particular, the objective of minimizing delays may be reduced to the following primary goal: Minimize the frequency of shortages. Here, shortage is defined as the excess of physician requests over the inventory immediately available for crossmatching with samples of prospective patients's blood to ensure compatibility.

Once a shortage occurs, the blood bank must seek to obtain the needed blood from external sources. Here, we shall not deal with specific means of acquiring blood in times of shortage but shall simply assume that it is obtained.

Since the second objective—maximizing the quality of the blood supply—involves primarily the medical and technical aspects of blood banking, we shall not consider it further.

The third objective—to minimize the burden of transfusion therapy—was divided into blood inputs and costs. With regard to the former, the only two ways in which banked whole blood may be disposed of are by transfusion or by outdating. Consistent with the objective of meeting all requests for blood, this aspect of the goal may be stated as: Minimize outdating. The second aspect of this goal is: Minimize inventory operating costs. Here, four types of costs may be identified: the losses associated with outdated blood, the costs of the information and transportation systems needed to support the routine inventory policies, the extra costs associated with expediting blood orders during a shortage, and the costs of carrying the blood inventory (for example, the costs of refrigeration, floor space, and so forth). However, since carrying costs are almost entirely fixed, determined by the decision to operate a blood bank and by the level of demand to which the blood bank responds, they will not be considered here.

The measures of effectiveness we shall use in evaluating alternative inventory policies are implied by the earlier cited goals:

1. Shortage: The amount of blood that is requested by physicians and not immediately available for crossmatch.
2. Outdating: The amount of blood entering a bank and not transfused before the expiration of the shelf life (21 days).
3. Support system requirements: Since the precise costs of supporting alternative policies vary considerably with the specific context in which the policy is used, we may instead use the following indices:
3a. The volume of information transmitted between facilities, the frequency and speed with which it must be transmitted, and the amount of processing (or computation) to be performed.

3b. The number of interhospital shipments of blood (or trips) and the speed with which they must be executed.

11.2 Inventory Control in an Individual Hospital Blood Bank

The first phase of a blood inventory control program must focus on the individual hospital. In order to evaluate the effects of alternative inventory policies without disturbing the operations of an on going facility, we shall study the effects of such policies on a mathematical model of a hospital blood bank. The development of this model, which is described in detail elsewhere [5], is summarized below.

The Hospital Blood Bank Model

The general model structure, developed on the basis of a survey of the operations of a number of hospitals in several localities, is presented diagrammatically in Figure 11.1. As shown, the inventory of blood is divided into two portions: the assigned inventory, which consists of crossmatched blood reserved for particular patients; and the unassigned inventory, which is available to meet new requests for blood.

The flow of blood through the system is as follows: The unassigned inventory is depleted by physician demands for blood to be crossmatched, by the outdating of blood and by the shipment of blood to other hospital blood banks. It is replenished with blood ordered from one or more central blood banks, with blood drawn from selected donors (or "ordered" from one or more

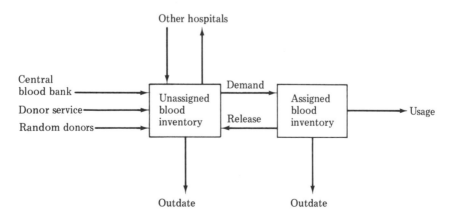

Figure 11.1   The hospital blood bank whole blood inventory model.

donor services), with blood drawn from random, or unsolicited, donors, with blood released (unused) from the assigned inventory, and with blood received from other hospital blood banks. The assigned inventory (which is assumed to include bloods in the process of being crossmatched or transfused) is supplied with blood demanded by physicians; it is depleted by blood usage (transfusions), by the release of blood demanded but not used, and by outdating.

This structure is capable of providing a good representation of the operation of most hospital blood banks. However, it now becomes impossible to continue to speak solely about blood banks in general, for no two blood banks are operated in exactly the same manner. Therefore, in order to obtain a consistent set of specifications for the inputs to and relationships in the model, we must use data derived from a particular hospital blood bank. It is true that the resulting combination of model and data will apply specifically to that blood bank only. However, by selecting for the data source a blood bank whose operations and problems are reasonably "typical" of those at a wide range of hospital blood banks, we should be able to draw reasonably general conclusions.

The specifications that are needed to define precisely the model include the policy for ordering blood from the central blood bank(s) and donor service(s), the age of the blood received, the rate at which blood is requested by physicians, and so on. The necessary data were collected at a large hospital blood bank in Boston (The Peter Bent Brigham Hospital Blood Bank). It was found that the eight major blood types could be treated independently, and here we shall report the results for type B+ that was used at the rate of about 800 units per year.

Because of the desire to avoid oversimplification, the model was left in a form that is too complex to permit a purely "analytical" approach to the study of its behavior. The model was, therefore, simulated on a digital computer. Each simulation represented the equivalent of a three-year period of operation. After this length of time, the average operating statistics were found to be quite stable.

In order to establish the statistical validity of the model, simulations were run under conditions representing those existing at the bank that served as the data source. In other words, the model, which was based on actual inputs and internal operating procedures, was tested to determine whether it yielded outputs resembling those which are found in the "real world." The correspondence was, in fact, found to be quite close.

Establishing an Inventory Ordering Level
The most basic inventory policy in a hospital blood bank is the establishment of the daily inventory ordering level, which we designate by S. With such a policy, the *unassigned* inventory is counted each morning, and, if it is less than S, the difference is ordered from available sources. If the unassigned inventory is equal to or greater than S, no blood is ordered. The ordering levels will be different for the various blood types.

Of the various criteria suggested earlier, the two which are significantly affected by this policy are shortage and outdating.

To demonstrate the simultaneous effects of the inventory ordering level on shortage and outdating, we shall represent the model's operating statistics in the form of a graph of attainable combinations of shortage and outdating, both expressed as percentages of the annual number of pints transfused, with the inventory ordering level S as a parameter. This graph, which we shall refer to as the shortage-outdating operating curve, is shown in Figure 11.2 for the basic model. In other words, for each value of S, the average annual shortage and outdating observed in the simulation of the model are plotted as a single operating point in Figure 11.2 and labeled with the appropriate value of S. Thus, for example, for an inventory ordering level of 18 units, shortage is 5.8 percent and outdating is 10.3 percent. (The blood bank which served as the source of the data for this model operated at a 15- to 18-unit ordering level.) As S is raised, the operating point moves up and to the left, corresponding to increased outdating and reduced shortage, and vice versa. This curve represents the tradeoff between the two most important measures of the blood bank's effectiveness, and the blood bank administration can select the most desirable operating point on this curve simply by specifying the daily inventory ordering level. This decision will depend on the administration's assessment of the relative tangible and intangible costs of shortage and outdating.

Investigating Alternative Inventory Policies
The model described above may now be used to investigate the effects of a variety of other inventory operating policies. Changes

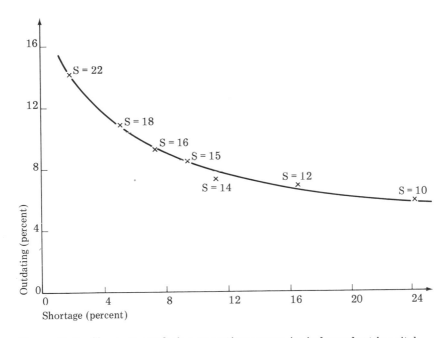

Figure 11.2   Shortage-outdating operating curve: An independent hospital.

in other practices will, in general, make it desirable to make a subsequent change in the ordering level. The effect of other changes,
such as extending the legal lifetime of blood, will be represented
as a shift of the blood bank's shortage-outdating operating curve,
and any subsequent changes in the ordering level will be indicated
by movements along the new curve. Clearly, the shortage-outdating performance of a blood bank can be improved only by policy
changes which result in downward and/or leftward (that is, toward the origin) shifts of the shortage-outdating operating curve.

A useful index of the extent of such an inward shift may be determined as follows: (1) Identify the most desirable operating
point on the curve for the basic model; (2) Draw a straight line
from the origin through this operating point; (3) Treat as the approximate most desirable operating point on any inner operating
curve that point at which the curve intersects the constructed line;
and (4) Take, as an index of improvement in shortage and outdating performance under the new policy, the percentage reduction in *both* shortage and outdating. Since the ratio of outdating

to shortage at the two operating points being compared is the same, both measures are reduced by the same percentage.

To illustrate this procedure, let us examine one potential policy change. Consider the possibility of replacing the central blood bank with another source which provides blood that is always freshly drawn. In the model, blood supplied by the central blood bank is an average of 5.5 days old when received at the hospital. Therefore, since approximately 60 percent of the hospital's supply is obtained from the central blood bank, this change effectively adds an average of 3.3 days to the useful life of all the units of blood entering the hospital. The shortage-outdating performance under this new situation is represented in Figure 11.3. As shown, when the inventory ordering level is held constant, outdating is everywhere reduced by about 30 percent while shortage is unchanged. However, by adjusting the ordering level, part or all of this outdating gain can be exchanged for a shortage reduction. For example, if the most desirable operating points are those at which the ratio of outdating to shortage is 1.0 (an ordering level in the basic model of about 16 units), a simultaneous reduction of shortage and outdating can be achieved in the amount of 24 percent. The costs involved in making this change in policy could be

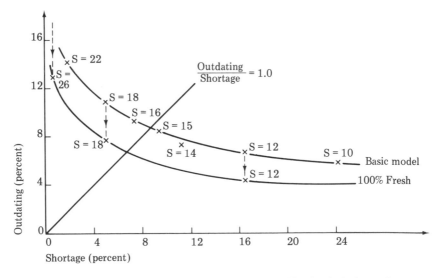

Figure 11.3 Shortage-outdating operating curves: The basic independent hospital model and the case of 100 percent fresh (21-day) blood.

analyzed for a specific blood bank and compared with the benefits of reduced shortage and outdating.

Some other policies that have been reported in [5] include the possibilities of ordering blood more often and of ordering when the inventory falls below some lower level. However, let us now turn our attention to regional inventory policies.

11.3 Regional Blood Inventory Control

In the case of an individual hospital blood bank, the range of available policy alternatives is relatively restricted. At the regional level, however, interactions are presently extremely limited in most areas, and there is a wide range of potential inventory strategies from which to choose. However, those that are capable of contributing to the goals discussed earlier fall into two classes:

1. *Shortage-anticipating transfers* of blood from one hospital to another. Policies in this class allow a hospital that is experiencing an unexpectedly large demand to avert (or end) a shortage by "borrowing" blood from relatively well-supplied neighbors.
2. *Outdating-anticipating transfers.* Under this class of policies, a blood bank which is passing through a period of low demand may seek to reduce outdating by "lending" blood to banks that are more likely to use it.

The benefits to be derived from such policies must, of course, be balanced against the costs of the systems required to support them. This tradeoff may be explored by investigating the effects of specific policies on a model of a regional system. Such a model, based on that developed for a single hospital, is described below.

The Regional Blood Banking System Model

As in the case of the individual blood bank model, we are now faced with the choice between the realism of a model of a particular operational system and the greater generality that is possible in a model of a hypothetical hospital blood bank. A hospital blood bank is a collection of numerous components with many complex interactions. The components did not develop, nor can they stand, independently; and it would make no sense to consider a mélange of ordering policies, demand patterns, and crossmatching procedures drawn from different hospital blood banks. On the other hand, most regional groups of blood banks today are not so interdependent. Most hospital blood banks have developed with very little routine, operational interaction with other hospital blood banks. Further, we are interested, here, in investigating presently non-existent forms of interaction between a variable number of relatively isolated units.

For simplicity, let us concentrate our attention on a model of a homogeneous system composed of, say, N identical hospital blood banks, all operating under exactly the same policies (including the inventory ordering level policy). This procedure has the advantage of facilitating our understanding of the effects of the policies to be examined. However, note that the methods and simulation program used can be easily adapted to the analysis of other configurations. Since we already have a validated model of one hospital blood bank, we shall use it as the archetype. The central blood suppliers are modeled implicitly, just as in the one-hospital model. Further details may be found in Reference [6].

A Policy of Maximum Interaction

A useful point to begin an analysis of regional inventory control policies is with the policies which specify minimum and maximum interaction, respectively. The former has already been examined: it is simply the case of the individual, independent hospital for which the shortage and outdating results are given in Figure 11.2.

The policy which maximizes interaction in terms of both shortage anticipation and outdating anticipation will be called the common-inventory policy. Under this policy, all hospital inventories are, in effect, fully shared by all participating blood banks. The oldest units of blood in the system are always crossmatched first, no matter where they might be located, thereby maximizing outdating-anticipating transfers. Shortage-anticipating transfers are also maximized, for the common-inventory structure requires that either all hospitals have blood available for crossmatch or all are out of stock.

The performance of the model under this policy, in terms of shortage and outdating, is the best attainable. Thus, if the implementation costs (both tangible and intangible) for such a policy were sufficiently low, we could terminate our analysis and recommend that this arrangement be adopted. On the contrary, however, we shall find that the costs of the necessary support systems—information as well as transportation—would be large, particularly since parts of the total inventory are usually maintained at each hospital.[3]

Thus far, we have ignored the precise way in which the blood is moved from one hospital to another. In order to simulate the operation of our model under such a policy, however, we must specify some precise set of rules governing these transfers. For simplicity, let us specify the following interactive procedure: Whenever a request for blood to be crossmatched is received at any of the blood banks under consideration, that bank determines the age of the oldest units of blood in the system, and, if it has a unit of that age, it crossmatches that unit. Otherwise, it "borrows" such a unit (one of the oldest in the system) from the hospital with the largest total inventory on hand. Since this rule automatically ensures that no bank is short unless all are short, no further forms of interhospital exchange need be explicitly included.

The shortage and outdating results of a number of one-year simulations are shown in Figure 11.4 as a family of shortage-outdating operating curves. The reader should recall that the curve for the independent hospital (or one-hospital) system that is also shown can be interpreted as the case of minimum (that is, no) interaction. Referring to Figure 11.4, it may be seen, for example, that two hospitals operating under the common-inventory policy described, at the 12-unit inventory ordering level, would be expected to outdate blood at the rate of 4.9 percent of annual usage and experience shortages in the amount of 5.0 percent of average annual usage. Five hospitals operating under these same policies would have 4.2 percent outdating and 0.5 percent shortage.

As shown, an increase in the number of participating hospitals in the regional system has the effect of shifting the shortage-outdating operating curve toward the origin. If one is interested in points at which the ratio of outdating to shortage is 1.0, for example, it may be seen that, with respect to the one-hospital starting point, a two-hospital common-inventory system reduces both outdating and shortage by about 45 percent, a five-hospital system

3. In only one system of blood banks in the country—that in Seattle—are all blood inventories centralized in a single location. Elsewhere, physicians, blood bank directors, and hospital administrators have become accustomed to hospital-based systems and are unwilling to sacrifice certain advantages associated with their present autonomy.

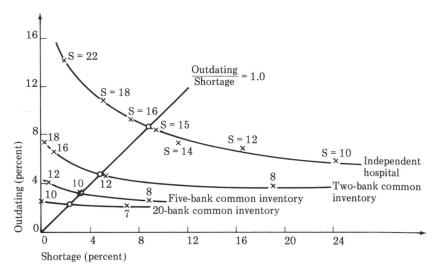

Figure 11.4   Shortage-outdating operating curves for common-inventory systems.

by about 64 percent, and a 20-hospital system reduces both measures by about 72 percent.

While we have shown the operating curves only for systems of 20 or fewer hospitals (one may interpolate between the four curves presented to estimate the results for intermediate-sized systems), there is clearly a very strong effect of diminishing returns as the size of the system is increased. We may conclude that, under this policy, a further increase of the size of the system to even 50 hospitals[4] would produce little additional gain.[5]

With regard to the support system requirements of the common-inventory policy, we find, as anticipated, that they are quite

4. It should be recalled that our hospital model represents a blood bank that provides blood for an average of about 800 transfusions per year to patients having just one of the eight blood types. Even in the largest metropolitan areas, hospitals of this size are not found in great numbers. For example, the American Medical Association's 1969 *Directory of Blood Banking and Transfusion Facilities and Services* lists fewer than 50 out of 250 hospitals in New York City at which transfusions of *all* blood types taken together total 1,000 or more per year.

5. Note, however, that further reductions of shortage and outdating can be achieved through changes in internal policies, particularly those that govern the entire crossmatch process.

heavy. The supporting information system must provide essentially continuously updated information on both the locations of the oldest units of blood of each type in the system and the total inventories at those hospitals. The transportation system is found to be required to transfer about 550 units of this type per bank per year in a two-bank system (that is, 1,100 units per year), about 900 units of this type per bank per year in a five-bank system (4,500 units per year), and almost 1,100 per bank per year in a 20-bank system (22,000 units per year). In evaluating these requirements, it must be recalled that, in this extreme case, these units must be transferred one at a time in response to requests as they are received, and that the total blood usage at each bank is about 800 units of this type per year.

Investigating Alternative Regional Inventory Policies

Clearly, the number of reasonable policies combining various forms of the two types of interactive transfers identified earlier is very large. While the simulation model used in this study is available for simulating any such combination, here we shall illustrate our method of analysis using one policy which was found to be relatively attractive in terms of the gain achieved and the support systems required.

The policy we shall review here will be referred to as a "threshold transfer policy" and is defined as follows:

1. Whenever the inventory level (for the blood type under consideration) at any bank falls below a lower threshold of one unit, a transfer is initiated.
2. Each bank is willing to lend only those units it may have in excess of a retention level of one unit.
3. When more than one bank is "willing" to lend blood, a single lender is selected as follows: Once each day in the middle of the day on weekdays and at the start of the day on weekends, the status of the inventory at each bank in the system is determined; when a lender is being sought, the hospitals are "polled," beginning with the one most recently known to have had the largest inventory (of the type under consideration), until a willing lender is identified.
4. The borrowing quantity is determined as follows: Five units are requested on each transfer occasion; the selected lender then

transfers as much of the request as it can without reducing its inventory below the retention level.

5. The selection of the specific units to be transferred is simply on the basis of age, oldest first.

In order to explore the effects of the threshold transfer policy described here on the relevant measures of effectiveness (shortage, outdating, and support system requirements), the operations of systems composed of various numbers of hospitals were simulated for several values of the inventory ordering level. As above, each simulation represents a one-year period of operation, all participating hospitals being assumed to be identical and to operate under identical inventory policies. The shortage and outdating results for this policy are shown in Figure 11.5.

As shown, there is a continuous shift of the shortage-outdating operating curve to the left (lower amounts of shortage) as the size of the system operating under this policy is expanded. The relationship between operating points corresponding to the same inventory ordering level is emphasized by dotted line "trajectories." The fact that the shift of the curves is primarily horizontal indicates that the sample threshold transfer policy has very little direct influence on outdating.

If, as in earlier examples, one happens to be interested in operat-

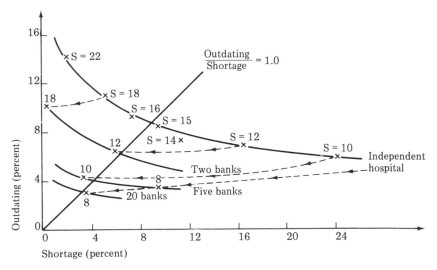

Figure 11.5   Shortage-outdating operating curves for the threshold transfer policy.

ing points at which the ratio of outdating to shortage is 1.0, the
following gains can be seen to result under this policy: a 29 percent reduction of both shortage and outdating in a two-bank system, a 54 percent reduction in a five-bank system, and a 61 percent reduction in a 20-bank system. Clearly, there is again quite a
strong effect of diminishing returns as the size of the system is
expanded. While these gains are not as large as those achieved
under the common-inventory policy, they are substantial: for the
two-bank case, the inward shift is two-thirds as large as that obtained in the common-inventory system; and, for the five- and 20-
bank cases, the inward shift is five-sixths as large.

Let us now examine the relationship between the policy's primary benefit—the inward shift of the shortage-outdating operating
curve—and the policy's primary variable cost—the cost of execut-
ing the necessary transfers. Specifically, let us examine the relationship between, on the one hand, the percentage reduction in
both shortage and outdating along the line representing operating
points for which the ratio of outdating to shortage is unity and,
on the other hand, the number of interhospital shipments, or trips,
required to execute the policy. The combinations of reductions
and numbers of shipments found in the simulations of the three
system-sizes simulated are plotted in Figure 11.6, and a curve is
sketched through them and the origin. This curve represents the
variable cost, in terms of interhospital shipments per bank per
year, of achieving various reductions of shortage and outdating
through the sample threshold transfer policy.[6] For example, the
five-bank point on this curve represents the combination: shortage
and outdating reduced by 54 percent; 90 interhospital shipments
per bank per year (for this blood type).

Also shown in this figure is the curve which applies to the common-inventory policy. Clearly, for reductions in shortage and outdating that can be achieved by the threshold transfer policy, this
policy requires far fewer interhospital shipments than does the
common-inventory policy. However, suppose that the size of the
system is limited to some number of banks N. In such a case, the
maximum reduction of shortage and outdating provided by the
threshold transfer policy alone is also limited and can be deter-

6. Strictly, only those points on this curve which correspond to an integer
number of blood banks are realizable. However, variants of this policy are
capable of yielding intermediate points.

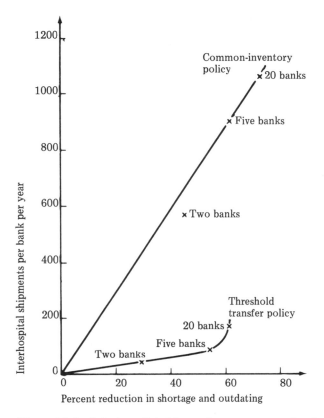

Figure 11.6   Interhospital shipments versus percent reduction in shortage and outdating: The threshold transfer policy and the common-inventory policy.

mined by referring to the appropriate point on the lower curve in Figure 11.6. If larger reductions are desired, this policy must be replaced by or combined with some other policy which is capable of shifting the N-bank point on the lower (threshold transfer) curve in Figure 11.6 towards the N-bank point on the upper (common-inventory) curve. Note, though, that the ratio of additional shipments to additional gain in such a shift would be extremely large.

Finally, the information requirements of the threshold transfer policy are less severe than those of the common-inventory policy. Specifically, the requirements of the former are the following: First, the total inventory of the type of blood under consideration at each blood bank must be determined once each day. Second, a means must be provided for initiating a transfer whenever the inventory of the appropriate type of blood falls below one unit. Third, other hospitals must be polled in order to locate a willing lender and the status information so obtained used to update the daily survey information. Fourth, the transfer must be coordinated and reported to the parties involved. Last, the necessary accounting information must be maintained.

11.4 Conclusions

The accomplishments of this study are threefold. First, the whole blood inventory problem for a single hospital has been structured and several classes of alternative policies identified. Second, a realistic model of the whole blood inventory system in a group of hospitals has been developed for use in the analysis of the operations of such systems. Third, the feasibility of testing the effects of specific policies using computer simulation has been demonstrated, a number of such policies have been examined in detail,[7] and the simulation programs have been documented for use in analyzing specific systems.

The analyses performed should provide useful insights with direct applicability in a variety of blood banking systems. Specifically, we have determined (1) the range of improvements in shortage and outdating performance that can be expected in systems of various sizes, (2) the nature of the corresponding support system capabilities that must be provided, and (3) the fact that a group of only five cooperating blood banks can achieve most of the gains available in larger coordinated systems.

The studies reported on here are not the last word in the investigation of blood bank inventory control. They should, however, establish a firm basis and the necessary tools for further analyses of specific operating systems and for the initiation of controlled experiments to test the effects of the most promising policies in the "real world."

7. Only some of those examined in References [5] and [6] have been described here.

References

1. Elston, R. C., "Blood Bank Inventories," *CRC Critical Reviews in Clinical Laboratory Sciences*, July 1970.

2. Elston, R. C., and J. C. Pickrel, "Guides to Inventory Levels for a Hospital Blood Bank, Determined by Electronic Computer Simulation," *Transfusion*, Vol. 5, 1965.

3. Hurlburt, E. L., and A. R. Jones, "Blood Bank Inventory Control," *Transfusion*, Vol. 4, 1964.

4. Jennings, J. B., *An Introduction to Blood Banking Systems*, Technical Report No. 21, M.I.T. Operations Research Center, Cambridge, Mass., July 1966.

5. _____ , *Hospital Blood Bank Whole Blood Inventory Control*, Technical Report No. 27, M.I.T. Operations Research Center, Cambridge, Mass., December 1967.

6. _____ , *Inventory Control in Regional Blood Banking Systems*, Technical Report No. 53, M.I.T. Operations Research Center, Cambridge, Mass., July 1970.

7. Millard, D. W., *Industrial Inventory Models as Applied to the Problem of Inventorying Whole Blood*, Bulletin No. 180, Ohio State University Engineering Experiment Station, Columbus, Ohio, March 1960.

8. Pegels, C. C., and A. E. Jelmert, "An Evaluation of Blood-Inventory Policies: A Markov Chain Application," *Operations Research*, Vol. 18, 1970.

9. Silver, A., and A. M. Silver, "An Empirical Inventory System for Hospital Blood Banks," *Hospitals*, Vol. 38, 1964.

10. Systems Research Group, Ohio State University, *Community Blood Banking Systems: An Application of Simulation Methodology*, Progress Report RF1234, Ohio State University Research Foundation, Columbus, Ohio, 1963.

12

Library Models

Philip M. Morse

12.1 Introduction

A public service of growing importance is the storage and later dissemination of the information generated by society. Since books are at present the most efficient means of storing information, the information storage-and-dissemination service is, to a great extent, performed by libraries—departmental, industrial, university, and public. Operating problems in libraries are now severe because of overcrowding and budget reductions on the one hand, and because of the impending changes consequent to computer applications on the other. As with other service operations thus bedeviled, it becomes all the more important to analyze library operations quantitatively and to devise models to represent and predict their behavior.

Administrative decisions, both major and minor, regarding all aspects of library planning and operation, can be wisely reached only in the light of knowledge of present library use and by the help of careful estimates of future use. Administrative questions regarding budget or space must be answered, either actively or by default, often or occasionally, by every librarian or library board. Much of the time the operating decisions, which should be based on an explicit analysis of such questions and their answers, are implicitly based on a reluctance to change past practices or a desire to emulate some other library, though it should be apparent that the answers may differ appreciably from library to library and even from time to time in the same library. Occasionally attempts are made to arrive at answers by "market surveys" of a sample of users. Experience is showing the dangers of such opinion surveys, unless they are very carefully worded and unless they are quantitatively checked against the actual behavior of the same users. Too often has the questionee persuaded both himself and the questioner that he would use some proposed new service, only to find that he seldom gets around to using it, once installed.

Many library operations are similar to those carried out in other service organizations: personnel recruitment and organization, individual consulting, purchasing, and financial accounting. Other operations are unique to libraries: the storage and preservation of books, the arrangement of books so they are accessible to library users, and the procedures whereby books are loaned or otherwise made available to the user of the library. Models for some of the latter operations will be described in this chapter. Discussion of other aspects of library operation will be found in library periodicals such as *Documentation, Journal of Documentation, College and Research Libraries*, the *Library Quarterly*, and *American Documentation*. At present none of the models have been carried far enough, or have been mutually integrated enough to assist the librarian adequately in reaching broad policy decisions. They do, however, represent necessary steps toward the attainment of a quantitative picture of library operation. It is hoped that future developments will fill out this kit of analytic tools so that the librarian may judge more accurately how well his library is satisfying the needs of his library users and may determine more rationally what policy decisions will improve the cost effectiveness of his operation.

12.2 Data
If any of the models are to be used, more data on library user habits must be gathered. How many "customers" use the card catalogue and how do they use it? What fraction of those who enter know the book they wish to peruse when they enter the library, and what fraction enter with a more general desire for some book on a particular subject? How many of them are willing to peruse the book in the library and how many wish to take the book home? What are the borrowing habits of the users: How long, on the average, do they keep the book out and what fraction of the time the book is out is it actually in use?

Similar questions regarding the use of individual books and classes of books in the library need to be answered. How often during the year does a person enter the library with a desire to peruse a specific book and how often does a person enter with a less specific desire, but which *would be satisfied* by this same book if he could find it? The sum of these two could be called the *demand rate* for this specific book. What fraction of this demand is satisfied by in-library perusal and what fraction requires taking the book out of the library? What is the relation between the demand rate this year and the demand rate for the same book in future years? Are there differing patterns of use and demand for books of different classes of subject matter? And so on.

Unfortunately, the one thing the usual librarian does *not* preserve is operating data. He tends to save out-of-date books, but he throws away the book cards that have recorded the number of times a book has been borrowed. Some of the questions raised in the preceding two paragraphs need special investigative techniques to answer, but many questions regarding book use can be answered by analysis of these book cards before they are thrown away. Of course computerization of the book-circulation process will make it much easier to collect data on book use *if* the computer system is designed in advance to record such data.

Thus, in practice the one datum most accessible to the operations analyst is the book *circulation rate R*, the number of times a particular book has been borrowed during the year. This is *not* the same as the *demand rate* λ for the book, though the two are related statistically. Part of the task of the analyst is to devise a model by which the demand for a book can be inferred from the more accessible figure on its circulation. The difference between demand and circulation is crucial; if demand is much greater than circulation, the user public is not being served effectively. Another task is to predict future from past circulation and still another is to estimate in-library use of a book from its recorded circulation. In other words, in advance of extensive computerization of the circulation department, the most useful models will be those using circulation figures as input data; these will still be useful models during and after computerization.

A few other data are relatively easy to measure and record: the total number of users entering the library each day and the number of books withdrawn per day; the number of books left on tables by in-library users, to be reshelved by library personnel, and the number of books, of each different class, out of the library on loan or being repaired at any time. This latter figure can be obtained by counting the book cards left at the circulation desk while the book is borrowed or being repaired. From the first two figures one can estimate the mean number of books borrowed per user per visit and, with more detailed analysis (obtained by sampling), the book classes that happen to be simultaneously of interest to an individual borrower. From this we can measure the *degree of connectivity* of different book classes (and thus avoid placing connected classes of books far apart). Knowing the mean yearly circulation $\overline{R}$ of a given class of books, the third figure enables one to estimate the average ratio of in-library use to circulation for that class.

A knowledge of mean circulation $\overline{R}$ for a given class plus a determination of the mean number $\overline{J}$ of books out on loan enables one to calculate the mean length of time $\overline{T}_R$ books of this class stay out per loan [4, page 121]. For a two-week book, if T_R is longer than (1/25)th of a year, then there is a large percentage of overdue books; if T_R is less than 1/25 then borrowers are "prompt" in returning books.

The reciprocal of the mean time per loan, $\overline{\mu} = 1/\overline{T}_R$, is the average number of circulations a book of the class could have if it were borrowed as soon as it was returned (so it never was on the shelf). The $\mu = 1/T_R$ for an individual book is the maximum number of loans this book can sustain. It is called the *maximum circulation rate* for the book or the *mean return rate*.

Note that all of these results are mean values, averaged over books of a class. This is not usually detrimental. The librarian must manage thousands of books; if his policies are satisfactory *on the average* he will be doing the best he can; in many cases he must operate as does an insurance company. Sometimes, of course, he must use the average value as a best estimate for the value for an individual book. For example, even though lengths of loan periods vary in a random manner from book to book and also from loan to loan for a particular book, we are probably justified in using the reciprocal of the mean loan period $\overline{T}_R$ for a class of books as being a good estimate for μ, the maximum circulation rate for any particular book of the class. At least its use will result in comparative estimates of behavior which may be sufficiently accurate to use for policy decisions.

Attainment of this "sufficient accuracy" (often no better than ±50 percent) for the least effort on the part of the library staff should be the goal of the data-gathering effort.

12.3 Inferences about Book Circulation

Libraries, like warehouses, have an inventory problem and, as with all inventory problems, a queuing model [1] may be used to analyze its behavior. For example, the model can indicate the relationship between the demand rate λ for a given book, its circulation rate R, and its maximum circulation rate (or return rate) μ.

The fraction of the year the book is out on loan, inaccessible to other library users who might also borrow it, is $RT_R = R/\mu$ (since $T_R = 1/\mu$ is the mean fraction of a year per loan). If the λ potential borrowers per year come at random during the year, then the number of these who *do not* find the book on the shelf and therefore do not borrow it, is $U = \lambda(R/\mu)$. If there is no book-reserving procedure to ensure that the book eventually gets to these "unsatisfied customers" none of the U will have borrowed the book and the difference between the demand rate λ and U will be equal to the circulation rate per year R, which measures the number who *did* find the book on the shelf and then borrowed it,

$$R = \lambda - U = \lambda - R\left(\frac{\lambda}{\mu}\right) \text{ or } R = \frac{\lambda\mu}{\lambda + \mu} . \tag{12.1}$$

This formula gives the expected value of the circulation rate R for a book in terms of its demand rate λ and its maximum circulation rate μ. The number U of "unsatisfied customers" per year for the book, the number who don't find it on the shelf when they come for it, is of course

$$U = \lambda - R = \frac{\lambda^2}{\lambda + \mu} \tag{12.2}$$

if the reserve-card procedure is not efficient. (A further discussion of this model is in [4, Chap. 4].)

It is reasonable to expect this simple model to represent fairly accurately the phenomenon of *circulation interference*, for in most (if not all) libraries the effect of book-reserve procedures is negligible. In the first place, as we noted, the demand λ for a book not only includes those who come to the library knowing exactly the book they want; it also includes those who do not know in advance the exact book they want but who *would* borrow the book in question if it were on the shelf. Since, in most libraries, fewer than 1/5 of the first category (those who know the book they want) fill out reserve cards if the book is out and since, in most cases, there are at least as many in the second category as in the first, it is not surprising to find that the fraction of the "unsatisfied customers" who do fill out a reserve card is less than 1 in 20. Thus the simple model, neglecting reserve cards, is sufficiently accurate for our purposes.

The simple model enables us to say, for example, that if a book is off the shelf more than half the time (if R/μ is greater than $1/2$), then a duplicate copy should be provided to satisfy the U unsatisfied customers. For if R/μ is greater than $1/2$, then U is greater than the number $R = \lambda - U$ who got the one copy. And if it is "worth it" to have one copy of the book on the shelf to satisfy R persons, it should be worth it to have another copy if it will satisfy U more persons when U is larger than R. Of course the problem is not quite that simple for, even if there are two copies of a popular book, the circulation process is random enough so that there will be times when *both* copies will be off the shelf and some potential borrowers will thus miss out even then [4, pp. 70–74].

If the expected value of circulation R is given in Equation 12.1 in terms of λ and μ, both considered as known, we cannot simply invert the formula to obtain $\lambda = R\mu/(\mu - R)$ for the expected value of λ, assuming R and μ as known. (The mean value of some function $F(x)$ of a random variable x is not usually the same function $F(\bar{x})$ of the mean of x.) In the present example one occasionally finds a book with a circulation R for a given year which is greater than the μ for the class, which will make nonsense of the use of $\lambda = R\mu/(\mu - R)$. What has happened is that, for this book for this year, demand happened to be larger than the mean λ and/or maximum circulation rate μ happened to be larger ($T_R = 1/\mu$ smaller) than its expected value, so that this one book achieved a circulation greater than its expected maximum circulation rate μ. If we wish to compute the conditional probability that demand for a book of a class is λ, given that the book's circulation is R, in terms of the conditional probability that the book's circulation is R, given that demand is λ, we must use Bayes's theorem, and also we must know the unconditional probability distributions for both λ and R [4, Chap. 8]. However, we do not usually need to know these for a single book; distributions for a whole class of books are sufficient for our purpose. Luckily the distributions for R and μ need only to be determined very approximately in order to work out what is useful in policy decisions. If, as seems to be the case, the distribution in circulation for a given class of books is a modified geometric distribution (related to the Bradford distribution [3]), then the distribution in demand is likely to be roughly exponential, with mean value given in terms of μ and of mean circulation for the class.

12.4 A Markov Model of Book Use

A logically satisfactory model for the attenuation of popularity of a book would be one which relates the demand λ for the book over time. As was just pointed out, we cannot measure λ directly for an individual book; we have to work with circulation figures—not demands. Therefore it is more convenient to set up an approximate model relating successive yearly circulations R; it is much easier to check this against data.

We know that a book's circulation usually decreases year by year. But there are exceptions, too important to neglect, where a book suddenly becomes popular, thereafter to "decay" again with time. *On the average*, book circulation drops off exponentially [9], but there are enough exceptions to indicate that a distribution about a decaying mean would not be sufficient for our purpose. Such a distribution does not connect a book's circulation this year with its own circulation last year; it only connects with the average circulation of all books of its class. We would like to know, given that a particular book had circulation m last year, the chance that *this book* has circulation n this year. Or, at least, we would like to know the expected total circulation of all the books in a class which circulated m times or less last year.

The simplest model of this sort is the Markov process. We start by setting up a matrix of "transition probabilities" T_{mn}. These are conditional probabilities; given that the book circulated m times last year, the chance it will circulate n times next year is T_{mn}. We might expect that the T change with the age of the book, but we can hope that they change slowly; otherwise the model requires more data than it is worth to determine the added parameters. Since the T are probabilities, if the T do not change with book age, we have

$$\sum_{n=0}^{\infty} T_{mn} = 1 \; ; (T^t)_{mn} = \sum_{k=0}^{\infty} T_{mk} \, (T^{t-1})_{kn}$$

$$\bar{R}(0) = \sum_{m=0}^{\infty} m P_m \; ; \bar{R}(t) = \sum_{m=0}^{\infty} P_m \sum_{n=0}^{\infty} n(T^t)_{mn}$$

(12.3)

where $(T^t)_{mn}$ is the conditional probability that, if a book of the class circulated m times in a given year, *the same book* will circulate n times yearly t years later. If the circulation distribution of a given collection of books is P_m then $\overline{R}(0)$ is their mean circulation during the year for which P_m was measured and $\overline{R}(t)$ is the expected mean yearly circulation of *the same collection* t years later.

It does turn out that, to a good approximation, the mean circulation next year of all the books in the class, which circulated m times this year, is a linear function of m,

$$\sum_{n=0}^{\infty} nT_{mn} = \alpha + \beta m \tag{12.4}$$

where β must be less than unity if the high-circulation books are to reduce in circulation, on the average. Then the mean circulation of a particular group of books will "decay" in the exponential manner actually found in practice. For if

$$\overline{R}(0) = \sum_{m=0}^{\infty} mP_m \text{, then } \overline{R}(1) = \sum_{m} P_m \sum_{n} nT_{mn} = \alpha + \beta\overline{R}(0),$$

$$\tag{12.5}$$

$$\overline{R}(2) = \alpha + \beta\overline{R}(1) = \alpha + \beta\left[\alpha + \beta R(0)\right] = \alpha(1 + \beta) + \beta^2\,\overline{R}(0), \text{ and}$$

$$\overline{R}(t) = \alpha(1 + \beta + \ldots + \beta^{t-1}) + \beta^t\overline{R}(0) = \alpha\,\frac{1 - \beta^t}{1 - \beta} + \beta^t\overline{R}(0).$$

Since β is less than unity, β^t will diminish as t increases, and the mean circulation will eventually reach the asymptotic value $\alpha/(1 - \beta)$. However, because of the model, there is always a chance that a low-circulation book suddenly gains popularity (T_{mn} for m small and n large is not zero), as is required by the real situation.

Study of the circulation records of classes of books shows that this model represents most of the behavior of interest for circulation history. One finds that α and β for various classes of books change slowly with age of the book, so that if one is predicting within a time span of five years or less, one can consider these parameters to be independent of book age and dependent only on the nature of the group of books chosen. Furthermore, because of the linearity of Equation 12.4, the average values of α and β for a combination of two groups is the mean of the values of α and β for the groups taken separately. This simplifies the application of the model considerably.

A certain amount of data (as well as Occam's razor!) indicates that a reasonable approximation to the transition probabilities T_{mn} is that they form a Poisson distribution about the mean value $\alpha + \beta m$,

$$T_{mn} \simeq \frac{(\alpha + \beta m)^n}{n!} \exp(\alpha + \beta m). \tag{12.6}$$

Detailed analysis of the properties of this distribution is given in [8]. Some of the consequences will be discussed here (see also [4, Chap. 5]). For example, if during their first year of accession the fraction of books of the group which circulated m or more times is γ^m, then the distribution in circulation of this same group in successive years can be calculated as shown in Figure 12.1. The degree to which such calculations check the data is shown in Figure 12.2; here the distribution in circulation of all the first-year chemistry books in a science library is plotted. The upper solid line corresponds to the best fit for a geometric distribution. The middle solid line is the distribution predicted for all books in the collection less than five years old. It is obtained using Equations 12.3 and 12.6, assuming that $P_m = (1 - \gamma)\gamma^m$ for all books in their first year and $P(\geqslant N, t) = \sum_{n=N}^{\infty} \sum_{m=0}^{\infty} P_m (T^t)_{mn}$ is the probability that a book t years old has circulation N or greater; these distributions are then combined to obtain the distribution $F(\geqslant N, 4)$ for all books in the collection less than five years of age. The whole collection consisted of roughly equal numbers of books of ages from zero to fifteen years. Again the distributions for different ages were combined to obtain the lower solid line for $F(\geqslant N)$. The dots, circles, and crosses constitute the data, which are reasonably well in accord with the predictions of the model.

This model has been of assistance whenever the future circulation of various classes of books is of interest. For example, the decision to duplicate a very popular book should be based on an estimate of its *future* popularity, not on its circulation during the previous year; it is too late to satisfy last year's potential users—next year's demand is what needs to be planned for. The Markov model can do this. If the parameters α and β are known for a class of book, one can predict the circulation during the next five years (for example) of those books which have a given circulation this year, and one can predict on the average the increase in satisfied users if a duplicate of the book is purchased now. Table 12.1 shows an example.

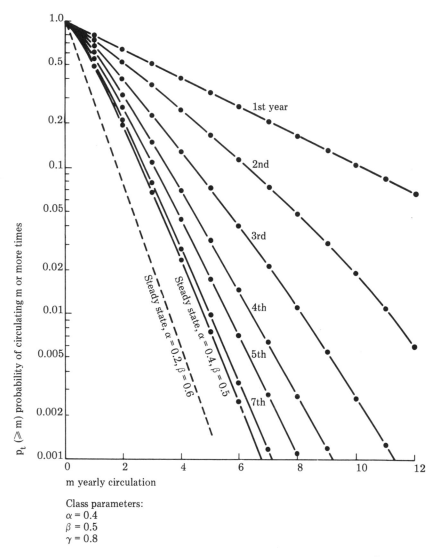

Figure 12.1   Example of the Markov model. Expected fraction P_t $(\geqslant m)$ of books of a class, t years old, that circulate m or more times in the year. From [4].

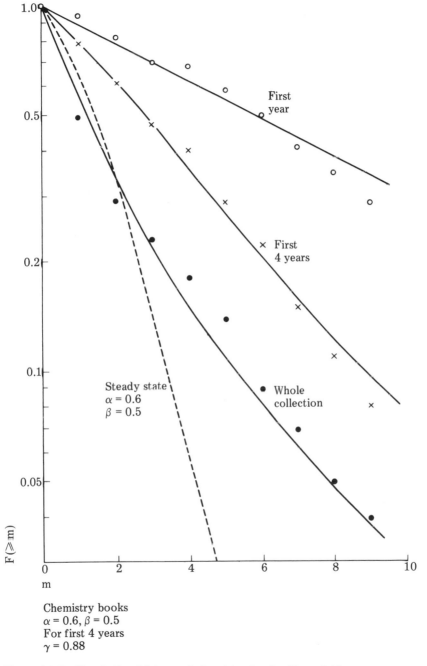

Figure 12.2   Circulation history of chemistry books. From [4].

Table 12.1   Expected Unsatisfied Demand for Two Typical Books*

Year of Circulation	1	2	3	4	5	Cumulative
Math. book expected circulation $R(t)$	12	7.5	4.8	3.2	2.2	29.7
Math. book unsatisfied demand, 1 copy, U_1	11.1	3.5	1.1	0.5	0.2	16.4
Math. book unsatisfied demand, 2 copies, U_2	4.2	0.6	0.1	—	—	4.9
Geol. book expected circulation $R(t)$	12	2.9	1.0	0.7	0.6	17.2
Geol. book unsatisfied demand, 1 copy, U_1	11.1	0.7	—	—	—	11.8
Geol. book unsatisfied demand, 2 copies, U_2	4.2	—	—	—	—	4.2

*From [4].

In both cases worked out in Table 12.1, the first-year circulation
is 12. Because of its slow decay in popularity (the β for mathematics books in this library is 0.6, whereas $\beta = 0.3$ for geology books)
the circulation of the mathematics book stays high enough to
justify buying a duplicate. If, for example, the high circulation is
discovered during the first year and a duplicate gets on the shelves
by the end of the first year, the 11 unsatisfied customers cannot
be mollified, but about 5 additional persons will be able to borrow
the book during the next five years. If the mean circulation of the
whole collection is one per year (which it was for this library),
then the duplicate would be expected to be as much used as the
average book, in the next five years, and would thus be worth having on the shelves. On the other hand, the geology book decreases
in circulation so rapidly it is hardly worthwhile to buy a duplicate
after the first year.

Of course predictions of this sort can be badly off in individual
cases, but they should be reasonably correct, on the average, for a
large number of books. If, for example, one were to decree that all
mathematics books which circulate five or more times in their first
six months on the shelf should be duplicated as quickly as possible,
then the prediction, that the number of additional borrowings will
be about five times the number of duplicates bought, should check
fairly well on the average.

Similar calculations are useful when one is forced, by space limitations, to retire some of the collection to a less-accessible location. If the selection is made according to circulation, if, for example, all books which did not circulate last year are relegated to the "basement," then the Markov model can predict the number of persons, next year, who will have to go to the basement to get the book or else will not borrow the book because they did not go to the basement to look for it. Examples of this sort are given in [4, Chap. 8].

12.5 A Search Model

We have mentioned several times that part of the "demand" for a given book consists of those library users who did not come to the library specifically to borrow that book, but who *would* borrow the book if they came across it on the shelf. The process of searching the shelves for a book of immediate interest may be called *browsing.* Sometimes a specific book is searched for; sometimes one looks for a likely book on a specific subject, not being sure in advance which book will look promising enough to borrow, or whether any will be found. This process of looking over the shelves to find a book of sufficient promise to withdraw is similar in nature to the process of searching over the ocean by aircraft observers for a surfaced submarine or a ship. The model developed in [2] is appropriate here, with the modifications required by the operational differences between air search and browsing.

During the search for a book somewhere in a section of shelves, the browser's eyes fixate momentarily for a glimpse of an area of the shelves, then jump to another area. The probability g that the book of interest is seen during a single glimpse is inversely proportional to the area which is to be searched over (that is, to the number N of books in the section searched) $g = \alpha/N$, and the chance it is not found in any one glimpse is $(1 - g)$. Constant α depends on the illumination of the shelves and on the degree of attentiveness of the browser (he may not "see" the book even if he is looking at it). During a time T minutes the browser will perform ωT glimpses, where ω is the mean glimpse rate. The chance he will *not* find the book of interest during the whole time is $(1 - g)^{\omega T}$ and his chance of success during the search is $1 - (1 - g)^{\omega T}$. Since g is usually a small quantity, this expression can be expressed in terms of the exponential, so the probability P_s of finding the book of interest among N others on the shelves during a time T is

$$P_s = 1 - e^{-\rho T/N} \; ; \; \rho = \alpha\omega \tag{12.7}$$

where ρ is called the *browsing rate*. It may be determined experimentally; its value usually ranges between 100 and 200 books per minute. The shape of the curve for P_s is given in Figure 12.3. The important fact about this formula is that the chance of success is subject to a law of diminishing returns; doubling the browsing time does not double the chance of success. The fraction $\gamma = \rho T/N$, the ratio of volumes searched to total number of volumes, may be called the *search coverage*. If γ is small, $P_s \simeq \gamma$; if γ is large, P_s is less than γ because of the inefficiencies inherent in search due to overlap and duplication of glimpses.

The usual browser takes this into account in his search. He presumably has come to the library with one or more desires in mind. They may be desires for specific books, which he will look for in the appropriate sections, or they may be more generalized desires, for a good book on helium II, for example, or a biography of Jean-sans-peur of Burgundy (which he may or may not recognize when he sees it on the shelf). In terms of the model, he has come with a set of estimates of interest potentials for different sections of the library, ratios $V = E/N$ between the expected number E of books of immediate interest likely to be in a given section, divided by the total number N of books in the section. And he allocates the time

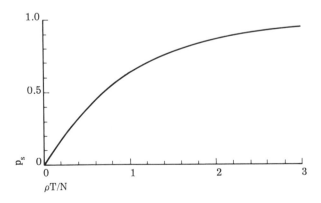

Figure 12.3   Chance of spotting one book of present interest, placed at random in N books, as a function of the ratio of search effort ρT to number of books scanned N.

he has available for browsing according to the different interest potentials he intuitively places on the different sections, going to the section of highest interest potential first, and so on. Given the interest potentials, one can work out the optimum allocation of effort [2,7]; the usual browser instinctively approximates the procedure, spending most time in the sections with highest interest potential for him this visit and neglecting entirely sections with interest potential less than some minimum, which is determined by the amount of time he has available this visit.

This very nonlinear method of searching sections of the library has important implications for library architects and planners. Each browser would prefer to spend his time in one or two small sections of the library, in which all the books he might want would happen to reside; such concentration of his search would produce optimum results for him that visit. Of course other browsers, and the same browser on another visit, will each have a different constellation of interests; thus each will frequent different sections and will desire to bring his immediate areas of interest into proximity.

Implications for Book Classification

Obviously, the worst arrangement possible of books on the shelves would be a random one, or one in order of accession; one alphabetic by author would be almost as bad. For such arrangements, every browser would have to dip at random over the whole collection. The interest potential would be nearly the same everywhere so he would not be able to concentrate his search, because the number of books over which he has to search is large, the search coverage ($\rho T/N$) for a given search time is small, and his chance of success is small. Also obviously, the arrangement of books by subject, Dewey or Library of Congress (LC) classification, is an attempt to gather together books that might be sought during one visit, so the browser can narrow his search area. One can imagine procedures for gathering data to improve the classification scheme and the arrangement of the sections in space. For example, every time a borrower takes out two or more books, it constitutes a "connectivity of interest" between that set of books. The number of times per year book i is borrowed at the same time, by the same borrower, as book j, might be called the *correlation index* n_{ij} of the pair ij. One could then work out a mathematical programming model to arrange the books in the library so that books with high degree of connectivity are close together. Data of this sort should be easy to gather when circulation is computerized, *if* the system is designed to record and process data of this sort.

One could then allot to each item *i* (book, report, article, or element of a computer store) in a set of Q items a number x_i on a classification scale, such that the items with largest correlation indices are closest together. For example, one could adjust the x_i so that

$$S(x) \equiv \frac{1}{2} \sum_{i,\,j=1}^{Q} n_{ij} (x_i - x_j)^2 \text{ be minimum,}$$

(12.8)

subject to the requirement that $\sum_{i=1}^{Q} x_i^2 = C$.

This variational problem has the solution that the x be solutions of the following set of simultaneous equations

$$\omega x_i = \sum_{j=1}^{Q} n_{ij} (x_i - x_j) \qquad (i=1, 2, \ldots, Q)$$

(12.9)

where ω is the Lagrange multiplier. There are Q allowed values of ω and thus Q different solutions to the x. For each allowed solution, the corresponding functional

$$S(x) = \omega C$$

(12.10)

showing that an allowed value of ω cannot be negative.

The smallest value of ω is, of course, zero, for which all x_i are equal. This trivial solution is of no operational use; the next lowest value for ω represents the solution of value. This classification scale x_i, for item i, (a solution of Equation 12.9 for the next lowest allowed value of ω) collects those items together which are most often used together. It thus would represent an ordering which would be of greatest convenience to the browser. In addition, if the x_i showed an appreciable amount of "clumping," groups of items being close together, with large gaps between the groups, this would provide a means for separating a library into sections (or even branch libraries) which would inconvenience the fewest users. For details see [5].

Until analyses of the sort just described are carried out, the different subject sections of the Dewey or LC classification can be considered to be sections of more or less uniform interest potential for the usual browser, one or more of which he will search through during any of his visits, the particular choice depending on his immediate interests. If any of these sections become too large, they cannot be searched efficiently by the average browser in the time he has available. If the usual browsing rate ρ of Equation 12.7 is 150 volumes per minute and if the browser has at most 20 minutes to spend on a particular section, then if the section contains more than about 3,000 volumes he will not be able to search the section very efficiently. In fact, if $(\rho T/N)$ is smaller than 1/2, his chance of finding a particular book is approximately equal to $(\rho T/N)$. For example, this ratio would be less than 1/2 if T were 10 minutes, ρ were 150 volumes per minute, and N were 5,000 volumes; a browser would be discouraged by such a poor chance.

Retiring Books

As open-shelf subject sections come to contain more than about 5,000 volumes, they begin to be inefficient for browsing. They can be subdivided by subject, which might help, or the books of less general interest can be removed from the open shelves and placed in a less accessible place. Often the influx of new books forces the librarian to do this "weeding" anyway, and he might as well do it in a way to benefit the browser. If the librarian leaves a fraction x of the original section in the open shelves and "retired" the $N(1 - x)$ remainder in the stacks or in some less accessible storehouse, the particular book of interest to the browser may or may not be left on the open shelf, but if it is it will be easier for him to find it among the smaller number of books. Thus the librarian might balance, for the browser, between the reduced chance that the book of immediate interest is still among the xN books left on the open shelves and the increasing chance of finding it (if there) among a smaller number of other books. He might adjust x to maximize the utility, to the average browser, of the books in the fraction x left on the open shelves.

If the choice of books to retire is a random one, a fraction $1 - x$ of the section being "retired," independent of age or popularity, then the hope of improving the returns for the average browser is illusory; the chance his book of immediate interest has been re-

tired more than counterbalances the increase in search coverage
($\rho T/xN$) which is provided by the smaller number xN left in the
open-shelf section. But if the choice is by potential interest to the
browser, the fraction x left on the open shelves being the books
more likely to be chosen by the average browser, then the open
shelves can be made more productive for the average browser by
"weeding out" the less popular books.

If the section has N books to begin with, the chance the browser
has of finding his book of interest in time t if it still is in the
browsing section, is $1 - \exp(-\rho t/xN)$ from Equation 12.7. This
increases as x is decreased. Of course different browsers spend different lengths of time looking for their book of interest; we should
average this probability over their different search times. Observation indicates that these times are distributed exponentially; the
probability density that a search time is t is $(1/T)e^{-t/T}$, where T
is the mean search time for the average browser, for this section.
Thus the chance the average browser finds his book in the "rejuvenated" fraction x, *if* his book is still in that section, is

$$P(x) = \frac{1}{T} \int_0^\infty e^{-t/T}(1 - e^{-\rho t/xN}) \ dt = 1 - \frac{x}{x + \gamma} = \frac{\gamma}{\gamma + x} \quad (12.11)$$

where $\gamma = \rho T/N$ is the search coverage of the original section of N
books, for an average browser spending an average time T looking
for his book. Presumably γ is less than unity, otherwise there
would be no particular advantage for the browser to "weed
out" the section.

If now the section is reduced in size by random choice, the
chance that the book of immediate interest for a browser is still on
the open shelves is x, the fraction of the books left on the open
shelves. The chance the average browser has of finding a book of
immediate interest to him in the average time T is then

$$xP(x) = \frac{\gamma x}{\gamma + x} \quad (12.12)$$

which has no maximum in the range $0 < x < 1$. But if the books in
the section are "weeded" in accordance with their potential likelihood of being a book of interest to the average browser, then an
optimization is possible.

The yearly circulation of a book is the best measure we have of
the likelihood that the average browser will choose that book as

his book of immediate interest, to borrow if he finds it. Thus if
we wish to remove from the oversize section the books which are
least likely to be chosen by browsers, we will remove the low-
circulation books first. We saw earlier that the circulation of books
in a section are distributed geometrically, or exponentially, if we
consider the number of books to be a continuous variable. Thus
the probability density that a book in the "unweeded" section has
circulation y is $(1/R) \exp(-y/R)$, where R is the mean circulation
per book of the "unweeded" section. To "weed" this section of a
fraction $1 - x$ of the lowest-circulation books, leaving the fraction
x made up of high-circulation books, we must "retire" all books
with circulation equal to or less than Y, where

$$\int_0^Y \left(\frac{1}{R}\right) e^{-y/R} \; dy = 1 - x \quad \text{or} \quad Y = R \; ln \; (1/x) \tag{12.13}$$

The mean circulation of the "rejuvenated" section (having books
with circulation *greater* than Y) is then

$$M(x) = \frac{1}{x} \int_Y^\infty \left(\frac{y}{R}\right) e^{-y/R} \; dy = R(1 - ln \; x) \tag{12.14}$$

which increases above R (the average for the full section) as the
fraction x of books left in the "rejuvenated" section is decreased,
leaving fewer and fewer books of higher and higher circulation.
   If the oversize section is "weeded" according to circulation, and
if we assume that the mean circulation of a collection is proportional to the probability that an average browser will find a book
of his immediate choice in the collection, then the probability
that the average browser, spending a mean time T searching the
"rejuvenated" section of Nx books, will find the book of immediate interest to him is

$$x[M(x)/R]P(x) = (1 - ln \; x) \frac{\gamma x}{\gamma + x}; \quad \gamma = \frac{\rho T}{N}. \tag{12.15}$$

This does have a maximum value when γ is less than unity and one
can therefore inquire what fractional size x_0 will be optimum for
the average browser. Letting the derivative of this expression be
equal to zero results in the equation

$$x_0 = \gamma \; ln \; (1/x_0) \tag{12.16}$$

and, for this optimum fractional size x_0, the chance of "success" for the average browser is given by

$$\overline{S_r}/\overline{S} = (1 - ln\ x_0)\ \frac{\gamma x_0}{\gamma + x_0} = x_0\left(1 + \frac{1}{\gamma}\right) \tag{12.17}$$

where $\overline{S}$ is the chance that the average browser will find a book of immediate interest to him in the oversize section of N books, and $\overline{S_r}$ is the chance that he will find that book in the "rejuvenated" section of Nx_0 books, obtained by removing the fraction $1 - x_0$ of lowest-circulation books. And for $x = x_0$ this ratio S_r/S is maximum.

Figure 12.4 plots this optimum fraction x_0 against γ, the search coverage for the full section. In Figure 12.5 we have plotted the corresponding expected gain in search success. As might be expected, x_0 decreases as N, the size of the full section, increases (as $\gamma = \rho T/N$ decreases). Since ρT is of the order of 3,000; if N is 10,000, then the "rejuvenated" section, left on the open shelves, should be about a third of this, or 3,000 volumes, if this section is to be of optimal size for browsing. At this size, the chance the browser has of finding his book of immediate interest has been increased by 50 percent by the "weeding" ($S_r/S = 1.5$). On the other hand, if $N = 30,000$, then x_0 is about 0.15, or the "rejuvenated"

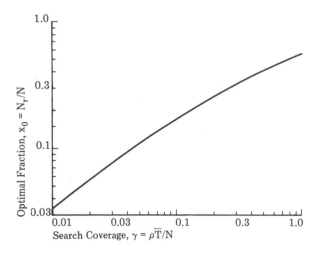

Figure 12.4   Optimal browsing fraction x as a function of coverage parameter γ for low-circulation retirement plan.

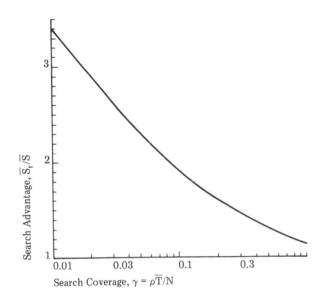

Figure 12.5   Search advantage as a function of search coverage parameter γ.

section should be 4,500 volumes and the search advantage $(\overline{S_r}/\overline{S})$ is nearly a factor of 2. Since it probably is not worth the trouble to make the separation unless it results in an improvement of at least a factor of 1.5, it is probably not worth dividing a section with $\gamma = \rho T/N$ greater than 0.3 (that is, with N smaller than about 10,000 volumes). Of course, other considerations may force the reduction in size, even if the advantage to the browser is less than 1.5. These questions, and others, are discussed in greater detail in [7]. It can be seen that these models, and others, which can be devised when we have more data on library operations, can assist in reaching decisions on library operating procedures, on library layout, and even on the architectural design of libraries.

12.6 Conclusions

These examples show what may be done to assist the librarian in making his library serve its users effectively, within the ever-present constraints of budget and space. The goal is to devise models which are easy to manipulate and which require the least manpower in gathering the necessary data. Since circulation figures are (or will be) relatively easy to obtain, models using these data should be among the first to be developed and utilized. The examples outlined here could be used to justify budget allocations, to plan alternative uses of space, or to institute new services in any library. What is needed is to set up procedures to gather the relatively small amount of data needed to determine the parameter values appropriate to that library. If manpower is in short supply, data from small random samples taken fairly regularly are more useful than detailed inventories taken every decade. The data-gathering program must, of course, include its insertion into the formulas of the model, so that a continuous surveillance is kept of the performance of the library in serving its users, so that one can see when new operating policies are required, and so that a check can be made as to whether the new policy is actually achieving the results expected of it.

References

1. Fussler, H. H., and J. L. Simon, *Patterns in the Use of Books*, Chicago, University of Chicago Press, 1961.

2. Koopman, B. O., "The Theory of Search," *Operations Research*, October 1956.

3. Leimkuhler, F. F., "The Bradford Distribution," *Journal of Documentation*, September 1967.

4. Morse, P. M., *Library Effectiveness*, Cambridge, Mass., M.I.T. Press, 1968. See also "Measures of Library Effectiveness," Library Quarterly, January 1972.

5. _____, *Optimal Linear Ordering of Information Items*, Technical Report No. 65, M.I.T. Operations Research Center, Cambridge, Mass., June 1971.

6. _____, *Queues, Inventories and Maintenance*, New York, John Wiley and Sons, 1958.

7. _____, "Search Theory and Browsing," *The Library Quarterly*, October 1970.

8. Morse, P. M., and C. Elston, "A Probabilistic Model for Obsolescence," *Operations Research*, January 1969.

9. Trueswell, R. W., "Two Characteristics of Circulation," *College and Research Libraries*, July 1964.

13

Efficient Operation of Runways

Amedeo Odoni

13.1 Introduction

Air traffic control (ATC) is an area in which such operations research disciplines as applied probability, queuing theory, scheduling, and network analysis can be used to good advantage. In this respect, problems related to the efficient use of the runways seem particularly suited for this type of analysis. Partly for this reason, the runway was the subject of most of the early OR work in this area, notably that of Blumstein [2], Oliver [7], and Simpson [9].

More recently, much attention within the OR community has been given to runway problems. This interest was, of course, stimulated by the well-publicized congestion problems that several major airports have been experiencing since the summer of 1967. It was not much before that date that the aviation industry itself began to become aware of the severity of the runway capacity limitations with which it was faced. The experience of the last decade in several localities throughout the United States and abroad has been that construction of new airports and runways is quite often infeasible (politically and/or economically) despite strong pressures from aviation officials and planners. The realization has dawned that, at least for the immediate future, the number of available runways at major hubs is not likely to increase substantially.

In this light, modeling and analysis of runway operations can be extremely helpful in (1) understanding the capabilities and limitations of the present system; (2) anticipating potential future problems; and (3) evaluating alternatives for improvement. The remainder of this chapter, after briefly describing operations in the terminal area, will discuss some work on runway usage that has been performed by the author and will briefly identify potential problems and improvements.

13.2 The Terminal Area

The terminal area is the location where most of air traffic's congestion and delays occur. Physically, a terminal area is the portion of airspace within a radius of 25 to 30 miles from an airport. Typically, the terminal airspace is supervised by an approach control center, as opposed to an air route traffice control center (ARTCC) which directs en route traffic, guiding aircraft during the arrival and departure stages of flights.

Approaching aircraft enter the terminal area at prescribed locations ("entry fixes") and, depending on traffic conditions, are either instructed to proceed directly toward the runways or to take delaying action by flying a longer route or, more often, by joining a "holding stack." In the latter case, aircraft await their turn to land. Once cleared, aircraft proceed through the regulator space to the glide path, the runway, the taxiway and, finally, the gate of the terminal building (see Figure 13.1).

The weather conditions in which most of the delays occur are those calling for the use of instrument flight rules (IFR)—as opposed to visual flight rules (VFR) in good weather conditions. In practice, IFR are used irrespective of weather conditions in high density terminal areas. This is because visual perception alone is inadequate to guarantee against the occurrence of a midair collision. As IFR flying implies adherence to strict separation standards, terminal area congestion is intensified in this way and delays become even worse.

Instrument flight rules call for three miles, horizontal separation

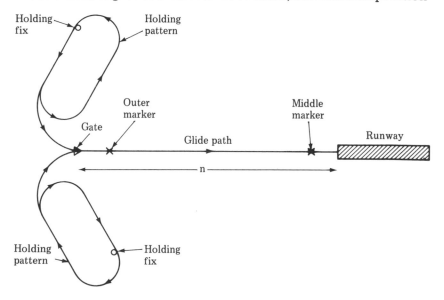

Figure 13.1   Idealized model of a runway used only for landings.

and 1,000 feet vertical separation as minimum safety standards for aviation in the terminal area. (For en route flights minimum horizontal IFR separation is set at five miles.) Thus aircraft flying in the terminal area can be visualized as "occupying" a cylinder of inviolable airspace. This cylinder is 1,000 feet tall and it has a radius of three miles.

The three-mile horizontal separation requirement combined with the rule that no two aircraft should occupy a runway simultaneously is the cause of considerable waste of time between successive landings of aircraft. This can be explained by studying the geometry of the final approach in Figure 13.2. Suppose that aircraft using a particular runway can be classified as "fast" and "slow" according to their final approach speeds (that speed can be

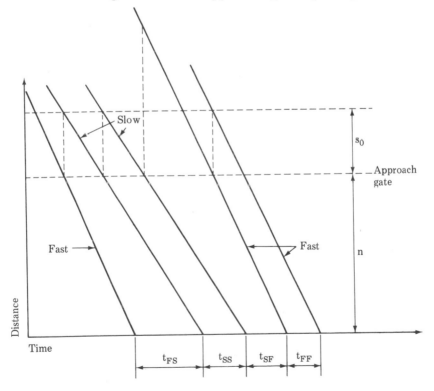

Figure 13.2 Effect of approach speeds on interarrival time gaps for two a/c classes (F and S). Here s_0 is the minimum separation required in the air. F = "fast" a/c, S = "slow" a/c.

assumed as being approximately constant throughout the final approach). Then if a "fast" aircraft reaches the outer marker ahead of a "slow" one, their distance will increase by the time they reach the runway. Conversely, if a "fast" aircraft follows a "slow" aircraft, the controller must intervene in order to space the two further apart than three miles at the outer marker, so that the two aircraft will not occupy the runway simultaneously. It should be obvious that the disparate approach speeds and the separation standards result in the loss of valuable time.

Priorities for service both on the ground and in the air are of the "first-come, first-served" type. In addition, when a runway is used both for landings and for takeoffs, priority is accorded to aircraft in the air unless the queue on the ground becomes unacceptably long.

13.3 Capacity of a Runway

The term "runway capacity," strangely enough, has been a controversial one over the years. At the root of the matter seems to be the rather imprecise and unfortunate definition of runway capacity first suggested in [1] and used by the FAA ever since. According to that definition the "practical capacity" of the runway is the hourly operations rate at which an average delay of four minutes occurs.

There are several problems with this definition: First, for the definition to be meaningful in practice, some kind of steady-state demand must be assumed for an extended period of time—a situation that is not currently observable at all but a few airports. Second, measurement of delays, in practice, is difficult, since a good fraction of delays due to runway congestion is disguised in the form of numerous path-stretching maneuvers in various stages of a flight. Third, and perhaps most important, average delay depends, among other things, on the arrival process—as we know from queuing theory. For instance, at a given service system, average delays would differ according to whether arrivals of prospective "customers" occur at random, or in groups, or at regular intervals (although the average number of "customer" arrivals per time unit may be the same in all three cases). One would like "capacity" to be a measure of runway "performance," and the arrival process certainly has nothing to do with the runway as a physical entity.

Because of the faults of the definition a variety of other terms have come into being, such as "peak hour" capacity, "sustained" capacity, "yearly" capacity, "theoretical" capacity, and so forth. By far the most natural definition, however, is the one first suggested by Blumstein [2], who defined capacity as "the hourly rate of accepting aircraft under continuous saturation conditions." In other words, assuming that aircraft seeking service are always present, capacity is equal to the hourly rate at which such aircraft can be serviced.

This definition has been gaining increasing acceptance over the years and most of the recent work in this area is aimed at estimating the "maximum throughput rate" or "saturation capacity" of the runway.

The following is a brief discussion of the problem of estimating the capacity of a runway which is used only for landings.[1] The intent here is to indicate a typical approach to problems in this area.

Assume first that a large number of aircraft are available in the vicinity of a single runway (possibly flying in holding patterns) and await clearance to land. Service is provided on a first-come, first-served basis. Assume further that the speed of a given aircraft flying the final approach remains substantially constant during that portion of a flight. Then, with reference to Figure 13.1, let us define:

n = length of the common glide path.

s_0 = minimum required distance separation between two aircraft in the air (currently s_0 = three miles).

t_0 = minimum required time separation between successive touchdowns of aircraft on the runway (currently t_o = 60 to 90 seconds).

We also define the random variables:

v = approach speed of landing aircraft using the runway. The probability density function $f_v(v_0)$ is assumed known.

x = distance between two successive landing aircraft at the instant when the first of the pair enters the common glide path. The probability density function $f_x(x_0)$ is also assumed known.

---

1. For details see [6]. The model discussed here is an extension of the pioneer work of Blumstein [2]. A recent National Bureau of Standards report [5] also suggests a model in the same spirit.

Let us focus attention now on an incoming pair of successive aircraft. If their approach speeds are defined as v_1 and v_2 for the first and second aircraft respectively and if we define t_{AA} as the time gap between the touchdowns of the two aircraft, we obtain

$$t_{AA} = \begin{cases} \dfrac{n+x}{v_2} - \dfrac{n}{v_1}, & \text{for } \dfrac{n+x}{v_2} - \dfrac{n}{v_1} \geqslant t_0, \\ t_0, & \text{otherwise,} \end{cases} \tag{13.1}$$

subject to the condition:

$$x \geqslant s_0. \tag{13.2}$$

Random variable t_{AA} describes, in effect, the landing process. Assuming that x, v_1, and v_2 are independent random variables,[2] the probability density function $f_{t_{AA}}(t)$ can be found, using Equation 13.2, $f_v(v_0)$ and $f_x(x_0)$. The required calculations are algebraically cumbersome, even for simple forms of $f_v(v_0)$ and $f_x(x_0)$, but quite straightforward.

Once the probability density function $f_{t_{AA}}(t)$ has been obtained, the first moment, $E[t_{AA}]$, can be used to estimate the capacity of the runway. According to our definition

$$\text{capacity} = \frac{1}{E[t_{AA}]}. \tag{13.3}$$

A general expression for $E[t_{AA}]$ can be given only for the case when the time separation requirement on the ground t_0 is so short that it never affects the rate of operations. Then

$$E[t_{AA}] = E[x] E\left[\frac{1}{v}\right]. \tag{13.4}$$

It is interesting to examine the factors that affect capacity. The probability density function, $f_v(v_0)$, for the approach speed obviously describes the mix of aircraft that use the runway in question. For major commercial airports, approach speeds can be expected

2. The assumption of independence of x from v_1 and v_2 is justifiable only as an approximation. Given the approach speeds of two successive aircraft, the controller will try to space them appropriately (thus affecting x). However, other factors such as aircraft/pilot performance, weather conditions, and imperfect information on the position of aircraft contribute to a decoupling of the spacing x from the approach speeds.

to concentrate in the 110 to 150 knot range (the approach speed range of commercial jet airplanes). On the other hand, random variable x, the distance between successive aircraft when the first of the two enters the glide path, reflects a number of items such as: the separation standards; the performance of pilots, aircraft, and controllers; the weather conditions; and the guidance and navigation systems used. Obtaining meaningful statistics on x is a difficult task. At best, by assuming various distributions for x, one can hope to demonstrate the marked effect that aircraft spacing has on the capacity of a runway.

In conclusion, it should be clear from this discussion that runway capacity depends on the separation standards, aircraft mix, performance of pilots, controllers, and instruments, weather conditions, and length of the glide path. Local noise abatement regulations may also play an important role in this respect.

There are several ways in which the above model can be extended for added realism. For instance, instead of assuming a fixed time t_0 as a minimum interval between successive touchdowns, one can postulate a random variable representing runway occupancy times for the mix of aircraft at hand. Also wind effects, and even aircraft load factors, can be accounted for by appropriately modifying the density function $f_v(v_0)$. Figures 13.3 and 13.4 show some typical results that explore the sensitivity of a runway's capacity to changes in various parameters.

Before concluding this section, it may be noted that similar models exist for estimating the capacity of a runway used only for departures [6], of a runway where departures alternate with arrivals [1,2,6], and of terminal and en route areas [10] in general.

13.4 A Queuing Model for the Runway

As noted above, the final approach-runway sequence is the "bottleneck" of terminal area traffic. In fact, it is presently the bottleneck of the whole air traffic control system. Delays related to the arrival and departure stages of flights probably account for more than ninety percent of all aircraft delays [8].

Considerable attention has, therefore, been focused recently on queuing models related to the runway as a service system. In this section, we will discuss in some detail a model of this type for a runway which is used only for landing. In particular, we will concentrate on the final stage of the sequence of "servers" pictured in

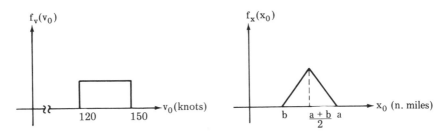

Figure 13.3   Sensitivity analysis of runway capacity. Figures 13.4 and 13.6 present capacity and delay curves for a runway with a n = 6 n. miles final approach. The density function for the approach speed $f_v(v_0)$ is given here. We examine four cases (four different sets of values for a and b of the $f_x(x_0)$ density function here):

Case a: $a = 5; b = 3$
Case b: $a = 3.5; b = 3$
Case c: $a = 3.0; b = 2.5$
Case d: $a = 2.5; b = 2.0$.

Case a can be considered as describing present ATC conditions. Future conditions may be better described by Cases c and d.

Figure 13.5, and will consider the preceding two stages (holding stack, regulator space) as only those portions of airspace where the queue of aircraft is temporarily accommodated.

As in all queuing analyses we must now provide a probabilistic description of (1) the arrival process of aircraft at the holding stacks (that is, at the periphery of the terminal area), and (2) the time required to serve an aircraft at the final approach and runway sequence.

With regard to (1), several previous studies [3,7] have shown that for *high-density terminal areas* the instants of aircraft arrivals at the area periphery can be accurately modeled by a Poisson process. Heuristic arguments can also be offered in support of this proposition [8]. The hourly rate of arrivals varies, of course, with the hour of the day. For a few of the busiest airports, however, it is fairly realistic to assume that for considerable periods of time during a day, the arrivals rate remains constant at a level of, say, λ arrivals per hour. We will, therefore, perform a steady-state type of analysis, while recognizing the limitations associated with this approach.

Turning now to service times, note that item (2) above has already been obtained in Section 13.3. In fact, the probability den-

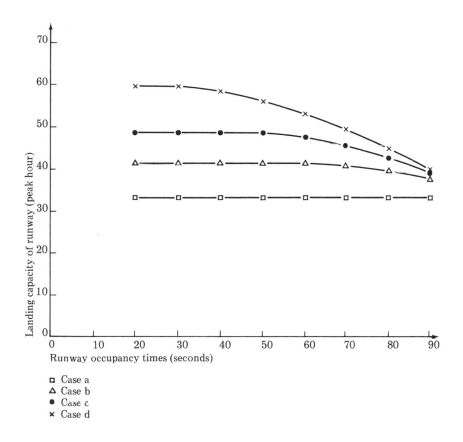

Figure 13.4   Landing capacity in terms of runway occupancy times.

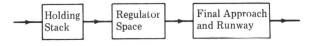

Figure 13.5   Sequence of "servers."

sity $f_{t_{AA}}(t)$ is precisely the description of service times at the final approach-runway that we are seeking.[3]

In summary, we have a queuing situation with Poisson arrivals and a general service time distribution. As service is provided on a first-come, first-served basis and as the maximum length of the queue can be considered infinite for all practical purposes, it would appear that the usual expressions related to the analysis of $M/G/1$ queues can be applied to this case. For instance, from the well-known Pollaszek-Khintchine formula, we obtain for the average waiting time per aircraft

$$E[w] = \frac{\lambda E[t_{AA}^2]}{2(1 - \lambda E[t_{AA}])}. \tag{13.5}$$

However, the following complication arises under closer examination: The random variable t_{AA} has been defined as the time gap between arrivals *under saturation conditions*. Hence the attendant density function $f_{t_{AA}}(t)$ is affected by the characteristics of both the first and the second of a pair of incoming aircraft. Thus $f_{t_{AA}}(t)$ does not describe the service time associated with aircraft that find an "idle" facility, that is, those that land without interacting with any preceding aircraft. We are, therefore, faced with a queuing situation in which the service time distribution depends on whether a prospective user of the facility finds the server idle or busy.

An investigation of this type of $M/G/1$ queue with state dependent service times as described above is presented in [6]. The analysis is performed for a facility with Poisson arrivals and service time distributions $b_0(t)$ and $b(t)$, respectively, depending on whether a prospective user finds the server idle or not. Explicit expressions are obtained for the geometric transform of the steady state probabilities, as well as for the expected queue length, the expected waiting time and the probability that the facility is idle at a random instant. Thus, if the first, second, third, and so forth moments of $b_0(t)$ and $b(t)$ are $\beta_0, \gamma_0, \delta_0, \ldots$ and $\beta, \gamma, \delta, \ldots$, respectively, we obtain,

Expected waiting time for a random "customer":

3. It may be added here that random variable x of Section 13.3 makes it possible to also account in the model for any secondary delays that may take place at the holding stack and regulator space.

$$E[w] = \frac{1}{1 - \lambda(\beta - \beta_0)} \left[\frac{\lambda \gamma_0}{2} + \frac{\lambda^2 \beta_0 \gamma}{2(1 - \lambda \beta)} \right].$$

(13.6)

Expected number of aircraft in queue (including the one being served):

$$E[N] = \frac{1}{1 - \lambda(\beta - \beta_0)} \left[\lambda \beta_0 + \frac{\lambda^2 \gamma_0}{2} + \frac{\lambda^3 \beta_0 \gamma}{2(1 - \lambda \beta)} \right].$$

(13.7)

Probability that the runway is idle:

$$\pi_0 = \frac{1 - \lambda \beta}{1 - \lambda(\beta - \beta_0)}.$$

(13.8)

In applying these results to the present case of the runway, we must, of course, set $b(t) = f_{t_{AA}}(t)$. It is also reasonable to assume that the service time of aircraft that find an idle runway is given by the minimal landing interval t_0 (no other aircraft can occupy the runway during this time period). Thus, we assume that

$$b_0(t) = \begin{cases} 1, & \text{for } t = t_0 \\ 0, & \text{otherwise} \end{cases}$$

(13.9)

which means that $\beta_0 = t_0$ and $\gamma_0 = t_0^2$.

Figure 13.6 shows curves obtained from Equation 13.6 for typical sets of parameters.

Before concluding this section, we might add that several attempts have been made recently to analyze the queuing problem with time-dependent arrival rates (see [4]). Although such efforts provide good opportunities to observe interesting phenomena like the build-up of queues during rush hours, they are still in the stage where further refinements are needed for a closer approximation to reality.

13.5 Improving the Runway

The preceding sections provide a strong base for understanding the effects of different parameters of the ATC system and meaningfully investigating possible improvements for the future. In what follows, we discuss briefly some possible future modifications of the final approach-runway sequence. The modifications are listed in the order of increasing sophistication and complexity:

1. *Fast-exit, fast-entry runways*: It has been suggested that run-

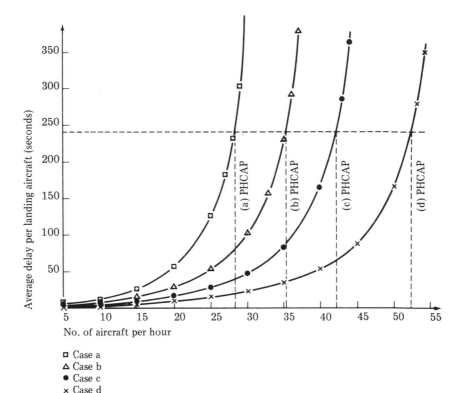

Figure 13.6   Delay curves obtained from Equation 13.6 (PHCAP = peak hour capacity).

ways be provided with exits that arriving aircraft can use at high speeds. Similarly, it is suggested that acceleration ramps be provided for departing aircraft so that they can enter the runway at a speed that will permit a faster takeoff. The effect of these modifications is a decrease in runway occupancy times (reduce t_0 in the landing model of Section 13.3).

2. *Shorter common final approach*: For the last few years work has been going on toward the development of a new microwave instrument landing system (microwave ILS) which, instead of a single corridor for an instrument approach to the runway (as in Figure 13.1), would define a volume of airspace that aircraft could use in the vicinity of the airport. The microwave ILS would then result in a reduction of the common flight path (reduce n in Sec-

tion 13.3) and consequently alleviate the problems caused by the different approach speeds of incoming aircraft.

3. *Abandoning the first-come, first-served rule*: It has often been argued that if the controller could select aircraft according to criteria other than first-come, first-served (for instance shortest-service-time, first-served or most passengers, first-served) some improvement in runway capacity or decrease in average delay could be achieved. Although this contention can be confirmed by methods similar to those of Section 13.3, this change in rules may cause other problems elsewhere in the ATC system.

4. *Regulating the flow of air traffic*: Through careful scheduling and sophisticated monitoring of flights, it is possible to derandomize substantially the pattern of arrivals at the terminal area. Although this does not have any effect on the capacity of the runway as defined here ("maximum throughput rate"), it will result in a reduction of terminal area delays. However, if the planning for a scheme of this type is not good, then we may only be disguising terminal area delays in the form of path-stretching maneuvers in the en route portion of the flight.

5. *Automatic sequencing and spacing of flights*: This has been a long cherished goal of ATC planners. It is argued that a sophisticated computer system will avert spacing errors (as represented by random variable x in Section 13.3) and also lead into sequences of landing aircraft that minimize the effects of different approach speeds at the final path. On the other hand, one can point out that the human controller provides valuable flexibility (not always going "by the book,") which only very sophisticated computer software can match.

6. *Reducing minimum separation standards*: This seems, at first sight, like the most obvious solution since any material reduction of the minimum separation standards (particularly of the three mile separation in the air) would result in significant increases in runway capacity. However, before a step of this kind can be taken, we need a much better understanding than we have presently of the quantitative relationship between safety and separation requirements. This is an extremely difficult problem. We can, therefore, say with certainty that it will be some time before ATC administrators feel on strong enough ground to alter these separation rules.

References

1. AIL, "Operational Evaluation of Airport Runway Design and Capacity (A Study of Methods and Techniques,)" Report 7601-6, Project 412-7-1R, January 1963.

2. Blumstein, A., "An Analytical Investigation of Airport Capacity," Cornell Aeronautical Laboratory, Report No. TA-1358-G-1, June 1960.

3. Bowen, E. G., and T. Pearcey, "Delays in the Flow of Air Traffic," *J. Royal Aeronautical Society*, vol. 52, no. 4, 1948.

4. A. D. Little, Inc., "A Study of Air Traffic Control System Capacity," Report No. FAA-RD-70-0, October 1970.

5. National Bureau of Standards, "Analysis of a Capacity Concept for Runway and Final Approach Path Airspace," Report No. NBS-10111, November 1969.

6. Odoni, A. R., "An Analytical Investigation of Air Traffic in the Vicinity of Terminal Areas," Technical Report No. 46, M.I.T. Operations Research Center, Cambridge, Mass., December 1969.

7. Oliver, R. M., "Delays in Terminal Air Traffic Control," *Journal of Aircraft*, vol. 1, no. 3, 1964.

8. Pestalozzi, G., "Delays to Air Traffic in a Terminal Area," University of California at Berkeley, Report No. N68-860674, June 1966.

9. Simpson, R. W., "An Analytical Investigation of Air Traffic Operations in the Terminal Area," Ph.D. dissertation, Aeronautics and Astronautics Department, Massachusetts Institute of Technology, May 1964.

10. Warskow, M. A., and I. S. Wiseport, "Capacity of Airport Systems in Metropolitan Areas," AIL Report No. 1400-5, January 1964.

14

Post Office Mail Processing Operations

Charles C. McBride

14.1 Introduction

The United States Postal Service (formerly the U.S. Post Office Department) is one of the largest industries in the country today. Approximately 80 billion pieces of mail are collected, transported, sorted, and delivered each year by roughly three-quarters of a million employees. Many large post offices in the country are operating near capacity levels in order to handle this volume.

The growth rate of this mail volume is currently higher than that for population growth; the 1980 mail volume is projected to be 120 billion pieces. Moreover, the cost of handling the mail is increasing at an even higher rate. As can be seen from Figure 14.1, average postal salaries have increased faster than their industry counterparts during the ten-year period 1956–1967, while postal productivity measured in terms of total volume handled per manhour worked, has remained relatively constant.

Explanations for the current problems of the Postal Service are plentiful. In *The Report of the President's Commission on Postal Organization* [6], the problems are traced primarily to the particular form of management system used by the old Post Office Department. The report recommends the replacement of the department by a largely nonpolitical postal corporation with powers adequate to determine its own policies and procedures for coping with current and future demands for service. The recent Postal Reform Act provides for the establishment of such a corporation— the U.S. Postal Service (USPS).

The Postal Service is now taking a systematic look at many areas of postal operations. Fundamental questions are being asked concerning what the goals of the USPS should be, what policies should be followed to achieve these goals, what measures of effectiveness should be used to evaluate various policies, and, finally, what models should be developed for examining the effects of each proposed policy. The construction of these models is perhaps the most difficult step in the analysis of the postal system, for it requires a thorough understanding of the interrelations between the various components of the system, as well as the relationships between the postal system and the outside world.

The purpose of this chapter is to describe some introductory efforts at developing models of components of the postal system.

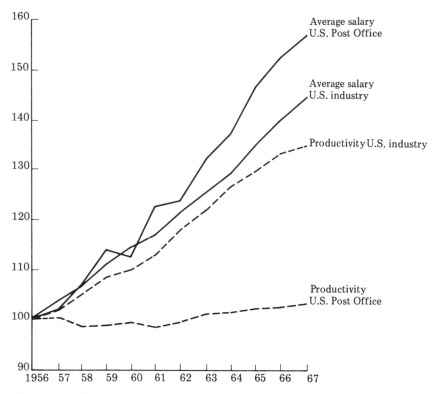

Figure 14.1   Productivity and salary trends (1956–1967). Source: Post office salary, Post Office Department Annual Report; Post Office productivity (weighted), Robert R. Nathan Associates; U. S. industry data, Economic Report of the President, February 1968.

More specifically, two models of the mail processing operations within a post office are considered here. The collection, transportation, and delivery subsystems of postal operations are not treated.

Mail processing costs constitute about 32 percent of the current postal budget [6]. Since most processing is currently performed in a manner that has not changed appreciably during the last century, it was felt that the mail processing system in a post office might offer a high potential for improvements through the application of the techniques of systems analysis.

The next section of this chapter consists of a brief description of the mail processing system. Some mail processing problem areas are discussed in Section 14.3. Two models suitable for analyzing these problems and results obtained from their application are presented in Section 14.4. Finally, a brief summary of related postal systems work is given.

14.2 Description of Postal Mail Processing System

The description of the mail processing system given in this section refers primarily to letter mail processing operations. Analogous operations exist for the other types of mail.

The mail processing system covers all mail handling operations that take place within post offices including mail preparation activities, sorting operations, and dispatching activities. The mail preparation operations cancel stamped mail that has not been previously handled, sort and open sacks, sort and open bundles, and place mail in trays. Dispatching units gather and package mail that has received its final sort in the office for transportation to another post office or to a local carrier station.

The principal mail processing activity by far is that of sorting the three types of mail that are normally found in a post office. *Collection and acceptance mail* consists of mail that is collected from local mail boxes or is brought to the post office by large mailers. This may be destined for local delivery or for another office. It is processed during the evening shift and normally leaves the office by midnight. *Transit mail* originates in, and is destined for, post offices other than the one doing the processing. This mail is processed on the day tour that ends about 4 P.M. *Incoming* mail originates in another city and is destined for local delivery; it is handled on the night tour and must be ready for the carriers at about 7 A.M.[1]

These three types of mail are normally distributed to various destinations by five letter mail sorting operations: the combined primary, the letter sorting machine operation, the outgoing secondary, the incoming primary, and the incoming secondary. The outputs of these operations are called outgoing if they are sent to another post office and local if they are destined for local delivery. The various configurations of these operations used for sorting the three mail types is shown in Figure 14.2.

1. The processing deadlines given for the three mail types are those currently used in the Postal Service. Other times could be specified by postal management.

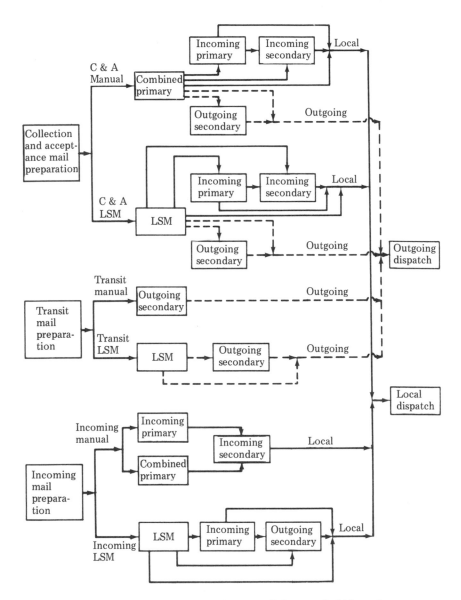

Figure 14.2 Letter mail processing. Source: Cohen et al. [1], p. 9.

All of the sorting operations except the letter sorting machine operation are entirely manual. The letter sorting machine (LSM) is a semiautomated sorting device which consists of twelve sorting consoles multiplexed to 277 output bins. At each console an operator sorts a letter by reading the address, using his scheme knowledge[2] to select an output bin number, and recording this bin number via a keyboard on the console.[3] The letter is then automatically routed to the selected output bin.

Both the combined primary and LSM operations separate local mail to zone (five digit zip code) and outgoing mail to distant states or groups of states, a few cities, and sectional centers[4] in the same state or nearby states. The outgoing secondary operation performs a finer sort of outgoing mail destined for the same state or nearby states than is done in either of the two primary operations.

Local mail that does not have a zip code on its address is sorted to zone in the incoming primary operation by experienced clerks with detailed city scheme knowledge. Local mail that has been previously sorted to zone is separated to carrier, post office box, or large firm in the incoming secondary operation.

14.3 Mail Processing Problem Areas

Two problem areas in mail processing are described in this section. The first area deals with the determination of disaggregated processing cost information that would provide postal managers with the data necessary to efficiently distribute the total volumes of the three mail types among the five sorting operations. The second problem area is that of evaluating the cost savings from mechanized sorting equipment in the face of large volume variations and performance requirements. Both of these areas were investigated in Cohen, et al. [1], a study in which the author participated.

Current Sorting Costs

A major problem in mail processing has been the lack of an accounting system that would allow the computation of costs at a

2. Scheme knowledge is acquired by memorizing the correspondence of all possible addresses to the various bin numbers.
3. During 1971, many LSMs were converted to ZIP Mail Translators (ZMTs). The ZMT console operator merely keys in the zip code given in the letter address; a computer is used to establish the correspondence between zip codes and bin numbers. The need for operator scheme knowledge is thus eliminated.
4. A sectional center serves as a distribution center for cities with the same first three digits in their zip codes.

suitably disaggregated level. Currently, mail volume and mail processing labor man-hour figures are kept for each sorting operation on a daily basis under an accounting system known as the Work Load Recording System (WLRS). This costing system ignores the basic network structure of the sorting operations. A letter of a particular type may initially be routed to any of two or sometimes three operations. For example, an outgoing collection and acceptance letter may be initially sent either to the combined primary or LSM operations. Not only do these two operations have different sorting costs, but their depth of sort is different; that is, the LSM has more outgoing bins than the combined primary and thus will send a smaller fraction of its output to the outgoing secondary operation for further sorting.

A more meaningful accounting system for postal management would provide the average sorting costs (including all sorts by all operations) as a function of mail type and initial operation.[5] This information could be used by postal managers to direct the flow of the three types of mail to the various initial operations so as to achieve lower sorting costs.

Cost Savings from Mechanized Sorting Equipment
An often-touted explanation for the lack of improvement in postal productivity in the last decade has been the lack of technological improvements in mail processing. The LSM is currently the only mechanized sorting device in widespread use across the country. Although improvements in sorting productivity [8] have been realized through the use of the LSM, the fact remains that clerks are still required for sorting mail with this machine.

This sorting function is performed automatically by the optical character reading machine. Currently, ten of these devices have been deployed in a few offices across the country. These optical character readers (OCRs) employ electronic scanning techniques to read a letter address and a computer to direct the letter to the proper output bin. The current OCR has had only limited success because it can only "read" a small number of type fonts.

In all post offices there are large daily and hourly mail volume fluctuations which have the effect of lowering the average utilization of the sorting machines.

5. Since a letter entering a particular operation for its primary sort may or may not receive secondary and/or tertiary sorts, an average cost weighted by the actual volume that received one, two, or three sorts must be computed.

As an example of the daily volume variations, Figure 14.3 shows a histogram of observed total daily mail volumes in the Cincinnati, Ohio, Post Office over a period of a year. It can be seen that these daily volumes range from a low of 400,000 pieces to a high of 4,000,000 pieces. The highly variable nature of the demand for these mechanized sorting devices makes it difficult to estimate their cost savings.

The demands for processing service also vary widely during the course of a day principally because of the arrival pattern of collection and acceptance mail. Many businesses send out their mail just before quitting time on each work day. As a result of this practice, the local post office receives from 40 to 60 percent of its collection and acceptance mail volume during the four-hour period from 4 P.M. to 8 P.M. Since the normal processing deadline for collection and acceptance mail is midnight, a severe peaking problem results. The arrival rates of transit and incoming mail are much more uniform throughout the day, thus resulting in relatively little further aggravation of the problem.

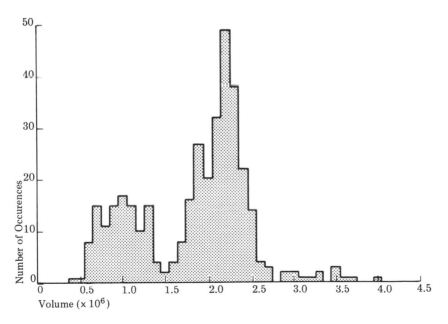

Figure 14.3 Histogram of daily letter mail volumes in Cincinnati. Source: Cohen et al. [1], p. 89.

Since sorting machines are rather expensive,[6] their cost effectiveness depends heavily on their utilization, which in turn depends on the variability of demand. Pigeonhole cases, on the other hand, are extremely cheap, and some clerks are paid to work on an hourly basis only. Furthermore, clerks working on low-priority (third or fourth class) mail can be sent to work in the high-priority letter mail processing operations during high demand periods. The manual sorting system is thus quite flexible in terms of handling highly variable demands.

A model that takes this lack of flexibility of mechanized sorting equipment into account when estimating the cost savings of the equipment is described in the next section.

14.4 Models of the Mail Processing System

A Model for Determining Sorting Costs

A simple Markov model will be described that is useful for determining the total intraoffice sorting cost per letter as a function of mail type and initial operation. It is assumed that an average value for this cost is a meaningful figure, that is, the daily and hourly cost variations cancel out when measured over a sufficiently long period. It is also assumed that all error flows result from missorts in the LSM operation.[7] Finally, the (Markov) assumption is made that the probability that a letter will go to operation j after being sorted in operation i depends only on i.

In order to determine the average sorting costs for a particular mail type, it is necessary to know the average productivity in pieces per man-hour in each sorting operation, the average labor cost per man-hour (including overhead) in each operation, and average values for the "branching probabilities" of flows to and from all the operations for that mail type.[8] The first two items can be determined in a straightforward manner from accounting information kept in each post office. The matrix of branching probabilities for a particular mail type k can be thought of as a simple Markov transition probability matrix, $\overline{P}(k)$ where the i,jth element of the matrix is the probability that a type k letter currently being handled in operation i will next be handled in opera-

6. About $130,000 for an LSM, $700,000 for an OCR.
7. From p. 53 [1], LSM error rates range from 6 to 18 percent manual error rates are about 1 percent.
8. Capital investment costs are not included: they are treated as sunk costs.

tion j. These transition probability matrices can be estimated using data from the WLRS.

Using the theory of Markov processes [2], the matrix $\overline{N}(k)$ can be determined, where the i,jth element, denoted $n_{ij}(k)$, is the average number of times a type k letter is handled in operation j, given that it was first handled in operation i. A simple model for determining the total sorting cost as a function of mail type and initial operation is then

$$C_i(k) = \sum_{j=1}^{5} n_{ij}(k)\,(L_j/R_j),$$

where

R_j = average productivity of operation i (pieces/man-hour);

L_j = average labor cost per man-hour for operation i (dollars/man-hour); and

$C_i(k)$ = average sorting cost for type k mail that is initially handled by operation i (dollars/piece).

This procedure was applied to find the sorting costs for two post offices, Cincinnati, Ohio and Washington, D.C. The resulting costs are given in Table 14.1.

Table 14.1   Total Sorting Cost by Mail Type and Initial Operation*
(dollars per thousand letters)

Office	Mail Type	Initial Operation[†]			
		Combined Primary	Outgoing Secondary	LSM	Incoming Primary
Cincinnati, Ohio	Collection and acceptance	18.20	—	11.90	NA[§]
	Transit	—	10.00	8.50	NA
	Incoming	20.10	—	16.00	NA
Washington, D.C.	Collection and acceptance	17.10	—	12.30	—
	Transit	—	13.00	9.30	—
	Incoming	24.90	—	23.00	29.40

*Source: Cohen, et al. [1], pp. A-45, 46.
†The incoming secondary operation is not normally an initial operation for first class mail.
§ Cincinnati's post office does not have an incoming primary operation.

Several observations can be made from the figures shown in Table 14.1. First, there are dramatic differences between corresponding cost elements in the two offices. The result is further substantiated by the WLRS monthly reports on productivity for 72 large post offices [8]. These reports show that the productivity for some operations may be as much as three times greater in some offices than in others. The reasons for this effect are not well understood at the present time.

The costs shown also vary widely by mail type. This is not very surprising, since the sorting requirements for each mail type vary considerably. A more interesting result is that the costs for a particular mail type in a particular office vary considerably by initial operation. For these two offices, it is always cheaper to send mail initially to the LSM for sorting, provided that the LSM has excess capacity at the time.

This cost accounting system could be implemented very easily on a routine basis using the Markov model described previously and a new Postal Service data collection system known as the Postal Source Data System (PSDS). The PSDS is a recording system in which the mail volume figures are entered into a central data bank via a number of time-sharing consoles in various locations around each of about 100 large post offices. Reports could be automatically prepared that would provide both local post office officials and central USPS management with useful data for making day-to-day decisions on man-power allocation by operation and mail type.

A Model for Estimating Cost Savings from Sorting Machinery

In this part a model is described that is useful for estimating realistic upper bounds on the cost savings derivable from sorting machinery. This model is designed to estimate the minimum total sorting costs in a post office over a period of one or more years, subject to current service requirements and projected demand requirements, for a combined manual and mechanized system. Clearly, this goal is not the only objective of a post office. The presentation in this part is only intended to illustrate how a model suitable for accomplishing this particular goal has been developed.

The model for estimating minimum total sorting costs is basically a standard linear programming model. The cost per piece in an office as a function of mail type and initial operation is assumed to be known as a result of applying the methods described previously. The daily volumes of the three mail types are assumed to be predictable over the period of interest.[9] The patterns of hourly demand requirements are assumed to be dictated by the arrival rates and the processing deadlines of the three types of mail. Figure 14.4 depicts typical cumulative arrival patterns with processing deadlines for collection and acceptance, transit, and incoming mail of 12 P.M., 4 P.M., and 7 A.M., respectively.[10] In the model, it is further assumed that all mail is processed by either the

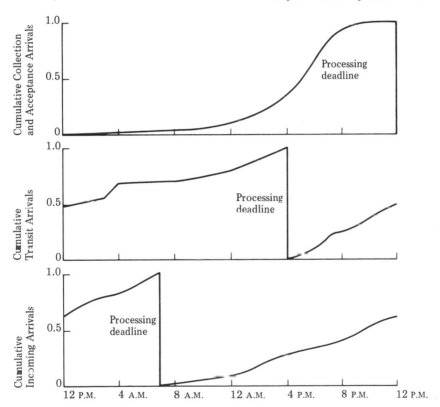

Figure 14.4   Mail arrivals for the Cincinnati, Ohio, Post Office. Source: Cohen et al. [1], p. 87.

9. Current daily volumes can be obtained from WLRS data; projections are based on a 3.4 percent annual increase. See Cohen, et al. p. 90 [1].
10. As mentioned in Section 14.2, other deadlines could be specified by postal management.

manual or the mechanized system in time to meet these processing deadlines.[11] Since the mechanized system has a fixed capacity based on the maximum number of operator positions and the sorting rate of each operator, this implies the manual system must meet the service requirements for the mail not processed by machine.

The basic linear programming model minimizes the total of hourly sorting costs over a 24-hour period as a function of total daily volume V. The objective function can be written

$$Z^*(V) = \min \sum_{i=1}^{3} \sum_{j=1}^{24} \{C_p(i)V_p(i,j) + C_m(i)V_m(i,j)\},$$

where

$Z^*(V)$ = minimum total cost of sorting a daily volume V,
$C_p(i)$ = manual sorting cost for type i mail,
$C_m(i)$ = machine sorting cost for type i mail,
$V_p(i,j)$ = volume of type i mail processed during hour j by the manual system,
$V_m(i,j)$ = volume of type i mail processed during hour j by the mechanized system.

The capacity constraint on the mechanized system can be stated

$$\sum_{i=1}^{3} \frac{V_m(i,j)}{R_m(i)} \leqslant 1, \text{ all } j,$$

where

$R_m(i)$ = capacity of mechanized system for type i mail (pieces/ hour).

Constraints due to arrival rate patterns and processing deadlines must also be written. For all feasible solutions to the linear program, the cumulative amount of type i mail processed since the last processing deadline must always be less than the cumulative arrival rate for type i mail. Stated mathematically, this constraint becomes

11. This assumption is generally verified by data; inventories of mail held from one day to the next are very small except for several days during the pre-Christmas rush.

$$\sum_{t_i=1}^{k} \{V_m\,(i,t_i) + V_p\,(i,t_i)\} \leqslant \sum_{t_i=1}^{k} A(i,t_i) \cdot V,$$

$i = 1, 2, 3; k = 1, 2, \ldots, 24$

where

t_i = hours since the last processing deadline for type i mail,
$A(i,t_i)$ = fraction of total daily mail volume which is type i mail arriving during hour t_i.

The minimum annual sorting cost is just the sum of the minimum costs for each day of the year. Thus

$$Y_1 = \sum_{T=1}^{365} Z^*(V_T)$$

where

Y_1 = minimum annual sorting cost, and
$Z^*(V_T)$ = minimum daily sorting cost for sorting a total daily mail volume V_T.

To estimate the minimum sorting cost for future years, three factors were taken into account. First, the nationwide mail volume has increased each year. Second, the real wage of postal employees has shown a steady growth. Finally, the time value of money was taken into account by discounting future costs at an appropriate discount rate. Combining the effects of these factors, we can evaluate the present value of the minimum sorting cost, call it Y_n, for any future year

$$Y_n = \frac{(1+w)^{n-1}}{(1+r)^{n-1}} \sum_{T=1}^{365} Z^*[(1+v)^{n-1} V_T],$$

where

w = annual real postal wage increase factor,
r = annual discount rate,
v = annual mail volume increase factor, and
V_T = mail volume on corresponding day of current year.

It must be remembered that the model described here estimates only the total operating cost of a manual system and a particular

mechanized system over a period of time. When making investment decisions, the initial equipment cost must be added to this
cost. Since this exercise can be done for mechanized systems with
different initial costs, different capacities, and so on, the model
can be used to determine the optimal size (capacity) of a mechanized system.

Results from the linear programming model for minimizing total
sorting costs over a period of time showed that cost savings from
mechanization may be seriously overstated if daily and hourly volume fluctuations and daily processing deadlines are not taken into
account. For example, assume that one wished to estimate the
yearly savings of an LSM system in Cincinnati with a daily capacity equal to the average daily total mail volume in Cincinnati. The
naive approach would be to take the difference in costs per letter
between the LSM and manual initial operations for each mail type
given in Table 14.1, multiply the difference by the corresponding
average yearly volume for that mail type, and sum the resulting
savings over the three mail types. The total yearly savings indicated by the linear programming model, however, are the 25
percent less than the total obtained from the naive method, since
with the proposed number of mechanized sorters, a significant
amount of mail must be manually sorted due to machine capacity
constraints.

One use for this model would be to improve the scheduling efficiency of existing mechanized equipment. It is possible that the
processing savings could be increased by changing the input mix
of mail types during certain periods of the day.

Perhaps the primary use of such a model, however, would be in
the area of investment decisions for new mechanized sorting equipment. The net present value of the savings from various alternative
systems would provide a convenient means for ranking various
equipment investment alternatives. The linear programming model
could be readily implemented on any moderate-sized computer.

14.5 Survey of Postal Systems Work

There have been surprisingly few articles or books written on the
subject of postal systems analysis in the professional literature of
systems analysis and operations research. The objective of a study
by Oliver and Samuel [3] was to find analytical methods for
minimizing intraoffice letter delays. Optimal man-power schedul-

ing and dispatching rules were derived as a means for reducing
these delays, subject to the restriction that total processing costs
remain constant. An operational test of these rules was conducted
in the Detroit, Michigan, Post Office. Intraoffice letter delays were
apparently reduced by 25 percent.

A brief follow-up to this paper written by Samuel [4] provides
an introductory analysis of the factors which should be considered
when total letter delay time (from collection to delivery) is the desired measure of effectiveness for postal performance.

A book by Tulkens [7] contains an exposition of several total
postal system problems using the framework of economic theory.
The techniques of mathematical programming are employed to
generate optimal solutions to resource allocation problems.
Duality theory is then applied to these solutions with the goal of
determining a meaningful pricing strategy for post office services.
The book provides a structure for formulating many problems involving the total postal system. However, the models described are
either too large in terms of computational requirements or are too
abstract to be of immediate use to the postal systems analyst.

The Kappel Commission Report [6] contains a great deal of
descriptive information about the post office which would be very
useful to the potential postal analyst. The deficiencies found in
the present state of mail service, postal employment, and postal
finance are itemized in the report. Recommendations are given
which suggest that a largely nonpolitical postal corporation be
formed which has the power to establish postal rates, subject to
veto by Congress.

References

1. Cohen, R., C. McBride, R. Thoronton, and T. White, *Letter Mail System
Reference Design: An Analytical Method for Evaluating Candidate Mechanization*, Institute for Defense Analyses, Report R-168, 1970.

2. Howard, R. A., *Dynamic Programming and Markov Processes*, Technology
Press, Massachusetts Institute of Technology, 1960.

3. Oliver, R. M., and A. H. Samuel, "Reducing Letter Delays in Post Offices,"
Operations Research, vol. 10, 1962.

4. Samuel, A. H., "Reduction of Letter Delays Between Post Offices," *Operations Research*, vol. 11, 1963.

5. *System Engineering Program*, Communications and Systems, Inc., Report
No. 105-68-4-1.

6. *Towards Postal Excellence: The Report of the President's Commission on
Postal Organization*, 1968.

7. Tulkens, H., *Programming Analysis of the Postal Service*, Librairie Universitaire, Louvain, Belgium, 1962.

8. *Work Load Recording System Accounting Period 9 Report*, Bureau of Operations, U.S. Post Office Department, 1970.

15

Driver Accident Models and Their Use in Policy Evaluation

Joseph Ferreira, Jr.

15.1 Introduction

This chapter presents two specific examples in which quantitative models are used as an aid in evaluating alternative government programs that affect the involvement of motorists in accidents and the compensation of selected accident victims for portions of their losses. Questions regarding driver licensing, traffic safety, emergency health services, liability for accident losses, and auto accident insurance have been debated for more than fifty years. However, it is only recently that such questions have been examined in the context of a comprehensive approach toward government involvement with the automobile accident and compensation issues [16,22].

Legislators and government administrators are faced with a choice between "fault" and "no-fault" insurance. They determine the level of expenditures on highway safety projects and driver training programs, and they establish criteria to be used in licensing drivers, adjusting insurance premium rates, and compensating accident victims. Most quantitative analyses have focused on resolving specific isolated questions and have been of limited value to the policy makers interested in comparing alternative, yet untried, programs. For example, such analyses—usually supported by either insurance companies, legal foundations, or state motor vehicle departments— have investigated the correlation between certain driver characteristics, the drivers' accident records, and the fraction of economic loss for which certain accident victims are compensated or the level of overhead costs involved in insuring drivers under the present system. The specialized studies provide factual information about the current system and identify factors that are important in predicting the effects of change. However, they do not explicitly relate their results to policy questions in terms of providing measures of effectiveness for predetermined objectives. An explicit model for the government's interaction with the accident and compensation process is absent, and consideration of the tradeoffs among critical factors is neglected.

To be sure, data problems and shortcomings in the understanding of behavioral patterns are many—a number of these difficulties will be discussed shortly. However, tens of millions of dollars are spent annually to collect data concerning automobile accidents and the compensation of accident victims; and it is an unfortunate fact that many of these data are collected without any particular evaluation program in mind and only to meet legal requirements set by independent agencies. Much useful work can be done to develop systematic and quantitative approaches toward evaluating alternative program choices.

This chapter investigates two problems of direct concern to policy makers. The problems were brought to the attention of the author while he served on the U.S. Department of Transportation's Federal Auto Insurance and Compensation Study, and they concern overrepresentation of particular groups of drivers in accidents and efforts to decrease accidents by retraining certain drivers. Many detailed results and models for driver behavior and accident involvement are available. The research reported here utilizes available data sources and builds on models and results already developed in specialized analyses. It was thought that working on such problems would best illustrate the potential role of the operations research analyst in formulating quantitative approaches to policy evaluation.

15.2 Overrepresentation in Accident Statistics
The National Safety Council [18] estimates that motorists in the United States account for 15 million accidents each year and, as a result, incur direct wage losses and medical expenses of 3.7 billion dollars and property damage losses of 3.8 billion dollars per year. Licensing authorities, state and federal legislators, and other officials are often advised that a small fraction of drivers account for the majority of accidents and that removing them from the road would reduce the total number of accidents dramatically. This advice is based on a popular notion concerning the role of chance and causal factors in automobile crashes that presumes all drivers are either "good" or "bad." Drivers who "cause" accidents are regarded as accident-prone and are thought to be a small, identifiable group that is guilty of hazardous driving, vastly overrepresented in accident statistics, and solely responsible for the "accident problem."

The policy implications of such an attitude are straightforward. If "chance" is thought to play a small role in accident causation, and if driver accident experience is regarded as a good indicator of driver risk, then a compensation system that charges "at fault" drivers for their accident losses is considered equitable, and programs that retrain hazardous drivers and/or remove them from the road are given priority.

Proponents of the overrepresentation theory cite statistics such as "the 6% of all families[1] with several accidents accounted for not less than 45% of all accidents" [20]. In searching for overrepresentation of groups of accident-involved drivers, it is quite natural to compare the size of the group of drivers with the fraction of accidents in which they are involved. Statistics such as the "6% cause 45%" figure just mentioned do, indeed, sound abnormally high. However, the time period included in the accident data is critical—a single week's data would surely indicate that less than 1% of all families accounted for all accidents recorded that week. The appropriate basis for comparison of the 6% subgroup of families is not the 45% figure but that percentage of accidents for which the 6% would be expected to account *if* all families were *equally likely* to be involved in accidents or *if* specific variations in accident likelihood existed.

The mathematical tools required to make such comparisons are well known, and the problem of identifying high-risk drivers has been the subject of many specialized studies. However, the available mathematical techniques have not been used to make careful interpretations of the "6% account for 45%" statistics in order to provide results in a form useful to policy makers. An attempt at such an analysis is made in the next several sections. A sample of six-year driver accident records is used to estimate the fraction of drivers involved in accidents during various time periods. The results are then compared with those that would be expected (1) if all drivers were equally likely to be involved in accidents and (2) if specific differences in accident likelihood among drivers existed.

Observations Based on ITTE Data

Most estimates of the fraction of drivers involved in accidents are developed from department of motor vehicle records, which indicate the number of accidents in which each individual driver has been involved. Since approximately 75% of all auto accidents in-

1. Individual family experience rather than driver experience was collected in this case for reasons connected with other aspects of the Michigan study. Similar statistics have been cited for individual drivers [11].

volve two or more drivers [18], the same accident will often appear on the records of two or more individuals. Thus a count of
the total number of *accident involvements* recorded on driver
accident records will produce a number almost twice as large as
the total number of *accidents*. Statistics such as "6% of the drivers
accounted for 45% of the accidents" are usually developed from
driver record samples. Though the term "45% of the accidents" is
used, the data really indicate involvement, and thus "45% of all
accident *involvements*" would be more appropriate. In this report,
the percentage of drivers accounting for various proportions of all
accident involvements is estimated. The sensitivity of the results
to this distinction is considered in another report by the author
[11].

Since the overall average time between individual involvements
in reported accidents is on the order of ten years, accident data
covering as long a time period as possible are desired. However,
obtaining large samples of driver accident data covering a period
of more than three years is quite difficult since, until recently,
most motor vehicle departments had purged records of information more than three years old, and insurance company records
had not been kept in a manner suitable for tabulation of accident
data for a controlled sample of drivers.

As a result of my association with the Department of Transportation's Federal Auto Insurance and Compensation Study, six-year
accident data for a random sample of 7,842 California licensed
drivers were made available by Dr. Albert Burg of the Institute for
Transportation and Traffic Engineering (ITTE) at the University
of California, Los Angeles [4,5]. These data covered the longest
time period of the available data sources and were developed from
records of the California Department of Motor Vehicles, widely
recognized as having reliable driver accident data suitable for research purposes [17].

The ITTE data identify the dates of all state-reported accidents
occurring between November 1959 and February 1968 and involving at least one of the 7,842 drivers. During that time, California state law required reporting of all accidents involving bodily
injury and/or property damage in excess of $100. (The minimum
has since been changed to $200.) The only exception is that an
accident was omitted from a driver's record if his car was stopped
and he was not at the wheel at the time of the accident.

A total of 3,877 accidents were recorded; the number of drivers involved in a total of 0, 1, 2, 3, . . . accidents is given in Table 15.1 (along with other information to be discussed shortly). The final list developed from the data for use in this report specified the number of drivers out of the total driver population described by each possible six-digit combination, $x(1), x(2), \ldots, x(6)$, where $x(i)$ = the number of accident involvements during the ith year i = 1, 2, 3, 4, 5, 6.[2] A list of 144 such combinations resulted.

Some shorthand notation for the percentage of drivers accounting for various percentages of all accidents will facilitate the discussion of overrepresentation. We define $D(X,T)$ to be the minimum percentage of ITTE drivers whose individual accident records during the first T years include $X\%$ of all ITTE accident involvements recorded during that time. The "minimum" percentage is specified, since we want to be sure that drivers most frequently involved in accidents are counted first.

The $D(X,T)$ figures were obtained by first sorting the 144 accident combinations in descending order according to the total number of accidents during the first T years. The list was scanned, and the number of drivers and accident involvements were totaled until $X\%$ of all involvements had been counted. Hence, the percentage of drivers included up to that point equals $D(X,T)$. For example, $D(50,6)$ = 10 would indicate that half of all accident involvements recorded during six years were accounted for by the 10% of the drivers whose accident records indicated, in this case, two or more involvements during the six years.

The observed $D(X,T)$ values are plotted in Figure 15.1 as a function of T for X = 25%, 75%, and 100%. A smooth curve has been drawn through each set of points to aid the reader. The difference between $D(X,T)$ and X is, in fact, quite large. For example, 20%, of the 7,842 drivers, accounted for all of the 1,911 accident involvements recorded during the first three years. During the entire

2. In the form in which it was made available, the ITTE data specified the date on which each accident occurred. However, the six-year period for each driver was not fixed, but centered around one of two possible interview dates. An extensive amount of data analysis was required to accurately define the number of accidents involving each driver during his six-year period. This analysis was done on two IBM 360/65 systems located at the Federal Highway Administration and at the Massachusetts Institute of Technology Information Processing Center and is described in Section 3.8 of another report by the author [12].

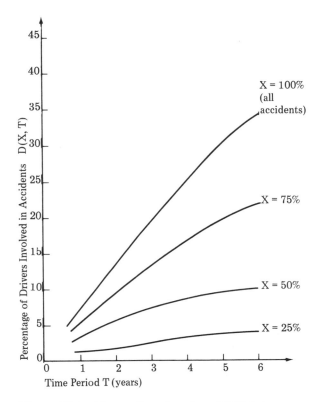

Figure 15.1   Observations based on ITTE data.

six years, 4% or 311 of the drivers, accounted for 25% of the 3,877 accidents.

The $D(X, T)$ values for the percentage of drivers accounting for X% of all accident involvements during T years depend strongly on T and, by themselves, are questionable indicators of overrepresentation in accidents. At first glance, one anticipates that $D(X, T)$ would differ from X unless all drivers were equally likely to be involved in accidents. However, $D(X, T)$ values obtained over short time periods are misleading. In order to make reliable comparisons and demonstrate the relationships among time, accident frequency, and $D(X, T)$, the next several sections develop predicted values for $D(X, T)$ based on certain assumptions about differences in accident likelihood among drivers.

An "Equally Likely" Accident Model

The first step is to predict the fraction of drivers that would be expected to account for various percentages of all accident involvements *if* all drivers were *equally likely* to be involved in accidents. Making such predictions requires explicit consideration of the manner by which individual motorists would be involved in accidents over time if the equally likely assumptions were true. The simplest such model is to regard all reported accidents as equivalent, to assume that the likelihood of being involved in accidents during separate time periods is independent, and to assume that the accident likelihood[3] of drivers may be characterized in terms of a single parameter r, which has the same value for each driver and remains constant from one year to the next.

Such assumptions amount to regarding individual involvement in accidents as independent renewal processes and assuming that each driver is involved in $i = 0, 1, 2, \ldots$ accidents during T years according to a Poisson probability distribution

$$P_1(i \mid T, r) = \frac{(rT)^i e^{-rT}}{i!}, \qquad i = 0, 1, 2, \ldots \tag{15.1}$$

where the parameter r is interpreted to be the driver's accident likelihood, or his expected number of accidents per year.

The Poisson distribution is well known among actuaries, biologists, and industrial safety researchers [3,13]. It is frequently used to model "pure chance" phenomena because of its underlying independent increments, homogeneity, and "one event at a time" assumptions.

One might suspect that any accident model that assigns the same accident likelihood to all drivers is an oversimplication of reality—indeed we shall find this to be the case. However, it is used in this section to provide base estimates of $D(X, T)$ values—estimates that would result *if* all drivers were *equally likely* to be involved in accidents. The contention is that the Poisson accident model provides a plausible description of the driver accident records that would be observed under such circumstances.

---

3. The term "accident likelihood" is used rather than "accident-proneness" since environmental factors as well as driver skill are included.

Predictions Based on the Poisson Model

For notational convenience, we shall use D_1 (X,T,r) to denote the predicted values for $D(X,T)$ obtained using the "equally likely" Poisson accident model with parameter r. Thus $D_1 (X,T,r)$ is the expected minimum percentage of drivers who would account for $X\%$ of all accident involvements reported during T years if accidents were a pure chance phenomenon and all drivers had the same accident likelihood r. Values of $D_1 (X,T,r)$ may be estimated using the Poisson accident model.

According to the Poisson model, the probability $P_1 (i \mid T,r)$ that any individual driver is involved in i accidents during T years may also be interpreted as the fraction of all drivers expected to have a total of exactly i accidents during T years. Thus, the percentage of drivers expected to have at least k accidents each during T years is

$$100 R_1 (k) \equiv 100 \sum_{i=k}^{\infty} P_1 (i \mid T,r).$$

The total number of accidents involving these drivers with k or more accidents each during T years is simply the total number of drivers times the right-tail expected value

$$G_1 (k) \equiv \sum_{i=k}^{\infty} iP_1 (i \mid T,r).$$

Thus the percentage

$$D_1 (X,T,r) = 100 R_1 (k)$$

of drivers with k or accidents is expected to account for

$$X = 100 \frac{G_1 (k)}{G_1 (0)} = 100 \frac{G_1 (k)}{rT}$$

percent of all accident involvements recorded during T years.

Since k is restricted to the values $0,1,2, \ldots$, it is not always possible, for any given X, to obtain an integer k such that

$$100 \frac{G_1 (k)}{rT} = X.$$

For example, X might be 50%, whereas all drivers with two or more accidents account for only 45% of all accident involvements; and some, but not all, of the one-accident drivers would have to be included to account for the last 5%. Where necessary, linear interpolation was used to take such considerations into account. Values for $D(X,T,r)$ were obtained for various values of X by using the CP 67/CMS time-sharing facility of the M.I.T. Information Processing Center. In order that $D_1 (X,T,r)$ values would be comparable to the results obtained using the ITTE data, r was set equal to 0.0822, the observed average annual accident rate.

Figure 15.2 compares the actual values of $D(X,T)$ for the ITTE data with the $D_1 (X,T,r)$ values predicted using the Poisson accident model. The shaded area represents the difference between the actual and expected results and may be explained in terms of some variation in accident likelihood among drivers. That is, the fraction of drivers accounting for, say, 75% of the accidents during a five-year period is not expected to be 75%. In fact, the 20% figure reported for the ITTE data differs by only 3.5% from the figure that would be expected if all drivers were equally likely to be involved in accidents.

At first glance, it is natural to suspect that the "equally likely" assumption would result in accidents distributed evenly among all drivers. That is, one anticipates that eventually all drivers would have at least one accident, about 50% of the drivers would be needed to account for 50% of the accidents, and so on. It is obvious from Figure 15.2, however, that the time period that would be needed before such results would occur is much longer than 10 years. In fact, $D_1 (X,T,r)$ lags behind X even for large T in cases where $X < 100\%$. When $T = 50$ years, for example, $D_1 (50,50, 0.0822) = 32\%$ and $D_1 (75,50,0.0822) = 56\%$. Reflection on the method used to calculate $D_1 (X,T,r)$ supports these findings. Eventually, we would expect all drivers to have at least one accident, so that $D_1 (100,T,r)$ should approach 100%. However, over any specified time period, some "unlucky" drivers would have more accidents than others, and $D_1 (X,T,r)$ would remain less than X for values of X less than 100%.

The Negative Binomial Accident Model
The Poisson accident model assumed that all drivers were equally likely to be involved in accidents and assigned to each the same

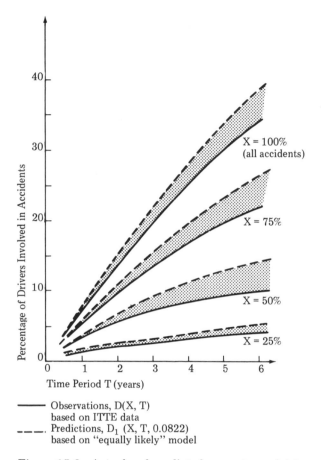

Figure 15.2   Actual and predicted percentage of drivers involved in X percent of all accidents occuring during T years (Case 1).

value for the accident likelihood r. To allow for differences among drivers, this assumption is now relaxed. Individuals are again assumed to be involved in accidents independently according to the Poisson distribution of Equation 15.1; however, the particular value of the parameter r is now permitted to vary among individual drivers in the population. In particular, the value of r associated with a generic driver is regarded as a random variable, the probability density function of which is the gamma-1 function,

$$f_r(\alpha) = f(\alpha|k,m) = \frac{k/m}{\Gamma(k)} \left(\alpha \frac{k}{m} \right)^{k-1} e^{-\alpha \frac{k}{m}}, \qquad a \geqslant 0, \tag{15.2}$$

where the two nonnegative parameters k and m may be fitted to
sample driver accident records [1,3]. The use of a gamma-1 function for the distribution of accident likelihood is desirable since it
is the natural conjugate family for Poisson sampling and will facilitate a Bayesian approach toward estimating accident likelihood,
which will be developed in subsequent sections.

Although this choice of parameters k and m to describe the
gamma-1 family differs from those commonly used in the literature, it facilitates their interpretation and also their estimation,
since estimates of k and m are very nearly independent [1]. The
m parameter of the gamma-1 family may be interpreted as the
average annual accident rate of the entire driver population (0.082
accidents per year in the ITTE sample). The larger the value of k,
the more concentrated the distribution. For the $k = 1.00$ case, a
simple negative exponential curve results. A graph of the gamma-1
function using values for the k and m parameters fitted to the
ITTE data will be presented later.

This compound Poisson accident model was first suggested by
Greenwood and Woods [13] in 1919 in a study of industrial accidents. It is sometimes referred to as a negative binomial model
since the resulting probability that a randomly selected driver is
involved in i accidents during T years is now a negative binomial
distribution,

$$P_2(i|T,k,m) = \int_0^\infty P_1(i|T,r) f_r(a)\, da$$

$$= \frac{\Gamma(k+i)}{i!\,\Gamma(k)} \left(\frac{k}{k+mT} \right)^k \left(\frac{mt}{k+mT} \right)^i \tag{15.3}$$

where $i = 0,1,2, \ldots ; k \geqslant 0$ and $m \geqslant 0$.[4]

In Table 15.1, the actual number of drivers in the ITTE sample
involved in a total of $0,1,2,3, \ldots$ accidents during all six years is
compared with predictions based on the simple Poisson model and

---

4. The model is also referred to as the "accident-proneness" model since it
assumes that a driver's accident likelihood does not change from year to year
and that some drivers have higher accident likelihoods than others.

Table 15.1   Theoretical and Actual Accident Distributions

No. of Accidents	Actual No. of Drivers*	Poisson Predictions[†]	Negative Binomial Predictions[§]
0	5,147	4,789	5,140
1	1,859	2,362	1,874
2	595	582	586
3	167	96	173
4	54	12	50
5	14	1	14
6+	6	0	5
	7,842	7,842	7,842

$$\chi^2 = 477 \ 4 \ \text{d.f.} \qquad \chi^2 = 0.99 \ 4 \ \text{d.f.}$$

*ITTE accident data for 7,842 drivers over six years.
[†]Predictions using the Poisson accident model assuming all drivers have the same accident likelihood $r = 0.0822$, the average accident rate observed in the ITTE sample.
[§]Predictions using the negative accident model where the k and m parameters have been fitted to the ITTE data using the method of moments; $k = 1.40$, $m = 0.0822$.

on the negative binomial model. The parameters are fitted using the method of moments. For the negative binomial model, this method [1] has been shown to be the most efficient for the observed range of values for k and m.

Several other tests of the accuracy of the negative binomial model were made. Specific results of these tests have been reported elsewhere by the author [12]. They indicated that (1) the times at which accident repeaters in the ITTE sample were involved in accidents during the six-year period were dispersed in a manner consistent with the Poisson model for individual accident experience; (2) the compound Poisson hypothesis appeared to be a more appropriate explanation of accident experience than did a "contagious" hypothesis that assumed accident likelihood was a linear function of past accidents; and (3) fits of the negative binomial distribution to various sample data indicated that variations in the estimates of the k and m parameters were not enough to significantly change the shape of the predicted distribution of accident likelihood.

In the next section, the negative binomial model will be used to predict another set of $D(X,T)$ values. Judging from the accuracy of the model indicated by the above results, we expect these predictions to be much closer to the actual $D(X,T)$ values than were those based on the Poisson model.

Predictions Based on the Negative Binomial Model

For notational convenience, we shall use D_2 (X,T,k,m) to denote the predicted values for $D(X,T)$ obtained using the negative binomial accident model with parameters k and m. Thus, D_2 (X,T, k,m) is the expected minimum percentage of drivers accounting for $X\%$ of all accident involvements during T years if the compound Poisson hypotheses underlying the negative binomial model with parameters k and m were valid.

The method used to obtain values for D_2 (X,T,k,m) is completely analogous to that used in calculating D_1 (X,T,r) for the Poisson accident model, though computationally more difficult. To make the values of D_2 (X,T,k,m) comparable to the $D(X,T)$ results obtained from the ITTE data, the fitted values of the k and m parameters from Table 15.1 were used ($k = 1.40$ and $m = 0.0822$). In Figure 15.3, these values for D_2 $(X,T,1.40,0.0822)$ are compared with the observed results $D(X,T)$. Note how well the predicted and actual figures agree.[5] The curves no longer diverge as T increases, as they did in Figure 15.2 where the equally likely model was used.

What distribution of accident likelihood among drivers is suggested by the fitted gamma-1 functions? Figure 15.4 graphs the distribution implied by the k and m values used to obtain the D_2 (X,T,k,m) predictions. (The height of the curve is scaled so that the area underneath equals 1.) Substantial differences in driver accident likelihood are, in fact, predicted; however, the vast majority of drivers have quite low accident likelihoods. For the $k = 1.40$ case, 93% of all drivers are predicted to have an accident likelihood $r \leqslant 0.10$.[6] The most likely value for r is about 0.025 (one reportable accident every 40 years).

The predicted accident distribution of Figure 15.4 may also be used to estimate the fraction of all accidents that involve drivers whose actual accident likelihood falls in a particular interval. Once

5. The standard error of the predictions, the results for other values of k and m, and a discussion of what constitutes a significant deviation are given in another report by the author [11].
6. That is, $\int_0^{0.2} f(a \mid k,m)\, da = 0.93$.

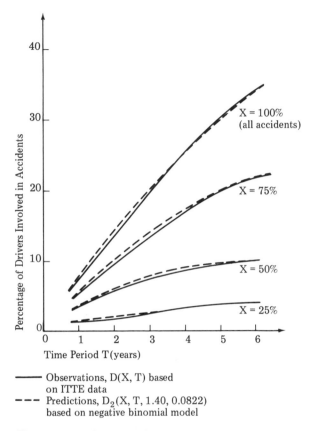

Figure 15.3   Actual and predicted percentage of drivers involved in X percent of all accidents occurring during T years (Case 2).

again the calculations are made by using right-tail cumulative and right-tail expected value functions, this time for the gamma-1 distribution $f(r|k,m)$. The predicted fraction of drivers with an actual accident likelihood $r \geqslant c$ may be expressed as $R_3(c) \equiv \int_c^\infty f(a|k,m)\,da$, the area under the right tail of the curve in the region where $r \geqslant c$. The right-tail expected value may be obtained by weighting the gamma-1 function by the accident rate r before integrating. The result, $G_3(c) \equiv \int_c^\infty af(a|k,m)\,da$, when normalized by dividing by m—the overall accident rate per driver per unit time—is the fraction of all accident involvements expected to involve the frac-

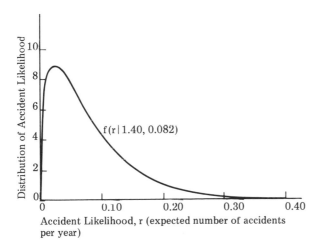

Figure 15.4   Theoretical accident likelihood distribution (based on ITTE data).

tion $R_3(c)$ of drivers with accident likelihood $r \geqslant c$. Values of $R_3(c)$ and $G_3(c)$ may be obtained using Pearson's Tables [19].

In Figure 15.5, both $R_3(c)$ and $G_3(c)$ are plotted as a function of c. We see that only 0.06% of the drivers are predicted to have accident likelihoods greater than one accident every two years and that these drivers are expected to account for only 0.38% of all accidents. Those 7% of the drivers with $r \geqslant 0.20$ (one accident every five years) are predicted to account for 22% of all accident involvements. This figure is substantial, although it is less startling than the "6% account for 45%" claim based on the estimates using accident data from short time periods.

The results of Figure 15.5 may be interpreted as long-term, steady-state estimates of the amount of overrepresentation in accidents by drivers with relatively high accident likelihood. However, the accident likelihood of any specific driver is not known. Those drivers who fit one's image of *chronic* accident repeaters— say, $r > 0.5$—are a very small group and account for a small fraction of all accident involvements. It is the drivers with accident likelihoods in the 0.1 to 0.3 range who account for a substantial proportion of the accidents. These drivers are harder to identify by examining accident records since they are infrequently involved

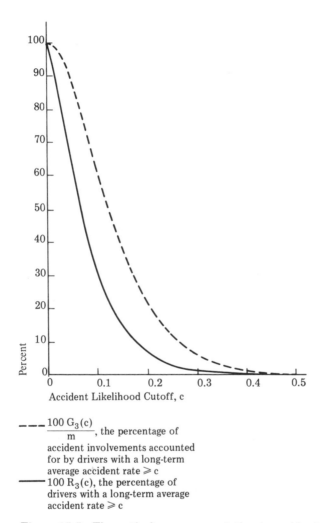

$- - -$ $\dfrac{100\ G_3(c)}{m}$, the percentage of
accident involvements accounted
for by drivers with a long-term
average accident rate $\geq c$

$-\!-$ 100 $R_3(c)$, the percentage of
drivers with a long-term average
accident rate $\geq c$

Figure 15.5   Theoretical overrepresentation in accidents.

in accidents and may be involved in no more than a handful of reported accidents during their entire lifetime.[7]

To illustrate the problem of identifying which specific drivers
are in the right tail, consider the following. As T increases, Figure 15.5 predicts that D $(22, T)$ will approach 7%. However, the
"equally likely" accident model predicts that 10% of the drivers
would account for 20% of all accident involvements occurring
during a fifty-year period. Thus, a driver's lifetime is still sufficiently short for misrepresentation due to purely chance factors
to distort the data on accident involvement by an amount similar
to the "7% account for 22%" prediction.

Section 15.2 has pointed out the extent to which statistics such
as "6% of the drivers account for 45% of the accidents" are misleading. Conclusions and policy implications based on the data
presented in Section 15.2 will be discussed in more detail in Section 15.4 after driver improvement programs have been considered.

15.3 Driver Improvement Programs

The second problem to be considered concerns the cumulative effect of operating specific driver improvement programs over several years. It is of much broader scope and will require the development of more elaborate models. Past evaluations of specific
driver improvement programs have focused on measuring a change
in accident frequency of that particular group of drivers included
in a program. To compare the merits of such programs with alternative accident reduction schemes, additional information is required. Suppose a driver training program were available that—for
a price—produced "perfect" drivers (or drivers with any specified
accident likelihood). What price should one be willing to pay for
such a program in view of the benefits likely to be obtained? How
much money should be diverted from other efforts at accident
prevention? Which drivers should be placed in the program? If
drivers were selected on the basis of accident history, what would
be the cumulative effect of such a program over several years of
operation? A systematic and quantitative approach toward answering such questions will be developed. Rather than attempting to

7. Criteria other than accident record have been used in attempts to identify
drivers with relatively high accident likelihoods [7,11]. However, the results
are far from perfect in distinguishing drivers in the $r = 0.1$ to 0.3 range, and
the low values of the absolute accident rates complicate efforts to evaluate
the usefulness of the selection criteria.

compare all possible programs and then to determine an "optimal" program, this analysis focuses on the development of classes of quantitative models that are useful in the evaluation of options available to licensing authorities. At a later stage, these models may be refined and calibrated for use in the resolution of specific issues.

Each of the fifty states provides for some type of motor vehicle authority (MVA) charged with licensing, investigating, and training motorists. An MVA might operate any of a number of "driver improvement programs" ranging from extensive remedial training courses and group or individual counseling to threatening actions such as warning letters, formal hearings, and license suspensions or revocations. Before using such programs the MVA must specify a strategy for reviewing driver record files and selecting those drivers to be included in each program. For example, California uses a "point count" as a means of selecting drivers. California state law defines an algorithm for converting the number and type of traffic convictions and accident involvements of each motorist into a personal point count and specifies the minimum number of points needed in various time periods for a driver to be classified as a negligent driver [8].

The next several sections will deal with selection strategies that utilize only accident involvement information. There are several reasons for choosing accident record as the one variable to consider. Driver record data have been found to be among the most significant predictors of future accident experience in multiple regression analyses [7]. Also, references are frequently made to "accident-prone" drivers and "accident repeaters" [3], and a treatment of licensing strategies based on accident record permits a discussion of some of these concepts. Finally, the justification for discriminatory treatment of drivers based on driver record information is not as questionable and controversial as is selective treatment based on biographic and psychological data.

Two additional assumptions that simplify the analysis will be made. First, we assume that records are reviewed at the end of each year and that only then are drivers selected for improvement.[8] The second assumption is that the training takes a negligi-

---

8. This is the cheapest method and the one commonly used. Recently, computer-aided file searches have made more frequent searches feasible.

ble amount of time, so that the full effect of the program will be realized during the next year as well as in subsequent years. Examining the effects of operating several such strategies and improvement programs will illustrate the use of probabilistic models in evaluating decision strategies that utilize streams of information as they become available over time.

The Objectives and Measures of Effectiveness
The MVA activities complement and compete with other aspects of the Automobile Accident Compensation System. Vehicle and highway safety efforts are sizable; and insurance rating plans, the fault system of reparations, and law enforcement activities are intended, in part, to deter motorists from hazardous driving. Indirectly, all branches of the system compete for funds.

In general, an MVA focuses on four primary objectives: (1) safe driving, (2) convenience to the public, (3) efficiency, and (4) "equitable" discrimination. The MVA is interested not only in reducing accident losses (presumably by means of licensing criteria and training programs) but also in minimizing the inconvenience to motorists of having to interact with the authority, and in operating its programs at minimum administrative cost. In addition, the MVA is concerned that selection strategies used to discriminate among motorists do in fact pinpoint drivers most likely to be involved in accidents.

Driver improvement programs are intended to reduce the driver's chances of causing or being involved in accidents. As a simple measure of their safe-driving effects, we shall estimate the total number of reportable accidents that are avoided during year m as a result of operating a particular program during years $1,2,\ldots,m$.

The number of drivers participating in a driver improvement program will be used as a proxy measure for the program's effect on the cost and convenience objectives listed at the beginning of this section. A typical statewide program would involve at least several hundred and more often several thousand drivers. Over such a range, operating costs are very nearly a linear function of the number of drivers included. Hence, the operating costs will depend upon the licensing strategy only in terms of the number of drivers selected, and we shall focus on estimating this number. If we assume that participation in a program is equally inconvenient to all drivers, then the total inconvenience to the public is also a linear function of the number of drivers selected.[9]

Ideally, a licensing strategy would select only those drivers with the highest accident likelihood for inclusion in the program. However, a driver's accident likelihood is not known for certain. The strategies to be considered here select drivers on the basis of their accident record. Some measure of the extent to which drivers with a particular accident history do, in fact, have high accident likelihoods is desired. The negative binomial accident model discussed in Section 15.2 will be used to obtain such a measure in terms of the probability that a driver selected for training would otherwise have had at least one accident during a subsequent time period.

Updating Accident Likelihood Estimates

Recall that the compound Poisson model provides an estimate $P_2(i \mid T,k,m)$, given in Equation 15.3, for the probability that a randomly selected driver is involved in i accidents during T years. Bayes' theorem may be used to obtain an updated estimate for drivers with any known accident history. Since the gamma-1 family is a natural conjugate family for Poisson sampling, the probability $P_2(i \mid T,k',t')$ that a generic driver with y accidents during the last τ years is involved in i accidents during the next T years again follows a negative binomial distribution. The parameters of this posterior distribution can be expressed in terms of those for the original, a priori distribution as

$$k' = k + y \qquad \text{and} \qquad t' = \left(\frac{k}{m}\right) + \tau.$$

These equations suggest that the gamma-1 prior with parameters k and m is equivalent to an initial accident "record" of k accidents in k/m years. The resulting gamma-1 function, $f''(r \mid y, \tau) \equiv f(r \mid k + y, (k/m) + \tau)$, provides an estimate of the accident likelihood distribution for drivers with accident record (y,τ).

The ITTE accident data may be used to check the accuracy of these posterior distributions. The six-year ITTE time period was divided into two periods of various lengths, and the number of

9. In actually running a program, such differences would in some cases warrant special consideration for certain drivers. For example, several states permit "occupational" licenses to be issued to drivers whose regular license has been suspended [2].

drivers out of the 7,842 total with y accidents during the first period and x during the second was obtained. If we let $N(y,\tau)$ equal the number of drivers with y accidents during the first τ years, then the number of these $N(y,\tau)$ drivers predicted to have an additional x accidents during the remaining $6 - \tau$ years is $P_2\left[x \mid 6 - \tau, k + y, (k/m) + \tau\right] \cdot N(y,\tau)$. Table 15.2 compares these predictions with the ITTE observations for the $\tau = 3$ case. The number of degrees of freedom of the chi-square estimate is con-servatively estimated by subtracting two extra degrees of freedom to account for using the same data to test the predictions as were used to fit the original k and m parameters of the accident model [9]. Since the tests are made on predictions for only a portion of the six-year period, one might argue that the full two degrees need not be subtracted. The results for all cases were consistently accu-rate, suggesting that this use of Bayesian analysis in conjunction with the compound Poisson model provides us with an apparently accurate method of predicting the accident experience of groups of drivers with similar accident histories. It also allows us to con-veniently update our estimate of a driver's accident likelihood as a function of the driver's accident record.

Table 15.2   The Accuracy of Updated Accident Likelihood Estimates

Record during First Three Years			Number of Drivers with an Additional x Accidents during the Last Three Years			
Number of Accidents	Number of Drivers		$x = 0$	$x = 1$	$x = 2$	$x = 2+$
0	6,306	Actual	5,147	965	165	29
		Predicted	5,187	945	148	26
1	1,231	Actual	894	266	59	12
		Predicted*	881	275	61	13
2	249	Actual	164	58	20	7
		Predicted*	155	69	20	6
2+	56	Actual	34	16	3	3
		Predicted	30	18	6	2

Actual: based on six-year ITTE sample of 7,842 drivers.
Predicted: based on a negative binomial distribution fitted to the six-year ITTE data and conditioned on the first three years' record.
Goodness of fit: $\chi^2 = 3.03$, 0.63, 2.44, and 2.76 with one degree of freedom for the first three-year cases of 0, 1, 2, and 2+ accidents, respectively. (The corresponding levels of significance vary between 0.4 and 0.05.)
*Totals differ by one because of rounding.

The Accident Likelihood of Trained Drivers

When the driver improvement program under consideration involves license suspension or revocation, the "trained" driver's accident likelihood presumably drops to zero, corresponding to $k' = 0$ in the model.[10] Modeling the effect of remedial driver training programs is more difficult. Only a few controlled studies have been made, and they are based on the aggregate number of accidents involving drivers during the one year before and after training [10]. Such studies do not follow drivers long enough to determine whether the effect of the training diminishes with time or is correlated with accident history.

In this chapter, we shall make use of the compound Poisson accident model to characterize the individual effects of a driver training program in terms of simple parameter changes that have plausible interpretations. The model will then be used to predict the cumulative effect on the three measures of effectiveness (determined earlier) of operating various selection strategies for training programs with any specified individual effect.

One simple description of how training might affect driving behavior is that trained drivers with a record of y accidents during the past τ years would, as a group, behave the same as untrained drivers with $y - d$ accidents during the τ years (where d is any integer less than $k + y$). In terms of the compound Poisson accident model, training would correspond to modifying the posterior accident likelihood distribution $f[r \mid k + y, (k/m) + \tau]$ by "erasing" d accidents to obtain $f[r \mid k + y - d, (k/m) + \tau]$. Alternative methods such as altering $(k/m) + \tau$, the effective time period of observation, are possible; however, the former method is more easily interpreted and computationally simpler and therefore will be used here.

A Model for Comparing Driver Improvement Programs

The compound Poisson accident model, together with the Bayesian approach toward updating accident likelihood estimates and the method of adjusting for individual training, provides the tools needed to compare alternative driver improvement programs in terms of the three measures of effectiveness presented earlier. To

10. Unfortunately, not all drivers whose licenses are suspended or revoked stop driving. A California Department of Motor Vehicle study indicated 55% compliance [6]. Thus a more realistic model would set $k' = 0$ in about half of all cases.

illustrate such a comparison, consider a class of MVA programs indexed L_{nj} and described as follows: At the end of each year beginning with year one, all drivers whose accident records meet the criteria of strategy n take part in driver improvement program j, which lasts an amount of time that is negligible compared to one year and has an individual effect characterized by $d = j$.

We shall consider selection strategies that are based on accident history and include in the program all previously untrained drivers with n or more accident involvements in the current year. Selection criteria based on (1) the total number of accident involvements during any specified time period or (2) the number of times a driver had taken an MVA program during previous years are easily handled using the same model, and this one case will be used to illustrate the method of analysis.

Suppose program L_{32} was put into effect beginning in year one. Let us estimate its effects on a hypothetical driver population of fixed size N. At the end of year one, we expect $N\Sigma_{x=3}^{\infty} P_2 (x|1,k, k/m)$ drivers to be selected—one out of every 3,000 drivers if the ITTE fits for k and m are used. After one year, then, the "number of drivers included" measure of effectiveness equals $N/3,000$.

Without training, the probability that a four-accident driver would have been involved in at least one accident during the next three years is $\{1 - P_2 [0| 3,k + 4, (k/m) + 1]\}$. Averaging this probability over all trained drivers produces a value for the "equitable discrimination" measure. When the ITTE values of k and m are used, a value of 0.52 results—that is, 52% of the selected drivers are in fact predicted to have an accident likelihood $r \geqslant 0.20$.

For each four-accident driver trained, we can expect to avoid

$$\sum_{x=0}^{\infty} \{x \cdot P_2 [x|1,k + 4,(k/m) + 1] - x \cdot P_2 [x|1,k + 2,(k/m) + 1]\}$$

accidents during year two since the training's effect is modeled by eliminating two accidents from the driver's record. Note that the number of accidents avoided as a result of training any individual driver is the difference in the expected value of the negative binomial distribution $P_2 (x|1,k',t')$ where $t' = (k/m) + 1$, and $k' = k + y - d$ after training and $k + y$ before. This expected value is simply k'/t' so that the difference $= d/[(k/m) + 1]$, indicating that the number of accidents avoided is a linear function of the effectiveness d. A "perfect" program corresponds to the $d = k + y$ case. If the ITTE values of k and m are used, we would expect to avoid one out of every 2,300 accidents that would otherwise have occurred during year two.

At the beginning of the second year we may characterize our driving population by a set of numbers $N(y,1,NR)$ = the number of drivers out of the original N who have an effective accident record $[k + y, (k/m) + 1]$ and have or have not been previously trained, depending upon whether $NR = 0$ or 1. The number of drivers trained at the end of year two, the new average "equity" measure, and the number of accidents avoided during the third year may then be calculated using the compound Poisson model in a manner similar to that used for year one. Ten-year calculations were carried out with the aid of a computer for a variety of training programs.

This ten-year model assumes no prior knowledge of accident experience before the first year and considers an unchanging driver population. More realistic cases are easily handled using the same model; however, the calculations and initial conditions are more complicated. Table 15.3 summarizes the predicted results for several programs. A driver population of size 1 million and the ITTE values of $k = 1.40$ and $m = 0.0822$ were used. The percentage of

Table 15.3 Ten-Year Predictions

Strategy		Number Trained (% of total)	Accidents Avoided (% of ten-year total)	Equity*
Cutoff n	Effect d			
1	1	47.6	26.0	28.7
1	Perfect	47.6	63.9	28.7
2	1	4.7	2.4	41.5
2	2	4.7	4.8	41.5
2	Perfect	4.7	9.6	41.5
3	1	0.3	0.2	50.9
3	2	0.3	0.3	50.9
3	3	0.3	0.5	50.9
3	Perfect	0.3	0.9	50.9
4	2	0.02	0.02	58.2
4	3	0.02	0.03	58.2
4	4	0.02	0.04	58.2
4	Perfect	0.02	0.07	58.2

*Percentage of trained drivers who, had they not been trained, would have been involved in at least one accident during the next three years.

accidents avoided is given for year ten—82,200 would have occurred in the absence of a program. Note that random selection of drivers for training would produce an equity measure of 20%.

The "perfect" training programs correspond to removing a driver from the population when he first meets the criteria of at least c accidents in any year. When cutoffs greater than one are considered, the savings in accidents drops off dramatically. Even after 10 years, ruling drivers with 2 or more accidents off the road avoids less than 10% of all accidents that would otherwise have occurred during that year.

The theoretical amount of overrepresentation in accidents, estimated earlier in Section 15.2 and presented in Figure 15.5, indicated that over a very long time period, the 7% of the drivers with accident likelihoods of 0.20 or more would account for 20% of all accidents involvements. However, which specific drivers make up this 7% is not known. Using the "2 or more accident" criterion, only 4.7% of all drivers would be selected for training during 10 years of operation. A majority of these trained drivers would have accident likelihoods less than 0.20, and many of the $r \geqslant 0.20$ drivers would not meet the selection criterion during the 10 years.

For the simple set of strategies considered here, many of the ten-year results could have been estimated accurately by examining the negative binomial distribution's predictions for one year's accident records. Except for the case where every driver involved in an accident is "trained," the percentage of drivers selected is small. Thus, approximately the same number are trained each year, and the number of accidents avoided each year increases approximately linearly. However, analysis of more complicated selection strategies that result in more interaction from year to year makes such extrapolation inaccurate.

The results of Table 15.3 permit one to evaluate a proposed MVA program in terms of its effect on all four MVA objectives and provide a common denominator with which to compare such programs with other accident reduction efforts. They also begin to answer the questions raised at the beginning of Section 15.3.

15.4 Conclusions and Policy Implications

When interviewing department of motor vehicle administrators, police officials, and other government and industry personnel, I would ask, "How large a percentage of all accidents could be avoided by prudent driving? Is the fault system of insurance worthwhile?" and "Would the total number of accidents drop dramatically if a small group of negligent accident repeaters were removed from the road?" The responses varied among individuals but consistently fell into either a high-yes-yes or a low-no-no category. Each person interviewed was familiar with the "10% of all drivers cause 50% of all accidents" type of statistic and was aware of analyses of accident data that correlated various driver characteristics and experience with accident record. However, the same "10% cause 50%" figures and regression and factor analysis results were used to substantiate different claims concerning the effects of license revocation programs and accident prevention efforts. This experience suggested a need for more systematic, policy-oriented work that would interpret and extend the results of specialized data analyses, and it provided the motivation for the work reported here.

The analysis described in Section 15.2 represents a different approach toward studying overrepresentation in accidents. Specific claims of particular interest to policy makers were studied, and observations over various time periods were matched with predictions of analytical models based on explicit assumptions about differences among drivers. The results produced a different picture of the accident involvement process. Statistics such as "6% of all drivers account for 45% of the accidents" were found to be grossly misleading. If all drivers were *equally likely* to be involved in accidents, and chance alone determined who was involved in accidents during a three-year period, roughly 8% of all drivers would be expected to account for half of all accidents. Since three years is much shorter than the average time between accidents per driver, these statistics are *not* a good indicator of the extent to which drivers with high accident likelihoods are overrepresented in accidents.

When time periods of more than the usual two or three years were considered, the fraction of drivers involved in accidents was more sensitive to individual differences in accident likelihood. However, the observed statistics could still be explained without assuming a group of chronic accident repeaters of sufficient size to account for more than 1% or 2% of all reported accident involvements. The results suggested that the frequent, misleading references to the "6% account for 45%" type of statistic have incorrectly reinforced the popular notion that a small group of bad drivers accounts for most of the "accident problem."

Section 15.3 studied alternative motor vehicle authority programs that selected accident-involved motorists for participation in various driver improvement programs. Four MVA objectives were considered—safe driving, convenience to the public, efficiency, and "equitable" discrimination. A compound Poisson accident model of Greenwood and Woods was used to measure the effects of various programs in terms of the number of accidents avoided, the number of drivers selected, and the likelihood that selected drivers would otherwise continue to be involved in accidents.

The model was calibrated by using a sample of California driver accident data, and the effects of several specific programs over a ten-year period were compared. The results indicated substantial tradeoffs among the three measures of effectiveness. "Perfect" training programs produced measurable savings in the total number of accidents only after a number of years of operation. Over a ten-year period, between three and ten drivers had to be trained for each accident avoided. The likelihood that selected drivers would otherwise have been involved in accidents was quite sensitive to the cutoff number of accidents required for selection.

The results of Section 15.2 indicated that license revocation and driver training programs would be only a partial solution to the accident problem. Section 15.3 produced a model for the effect of such programs that enabled them to be compared on the same scale as other accident reduction efforts. The cumulative effect of operating a specific program over several years was considered, and this effect was related not only to the number of accidents avoided but also to the cost of the program, its public acceptance, and the extent to which its differential treatment of drivers was justified.

15.5 Future Research
This chapter has addressed only a few questions of interest to policy makers concerned with automobile accidents and compensation. It may be helpful to suggest more refined methods that may be developed for studying the problems discussed here as well as other questions that lend themselves to similar analyses. Personality traits, traffic violation records, and other driver characteristics

have been correlated with accident involvement records and used to distinguish drivers with low and high accident likelihoods. Accident models more elaborate than the compound Poisson model presented here might be developed to determine the added advantage of using such information in selecting drivers for special treatment.

A decision theoretic approach such as that used in Section 15.3 might be developed to compare alternative risk classification systems and underwriting strategies. The premium schedule affects insurance company profits, the distribution of costs among policy holders, and the number of uninsured motorists on the road; it must be established under conditions of uncertainty. A classification system based only on accident experience may be modeled with the compound Poisson model; however, consideration of other characteristics is desirable.

Finally, in shifting from a "fault" to a "no-fault" system of automobile accident insurance, it is argued that relatively low-risk drivers will pay a larger share of the claims payments. The argument assumes that high-risk drivers are more likely to be judged "at fault" in any particular accident in which they are involved. The extent to which this correlation exists and its cost implications are debatable. Whether or not the shift in costs is more than offset by the reduced operating costs experienced under a "no-fault" system is also important. Data needed to answer such questions are rare, but improved and expanded data processing within insurance companies and recent experience with "no-fault" systems (for example, Massachusetts, Puerto Rico, and Florida) should offer new opportunities for research.

Acknowledgment
This chapter is based on the author's graduate research, supervised by Professor Alvin W. Drake, at the M.I.T. Operations Research Center and on his work on the staff of the U.S. Department of Transportation Auto Insurance and Compensation Study. The author's graduate research was supported in part by the National Science Foundation under Grants GK-1685 and GK-16471 and in part by the M.I.T. Department of Electrical Engineering. The author wishes to thank each of the many individuals who contributed to this research and, in particular, Professor Alvin W. Drake and the staff of the Federal Auto Insurance Study.

References

1. Anscombe, F., "Sampling Theory of the Negative Binomial and Logarithmic Series Distributions," *Biometrika*, vol. 37, 1950.

2. Antony, A., *Suspension and Revocation of Drivers' Licenses, A Comparative Study of State Laws*, Automotive Safety Foundation, Washington, 1966.

3. Arbous, A., and J. Kerrich. "Accident Statistics and the Concept of Accident-Proneness," *Biometrics*, December 1951.

4. Burg, A., *The Relationship Between Vision Test Scores and Driving Record: General Findings*, Department of Engineering, University of California, Los Angeles, June 1967.

5. _____ , *Vision Test Scores and Driving Record: Additional Findings*, Department of Engineering, University of California, Los Angeles, December 1968.

6. California Department of Motor Vehicles, State of, *The California Driver Fact Book*, Sacramento, 1969.

7. _____ , *The 1964 California Driver Record Study*, Parts 1-9, Sacramento, 1964-1967.

8. California Vehicle Code, Section 12810.

9. Cramer, H., *Mathematical Methods of Statistics*, Princeton University Press, 1958.

10. Dunlap and Associates, Inc., Darien, Connecticut, *Driver Education and Training*, prepared for the National Highway Safety Bureau, PB 180 932, May 1968.

11. Ferreira, J., Jr., "Some Analytical Aspects of Driver Licensing and Insurance Regulation," Technical Report No. 58, Operations Research Center, M.I.T., Cambridge, Mass., September 1971.

12. _____ , *Quantitative Models for Automobile Accidents and Insurance*, Report to U.S. Department of Transportation, Auto Insurance and Compensation Study, GPO Cat. No. -TD1.17:Q2, 1970.

13. Greenwood, M., and H. M. Woods, "The Incidence of Industrial Accidents with Specific Reference to Multiple Accidents," *Industrial Fatigue Research Board Report*, No. 4, 1919.

14. Hakkinen, S., *Traffic Accidents and Driver Characteristics*, Finland's Institute of Technology, Scientific Researchers No. 13, Helsinki, 1958.

15. Harwayne, F., *The Relative Cost of Basic Protection Insurance in New York State—An Objective Determination*, 1968 (unpublished).

16. Keeton, R., and J. O'Connell, *Basic Protection for the Traffic Victim*, Little, Brown and Company, Boston, 1965.

17. Klein, D., and J. Waller, *Causation, Culpability, and Deterrence in Highway Crashes*, Department of Transportation, Washington, D.C., 1970.

18. National Safety Council, *Accident Facts*, Chicago, 1969.

19. Pearson, K., ed., *Tables of the Incomplete Γ-Function*, University Press, Cambridge, England, 1965.

20. Survey Research Center, *Public Attitudes Toward Auto Insurance*, U.S. Department of Transportation, Washington, D.C., March 1970.

21. U.S. Department of Transportation, Auto Insurance and Compensation Study, "Accidents and the Accident Repeater," *Driver Behavior and Accident*

Involvement: Implications for Tort Liability, GPO Cat. No. -TD1.17:D83, 1970.

22. _____ , *Motor Vehicle Crash Losses and Their Compensation in the United States*, Report of the Secretary of Transportation to Congress and the President, Washington, D.C., March 1971.

16

Analysis of a Total Criminal Justice System

Alfred Blumstein and Richard C. Larson

16.1 Introduction

The criminal justice system (CJS), comprising the agencies of police, prosecution, courts, and corrections, has remained remarkably unchanged through the significant social, technological, and managerial changes of recent decades. This stability results partly from the insularity of these institutions, and their relative freedom from external examination and influence; but it also results from the independence of the individual components of the system, each of which operates within a set of prescribed rules to approach its own suboptimized objective. Nowhere is there a single manager of a CJS with control over all the constituent parts.[1]

In the past few years, there has been an increasing trend toward examining the interactions among the parts of the CJS. The report of the President's Commission on Law Enforcement and Administration of Justice [2] urged much closer relations among the parts of the system. The Omnibus Crime Control and Safe Streets Act of 1968 [10] provides federal funds to State planning agencies to develop "a comprehensive statewide plan for the improvement of law enforcement throughout the State [11]." Federal subsidy grants are provided on the basis of these plans. Thus, there is an especially strong need for models permitting one to study a total CJS. Such models are needed only partly for reasons of resource allocation; perhaps even more importantly, they can provide tools for examining the effects on crime of actions taken by the CJS, for most crimes are committed by people who have previously been arrested. Thus, an examination of the feedback process is central to an improvement in the system's performance. In the

The first part of this chapter, outlining the models, their uses, and applications to a single state, is reprinted with only minor modification from "Models of a Total Criminal Justice System," *Operations Research*, vol. 17, March–April 1969, pp. 199–232. This is followed by a discussion of the implementation of the linear model.
1. The closest to which the existence of a single manager is approached is in the federal CJS, in which the police (Federal Bureau of Investigation), prosecutors (U. S. Attorneys), and corrections (Federal Bureau of Prisons) all report to the Attorney General. The courts, however, are completely independent. We do not suggest that a single manager would be desirable: there are strong checks-and-balances reasons for retaining the institutional independence.

present state of extensive ignorance on the cause-and-effect relations, the model of this chapter will at least identify the data
needs and the research questions that will permit analyses of the
crime consequences of the actions taken.

Description of Criminal Justice System

The CJS comprises the public agencies concerned with apprehending and dealing with the persons, both adult and juvenile, who violate the criminal law. The basic structure of the CJS is depicted in
Figure 16.1; this outline is, of course, a highly simplified version
of a very complicated procedure (for a more detailed description,
see McIntyre [8] or for a more condensed version, Hazard [7]).

Society, comprising former offenders (recidivists) and those not
previously so identified, gives rise to criminal acts. Of all crimes
which are detected (and many like shoplifting go largely unde-
tected) and reported to the police (and many go unreported)[2]
only a fraction lead to the arrest of a suspect.

An arrested person may simply be admonished at the police station and returned home, or he may be referred to some social-
service agency outside the CJS. An arrested adult is usually
brought before a magistrate, who may dismiss the case or formally
accuse the suspect of the original or a lesser charge and set his bail.

The district attorney, who is responsible for prosecution of an
accused adult, may dismiss the complaint against the defendant at
any time prior to the trial. Those defendants who are not dismissed may plead guilty or stand trial either by a jury or a judge.
Those who are not acquitted can receive a sentence by a judge that
can be of various forms, but usually one of the following:

1. A monetary fine.
2. Probation, usually with a suspended sentence.
3. Probation, following a fairly short jail term.
4. Assignment to a state youth authority.
5. A jail term (usually of less than one year).
6. A prison term (usually of no less than one year at a state institution).
7. Civil commitment for some specified treatment.

In addition to newly sentenced offenders from court, prisons
can also receive probation and parole violators. Release from

2. A Crime Commission survey in three Washington, D. C., precincts found a
victimization rate 3 to 10 times (depending on type of crime) that reported
to the police [16].

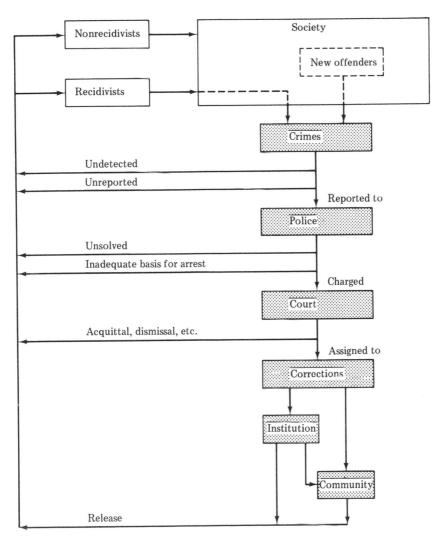

Figure 16.1   The criminal justice system.

prison is usually under parole supervision. Parole violators, if returned to prison, may subsequently be released either on another period of parole, or unconditionally if their sentence has been served.

The processing of juveniles is similar to that of adults, but it is far less formal, with far more freedom of choice exercised by the juvenile authorities.

This processing by the CJS typically involves a series of stages, with the alternatives at most of these stages being either return to the community or further penetration into the CJS. Since virtually all offenders return to society eventually, they are afforded repeated opportunities to return to the CJS by a subsequent arrest, followed by a recycling through the system.

This cursory description suggests two approaches to modeling the CJS. First, there is the simple production process, in which the principal concern is the flow through the system, and the accumulation of costs flowing from a single arrest. Such a linear model provides an opportunity (1) to examine at each stage the workload, the personnel requirements that result, and the associated costs, (2) to attribute these to types of crimes, and (3) to project all of these planning variables as functions of future arrest rates (Roy [14] has discussed such models in a preliminary way).

The second is a feedback model, which considers the recidivism probability associated with each released defendant, and his subsequent processing for future arrests after he has once been released by the CJS. Such a feedback model building on the work of the Space-General Corporation [12] permits estimating the costs of a total criminal career (considering the succession of rearrests of an individual) and the consequences of alternative actions within the CJS to lower recidivism probabilities.

Some preliminary results with these two models on aggregated U.S. data have been reported previously [1]. This paper provides some of the details on the form of these models, and presents some results for California, the single state that comes closest to having an adequate data base. Hopefully, as the use of such models increases, more complete data will begin to become available and the results will increase in reliability and usefulness.

16.2 The Linear Model
A steady-state, linear model is used to compute the costs and workloads at the various processing stages and to establish manpower

requirements to meet the anticipated workloads. The *workload* is the annual demand for service at the various processing stages (courtroom hours, detective man-hours); the *manpower require-ment* is derived from the workload by dividing by the annual working time per man (or other resource); total operating *costs* are allocated to offenders by standard cost-accounting procedures (these allocated costs are then assumed to be variable costs).

The flow of persons through each processing stage is described by a vector whose ith component represents the yearly flow associated with characteristic type i ($i = 1, \cdots, I$). These characteristics can be any attribute associated with individual offenders, their crimes, or their previous processing by the CJS. In most of our studies, there have been seven characteristics ($I = 7$), corresponding to the seven *index* crimes (the seven types of crimes which the FBI annually tabulates [3] to get an "index" of crime in the United States are willful homicide, forcible rape, aggravated assault, robbery, burglary, larceny of \$50 or over, and auto theft).

The independent flow vector to the model, which must be specified as input, is the number of crimes reported to police during one year (hereafter, unless stated otherwise, all computed variables and data are considered as seven-component vectors; the flow variables represent annual flow rates). The outputs are the computed flows, costs, and manpower requirements that would result if the input and the system were in steady state.

Each processing stage is characterized by vector cost rates (per unit flow) and branching probabilities (or branching ratios). The input flow at each processing stage is partitioned into the appropriate output flows by element-by-element vector multiplication of the input flow and the branching probability ($F_{i,mn} = F_{i,m} P_{i,mn}$), where

$F_{i,m}$ = number of offenders associated with crime-type i entering processing stage m during one year,

$F_{i,mn}$ = number of offenders associated with crime-type i following route n out of processing stage m, and

$P_{i,mn}$ = probability that an offender associated with crime-type i input at stage m will exit through route n ($\Sigma_n P_{i,mn} = 1$).

A simple processing stage, representing the verdict of a jury trial, is depicted in Figure 16.2. The input N_{t_1} is the number of defendants who receive a jury trial. The outputs $N_{t_{g_1}}$ and $N_{t_{\bar{g}_1}}$ are the numbers found guilty and not found guilty, respectively. The

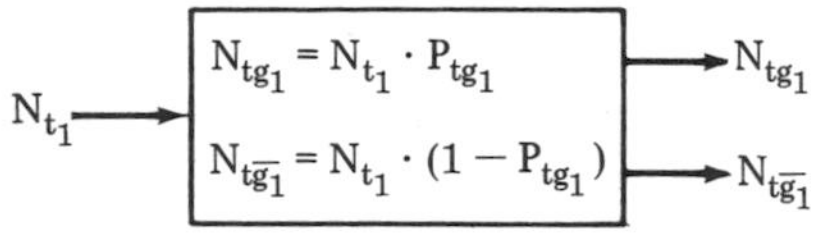

$$N_{t_1} \longrightarrow \boxed{\begin{array}{l} N_{tg_1} = N_{t_1} \cdot P_{tg_1} \\ \\ N_{t\overline{g_1}} = N_{t_1} \cdot (1 - P_{tg_1}) \end{array}} \begin{array}{l} \longrightarrow N_{tg_1} \\ \\ \longrightarrow N_{t\overline{g_1}} \end{array}$$

Figure 16.2 The jury-trial stage.
Definitions:
N_{t_1} = Number of defendants who receive jury trials
N_{tg_1} = Number of jury trial defendants found guilty
$N_{t\overline{g}_1}$ = Number of jury trial defendants not found guilty
P_{tg_1} = Probability that a jury trial defendant is found guilty

branching probability P_{tg_1} is the probability that a jury trial defendant will be found guilty. With seven crime types, the seven components of P_{tg_1} are required as input data for this stage.[3]

Describing the entire model in detail is not warranted here. To illustrate the details, however, we briefly discuss the prosecution and courts submodel. The flow diagram is given in Figure 16.3. The input to this part of the model is the vector, N_{ad_1}, the number of adult arrestees who are formally charged with index crimes. This submodel produces seven output vectors corresponding to the seven sentence types. These provide the inputs to the subsequent processing stages. In addition, there are four intermediate output vectors characterizing defendants who never reach the sentencing stage, namely:

1. $N_{\overline{f}}$ = number of adults formally charged who do not reach trial stage.
2. N_{td} = number of defendants whose cases are dismissed or placed off calendar at the trial stage.
3. $N_{t\overline{g}_1}$ = number of jury-trial defendants not found guilty.
4. $N_{t\overline{g}_2}$ = number of bench- and transcript-trial defendants not found guilty.

Clearly, any other intermediate flows can also be calculated, if desired.

This submodel calls for four classes of branching probabilities.

3. A more general model would define each branching probability as a function of an offender's prior path through the system and other information which had become known since arrest. The branching probabilities describing the sentencing decision, for instance, would depend on whether the defendant had pleaded guilty, had a jury trial, or a bench or transcript trial. In effect, the possible number of characteristics that could be associated with a flow variable could grow exponentially with the depth of system penetration; the demands for data, of course, grow comparably.

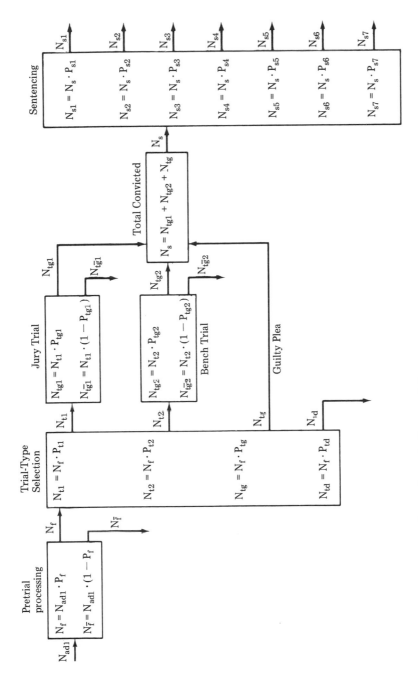

Figure 16.3   The prosecution and courts flow model.

These refer to:

1. Whether or not the defendant reaches the trial stage.
2. The type of trial (or whether dismissed at trial stage).
3. The trial verdict.
4. The sentencing decision.

The definitions of all the flow-and-branching probability variables of Figure 16.3 are given in Table 16.1.

Having determined the flow through each processing stage, we can determine the total costs simply as the product of the unit costs and the flow rates. Costs are separated into pretrial and trial costs, and for each, court and prosecutor's costs.[4] In addition, there is a cost of pretrial detention.

The flows through the appropriate processing stages permit calculating annual workloads in terms of total trial-days for jury-and-bench (that is, judge) trials and man-days for pretrial detention in jail. The annual manpower requirements (for example, the required number of prosecutors, judges, and jurors) are then calculated on the basis of unit productivity (e.g., annual trial days available per prosecutor).

Some illustrative results were developed based on data principally from California [15]. In some cases, where California data were unavailable, data from other jurisdictions were invoked. The input data are presented in Table 16.2.

It is interesting to note, for instance, that P_{t_1}, the probability that a defendant will receive a jury trial, increases with the severity of the offense, but never exceeds 0.25 [the numerical estimate of P_{t_1} is formed by computing the ratio (number of jury-trial defendants/total number of defendants) for a given year]. Regardless of crime type, a majority of those who reach trial plead guilty. Probabilities of being found guilty in a trial are roughly three-quarters.

Table 16.2 also shows time and cost data. The average jury-trial length, T_1, ranges between 4.6 and 1.6 days (a trial day is typically five hours long), depending on the type of crime. The average cost per day of jury trial was computed by first allocating the total court costs to "judgeships," and then dividing the judgeship annual cost by the annual number of judge working days spent in trial. (There are additional court costs to the prosecutor and to

4. Much of the court-cost data was estimated from other jurisdictions, particularly Washington, D. C., and the federal court system.

Table 16.1   Definitions of Flows and Branching Probabilities in the Prosecution and Court Submodel (Output flows and corresponding branching probabilities are given as matched pairs. Only the definition of the flow is stated.)

N_{ad_1}	The number of adult arrests who are formally charged by the magistrate.
(N_f, P_f)	The number of adults formally charged who receive a Superior Court felony disposition.
$(N_{\bar{f}}, 1 - P_f)$	The number of adults formally charged who do not receive a Superior Court felony disposition.
(N_{t_1}, P_{t_1})	Number of defendants who reach trial stage and who receive *jury trials*.
(N_{t_2}, P_{t_2})	Number of defendants who reach trial stage and who receive *bench* or *transcript trials*.
(N_{tg}, P_{tg})	Number of defendants who reach trial stage and who plead guilty.
(N_{td}, P_{td})	Number of defendants who reach trial stage and who are dismissed or placed off calendar.
(N_{tg_1}, P_{tg_1})	Number of defendants who receive jury trials who are found guilty.
$(N_{t\bar{g}_1}, 1 - P_{tg_1})$	Number of defendants who receive jury trials who are not found guilty.
(N_{tg_2}, P_{tg_2})	Number of defendants who receive bench or transcript trials who are found guilty.
$(N_{t\bar{g}_2}, 1 - P_{tg_2})$	Number of defendants who receive bench or transcript trials who are not found guilty.
N_S	The number of defendants who are sentenced.
(N_{Sj}, P_{Sj})	The number of sentenced defendants who receive sentence type j ($j = 1, 2, \cdots, 7$).

Table 16.2   California Input Data to the Prosecution and Courts Model

	Homicide	Robbery	Assault	Burglary	Larceny	Auto theft	Rape
P_{t1}	0.25	0.18	0.12	0.07	0.06	0.03	0.11
P_{t2}	0.18	0.13	0.25	0.17	0.20	0.16	0.21
P_{tg}	0.50	0.61	0.52	0.67	0.66	0.75	0.58
P_{tg1}	0.81	0.81	0.75	0.78	0.68	0.83	0.54
P_{tg2}	0.68	0.71	0.77	0.71	0.89	0.75	0.61
T_1	4.6	3.1	2.3	2.2	3.0	1.6	2.9
C_j	3680	2480	1840	1760	2400	1280	2320
T_2	1.1	1.1	1.0	1.0	1.1	1.0	0.8
C_b	620	620	560	560	620	560	450

T_1, T_2 = Average number of jury (T_1) and bench trial (T_2) days per case.
C_j, C_b = Average jury (C_j) and bench trial (C_b) cost per trial, including prosecution and court costs.

police investigators, attributed before and during trial.) This obviously simplified cost-allocation procedure clearly needs much more refinement when the necessary cost data become available.

Limitations of the Model
However complex this model may appear, it is still a gross simplification of reality. Each processing stage represents a number of detailed processing stages in the real system; the description could have been made more detailed, but the finer data were not available, and little but complexity would have been gained.

The unit costs at each processing stage have been calculated simply by dividing current total yearly cost by current yearly workload. This implied linear relation between flow and cost (that is, all costs are variable) ignores the fact that many costs are fixed and independent of flow (e.g., the cost of courthouses). However, this simplification also avoids the problem of having to identify which costs are fixed and which are variable, since many costs that are fixed over a slight variation in flow become variable if there is a large variation in flow. By this costing procedure, certain facilities that may currently be operating well below capacity (e.g., rural courts) would show an excessively high unit cost.

The variables in the model are assumed to be constant over time (a steady-state assumption) and independent of each other or of exogenous variables. There undoubtedly are interactions that limit the validity of this simplification. Certain service times (for example, detention times) and branching ratios (e.g., probability of prison sentence) are functions of the magnitudes of demands. Such interactions need further examination.

Despite these limitations, the model does permit a reasonable first estimate of costs, workloads, and flows, and allocation of these to crime type and processing stage. Furthermore, these planning variables can be projected into the future if the crime or arrest rate can be projected, and if the branching probabilities are either constant or can be projected.

16.3 Sensitivity Analyses

An important phase of the analysis is to determine the effects of changes in one subsystem on the workload, costs, and manpower requirements of another subsystem; for instance, if there were indications that an improved fingerprint-detection system would increase the burglary arrest rate (i.e., arrests per burglary), it would be necessary to plan for the increased cost-and-workload effect on the subsequent court and corrections subsystems. In addition, the allocation of costs to various subfunctions is of interest in considering possible reallocation of resources. A sensitivity analysis permits an examination of this distribution.

Given any two system flows, C_i and $N_i (i = 1, 2, \ldots, I)$ we find it useful to define the following two quantities:

$\partial C_i / \partial N_i$ = incremental change in C_i per unit change in N_i (first partial derivative of C_i with respect to N_i);

$(\partial C_i / \partial N_i) / (C_i / N_i)$ = incremental fractional change in C_i per unit fractional change in N_i ("elasticity" of C_i with respect to N_i); a "unit fractional change" could be, for instance, a 1 percent change.

To indicate the interpretation of these two quantities, suppose C_i represents the cost at stage 12 associated with processing individuals charged with crime i. Consider that N_i represents the flow of persons into stage 6. In terms of N_i, suppose C_i is linearly related to N_i, i.e., it can be written as follows: $C_i = A_i + B_i N_i$. Then,

$\partial C_i / \partial N_i = B_i$ = average additional cost incurred for processing at stage 12 per additional individual charged with crime i inserted at stage 6.[5]

$(\partial C_i/\partial N_i)/(C_i/N_i) = B_i N_i/(A_i + B_i N_i)$ = average fractional increase in cost incurred at stage 12 for processing individuals charged with crime i per unit fractional increase in individuals charged with crime i inserted at stage 6.

More succinctly, the first partial derivative in this case is an incremental *cost per person* and the elasticity is the *fractional increase in cost per unit fractional increase in the number of persons*.

As an example, we may be interested in the incremental change in total system direct operating cost (C_t) caused by the addition of one robbery defendant in the flow N_{ad_1}, the number of adults who are charged with a felony in magistrate's court. For this case, the incremental cost per additional robbery defendant (that is, $\partial C_t/\partial N_{ad_1}$ for robbery) is calculated to be $4800. This means that an average robbery defendant charged by a magistrate's court costs the system $4800 (for the current offense) in addition to costs already incurred in previous stages. The value of $4800 is the expected value of the total subsequent costs (that is, the sum of each of the unit costs at the magistrate's court and later stages weighted by the probability that the defendant passes through each particular processing stage).

If C_i is a flow, then $\partial C_i/\partial N_i$ is an incremental flow per additional person inserted. For instance, if we let C_i be the number of jury trials for robbery defendants (the robbery component of N_{t_1}) and N_i be the robbery component of N_{ad_1} (the number of adults charged with a felony in magistrate's court), then the incremental number of robbery jury trials per additional robbery defendant from magistrate's court is calculated to be 0.10. This figure can also be interpreted as the probability that a randomly selected robbery defendant from magistrate's court will proceed to and have a jury trial.

Now let us consider an example involving elasticity. Suppose that C_i is the number of burglary defendants placed on straight probation, the burglary component of N_{s_1} and that N_i is the number of defendants found guilty of burglary in jury trials, the burglary component of N_{tg_1}. We calculate that $(\partial C_i/\partial N_i)/(C_i/N_i) =$

5. This cost could be calculated directly as the product of the unit cost of processing at stage 12 and the probability that an individual inserted at stage 6 will reach stage 12; this latter probability is not explicitly calculated.

0.07. This means that a one percent increase in the number of burglary defendants found guilty in jury trials would cause a 0.07 percent increase in the number of burglary defendants placed on straight probation.

Other illustrative calculations made for the 1965 California CJS system are shown in Tables 16.3 and 16.4. Table 16.3 shows various incremental costs per additional reported crime. Of the crimes presented,[6] robbery costs are highest ($1083), primarily because of the high increment in correction costs; the incremental costs for auto theft are lowest. These calculated costs combine many fac-

Table 16.3   Incremental Costs per Reported Crime

	Robbery	Assault	Burglary	Auto theft	Rape
C_t	$1083	$437	$169	$170	$904
C_{co}	760	197	87	58	534
C_{ct}	59	34	9	8	108
C_p	82	52	37	25	124
C_{pd}	71	44	25	16	108

C_i = total system cost. C_{co} = cost of the correction system. C_{ct} = cost of the prosecution and courts system. C_p = cost of police. C_{pd} = cost of police detectives.

Table 16.4   Incremental Flows per Arrest (including juvenile arrests)

	Robbery	Assault	Burglary	Auto theft	Rape
N_I	0.41	0.09	0.09	0.04	0.16
N_P	0.10	0.02	0.03	0.02	0.03
N_{t_2}	0.02	0.04	0.02	0.02	0.06
N_{tg}	0.12	0.07	0.09	0.08	0.16
N_f	0.19	0.14	0.14	0.11	0.28

N_I = number of adult-years served in prison. N_P = number of adults sentenced to prison directly from Superior Court. N_{t_2} = number of adults having bench trials. N_{tg} = number of adults who plead guilty. N_f = number of adults who receive a Superior Court felony disposition.

6. No entries are given in Table 16.3 for homicide or larceny because of the lack of uniformity of definition of these two crimes in the various processing stages. For instance, police report the incidence of "grand theft, except auto" whereas most (but not all) other processing stages report the number of defendants associated with "theft except auto," a larger category which includes petty theft with prior and receiving-stolen-property offenses (see [15] 1965, pp. 207–209). Even for the five crime types considered here there are minor deviations of definitions in various parts of the system.

tors, including the probability of apprehending a suspect, the dismissal probabilities along the way, and the costing procedure.[7]

Table 16.4 presents incremental flows resulting from one additional arrest. The first-row entry (additional number of adult-years in prison) is the average man-years served in prison per additional arrest. This can also be interpreted to be the incremental prison population per additional arrest. All other entries have a probabilistic interpretation; for instance, entries in the second row indicate that 10 percent of those arrested for robbery are sentenced to prison from Superior Court and only 2 percent of those arrested for assault.

16.4 Estimation of Future Requirements

Administrators of the CJS at all levels, from state attorneys general, crime commissions, and budget directors to planners in the various local agencies, require projections of future workloads, costs, and manpower requirements. These projections are needed for earlier decisions that must be made in anticipation of future changes in workload. For instance, new buildings (courts or correctional institutions) can be designed and constructed or additional personnel can be hired and trained.

In this section we report two applications of the model, using data from the State of California. First, we investigate the degree to which the branching probabilities are constant. Following that, we project for California workloads, costs, and manpower requirements into the year 1970, on the basis of data collected through 1965. Since the number of reported crimes is a basic input to the model, we must independently project the number of crimes that will be reported; a linear extrapolation is used for that projection. Then we develop estimates of the number of arrests per year, and use the model to obtain projections of CJS workloads, costs, and manpower requirements.

7. The procedure for calculating police costs was a product of time components and time pay rates. For detectives, the time components were preliminary investigation, arrest, and case development. Cost assignment for the police patrol force is somewhat more troublesome. The force spends a large fraction of its time on "preventive patrol," and it is difficult to apportion this time to individual crimes. In the current model, a lower bound on patrol costs was used. The time allocated to crimes was taken as twice the average time to service a call.

Trend in the Number of Arrests Per Reported Crime
A comparison of system branching ratios over a five-year period indicated that system workload is most sensitive to changes in the average number of arrests per reported crime.

The branching probabilities P_{AC} (the number of arrests per reported crime)[8] for California in the years 1961–1965 are shown in Figure 16.4 for aggravated assault, robbery, auto theft, grand theft (in California, larceny of $200 or more), and burglary. (The crimes of homicide and rape are not included because the definition of these crimes changes from the crime report to the arrest stages.) Each rate exhibits a negative slope, with robbery showing the greatest rate of decrease. Indeed, arrests for robbery have shown a marked decline of about 32 percent from 0.83 per reported crime in 1961 to 0.57 per reported crime in 1965. The burglary arrest probability has decreased by approximately 20 percent.[9] The general downward trends could be caused by a combination of several factors:

1. More frequent reporting of crimes to or by police.

2. More accurate police classification of reported crimes.

3. Fewer arrests of individuals not associated with the crimes.

4. Saturation of limited police manpower resources.

5. Greater difficulty in solving crimes, caused by such problems as mobility of criminals, lowered citizen cooperation, and so on.

Many other possible reasons could be advanced. Without having to attribute cause, however, it is possible to project P_{AC} somewhat into the future. This parameter describes the system's first processing stage of arrest, and its value linearly affects workloads and costs in all other system stages.

8. Numerical values for P_{AC} are computed simply by dividing the total number of arrests (adults and juveniles) by the total number of crimes reported. Strictly speaking, it is an estimate of the average number of arrests per reported crime. We often refer to it as the 'arrest probability,' knowing that some crimes generate more than one arrest and that the suspect arrested may not be the perpetrator of that particular reported crime.
9. More recent data that have since become available indicate a continuation in these trends. For the year 1966, the number of arrests per reported robbery dropped to 0.52, per burglary to 0.21, and per assault to 0.59. Auto-theft and grand-theft probabilities remained about constant.

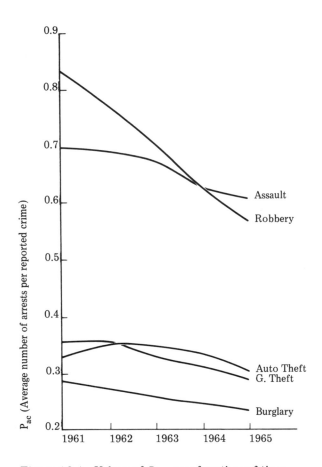

Figure 16.4   Values of P_{AC} as a function of time.

Trends in Final Disposition Percentages

To test the constancy of the branching ratios further, a linear extrapolation was performed to estimate trends in the other branching ratios for California. Specifically, for each of the years 1960–1965, the ratios of final disposition of adult felony arrests to total arrests were investigated. The final dispositions were:

1. Released.
2. Assigned to other jurisdiction.
3. Dismissed.
4. Acquitted.
5. Misdemeanor prosecution.
6. Superior Court conviction.
   a. Civil commitment.
   b. Prison.
   c. Youth Authority.
   d. Probation.
   e. Jail and fine.

The most significant trend ($t = 5.3$) was found in the fraction receiving probation. (Significance was tested with a student's t-test of the difference from zero of the linear time term; the value $t = 5.3$ causes us to reject, even at the $\alpha = 0.001$ level of significance, the hypothesis that there is no linear time trend in the fraction receiving probation.) During 1960–1965, a fraction of approximately 0.13 of felony arrests received probation at the sentencing stage, and this value is increasing 0.00631 per year. No other trends were significant (at the 0.05 level), and none was as important as the trend in P_{AC}.

Although not all of the individual branching ratios were examined in detail, the steady-state assumption appeared justified for all important branching ratios except P_{AC} and those relating to the probation decision.

In making projections with the model, it was especially important to consider the downward trend in P_{AC}, since changes in this fraction propagate throughout the entire system. It was felt that for short-range projections, it would not be necessary to adjust the probation or other branching ratios.

For short-range projections, it was decided to compute output in two ways:

1. Linearly extrapolate the trends in P_{AC} and use the resulting projection of P_{AC}.
2. Use the 1965 value of P_{AC}.

These two projections can be expected to bound the actual future values. In our calculations we use the average of the two projections.

Crime projection

The future numbers of crimes reported to police were projected using a linear time extrapolation of the reported crimes for the years 1958-1966[10]; the results of this analysis are shown in Table 16.5. All the correlation coefficients (except for the crime of forcible rape)[11] exceed 0.95, indicating that the linear fit is a good one. Particularly important to criminal justice system administrators in this table are the yearly growth coefficients in the next-to-last column. Note that the number of reported burglaries is increasing by the largest magnitude at 16,534 per year (with 95 per-

Table 16.5   Linear Projection of Index Crimes Reported to Police in California

Offense	Mean no. of reported crimes 1958-1966 ($N = 9$)	Standard deviation of reported crimes 1958-1966	Standard error of linear estimate	Correlation coefficient of estimating equation	Constant term in equation	Linear coefficient in equation (yearly increment)	T-value of linear term
Criminal homicide	677	128	42	0.956	440	47	9
Forcible rape	3309	528	302	0.863	2427	177	5
Robbery	16501	3402	1144	0.955	10209	1259	9
Aggravated assault	21724	4402	1046	0.978	13388	1667	12
Burglary	168022	43408	8910	0.983	85351	16534	14
Grand larceny	97146	27795	7948	0.968	45060	10417	10
Auto theft	62059	14957	4565	0.963	34163	5579	9

Data Source: Uniform Crime Reports for 1958 through 1966.

10. UCR figures for California were used. The definitions of some of the seven crimes are different from the "seven major offenses" of California. Most notably, larceny of $50 and over is counted by the FBI as an index offense whereas "grand larceny" in California requires theft of property valued at $200 and over.
11. In contrast to a simple linear relation, the number of reported rapes was found to remain approximately constant (about 3000 per year) until 1964, when it jumped to 3621, and then to 4432 in 1966.

cent confidence, the yearly growth coefficient is between 13,000 and 20,000 burglaries per year).

Arrest projection

Using the projections of reported crimes from the linear extrapolation, we obtained the approximate upper and lower estimates (keeping P_{AC} constant and projecting its trend, respectively) for the number of arrests in 1970 given in Table 16.6. The results are expressed as percentages of the numbers of arrests in 1965. The upper estimate indicates about a 30 percent increase in system workload during this five-year interval while the lower estimate indicates that the increasing trend in reported crimes is almost compensated by the decreasing trend in arrest probability, and so system workloads will remain about constant (with some fluctuations by crime type, of course). If the declining trend in robbery arrest probability were to continue, the robbery-arrest workload in 1970 would be about half that of 1965. On the other hand, it appears that the arrest probability for auto theft has almost kept pace with the increasing number of reported auto thefts; auto theft exhibits the largest lower estimate in Table 16.6.

To project a numerical value for arrests in 1970, we arbitrarily average the upper and lower bounds in Table 16.6; these results are shown in Table 16.6a.

Projections of System Variables

Using these arrest projections we can compute, using the steady-state model, projected values of system variables in 1970; several of these calculations are shown in Table 16.7. We see that a projected total of 119 additional detectives and 73.9 additional patrolmen will be required to handle increases in the seven major crimes. A projected total of 1393 additional defendants will be placed on probation in 1970. The additional yearly cost to California's criminal justice agencies for increases in the seven major crimes is computed to be $17.3 million. About 41.6 percent of

Table 16.6   Projected Number of Arrests by Crime Type in 1970 (Expressed as a percentage of the number of arrests in 1965)

	Homicide	Forcible rape	Robbery	Aggra- vated assault	Burglary	Grand larceny	Auto theft
Upper estimate	129.6	124.2	129.8	132.0	138.0	140.4	134.2
Lower estimate	—	—	55.7	109.0	100.0	93.5	121.0

Table 16.6a Projected Number of Arrests in 1970 (Obtained by averaging the upper and lower estimates)

Crime type	Projected number of arrests in 1970, expressed as a percentage of the number of 1965 arrests
Homicide	130
Forcible rape	124
Robbery	93
Aggravated assault	120
Burglary	119
Grand larceny	117
Auto theft	128

this additional cost is due to additional burglary workloads, about 22.5 percent to additional auto-theft workloads. In the 1965 calculations, burglary costs accounted for 31 percent of the total and auto theft costs 10 percent. Grouping auto theft, burglary, and larceny as the 'property crimes,' we see that they accounted for 54 percent of the cost in 1965 but are projected to account for 57 percent in 1970.

Extensions and Further Analyses with the Linear Model

These projections can be expected to deviate from the future observations. The differences will result from inadequacies of the current model, errors and incompleteness in the reported data, and basic changes in the operation of the California CJS. As actual results are compared with past projections, calibration of the model and the data sources will result, leading to an improved projection methodology.

As the model is improved, other useful analyses can be performed. The effects on CJS operations of significant changes in system branching ratios can be explored. For instance, introduction of new police hardware (for example, an electronic automobile-license-plate scanner or automated fingerprint files) might dramatically change one or more branching ratios (for example, the probability of arrest for auto theft or burglary) and thus affect the workloads at subsequent stages. More widespread provision of free defense counsel, especially for juveniles as a result of recent court decisions, might provide additional strain on prosecution and court workloads. Greater use of nonadjudicative treatment

Table 16.7 Projected Increases in Values of CJS Variables in California from 1965 to 1970

	Homicide	Rape	Robbery	Assault	Burglary	Theft	Auto theft	Total
N_{ad1}	900*	1700	4200	4600	13700	4400	4400	33900
	+270	+400	−300	+920	+2600	+750	+1200	+5840
M_d	24	22	85	65	310	115	75	696
	+7	+5	−6	+13	+60	+19	+21	+119
U_p	3600	9100	35000	31000	415,000	45000	115,000	654,000
	+1000	+2200	−2600	+6200	+78000	+7400	+32000	+124,000
N_{t1}	180	100	420	260	500	195	77	1730
	+54	+25	−30	+53	+94	+33	+22	+251
M_p	2.1	5.3	21	18	240	26	67	379
	+0.6	+1.3	−1.5	+4	+46	+4.5	+19	+73.9
N_{t2}	130	190	290	570	1200	700	410	3490
	+40	+50	−20	+110	+220	+120	+115	+635
N_s	590	700	1950	1800	5900	3000	2300	16200
	+180	+170	−140	+360	+1200	+520	+640	+2930
N_{s1}	90	280	95	600	1200	1000	500	3770
	+30	+70	−7	+120	+230	+170	+140	+753
N_{s2}	140	150	290	420	1400	660	440	3500
	+40	+40	−20	+75	+270	+110	+125	+640
N_{s4}	320	110	1200	340	1450	420	400	4240
	+100	+30	−85	+70	+280	+70	+110	+575
C_t	8.1	3.3	23	11	38	15	14	112.4
($ million)	+2.4	+0.8	−1.7	+2.2	+7.2	+2.5	+3.9	+17.3

*For each pair of entries, the projected increase is given below the 1965 value.
N_{ad1} = number of adult felony arrests which result in a felony charge.
M_d = total number of detectives required.
U_p = total number of patrolman manhours allocated (to these crimes).
M_p = total number of patrolmen required (for these crimes).
N_{t1} = number of jury trial defendants.
N_{t2} = number of bench or transcript trial defendants.
N_s = number of convicted defendants.
N_{s1} = number of convicted defendants granted straight probation.
N_{s2} = number of convicted defendants granted probation with jail as a condition.
N_{s4} = number of convicted defendants sentenced to state prison.
C_t = total system direct operating costs.

(for example, use of social service agencies as an alternative to prosecution) will require the introduction of additional flow routes in the model and can be expected to reduce court workloads. A change in sentencing policies (for example, more use of community treatment or longer sentences) might affect decisions on construction of new correctional facilities or hiring and training of additional parole and probation personnel.

Crime projections can be improved by taking into account changes in such demographic characteristics as age, income, education, and urbanization. Similarly, since many of the branching ratios also depend on these characteristics, they can be used for more accurate estimation throughout the system.

In our model, the branching ratios were assumed to be mutually independent. In a number of cases, interaction can be expected. For instance, if the number of convictions increases, and if prisons operate near capacity, one might expect a reduction in probability of prison sentence or the time served. Such interaction must be explored to improve the model.

16.5 Feedback Model

This section summarizes a feedback model that describes the recycling through the CJS during the course of an individual's criminal career. The model has several important applications. First, given the age of an offender at first arrest and the crime for which he is arrested, the model computes his expected criminal career profile (that is, the expected crimes for which he will be arrested at each age). Second, using the cost results of the linear model, the model computes the average costs incurred by the CJS over a criminal career. Third, recidivism parameters (e.g.; rearrest probabilities) can be varied to assess how each parameter affects criminal careers and cost. For instance, we can study the effect of an intensive rehabilitative program that reduces rearrest probability by a specified amount. Fourth, and most fundamental, the model provides a unified framework in which to study the process of recidivism and in which to test the effects of proposed alternative CJS policies on recidivism.

Overall Structure of the Model

As in the linear model, flows are distinguished by crime type. In addition, each flow variable is broken down by the offender's age.

The input to the model, rather than crimes reported to police, is the numbers of arrests during a year, by crime type and by age, of individuals who have never previously been arrested for one of the crimes being considered. In the model, these "virgin" arrests are added to recidivist arrests (that is, arrests of individuals who have previously been arrested) to obtain the total arrests during the year.[12] The total arrests then proceed through the CJS just as they do in the linear model. The model flow calculations are done recursively on a computer, starting at the lowest possible offender age and iterating the flow calculations in time steps corresponding to one-year intervals.

Since the offender flows comprise individuals who cycle back into the system after dismissal or release from the CJS, it is necessary to compute the number that do recycle, when they are rearrested, and for what crime. At each possible dismissal point, the offender is characterized by a probability of rearrest that is, in general, a function of his age and his prior criminal record. The expected number who will be rearrested at some later time is computed by multiplying the number in the flow by the appropriate rearrest probability. Then, the age at rearrest is computed by using the distribution of delay between release and the next arrest. Finally, the crime type of the next arrest is computed from a rearrest crime-switch matrix, where the matrix element p_{ij} is the condi-

12. Although reported *crimes* are a more adequate variable upon which to compute police workloads and the overall magnitude of the crime problem, *arrest* is the first event linking crime to a specific individual. Statistics describing recidivism often use arrest as the index of recidivism, even though the arrest may not necessarily indicate that one or more crimes have been committed by the individual arrested. In this model, recidivism is consistently measured by rearrest. Using arrest as the basis for measuring recidivism introduces two types of error: crimes for which no offender is arrested are not counted, and offenders who are erroneously arrested are counted. Using a later stage for counting (conviction) would introduce the additional, more serious error of omitting the many crimes for which evidence is insufficient to warrant conviction. In much of the criminological literature, where the concern is principally on the correction process (Glaser [6]), recidivism is often defined in terms of the imprisonment-to-imprisonment cycle. It should be clear that, for the same amount of crime repetition, the measured probability of recidivism decreases as one measures it at stages of successively deeper penetration into the CJS. Thus, FBI estimates [17] of rearrest recidivism of about three-quarters are consistent with Glaser's [6] estimate of reimprisonment recidivism of about one-third due to the arrests that do not result in imprisonment. A simple Markov model, using a reasonable value of 0.75 for arrest-to-imprisonment attrition probability, shows this compatibility.

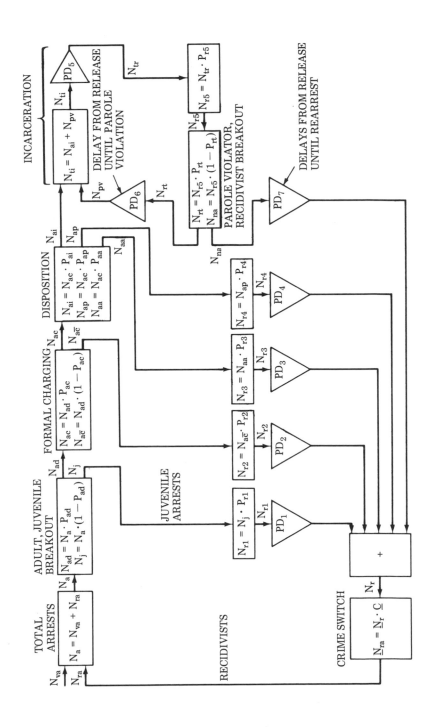

Variable or parameter name	Definition
N_{va}	Number of virgin arrests
N_{ra}	Number of recidivist arrests
N_a	Total number of arrests
N_{ad}, P_{ad}	Number (proportion) of arrests which are adult arrests
N_j	Number of arrests which are juvenile arrests
N_{ac}, P_{ac}	Number (proportion) of adult arrests formally charged
$N_{\overline{ac}}$	Number of adult arrests not formally charged
N_{ai}, P_{ai}	Number (proportion) of charged adults incarcerated
N_{ap}, P_{ap}	Number (proportion) of charged adults granted probation
N_{aa}, P_{aa}	Number (proportion) of charged adults released or acquitted
N_{ti}	Total number of adults who are incarcerated
N_{tr}	Number of adults released from incarceration
N_{r1}, P_{r1}	Number (proportion) of arrested juveniles who are rearrested
N_{r2}, P_{r2}	Number (proportion) of adults arrested but not formally charged who are rearrested
N_{r3}, P_{r3}	Number (proportion) of adults released or acquitted who are rearrested
N_{r4}, P_{r4}	Number (proportion) of adults granted probation who are rearrested

Variable or parameter name	Definition
N_{r5}, P_{r5}	Number (proportion) of adults released from incarceration who recidivate*
N_{rt}, P_{rt}	Number (proportion) of adults released who violate parole and are reincarcerated
N_{pv}	Number of adult parole violators who reenter prison
N_{na}	Number of adult releases who are rearrested
N_r	Total number of those who will be rearrested
C	Rearrest crime-switch matrix
PD_1	Distribution of time until rearrest of juvenile recidivists
PD_2	Distribution of time until rearrest of adults not formally charged and who are rearrested
PD_3	Distribution of time until rearrest of adults acquitted or released and who are rearrested
PD_4	Distribution of time until rearrest of adults granted probation and who are rearrested
PD_5	Distribution of time from entrance until release from prison
PD_6	Distribution of time from prison release until parole violation, for those adults who violate parole
PD_7	Distribution of time until rearrest of adults released from prison and who are rearrested

*Adults released from incarceration who recidivate either violate parole or are rearrested

Figure 16.5   Flow diagram of the feedback model.

tional probability that the next arrest is for crime type j, given that rearrest occurs and the previous arrest was for crime type i $i(1 \leqslant i, j \leqslant I)$. A flow diagram of the model is given in Figure 16.5.

There are two different interpretations of the computed flows: as a cohort-tracing model or as a population-simulation model. In the first, a cohort of virgin arrests can be inserted at some age and the aggregate criminal career of that cohort can be traced. For a 15-year-old cohort, for instance, the model will compute the expected number of arrests by crime type incurred at ages 16, 17, and so on. Alternatively, in the second case, we can input as virgin arrests the total present distribution of such arrests, by age and by crime type; in this case, invoking a steady-state assumption, the computed flows represent the current distribution of all individuals (including recidivists) processed by the CJS. With this interpretation, the computed number of arrested 20-year olds, for instance, represents arrests of both virgins and recidivists. If the virgin-arrest distribution were known for the United States, this use of the model would be a good check on the validity of the model.

Feedback Branching Ratios
Many details treated explicitly in the linear model are aggregated in the feedback model. Only four branching probabilities are required to determine flows through the trial stage:

1. P_c = probability that an arrested adult is formally charged with a felony.
2. P_i = probability that an adult who is charged will be incarcerated in a state correctional institution.
3. P_p = probability that an adult who is charged will be placed on probation or in a local jail.
4. P_a = probability that an adult who is charged is dismissed before or during trial or is acquitted.

The values of these probabilities that were used in the current model are given in Table 16.8, based on California statistics [15].

One of the facts noted from these data is that assault charges, most of which result from attacks on relatives or acquaintances, frequently result in dismissal and only rarely in incarceration. A similar situation exists for rape charges. Larceny charges, probably

Table 16.8   Branching Ratios for the Feedback Model

	Homicide	Robbery	Assault	Burglary	Larceny	Auto theft	Rape
P_c	0.68	0.41	0.34	0.50	0.53	0.42	0.59
P_i	0.43	0.35	0.09	0.15	0.12	0.17	0.10
P_p	0.26	0.22	0.31	0.27	0.55	0.35	0.30
P_a	0.28	0.43	0.60	0.58	0.33	0.48	0.60

Reference: Approximated from 1965 California data [15].

many of which are against first offenders, most often lead to probation.

Rearrest Probabilities

Rearrest probabilities are specified at each point of dismissal and are functions of age and crime of last arrest.[13] The variation with age of the offender is typically a gradual decrease after about 30 years of age. To approximate this decrease, we allowed the rearrest probability to be the following function of age:

$P_R(a)$ = probability that an offender dismissed at age a would be rearrested for an index crime
= $P \min \{1, [1/(T - C)] \max (T - a, 0)\}$.

This function is plotted in Figure 16.6. The three parameters of this function have intuitive definitions:

P = probability of rearrest of individuals released who are less than C years of age at time of release.
C = age at which the rearrest probability starts declining linearly to zero.
T = age beyond which rearrest does not occur.

Table 16.9 shows estimated values of these parameters for two types of dispositions:

1. Adults who are formally charged but not found guilty.
2. Adults who are found guilty and who are placed on probation or in a local jail.

These values were estimated from data presented in [17],

13. Rearrest probability data (the data on criminal careers in UCR, 1966) exhibit a marked variation by type of crime of the last arrest and the type of disposition.

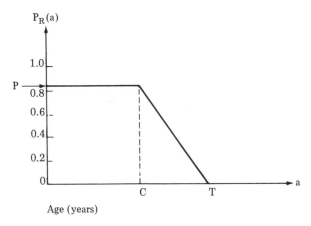

Figure 16.6   Rearrest probability as a function of age.

Table 16.9   Parameter Values for the Rearrest Probability Function

		Homicide	Robbery	Assault	Burglary	Larceny	Auto theft	Rape
Disposition 1	P	0.65	0.80	0.785	0.833	0.770	0.833	0.65
	C	40	35	40	35	40	60	25
	T	100	80	65	80	75	100	55
Disposition 2	P	0.25	0.573	0.375	0.572	0.539	0.675	0.33
	C	35	30	30	30	35	40	25
	T	100	80	64	75	75	100	55

Disposition 1: Adults who are formally charged but not found guilty.
Disposition 2: Adults who are found guilty and who are placed on probation or in a local jail.

pp. 32–42. There is a marked decrease in likelihood of recidivism for those placed on probation, even though they were found guilty.[14]

Time Between Release and Rearrest
Data describing times between release and rearrest are sketchy, at best, and the distributions which were used were chosen to have a

14. It may be that supervision during the probationary period provided a relatively successful rehabilitative environment. Part of the effect noted, however, must be attributed to the selection of probationers, since those granted probation were judged good risks during the presentence investigation.

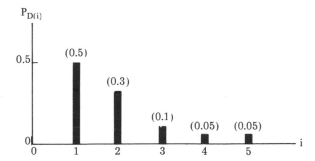

Figure 16.7   Illustrative distribution of delay from dismissal until rearrest.
$P_{D(i)}$ = probability that the delay from dismissal until rearrest is i years, given
that rearrest occurs (i is a positive integer).

mean of about two years.[15]   An illustrative delay distribution function of this time interval is given in Figure 16.7.

Rearrest Crime-Switch Matrix

In the present model, the same crime-switch matrix is used for all
recidivists, regardless of age and number of prior arrests. Even with
this simplification, 42 independent probability estimates are required to specify the matrix for seven types of crime. Thus, a relatively large sample of recidivists is required for accurate estimation. Those few studies that have reported data from which a
crime-switch matrix can be developed have either had an inadequate sample size or their sample was biased in some important
sense. Table 16.10 presents the rearrest crime-switch matrix that
was used in most of our studies. This matrix was based primarily
on a sample of about 500 recidivists who were studied by the Minnesota Board of Corrections.[16]   In this matrix, none of the on-

15. A mean of two years was chosen to match the UCR/1966 statistics which
showed that about 0.5 index arrests per year occurred from the start of an
individual's criminal career. Delay-distribution data for time from release on
parole until parole suspension for parole violation are published for California
[4]. These data, because of many unique characteristics about the parole
process, are inadequate for the model.
16. The data were obtained from *Crime Revisited* [9], Minnesota Board of
Corrections. The estimates for murder and nonnegligent manslaughter, forcible rape, and aggravated assault were best estimates based on inadequate data.
The Federal Bureau of Prisons statistical tables [5] for fiscal year 1965 were
also used in estimating the matrix where the Minnesota sample was too small.

Table 16.10   Rearrest Crime-Switch Matrix 1*

Last index arrest for:	If arrested again for an index crime, the probability it will be for:						
	Murder and non-negligent man-slaugh-ter	Forcible rape	Rob-bery	Aggra-vated assault	Bur-glary	Larceny ($50 and over)	Auto theft
Murder and nonnegligent manslaughter†	0.025	0.025	0.150	0.400	0.200	0.100	0.100
Forcible rape†	0.020	0.150	0.110	0.260	0.200	0.140	0.120
Robbery	0.015	0.010	0.350	0.060	0.350	0.115	0.100
Aggravated assault†	0.025	0.040	0.150	0.300	0.085	0.200	0.200
Burglary	0.010	0.020	0.135	0.063	0.459	0.282	0.031
Larceny ($50 and over)	0.010	0.020	0.140	0.025	0.400	0.275	0.130
Auto theft	0.010	0.027	0.045	0.028	0.390	0.222	0.278

*Based on data from *Crime Revisited: Minnesota Board of Corrections*; 1965 "Uniform Crime Reports," pp. 29–31; and Federal Bureau of Prisons, statistical tables, fiscal year, 1965.
†Best estimates based on inadequate data.

diagonal terms is greater than 0.50, indicating a strong tendency to commit (or at least to be arrested for) different types of crimes.

Table 16.11 presents a rearrest crime-switch matrix based on a sample of several thousand recidivists; it was computed primarily from the Federal Bureau of Prisons statistical tables for the years 1961–1965 [5].[17] The sample was biased in the sense that a disproportionate number of offenders had been arrested for federal offenses, the definitions of which often differ from those of local jurisdictions (an example is inter-state auto theft, the perpetrator of which is prosecuted under the federal Dyer Act). In this matrix, the on-diagonal terms for both burglary and auto theft are greater than 0.50, the burglary probability being higher at 0.63. We will compare results computed from the model using each of these matrices to see how the matrix affects the criminal careers depicted.

17. The entries for robbery, burglary, grand larceny, and auto theft were calculated from the Federal Bureau of Prisons statistical tables for the years 1961–65. The entries for forcible rape and aggravated assault were estimated from reference 13. The row for murder and nonnegligent manslaughter was set equal to the row for aggravated assault.

Table 16.11   Rearrest Crime-Switch Matrix 2

Last index arrest for:	If arrested again for an index crime, the probability it will be for:						
	Murder and non-negligent man-slaugh-ter	Forcible rape	Rob-bery	Aggra-vated assault	Bur-glary	Larceny ($50 and over)	Auto theft
Murder and nonnegligent manslaughter*	0.03	0.03	0.12	0.31	0.26	0.14	0.11
Forcible rape†	0.03	0.10	0.08	0.30	0.21	0.20	0.08
Robbery §	0.03	0.00	0.42	0.06	0.34	0.04	0.11
Aggravated assault†	0.03	0.03	0.12	0.31	0.26	0.14	0.11
Burglary §	0.02	0.00	0.15	0.04	0.63	0.04	0.12
Larceny ($50 and over) §	0.01	0.01	0.12	0.06	0.40	0.15	0.25
Auto theft §	0.01	0.00	0.10	0.03	0.29	0.06	0.51

*Set equal to the row for aggravated assault.
†Forcible rape and aggravated assault based on District of Columbia data [4, p. 605].
§Robbery, burglary, grand larceny and auto theft based on Bureau of Prisons statistical tables for the years 1961, 1962, 1963, 1964, 1965.

Simplifying the Assumptions of the Current Model

Before this feedback model can be used confidently to make decisions regarding rehabilitative programs and overall allocation of resources, appropriate data must be collected and analyzed. Limitations of existing data have required that we make a number of simplifying assumptions in our model such as the following:

1. Future criminal behavior is determined solely by the age of the offender, the crime for which he was last arrested, and the disposition of his last arrest.
2. The crime-switch matrix depends only on the crime type of the last arrest, not upon age, disposition, or otherwise upon prior criminal career.
3. CJS branching ratios are not a function of age or prior criminal career.
4. Delay until rearrest is a function only of disposition.

Because of these assumptions, the numerical results must still be treated with caution. The model, however, has identified the required data and provides the framework in which to use them once they become available.

Some Results From the Feedback Model

Recognizing these limitations, we computed some illustrative results by using the feedback model. In the first set of runs, 1000 20-year-olds are first arrested for crime i ($i = 1, 2, \cdots , 7$) and their criminal careers are traced. Table 16.12 presents the mean number of subsequent career arrests for crime type j (the columns) among the population of 1000 people first arrested at age 20 for crime type i (the rows). This matrix was computed using the rearrest crime-switch matrix of Table 16.10.

Those who are initially arrested for auto theft have the greatest average number of career arrests (3.76) and represent the only type of initial arrests that has an off-diagonal term greater than one (that is, those initially arrested for auto theft will commit an average of 1.084 burglaries). Table 16.12 also presents the total average number of career arrests for the seven crimes, the career costs using results from the linear model.

For comparative purposes, we show in Table 16.13 the career arrest matrix for the same cohort, but using the rearrest crime-switch matrix of Table 16.11. Overall, the total number of career arrests appears to be only slightly greater; the number of career grand theft and rape arrests appears to be significantly less. As we would expect, the total numbers of arrests (which depend principally on the rearrest probability) are much less sensitive to the crime-switch matrix than are the crime-type distributions.

In another run, 1000 15-year-old virgin arrestees were taken as the cohort. The distribution of initial arrests, by crime type, was

Table 16.12 Career Matrix for 1000 20-Year-Old New Arrestees (Using rearrest crime-switch matrix 1)

Crime of original arrest	Total number of career arrests							Total career arrests per person	CJS direct operating costs, $
	Homicide	Robbery	Assault	Burglary	Theft	Auto theft	Rape		
Homicide	1038	330	426	645	412	262	57	3.17	8100
Robbery	28	1486	154	816	427	230	41	3.18	4500
Assault	43	379	1402	687	561	395	78	3.55	3600
Burglary	28	371	176	2021	634	200	56	3.49	3500
Theft	26	336	128	900	1574	261	51	3.28	4000
Auto theft	31	309	157	1084	657	1455	70	3.76	3500
Rape	34	196	326	656	437	269	1144	3.16	3400

Table 16.13   Career Matrix of 1000 20-Year-Old New Arrestees (Using rearrest crime-switch matrix 2)

Crime of original arrest	Total number of career arrests							Total arrests per person	CJS direct operating costs, $
	Homicide	Robbery	Assault	Burglary	Theft	Auto theft	Rape		
Homicide	1052	338	353	860	209	404	32	3.25	8100
Robbery	52	1569	145	909	117	384	5	3.18	4400
Assault	61	395	1413	1005	245	472	37	3.63	3500
Burglary	52	435	148	2385	138	475	5	3.64	3400
Theft	39	365	151	1060	1211	576	13	3.42	3900
Auto theft	46	416	146	1162	177	1993	5	3.95	3400
Rape	52	302	355	810	256	377	1081	3.23	3400

Table 16.14   Arrest Distributions over Crime Type for a 15-Year-Old Cohort

	Age 15 input distribution from UCR/1965	Model-derived distributions for ages		Arrest distributions for all 20-year-old arrests
		16	20	
Homicide	0.002	0.011	0.01	0.01
Robbery	0.047	0.115	0.15	0.11
Assault	0.045	0.054	0.07	0.14
Burglary	0.335	0.398	0.39	0.35
Grand theft	0.246	0.248	0.24	0.19
Auto theft	0.317	0.149	0.11	0.17
Rape	0.008	0.024	0.02	0.03

made to approximate the actual distribution of total 15-year-old arrests reported in UCR/1965. Because of low age, this distribution is probably based largely on virgin arrests. The output distributions are shown in Table 16.14 for ages 16 and 20. Also shown in Table 16.14 is the arrest distribution of all arrests of 20-year-olds as reported in the UCR/1965 (this distribution is made up of virgin arrestees as well as recidivists with various lengths of prior criminal careers). Even though the model-derived distribution is only for those with five-year-old criminal careers, and the UCR distribution includes all arrestees, we would expect a similarity in the two distributions to be a modest validation check. We see that the distributions are roughly similar, with only the fraction that are assaults deviating significantly from the UCR value.

The recidivism model also permits examination of a crucial question confronting CJS administrators: How does reduction of recidivism probability affect a criminal career? Many experimental programs have been run to try to discover how various rehabilitative programs affect recidivism probability. For instance, one study of youthful offenders, which was part of the California Community Treatment Project, included randomly separated treatment and control groups. During a 24-month period, the institutionalized control group had a failure probability of 0.61 and the Community Treatment Group had a rate of 0.38, or about a one-third reduction in recidivism probability [18]. To investigate what a factor of a one-third reduction of recidivism probability implies in terms of criminal careers, the model was run with 20-year-olds first arrested for crime type i, with the rearrest crime-switch matrix of Table 16.10. and with all of the rearrest probabilities reduced by one-third. The results are given in Table 16.15. The total career arrests are reduced by about a factor of 2 by reducing recidivism probability by one-third.

16.6 Implementing the Model

Models such as those presented in this chapter can be used as design tools by planners in the criminal justice system. A contemplated system change may be introduced, its consequences considered, and one can hope to evolve quite desirable changes from experimentation with the model. Such design tools should be made accessible and understandable to planners at the state, regional, and city levels.

In working with one state, some of the problems of implementation became clear. These planning agencies are rarely staffed by individuals with analytical skills or with experience in using com-

Table 16.15   Career Matrix for 1000 20-Year-Old New Arrestees (Assuming a one-third reduction in rearrest probabilities)

Crime of original arrest	Total number of career arrests							Total career arrests per person	*
	Homicide	Robbery	Assault	Burglary	Larceny	Auto theft	Rape		
Homicide	1017	124	223	205	128	96	22	1.81	$6600
Robbery	11	1223	55	301	136	85	13	1.82	2900
Assault	19	142	1202	188	200	168	33	1.95	1800
Burglary	10	136	63	1400	248	57	20	1.93	1800
Larceny	9	123	38	340	1222	102	18	1.85	2400
Auto theft	11	88	46	402	239	1209	27	2.02	1600
Rape	14	103	159	209	145	103	1079	1.81	1900

*CJS direct operating costs per arrestee career.

puters. Officials are properly skeptical of any results derived from masses of input data they know to be of questionable validity. They are not sure which data to believe and which to question. Particularly in projecting future values of system inputs or parameters—an essential part of "planning"—any projection is bound to be based on unverified assumptions in a system with so little cause-and-effect knowledge. Furthermore, the effort required to collect input parameter values in the largely undocumented CJS is a major task that is not undertaken lightly.

Many of these implementation problems can be significantly alleviated by translating the model into an interactive computer program having a natural-language input-output capability. Then the model becomes usable by managers and planners untrained in either systems analysis or computer programming. Such a program, named "JUSSIM,"[18] has been developed for the linear model.

The program is used principally as a design tool for testing a variety of contemplated parametric changes in the operation of the CJS. These changes might include introduction of additional public defenders, discontinuation of arrests for certain types of crimes, introduction of additional judges to speed processing in the courts and thereby reduce costs of detention, or introduction of innovative correctional programs. Most changes can be reflected by modification of the branching ratios at the affected stages, changes in the unit costs (for example, using more expensive or less expensive personnel) or changes in the workloads imposed on the various system resources (for example, decrease in the time detectives spend investigating a crime).

In many cases, there is no theoretical or empirical basis for assessing the detailed consequences of a contemplated change. For example, what happens to the plea-bargaining process and the conviction probabilities when additional public defenders are made available to defendants? An analyst will have difficulty making such estimates. (This problem, of course, is shared by virtually all social systems, where consequences are dominated by responses of the human participants.) In view of this difficulty, the appropriate

18. Belkin, J., A. Blumstein and W. Glass, "JUSSIM: An Interactive Criminal Justice System Design Tool," presented at Spring Joint Computer Conference, Atlantic City, May 18, 1971. The operation of the model is detailed in Glass, W., "A User's Manual for JUSSIM, An Interactive Computer Model for Criminal Justice System Planning," Urban Systems Institute, School of Urban and Public Affairs, Carnegie-Mellon University, March 1971.

persons to make these estimates are the CJS planners and they can do this with an interactive model.

It is usually feasible, for instance, to introduce reasonable upper and lower bounds of the effect of a change being considered and thereby see if the proposed change dominates current operations regardless of particular parameter values assumed within the bounds. If an analysis for dominance is inconclusive, indicating neither acceptance nor rejection of the proposed change, then additional consideration, data collection or experimentation (depending on the resources available to assess the issue) is required to determine whether the proposed change is a satisfactory one.

With JUSSIM, the criminal justice planner sits at a terminal in his office and in response to inquiries from the program, makes changes to the system parameters, runs the model, and then notes the resource implications of those changes. Thus, he can quickly try a variety of changes, evaluate their consequences, and use that feedback of consequences to try further modifications.

In the JUSSIM program, a "base case" (or current operation) of a particular CJS is represented in a data file that contains values for the following system characteristics:

1. A listing of stages and their name designations;
2. For each stage, the output paths from that stage and the names of each output path;
3. Elementary crime types and "standard" crime type groupings (for example, felonies and misdemeanors, Part I and Part II crimes, and so on);
4. Number of reported crimes for each crime type;
5. For each stage, the branching ratios along the output paths for that stage by crime type;
6. Processing time for a unit of flow for each resource at each processing stage or flow path;
7. Resource costs per unit time for processing at each stage;
8. Annual availability per unit of each type of resource (for example, police, detectives, prosecutors, jail cells);
9. Formulas for computing possible output tables.

In the operation of the program, the user is taken through a series of phases to create a "test case" that will be compared with the stored base case. He is asked if he wants to change the base-case parameters in the following phases:

1. Crime groupings
2. CJS structure
3. Branching ratios
4. Number of reported crimes
5. Unit costs
6. Annual unit resource availability
7. Resource workload per unit of flow

For those phases in which the user wishes to make changes, he is asked to specify which parameters he wants to change and for which crime groups. He is then presented with the current test-case values[19] of those parameters and asked to input the new test-case values.

The user is then asked to specify what output tables he wants to see displayed, thereby avoiding the waste of printing time on material not of immediate interest. The printed tables can present costs, total workloads by resource, and resource requirements for various subsystems or for the total system. Then, for the base case and the test case these data and their percentage differences are presented.

After a run, the user can make several choices for his next run. For example, the most recently completed test case can be rewritten as the "base case" so that future changes will be perturbations on the latest one. Test cases can be saved as data files to be recalled at a later time as base or test cases.

JUSSIM was presented to a group of CJS planners from eight state criminal justice planning agencies at a one-week course at Carnegie-Mellon University in September 1970. These people were readily able to use the program with a minimum of training. The planners easily learned to translate proposed new CJS programs into changes in model parameters. It was particularly interesting to observe the intensity of the interactions among the participants in estimating these parameters and the sophistication they displayed in dealing with the *total* CJS that resulted from being forced to consider total-system consequences of a contemplated change. As

19. At the beginning of a sequence of runs with the program, the base case and test case are identical.

one of the participants, a former police officer, put it, "This is the first time I've thought about what happens to the people I arrest."

As a result of that course and the introduction to JUSSIM, at least two states and two cities are collecting the required data and planning to use the JUSSIM program in developing their criminal justice plans. The JUSSIM program is also being extended to include feedback features.

16.7 Summary

This chapter has described means of modeling the CJS—both in a detailed way with the linear model and in a more aggregated way using feedback to account for recidivism. Clearly, the focus here was on the CJS itself, and so we did not address the many public and private means outside the CJS by which criminal behavior is controlled, nor did we address the deterrent effects of the CJS. Within the constraints of the available data, these models allow us to study questions regarding the CJS and to explore parametric changes in a CJS. These issues would be examined in terms of the system's costs, workloads, and resource requirements, and the effects of alternative rehabilitative procedures on criminal careers.

Future studies can include more realistic assumptions within the framework of these models, and more complete and accurate data for performing the calculations. The end goal of such studies should be to improve the management of the system, including appropriate allocation of public resources to minimize the total social and dollar costs of crime and its control. The models also provide a research tool for examining the behavior of the CJS in order to understand its impact on the problem of crime.

Acknowledgments

The suggestions and contributions of Ronald A. Christensen and Sue Johnson and the programming assistance of Charles McBride are gratefully acknowledged. The JUSSIM model was developed and programmed by William Glass and benefited from important contributions by Jack Belkin. The authors also acknowledge with appreciation the support of the Office of Law Enforcement Assistance and its successor, the Law Enforcement Assistance Administration of the U.S. Department of Justice.

References

1. Blumstein, A., R. Christensen, S. Johnson, and R. Larson, "Analysis of Crime and the Overall Criminal Justice System," Chap. 5 of *Task Force Report: Science and Technology*, President's Commission on Law Enforcement and Administration of Justice, U.S. Government Printing Office, Washington, D. C., June 1967.

2. *The Challenge of Crime in a Free Society*, President's Commission on Law Enforcement and Administration of Justice, U.S. Government Printing Office, Washington, D. C., 1967.

3. *Crime in the United States: Uniform Crime Reports*, published annually by the Federal Bureau of Investigation, U.S. Department of Justice, Washington, D. C. (U.S. Government Printing Office). Hereafter referred to as UCR or UCR/j, where j is the year of publication.

4. Department of Correction, Research Division, Administrative Statistics Section, *California Prisoners 1961, 1962, 1963*, (summary of statistics of felon prisoners and parolees), Sacramento, California, 1963.

5. Federal Bureau of Prisons, statistical tables, published each fiscal year.

6. Glaser, D., *The Effectiveness of a Prison and Parole System*. Bobbs-Merrill Co., New York, 1964.

7. Hazard, G. C., "The Sequence of Criminal Prosecution," *Proc. National Symposium on Science and Criminal Justice*, June 22–23, 1966, U. S. Government Printing Office, Washington, D. C.

8. McIntyre, D. M., *Law Enforcement in the Metropolis*, American Bar Foundation, Chicago, Illinois, 1967.

9. Mundel, M. G., Beverly S. Collins, Mark R. Moran, Alfred J. Barron, Frederick J. Gelbmann, Charles B. Gadbois, Philip Kaminstein, *Crime Revisited*, Minnesota Department of Corrections, 1963.

10. Omnibus Crime Control and Safe Streets Act of 1968, Public Law 90-351, enacted on June 19, 1968.

11. *Ibid.*, Section 203 (*b*) (1).

12. "Prevention and Control of Crime and Delinquency in California," Space-General Corporation, El Monte, California, July 29, 1965.

13. *Report of the President's Commission on Crime in the District of Columbia*, Government Printing Office, Washington, D. C., Appendix, 1966.

14. Roy, R. H., "An Outline for Research in Penology," *Opns. Res.*, vol. 12, 1964.

15. State of California, Department of Justice, Division of Criminal Law and Enforcement, *Crime and Delinquency in California*, Bureau of Criminal Statistics, published annually.

16. *Task Force Report: Crime and Its Assessment*, President's Commission on Law Enforcement and Administration of Justice, U.S. Government Printing Office, June 1967.

17. UCR/1966. (See Reference 3.)

18. Warren, M., et al., "Community Treatment Project, An Evaluation of Community Treatment for Delinquents, Fifth Progress Report," State of California, Youth and Adult Corrections Agency, Department of the Youth Authority, Division of Parole and Division of Research, August 1968.

17   Water Quality Management

David H. Marks

17.1 Introduction

Environmental quality—or lack of it—has been the focus of many controversies during the last few years. The problem of what we should do about our environment is likely to tax our ingenuity for quite some time. Decision makers facing such questions quickly become immersed in a host of highly subjective and qualitative issues in the attempt to understand the complex technical, political, social, and economic system with which they must interact. This chapter deals with two main themes directed at the nature of the problems and the place of operations research in the realization and implementation of improvements.

The first is that even in complex, ill-defined systems where goals, objectives, constraints, and measures of effectiveness are difficult to identify, much less to quantify in meaningful units, the set of analytic techniques we know as operations research can provide great insight and quantitative information for decision making. The approaches and the applications to be discussed are at once problem specific in their adaptation for issues in water quality management while at the same time suggesting a general methodology for approaching a whole series of public sector problems.

The second theme involves specific issues in water quality management. The state of the art in the analysis of those issues is presented to give some appreciation of the richness of their applicability and the vastness of the problem area still to be approached. Our intent is to motivate new interest and research in water quality management and in the general area of quantitative analysis for public system decision problems.

17.2 Quality of Our Environment

A conflict exists between the desires for development, as measured in terms of production of material goods and services, and for a pleasant environment as measured in terms of aesthetic landscapes, clean water and air, abundant recreational opportunities, and individual privacy. The concept that an environmental resource is a free common good is tenable only as long as it is not deteriorated by overuse or congestion. It does not take much observation of the quality of our environment to see that such an overused state has been reached.

One fact is painfully evident. Every activity involved in the generation of material goods for our basic survival and needs (as well as for the further trappings of material well-being) causes the production of waste residuals that must be accounted for either in recycling or in the environment. To ignore this and require the stopping of pollution by merely technical means or by legislation, without suggesting a means for readjusting our standard of living and mechanisms of production, is as foolish as the situation we are presently in. An excellent reference in this area is Russell and Spofford [27].

Because no mechanism exists for the private sector to maintain environmental quality, it is up to the public sector to find some means for bringing environmental considerations within the scope of private decisions. Such action usually requires legislation that either modifies individual behavior, establishes standards of quality for resource use, or internalizes the effects of public resource use in private investment decisions through economic incentives such as taxes or subsidies. Often major legislation is made in the absence of real information as to the effects of new policies—much less the clear definition of objectives for making particular policy changes. Good analysis should provide some insight into the potential effects of the alternative policies, and thus, represent a basis for responsible decision making.

17.3 The Water Quality Management Problem
To understand the scope and nature of the water quality management problem, it is first necessary to see how the quality of water affects the uses it may support. Each day approximately 800 billion gallons of water in lakes, streams, estuaries, and groundwater supplies in the United States are "used." Uses include domestic water supply; industrial water supply for processing, waste removal, and cooling; agricultural usage including irrigation; support of fish and wildlife populations; recreation; navigation; a major component in our aesthetic appreciation of the environment; and waste disposal. It is easily seen that not only are some of these uses conflicting in nature but that water used for a particular objective is rarely returned to the water body in the same quantity or quality as obtained. Thus use itself contributes to the addition of wastes to water. In addition, the combination of our land and air use policies and its interaction with rain and groundwater also results in waste materials reaching water bodies. Urban storm drain-

age and agricultural land runoff contain surprisingly high levels of
waste material as does groundwater from abandoned mines and
solid waste land fills. The numbers here are enormous. The average
municipal waste is 120 gallons per person per day. But this is small
in comparison to the 400 billion gallons per day withdrawn by industry for power and cooling and an almost equivalent amount for
irrigation and agricultural use [40]. Looking at projections for future water needs makes it even clearer that to satisfy those needs
careful attention must be brought to the improvement of water
quality to allow its efficient reuse.

Before thinking about abating pollutants, the objectives relevant
to water quality control must be identified. On a broad level, this
is a true "motherhood" issue, and any grade school student can
tell us we want clean water. But progressing to specifics, a great
many people have spent years arguing over the definitions for and
characteristics of water for a particular use. An interesting compi-
lation of such criteria is shown in a major federally sponsored attempt [39] at integrating all known data to try and answer the
question "What physical parameters of water specify whether it
can or cannot be used for a particular activity?"

Kneese and Bower [17] feel the three basic problems in water
quality management are:

1. What water quality do we want?
2. How is that quality to be obtained at least cost?
3. What institutions and arrangements are necessary to implement
the procedure chosen?

Problem 1 addresses the crucial step of defining preferences for
water use and stating them in terms of physical parameters. An attempt in a large scale study to define preferences in terms of participation in the planning process by various interest groups representing the region's water users has been reported in [30]. Thus,
an important question is how analysis can aid in the determination
of the tradeoffs between competing uses. Other references will be
made later regarding the role of analytic techniques in this area.

It is in response to questions 2 and 3 that operations research
has had its greatest impact. There are many alternative means for
improving the quality of water, ranging from the traditional and
highly technical, such as waste treatment at a source through
piping to points on the water body of less sensitivity for joint

treatment and discharge, flow augmentation, and stream aeration to economic measures such as taxation to shift resource consumption away from those processes that create excessive wastes. Given that one or some combination of these alternatives is chosen there are many different ways that a particular goal might be reached, each implying a different distribution of the costs of the project among the participants. Investigations of how a given quality goal might be obtained to minimize cost have been of considerable interest to engineers working in this area for many years but only with the introduction of operations research techniques was progress obtained towards solution. The question of how costs of a program are to be allocated is a practical issue as complex as that of choosing the level of quality desired and the means of achieving it. These issues will be discussed in greater detail in Section 17.5.

17.4 Agencies Responsible for Water Quality Management
Before turning to a more specific discussion of modeling in these areas, it will be helpful to understand the institutional arrangements and governmental control agencies active in water quality management. Such institutions with their structure, perceived clients and power bases weave a delicate but strong framework of implicit constraints which may alter proposed control plans.

The main federal agency is the newly formed Environmental Protection Agency—Office of Water Quality (EPA-WQO) which has absorbed the previous agency, the Federal Water Quality Control Administration of the Department of the Interior. EPA-WQO has a multitude of missions ranging from inhouse and sponsored research in advanced waste treatment and other abatement procedures through a multimillion dollar per year treatment plant construction approval and aid activity. It has responsibility for the maintenance of water quality standards and for control of federal activities that cause pollution problems through consultation on environmental impact statements as required by the National Environmental Protection Act of 1969. Under an 1899 law, the U.S. Army Corps of Engineers is given the power to license all waste discharges in navigable waters. Obviously such power could be used effectively in controlling pollution, and current governmental thinking is to have the Corps exercise this power with technical assistance from the EPA. While the sheer enormity of dealing with the hundreds of thousands of such discharges may well defeat im-

mediate implementation, there is no question that a new avenue
for enforcement has been opened.

On the state level, water quality management is guided by state
boards with a very mixed bag of good and weak structures. Many
of the state boards have done little to promote effective control,
either through apathy or through major industrial representation
on the board. All are hindered to some extent by lack of sufficient
funds, the predominancy of the federal agencies, and an inability
to deal with problems that occur outside their political jurisdiction.

Because of the regional nature of water quality problems which
tend to involve several states, a new type of institution has been
formed specifically to deal with water resource problems. These
are the regional compacts, drawn up to provide an administrative
level between the federal and state responsibilities. Such an agency
is the Delaware River Basin Commission (DRBC), formed by an
agreement between the states of New York, New Jersey, Pennsylvania, and Delaware and the federal government as equal partners.
The DRBC has broad powers to administer programs and sufficient jurisdiction to make far reaching policy changes in the entire
water resources plan for the Delaware River basin and is the prede-
cessor of many similar arrangements. All told, it provides a novel
way for internalizing many of the political problems encountered
in gaining cooperation with neighbors.

17.5 Analytic Modeling for Examining the Effects of Alternative Policies to Achieve Desired Water Quality

In this section, two classes of analytic modeling approaches to the
management of water quality are outlined. The first includes the
detailed models describing physical processes, optimization of
treatment plants, and so on which have very little policy content.
The second class is the regional control models which sometimes
include strategy and behavioral questions directly in the modeling
process.

Simulation Models of Physical and Social Systems

An important aspect of any study of policy implications and decision analysis is being able to predict the cause and effect relationship of various actions. An accurate understanding of the system
must be demonstrated so that outcome of policy and system
change may be predicted. Such modeling has taken place on two
very different levels.

Physical models have been used to describe the cause and effect relationships in a physical system such as the waste discharge— water body quality response system. Problems of this sort have always intrigued scientists and engineers, and the relatively simple approaches of intuitive modeling and building of small scale prototypes has long since given way to sophisticated computer-oriented mathematical modeling.

In particular, Thomann [34] and O'Connor [23] have applied the techniques such as power spectrum analysis and autocorrelation to obtain the frequency transfer function including amplitude characteristics and phase shift for water body in terms of an input harmonic of waste discharge. Others such as Pence, Jeglic, and Thomann [25] use a finite difference approach and simulation to predict quality response over time. Loucks [20] uses a Markov chain approach to deal with the stochastic nature of streamflow used for dilution of wastes and for studying waste release strategies. Harleman [12] summarizes estuarine models from a computational and theoretical view point.

Of great interest, but considerably less sophisticated because of the scope of the problem, have been recent attempts to prescribe analytical models of the social and political processes involved in management. Here the shift from intuitive to analytic models has taken place slowly because of the great complexity of the problem but nonetheless several recent developments show a whole new line of approach.

Gates, Males, and Walker [9] used systems dynamics techniques based on feedback system analogies to examine California's response to new water quality legislation. A regional water quality board composed of groups having conflicting interests was modeled with the actual decision process formulated as a continuous interaction among the groups. Input-output studies for a regional trade model to show the economic impact of various proposed water quality control programs for the western basin of Lake Erie were made by Stillson [32]. Similar work by Miernyk [22] to show the effect on regional economics in the Colorado River Basin of water quality and quantity has also been reported.

Mathematical Programming Models for Policy Analysis and System Identification

Several researchers have been working with optimization models of treatment facilities to find the minimum cost configuration at a particular site that will meet a desired requirement for waste reduction. Such models require a detailed knowledge of the physical, biologic, and chemical processes involved in waste treatment and are seldom used for any form of policy analysis above the individual unit design level. Examples of such work are [6] and [29]. Both employ dynamic programming to solve essentially a process optimization question.

On another level, considerable attention has been focused on the problem of the regional control authority such as the DRBC mentioned in the last section. Here the policy implications are greater as the various management alternatives open to the regional authority are formulated. The main thrust of most work has been towards attempting to find an optimal solution to overall regional control without considering administrative arrangements such as allocation of costs explicitly. Such models have great value in gaining understanding of system interactions, data requirements and, implicitly, the tradeoffs necessary in various policy alternatives through repeated manipulation of the model in sensitivity analysis.

The basic model formulation first attempted was to define a quality level that maximized the net benefits of pollution control. Since the benefits of water pollution control are difficult to qualify, much less to put in commensurate units, the question of finding a quality level that would maximize net benefits was soon abandoned. Instead, a surrogate problem, that of finding the least cost mix of alternatives that satisfy a given goal, was attacked. Such a problem statement immediately suggests an optimization approach and several authors have suggested similar formulations for the problem of selecting treatment alternatives. These are of the form:

$$\text{Minimize } z = \sum_{j=1}^{n} f_j(x_j) \tag{17.1}$$

subject to

$$\sum_{j=1}^{n} A_{ij}(x_j) \geqslant b_i \qquad i = 1, \ldots, m \tag{17.2}$$

$$u_j \geqslant x_j \geqslant 0 \qquad j = 1, \ldots, n \tag{17.3}$$

where

x_j = the amount of waste removed at source j in pounds per day of biochemical oxygen demand (decision variable).

u_j = the upper bound on waste that can be removed at source j in pounds per day of biochemical oxygen demand (known).

$f_j(x_j)$ = the cost of removal of x_j (known).

$A_{ij}(x_j)$ = the quality response at some point i in the water body caused by a waste loading of x_j, at source j, for a given set of physical system parameters.

b_i = the minimum desired improvement in quality at point i.

There are several important assumptions buried in this simple formulation that bear discussion and examination. Notice first that the objective function Equation 17.1 calls for the minimization of costs for the region under investigation as a whole. The choice of which sources will be reduced will be based on a combination of strategic location and efficient means for treating wastes rather than on some notion of how much damage is being caused by the waste source. The formulation stresses an overall efficiency objective without taking into consideration equity or distributional problems. Thus, it would be possible and has in fact occurred in several applications studies that large, inefficient sources which have done little to reduce their waste flows are required to do nothing even though the damage they cause is great while small highly efficient sources where investment has already been made will be called on to treat further. This calls for some means to reallocate the efficiency costs of the improvement either among the polluters or among the beneficiaries, and some regional institution to administer and collect that cost. Neither the establishment of an allocation scheme that is satisfactory to all concerned nor of a strong regional institution to force such a scheme has been achieved with any particular success. This problem will be discussed in detail later.

Another important aspect of the formulation is Inequality 17.2. This states that improvements in quality must be at least as great as desired. It is interesting to note that the whole argument about establishing preferences for water use has been reduced to a question of meeting a measure of effectiveness in terms of a single physical parameter. Usually, this parameter is the dissolved oxygen

(D.O.) concentration in water. The biologic activity associated with waste reduction requires D.O. Thus the level of this parameter in the water is a good indication of the general pollution aspects in the surrounding areas. The means for treating wastes to raise stream D.O. also take care of many other important parameters such as acidic content, solids and pathogenic disease organisms.

Notice that quality is only considered at a set of discrete points. Further, there is no aspect of time in the formulation, that is, the problem is viewed as steady state under some conservative definition of water body parameters rather than reflecting the stochastic nature and uncertainty of stream flow, waste flows, and physical parameters.

Attempts to extend the model to the stochastic case will be discussed, but they are very limited. The definition of the transfer function $A_{ij}(x_j)$ as a function of the waste load removal is one that can be easily relaxed, and all authors have used a linear systems approach with superposition of waste effects. Notice also that the problem as considered here contains only those alternatives that might be considered at a particular source and allows for no joint treatment, no treatment external to a source, and no changes in waste loads at a source other than known and established methods. In addition, waste loadings are assumed constant when in fact they vary stochastically. The decision variables x_j represent the amount of present waste discharge that will be removed and are specified to always be non-negative. Thus, no source is allowed to reduce its treatment level and there can be no further degradation of quality conditions. Where present quality levels are presently high they must remain high. This leads to interesting questions of whether new industry could be allowed to use the water body's assimilative capacity without violating this constraint. Is the strategy here to cause the new industry to treat its wastes totally, to buy rights to the assimilative capacity owned by others, to reallocate the resources of the water body with the newcomer included, or possibly to prepare for such an occurrence by setting goals higher than desired? None of these cases seem completely equitable.

Attempts at solving the problem are aided by the linear assumption for the constraints and by the form of $f_j(x_j)$. While investment of this nature is rather lumpy because of the fixed charge character of design improvements, it is fairly easy to see the function as being convex (that is, with the marginal cost of treatment increasing with increasing waste removal). From that point, Thomann and Sobel [36] took the course of linear approximations of the convex function and used linear programming. Later, Liebman and Lynn [26] chose discrete dynamic programming. Deininger [4] used chance constrained programming to account for stochastic variation but presents no large-scale computational evidence. Falkner [7] suggests a primal dual heuristic for the stochastic problem. One use of this model is described in the next section.

The model that consists of Equations 17.1 through 17.3 has been adapted to reflect a different allocation of costs than those chosen under the efficiency objective of minimizing regional costs without regard to the sources chosen for abatement. One such attempt was the "equity" or uniform treatment formulation which required that each waste source in the region remove the same percentage of its waste load. The uniform treatment level for the region was to be chosen as the least level at which the given goals could be reached. The model can be written as

Minimize S (17.4)

subject to:

$$\sum_j B_{ij} x_j \geqslant b_i \qquad i = 1, \ldots, m \qquad (17.5)$$

$$\left. \begin{array}{ll} P_j + \dfrac{x_j (1 - P_j)}{\ell_j} = S & \text{if } S \geqslant P_j \\[2ex] x_j = 0 & \text{if } S < P_j \end{array} \right\} \qquad (17.6)$$

$$0 \leqslant x_j \leqslant \ell_j \qquad j = 1, \ldots, n \qquad (17.7)$$

where

B_{ij} = the unit response of water quality in section i due to a unit change in load at source j;

S = the uniform treatment level for the region defined as percent removal of the initial waste u_j at each source;

P_j = the present percent of waste u_j removed;

ℓ_j = the amount of waste presently being discharged at source j after P_j percent removal of the original waste loads;

x_j = the amount of the presently discharged waste at j to be removed;

and the other symbols are as previously defined. Note that $\ell_j = (1 - P_j)u_j$ for each source.

This formulation presents no problems if no treatment facilities already exist in which case the total waste discharge ℓ_j from each source is u_j. But if some treatment already exists, a constraint such as Equations 17.6 is needed. That allows the choice of a uniform treatment level below the existing treatment if it is acceptable. While the problem of solving Equations 17.4 through 17.7 would appear quite difficult as there are discontinuities in the constraint set, in fact optimal solution is obtained by a simple iterative process in which S is increased incrementally until the goals are met.

This uniform model is essentially the same as the efficiency model in Equations 17.1 through 17.3 but has an added constraint, Equation 17.6, which means that the regional treatment cost for the uniform model must be at least as great as that for the efficiency model. The uniform model's "equity" feature of allocating costs to users more fairly by requiring all users to provide treatment to the same specified treatment level is the reason for this increase in regional cost. However, closer examination of the features of the plan reveals it has its faults. Requiring the same percentage of waste reduction ignores the fact that the size of waste discharges and the costs associated with fixed improvements vary greatly from source to source. Thus a high degree of removal at a site of a small waste source contributes little to quality but does increase costs at that source. Similarly, the use of a uniform treatment level requires that all sources including those having no effect because of their location must raise their treatment level to obtain increased quality at a particular point. However, the model does have the appeal that it is easy to administer in the sense that each polluter is told directly the percentage of waste he must remove and no attention need be given to cost allocation as it has to be internalized.

A compromise between these two extremes has been suggested. It is the zoned uniform model and requires that sources be divided into zones which reflect equivalent activity, location and/or damages created and that uniform treatment levels be found for each of these zones so that a given quality goal is reached for the region at least cost. This model is formulated as:

Minimize $\sum_{j=1}^{n} f_j(x_j)$

subject to:

$$\sum_j B_{ij} x_j \geq b_i \quad i = 1, \ldots, m$$

$$\left.\begin{array}{ll} P_j + \dfrac{x_j(1 - P_j)}{\ell_j} = S_k & \text{if } S_k \geq P_j \\[2mm] x_j = 0 & \text{if } S_k < P_j \end{array}\right\} \quad \begin{array}{l} k = 1, \ldots, K \text{ and} \\ j \in R_k \end{array}$$

$$0 \leq x_j \leq \ell_j \qquad\qquad\qquad j = 1, \ldots, n$$

where

S_k = the uniform treatment level in zone k;
R_k = the set of sources j in zone k;
K = number of zones;

and all other symbols are as defined previously.

An optimal solution method based on a branch and bound method has been suggested for this problem by Liebman and Marks [19]. Obviously, the solution obtained depends greatly on the way the waste sources have been assigned to zones. If each zone were an individual source, the problem becomes the least cost model, while with only one zone the problem becomes the uniform cost model.

17.6 The Delaware River Basin Experience

Actual use of a management model (such as those just described) for analysis in large-scale planning was first accomplished on a study of the Delaware Estuary, which runs through New Jersey, Pennsylvania, and Delaware, by the Federal Water Quality Administration (now Environmental Protection Agency) in the period 1964 to 1967. Here a problem with 90 major waste sources, approximately 24 quality constraints, and piecewise linear approximations for cost functions was solved using linear programming for a variety of different assumptions about goals, stream parameters, and economic parameters. Results of the sensitivity analysis were reported by Thomann and Marks [35].

In designing water quality improvement programs for the Delaware Estuary, the federal Water Quality Administration generated several alternative schemes to reach a range of quality goals. They considered only the possibility of waste treatment at a source over other technical alternatives such as low flow augmentation, piping, stream aeration, and storm water control, because they could demonstrate that these alternatives were clearly dominated for the particular conditions on the Delaware. No consideration was given to taxing or incentive schemes or to the possibility of regional treatment.

Six sets of alternative water quality goals were chosen with the help of citizens' groups, conservationists, industrialists, and governmental representatives. These are shown in Table 17.1 along with the cost to meet the goals under different cost allocation assumptions and with some estimates of benefits. Objective set I represented the best that could technically be obtained by requiring maximum waste reduction from the 90 largest waste producers using the estuary. At the other extreme, objective set V represented the cost to keep the conditions as they were at the time. As can be seen in Table 17.1, a considerable expense is needed just to maintain the status quo. The objective sets II, IIA, III, and IV represent various possible alternatives in between.

Costs including capital costs and the present value of operation and maintenance expenditures were estimated to obtain each quality objective set using the least cost, uniform, and zoned uniform treatment models. Enumeration of the quality to be obtained from each objective set including an accounting of the visual, esthetic, and public health benefits, and an attempt at quantifying dollar values for fisheries, recreation, and water supply was made. These costs and benefits are presented in Table 17.1. The data is from Smith and Morris [30].

Table 17.1   Capital and Present Value of Operation and Maintenance Costs in Million Dollars to Obtain Stated Objectives under Three Types of Management Models (Dollar value of some of the benefits for each objective are given.)

Objective Set	Least Cost Model	Zoned Uniform Model	Uniform Model	Evaluation of Some Benefits ($ Million)
I	695	695	695	492
II	442	493	509	430
IIA	387	430	439	430
III	291	326	383	303
IV	238	256	319	282
V	140	140	140	162

There are several important factors to be noted about the costs. First, the cost of maintaining present conditions over the next 15 to 20 years is significant. Without action things will get worse. In the lower quality ranges, the difference between a least cost and uniform treatment model is quite significant. To reach higher quality levels, it must be remembered that there are many waste sources over which there is no control readily available. Thus, to account for these, more of the treatable wastes must be removed. Since the cost of treatment versus the percentage of waste at a source removed is highly convex, costs go up quite quickly. As well, there are relatively few waste sources under control and meeting higher goals requires that almost all be removed, thus giving little difference between allocation models.

As noted previously, an institution exists for the region specifically designed and empowered to deal with water resource problems, the Delaware River Basin Commission. Such figures as those in Table 17.1 provide excellent information for such a decision-making body to use as input for its planning along with its comprehension of the region and its political, social and economic complexity. The plan finally chosen by the DRBC was a compromise between two originally specified. Objective set III was strongly championed by industrial and governmental interests who had a large economic stake in the outcome. Objective set II or I was the choice of the various conservation and civic groups. A compromise, objective set IIA, was selected and the DRBC is now involved in the problems of implementing, financing and overseeing the results for these objectives.

17.7 Related Research
Recently, other researchers have begun to investigate additional methods of waste management at the source using operations research techniques. Graves, Hatfield, and Whinston [11] have suggested a large-scale decomposition method with column generation for the problem of choosing pipe networks for the transportation of wastes to less sensitive points in a water body. They were not able to consider the problem of treatment as well as piping because of the extreme nonlinearities this introduces. Thus the problem of locating regional treatment facilities that minimize the cost to meet quality goals and the problem of finding measures for allocating those costs remain two major unsolved problems. Hope-

fully advancement in operations research techniques will someday provide methods for these. Currently, some work by Schaake, Marks, and Leclerc [28] is directed towards the management and control of the highly stochastic storm water overflow problems that plague Boston harbor with sudden shock loads of street washings and sewage bypasses whenever storms occur. With increasing urbanization that concentrates wastes and drainage, such problems are increasing rapidly and alternatives in control by storage to reduce peaks and treatment to improve quality are under investigation. Problems in limiting thermal pollution caused by electric power generation are also under investigation. The effects of water-body temperature standards on locational patterns and equipment investment are analyzed using an efficiency based optimization model by Jirka and Marks [15].

Turning to alternatives that change the assimilative capacity of water bodies, we see that several different research directions involving operations research have developed. Tassarov, Perlis, and Davidson [33] have investigated the optimal means of introducing oxygen into polluted streams using control theory methods. Davis [3] has also done a detailed analysis of stream oxygen alternatives on the Potomac. Ortolano and Thomas [24] have looked at other nontreatment alternatives such as the removal of bottom deposits. Jaworski, Weber, and Deininger [14] have investigated optimal release sequences from reservoirs to provide downstream dilution water for wastes using dynamic programming while Grantham et al. [10] have used linear programming to estimate the benefits of low flow release. Young and Gitto [38] considered the problem of optimal reservoir releases for acid mine drainage control. Several researchers have addressed the problem of recycling, renovation and reuse of water. Bishop and Hendricks [1] have proposed a transshipment type model for allocating waste water to treatment and transportation.

A third and more recent level of development has been models to demonstrate the effects of cost distribution policy explicitly in the model formulation. One possible alternative for pollution control is the use of effluent charges or incentives to change waste production patterns either through changes in processes in industry, changes in resource use, or treatment of wastes. Here the individual, faced with a charge for using the stream assimilative capacity, optimizes his production investment decision taking social costs into account as well. Kneese and Bower [17] support the idea that such economic schemes present an excellent means for internalizing the externalities of pollution and allowing the polluter to make the most efficient decision about controlling his pollution production. Several writers have joined in with comments on economic schemes such as Johnson [6] and Brown and Mar [2]. Others have looked at various methods for decentralizing investment decisions. Upton [37] looked at the stochastic stream-flow problem and its influence on a combination of effluent changes and waste treatment using a simple model. Hass [13] showed how a decentralized taxation scheme could be established with imperfect knowledge of individual's cost functions. Dorfman and Jacoby [5] used a very simple model to generate the transformation surface between different objectives for water quality control. By weighting objectives differently, they were able to show how solutions varied as objectives changed.

17.8 Implementation and Prospects for the Future

The impact of operations research on water quality management over the last 6 to 8 years has been profound in the sense that it has completely revamped the tools and analytic procedures for analysts. We would like to say that there has been complete and total success, but unfortunately there is a growing concern among professionals about the proper way of implementing solutions in this complex environment. From its conception, systems analysis has been sold almost evangelically as a panacea, as a means for isolating and systematizing all possible problems. We know now that this is not true; we should use analytic techniques as some of our many available tools for gaining information about a problem rather than as a way for having the computer pour out optimal solutions. Too little attention has been brought to bear on the relationship, or lack thereof, between the mathematically optimal solution to a contrived formulation and the actual solution. What is important here is the demonstration that analytic techniques may be used in very complex problems to help a decision maker in a very subjective planning process. Even though a universal formulation including all possible alternatives, variations, and constraints cannot be accomplished, more modest analyses can abstract the essence of the tradeoffs between conflicting objectives and competing alternatives. Particularly in the field of water quality management, such tasks are being carried out routinely, and the demand for more and better techniques and applications, as well as the right atmosphere for their use, will continue to expand.

The problems of implementing and operating a water quality management plan present many ways the analyst can contribute. Large-scale monitoring systems will be necessary to ward off long-term trends and short-run emergencies. Control and economic alternatives for both these conditions must be studied. In addition, questions of cost allocation and development activities in the region must be understood. Can rights for the assimilative capacity of the stream be owned and traded? How does the management system react to new waste sources that enter the system or old waste sources that are removed?

A promising area of new research is that of modeling and optimizing in the context of social and political systems. The earlier work mentioned involving systems dynamics modeling combined with attempts at choosing optimal control schemes that can be successfully implemented presents an important challenge, but little has been done to promote actual planning for such use. One roadblock is the lack of strong effective institutional bodies. The Delaware River Basin Commission chose to go to regulation and enforcement in terms of specific treatment requests rather than try economic means because it felt stronger in taking a more traditional approach. In most areas, for that matter, regional institutions that could administer such a plan do not exist. Another roadblock lies in the computational and analysis question. What should be the level and structure of charges? Should there be some form of market mechanism for establishing prices? How are short-run (daily and weekly) problems and long-run (multiyear) problems handled? Such problems may well be attacked in the future using operations research techniques.

In terms of management models, much more development in techniques is needed. Most important is the consideration of the stochastic nature of the problem and of the control of pollution away from the source such as in a regional treatment system. Work in many directions has been started but requires additional input in terms of techniques and analysis.

In conclusion, there is a growing need for further application of quantitative analysis in public sector problems. One would almost suggest that we are on the verge of "putting it all together," of deriving the essence of the generalized methodology. Certainly, in water quality management, such techniques have not only been successfully adopted but have found their way into every facet of planning and design. Hopefully, such an exercise will prompt more development and a greater realization of the place for quantitative analysis in decision making in complex systems.

References

1. Bishop, A., and D. Hendricks, "Water Reuse Systems Analysis," *Journal of the Sanitary Engineering Division, American Society of Civil Engineers,* vol. 97, SA1, February 1971.

2. Brown, G., and B. Mar, "Dynamic Economic Efficiency of Water Quality Standards or Changes," *Water Resources Research,* December 1968.

3. Davis, Robert K., *The Range of Choice in Water Management: A Study of Dissolved Oxygen in the Potomac Estuary,* The Johns Hopkins Press, Baltimore, Md., 1968.

4. Deininger, R. A., "Water Quality Management: The Planning of Economically Optimal Pollution Control Systems," Ph.D. thesis, Northwestern University, Evanston, Ill., 1965.

5. Dorfman, R., and H. D. Jacoby, "A Model of Public Decisions Illustrated by a Water Pollution Policy Problem," in *Analysis and Evaluation of Public Expenditures: The PPB System,* U.S. Government Printing Office, Washington, D.C., vol. 1, 1969.

6. Evenson, D. E., G. T. Orlob, and J. R. Monser, "Preliminary Selection of Waste Treatment Systems," *Journal of the Water Pollution Control Federation,* vol. 41, November 1969.

7. Falkner, C., "Linear Programming in Water Quality Management: Problems under Uncertainty," Water Resources Center, University of Wisconsin, Madison, Wis., December 1969.

8. Frankel, R., "Viewing Water Renovation and Reuse in Regional Water Resource Systems," *Water Resources Research,* vol. 3, no. 1, 1967.

9. Gates, W. E., R. M. Males, and J. F. Walker, "Application of Industrial Dynamics Concepts to Decision Making in Environmental Management," *Water Resources Research,* vol. 6, December 1970.

10. Grantham, G., E. E. Pyatt, J. P. Heaney, and B. J. Carter, "Model for Flow Augmentation Analysis—An Overview," *Journal of the Sanitary Engineering Division, American Society of Civil Engineers,* vol. 90, SA5, October 1970.

11. Graves, G., G. Hatfield, and A. Whinston, "Water Pollution Control Using By-Pass Piping," *Water Resources Research,* vol. 5, no. 1, 1969.

12. Harleman, D. R. F., "Water Quality Analysis in Estuaries—Outline of Methodology," Notes for a Summer Short Course in Systematic Analysis of Water Resource Problems, M.I.T., Cambridge, Massachusetts, August 29 to September 3, 1970 (mimeo).

13. Hass, J. E., "Optimal Taxing for the Abatement of Water Pollution," *Water Resources Research*, vol. 6, no. 353, 1970.

14. Jaworski, H. A., W. J. Weber, and R. A. Deininger, "Optimal Release Sequences for Water Quality Control in Multiple Reservoir Systems," *Journal of the Sanitary Engineering Division, American Society of Civil Engineers*, vol. 96, SA2, April 1970.

15. Jirka, G., and D. H. Marks, "Location of Thermal Generating Facilities under Environmental Considerations," Technical Report 71-1, Urban Systems Laboratory, M.I.T., Cambridge, Massachusetts, January 1971.

16. Johnson, E. L., "A Study in the Economics of Water Quality Management," *Water Resources Research*, vol. 3, no. 2, 1967.

17. Kneese, A. V., and B. T. Bower, *Managing Water Quality, Economics, Technology, Institutions*, The Johns Hopkins Press, Baltimore, Maryland, 1968.

18. Liebman, J. C., and W. R. Lynn, "The Optimal Allocation of Stream Dissolved Oxygen Resources," *Water Resources Research*, vol. 2, no. 3, 1966.

19. Liebman, J. C., and D. H. Marks, "A Balas Algorithm for Zoned Uniform Treatment," *Journal of the Sanitary Engineering Division, American Society of Civil Engineers*, vol. 94, August 1968.

20. Loucks, D. P., and W. R. Lynn, "Probabilistic Models for Predicting Stream Quality," *Water Resources Research*, vol. 2, no. 3, 1966.

21. Loucks, D. P., C. S. ReVelle, and W. Lynn, "Linear Programming Models for Water Pollution Control," *Management Science*, vol. 14, December 1967.

22. Miernyk, W., "An Inter-industry Forecasting Model with Water Quantity and Quality Constraints," Systems Analysis for Great Lakes Water Resources, Proceedings, Fourth Symposium on Water Resources Research, Water Resources Center, Ohio State University, Columbus, Ohio, 1969.

23. O'Conner, D. J., "The Temporal and Spatial Distribution of Dissolved Oxygen in Streams," *Water Resources Research*, vol. 3, no. 1, 1967.

24. Ortolano, L., and H. Thomas, "An Examination of Non-Treatment Plant Alternatives in Water Pollution Control," Chemical Engineering Progress Symposium, American Institute of Chemical Engineers, 1968.

25. Pence, G., J. M. Jeglic, and R. V. Thomann, "The Development and Application of a Time Varying Dissolved Oxygen Model," *Journal of the Sanitary Engineering Division, American Society of Civil Engineers*, vol. 94, SA2, April 1968.

26. ReVelle, C. S., D. P. Loucks, and W. Lynn, "Linear Programming Applied to Water Quality Management," *Water Resources Research*, vol. 4, February 1968.

27. Russell, C. S., and W. O. Spofford, "A Quantitative Framework for Residuals—Environmental Quality Management," Proceedings of the 1969 Water Resources Seminar, Water Resources Research Center, Purdue University, Lafayette, Indiana, 1969.

28. Schaake, J. C., D. H. Marks, and G. Leclerc, "Management of Storm Water Overflows," Report on Research for the Office of Water Resources Research, M.I.T., Cambridge, Massachusetts, 1971 (mimeo).

29. Shih, Chia Shun, and P. Krishnan, "Dynamic Optimization for Industrial Waste Treatment Design," *Journal of the Water Pollution Control Federation*, vol. 41, October 1969.

30. Smith, E. T., and A. L. Morris, "Systems Analysis of Water Quality Management," *Journal of the Water Pollution Control Federation*, vol. 41, September 1969.

31. Sobel, M. T., "Water Quality Improvement Programming Problems," *Water Resources Research*, vol. 1, no. 4, 1965.

32. Stillson, R. T., "Regional Trade and Structure Model for Pollution Abatement Study," Systems Analysis for Great Lakes Water Resources, Proceedings, Fourth Symposium on Water Resources Research, Water Resources, Center, Ohio State University, Columbus, Ohio, 1969.

33. Tarassov, V., H. J. Perlis, and B. Davidson, "Optimization of a Class of River Aeration Problems by Use of Multivariable Distributed Parameters, Control Theory," *Water Resources Research*, vol. 5, no. 3, June 1969.

34. Thomann, R. V., "Mathematical Model for Dissolved Oxygen," *Journal of the Sanitary Engineering Division, American Society of Civil Engineers*, vol. 89, SA5, 1963.

35. Thomann, R. V., and D. H. Marks, "Recent Results from a Systems Analysis," Third International Conference, Water Pollution Control Federation, Munich, Germany, 1966.

36. Thomann, R. V., and M. J. Sobel, "Estuarine Water Quality Management and Forecasting," *Journal of the Sanitary Engineering Division, American Society of Civil Engineers*, vol. 90, SA5, October 1964.

37. Upton, C., "A Model of Water Quality Management Under Uncertainty," *Water Resources Research*, vol. 6, no. 3, 1970.

38. Young, G. K., and L. T. Gitto, "Stream Flow Regulation for Acid Control," IBM Symposium on Water and Air Resources Management, October 1967.

39. "Water Quality Criteria," Report of the National Technical Advisory Committee to the Secretary of the Interior, U.S. Government Printing Office, April 1968.

40. Wolman, A., "The Metabolism of Cities," *Scientific American*, vol. 218, no. 3, September 1965.

18

A Rational Approach for Government Decisions concerning Air Pollution

Howard M. Ellis and Ralph L. Keeney

18.1 Introduction

In New York City, the mayor must decide whether to approve a proposed major addition to Consolidated Edison's electric-power generating station in Astoria, Queens. If this addition is approved, city residents, over the next several years, would be reasonably assured of receiving at fair economic cost the growing quantity of electricity that they demand. However, approval of the addition would lead to a further worsening of the city's air quality, particularly in terms of the air pollutants sulfur dioxide, particulates, and nitrogen oxides. Should this addition be approved?

In both Boston and New York City, the respective city councils must decide whether to pass legislation that would place stringent limits on the sulfur content of fuels burned in the city. If passed, the legislation would lead to a definite improvement in the city's air quality—especially in terms of the air pollutant sulfur dioxide. However, passage of this legislation would require residents to incur added annual costs for heating and electricity to pay for the more expensive low-sulfur-content fuels. Should these city councils pass such legislation?

In Washington, D.C., the U.S. Congress must decide whether to establish very stringent emission standards for carbon monoxide, hydrocarbons, and nitrogen oxides for all motor vehicles manufactured and sold in this country after January 1, 1975. Establishment of these standards would contribute toward improving our air quality. On the other hand, they would require the public to pay significantly more money for new automobiles. Should Congress adopt these stringent standards?

Each of these decision problems is faced presently or has been faced recently by public officials. Moreover, they are representative of a host of similar problems that public officials are increasingly being asked to confront, namely, "Should government adopt a specific, proposed program intended to improve the air quality?" With each, there is the additional question, "What should the air quality standard be?" Due to the complex nature of these problems, an individual finds it difficult to decide which, if any, of a series of proposed air pollution control programs to support.

The purpose of this work is to describe how a public official, by using the concept of decision analysis,[1] can obtain help in choosing an air pollution control program. To illustrate the method of analysis we focus on one specific problem faced by one particular individual, namely the mayor of New York City. A survey of air pollution problems and current air pollution control programs in New York is given in Eisenbud [3].

Before beginning, we should make clear our views on the contribution of this chapter. We do not claim to have the solution to any of the current air pollution problems, nor do we think decision analysis is the panacea, or even a useful approach, for analyzing proposed solutions to all of these problems. However, in certain cases, it may be worthwhile to examine proposed policies in more detail than is currently done, and decision analysis may prove to be a useful approach for this.

Our work here is meant to be somewhat exploratory—an attempt to find out if in fact decision analysis is useful for certain problems. As such, our results and conclusions must be interpreted as preliminary. We believe they do represent a good basis upon which others can comment and critically review. This will hopefully begin a process of modification and improvement of the work presented here.

Motivation for This Work

Three of the main reasons for the difficulty experienced by public officials in selecting an air pollution control strategy are as follows:

1. The official has several conflicting objectives, such as improving air quality and limiting total program costs, that he wishes to satisfy. These objectives must be identified and clearly defined.
2. The extent to which any alternative program will achieve these objectives cannot be precisely specified. Said another way, there are inherent uncertainties in the effectiveness of any proposed program.
3. Because of conflicting objectives, the official is faced with the complex task of deciding how much achievement on each objective he is willing to forego in order to achieve specified amounts on other objectives. That is, the trade-offs between the conflicting objectives must be considered.

1. Two easily readable introductions to decision analysis are Howard [8] and Raiffa [18].

Notwithstanding these complexities, an air pollution control program must still be evaluated. However, it seems unreasonable to assume that a busy public official has the facility or the time to process rationally all the relevant information informally in his mind and then to come up with a responsible decision. The alternative we suggest, decision analysis, is designed to assist the official in examining proposed programs and analyzing their overall implications. Many of the pros and cons of this approach are discussed in detail in Chapter 5 in this volume. [11]

One would like the analysis to aid the public official in dealing with the particularly difficult aspects of choosing an air pollution control program identified earlier. The approach we suggest involves the following steps:

1. *Structuring the decision problem.* This includes identifying all objectives and selecting, for each of these, a measure of effectiveness which can be used to indicate the degree to which the objective is met.
2. *Describing the possible consequences* of each alternative program in terms of the effectiveness measures. Thus, the uncertainties associated with the proposed programs are specified.
3. *Prescribing the relative preferences* of the public official for each possible consequence. Here, the trade-offs among the conflicting objectives are precisely identified.
4. *Rationally synthesizing the information* from the first three steps to decide which of the proposed programs to support.

Note that the first three steps correspond with the three main difficulties identified in choosing among alternative air pollution control programs. The basic idea is, then, to break the problem into parts, which by themselves are still quite complex but presumably easier than the entire problem tackled as a whole; separately work on these parts; and then put the parts together to make implications about the best course of action for the public official.

Looking at the four steps, a public official might say, "But that's the way I make all my decisions." It may well be. However, the distinction between our approach and more traditional procedures is the degree of formality of each step. For instance, with decision analysis, the uncertainties are quantified using subjective or judgmental probabilities and the official's preferences are represented by utilities. In step four, the best alternative is that which has the greatest expected utility. The difference between decision analysis and the current approaches for choosing an air pollution control program are discussed in more detail in Section 18.3.

Outline of the Chapter
A brief overview of the air pollution control problem in New York City is given in Section 18.2. The specific problem which we use for our discussion in the rest of the paper is also introduced.

Section 18.3 is concerned with identifying objectives and selecting an adequate measure of effectiveness for each of these. The end result is a set of objectives and associated effectiveness measures for the analysis of our decision problem. These concern the physical (health), economic, and psychological well-being of the residents of New York City as well as costs to the government and the political implications of each program alternative.

In Section 18.4, the methods which were used to describe the possible consequences of each alternative program in terms of a probability distribution over the measures of effectiveness are discussed. Then, in Section 18.5, we indicate how the public official can decide with some conviction which of the program alternatives he prefers.

A few remarks on the impacts of the results of the study on which this chapter is principally based are given in Section 18.6. Our conclusions are presented in Section 18.7.

18.2 The Air Pollution Control Problem of New York City
A general model of the process by which air pollution control programs are designed and evaluated is shown in Figure 18.1. The major inputs are the standard of living that affects demand for electric power, and so on, weather, air pollution technology, and current air pollution programs and legislation. These directly influence the pollutant emissions, and thus the pollution concentrations, which are measured. The pollution concentrations influence what can be considered as outputs of the process, namely, adverse effects on the residents of the city and adverse effects on the city's economy.

Public officials control this process through the enactment of laws and programs concerning air pollution. In addition to the outputs in Figure 18.1, other major determinants of the air pollution control program are the costs of the various alternatives, the exist-

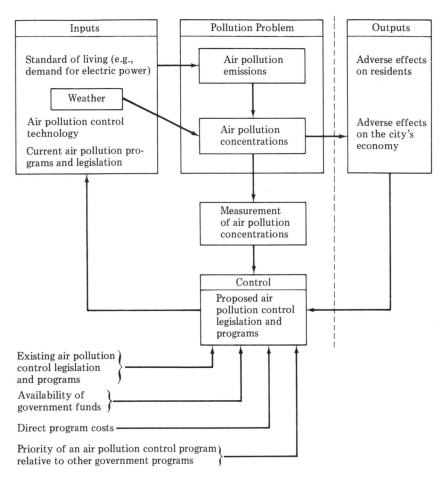

Figure 18.1   General model for evaluating air pollution control programs.
Note: the arrow symbol ⟶ reads "influences."

ing legislation on air pollution, the overall availability of municipal funds and the priority for air pollution control relative to other municipal needs. As the result of these interacting elements, an air pollution control program is developed.

The main problem with this control process as it is now practiced is that the outputs are not considered much in choosing air pollution policy. The reason is, of course, the complexities indicated in the introduction: the difficulty in defining output measures, establishing the relationships between pollution concentrations and these measures, and specifying preferences for the various possible outputs. As a substitute for this information, the public official must rely on the measured air pollution concentrations. In a sense, the process can be thought of as being short-circuited at the dashed line in Figure 18.1. Thus, the current decision-making process excludes the most important information necessary for rational control. Our efforts are meant to eliminate the short circuit and bring the outputs into the decision-making process.

The Sulfur Decision Problem

In 1970, major decisions still to be made in New York City's air pollution control program included those concerning the control of sulfur dioxide. Table 18.1 presents a breakdown of the estimated 1972 emissions of sulfur dioxide from sources within the city. These estimations account for all provisions of existing laws enacted through mid-1971.

Over 90 percent of these emissions arise from the burning of fuels for space heating and power generation. Also, the only current, practical way to reduce emissions from these sources is to lower the sulfur content of the fuels burned. Therefore, one major

Table 18.1   Estimated 1972 Emissions of Sulfur Dioxide in New York City [16]

Source of Emissions	Emissions of Sulfur Dioxide	
	(tons)	(percent of total)
Incineration of refuse	2,500	0.6
Motor vehicles	20,400	5.1
Industrial processes	9,900	2.5
Space heating	195,300	49.2
Power generation	169,500	42.6
Total	397,600	100.0

decision still faced by the city with regard to its air pollution control program is the "sulfur decision problem." That problem refers to whether and how much to lower the legal limit on the sulfur content of fuels burned in the city below the present legal limit of 1 percent. In what follows we will use the sulfur decision problem to illustrate the proposed methods for analysis.

18.3 Specification of Objectives and Measures of Effectiveness for the Analysis

In this section we specify what we believe is a reasonable set of objectives and measures of effectiveness for an air pollution control program in New York City. The manner by which these were chosen is important, and so this section follows the thought process used to arrive at the results. The discussion begins with a presentation of objectives currently in common use by public officials. These are rejected as inadequate, and an alternative set of objectives are suggested. This set represents the basis for what is "an evolutionary process" to a final set of major objectives. Then, we begin to associate measures of effectiveness with each objective. This forces us to specify the objectives further. The final result is seven objectives and measures of effectiveness which are used to describe the consequences of each of the alternative courses of action.

Inadequacy of the Objectives Currently Used by Public Officials
One might understandably ask why so much effort is being devoted to specifying objectives for an air pollution control program. Surely with all the experience certain public officials have had with such problems, the objectives must be well known? Table 18.2 indicates the kinds of objectives and measures of effectiveness principally used in making policy relating to air pollution control programs.

The main problems with this set of objectives and effectiveness measures can be illustrated by the following: Almost any public official will state that his primary objective in decisions relating to air pollution is to improve air quality. Of course, air quality *per se* is of very little, if any, concern to the official. What is of concern are the fundamental human benefits to his constituency and the direct and indirect costs that result from a given air quality. Air quality, as measured by pollutant concentration levels, merely

Table 18.2   The Objectives and Measures of Effectiveness Currently Used by Public Officials in the Analysis of Air Pollution Decisions

Objective	Associated Measure of Effectiveness
1. Improve air quality	Citywide concentrations of air pollutants
2. "Minimize" the costs to the city government of improving the air quality	Direct costs to the city government
3. "Minimize" the costs to city residents of improving the air quality	Direct costs to city residents

serves as a convenient, but inadequate, proxy for these fundamental benefits and costs. And only when the public official begins grappling with such basic questions as "How much should we improve air quality?" or "Should we spend $X of government money to reduce emissions of air pollutants by Y percent?" Does the inadequacy of the traditional objectives and their associated measures of effectiveness become apparent?

What the public official needs for choosing among air pollution control programs is a much clearer understanding of how each of these alternatives affects the fundamental human benefits and costs of concern to him. Whether he uses this understanding explicitly or implicitly in the subsequent analysis is not important at this point. What is important is that he understand as clearly as possible the package of fundamental benefits and costs associated with each alternative in his decision problem so that he has a meaningful basis for making a responsible decision.

To provide this meaningful basis, it is necessary to move behind the traditional objectives used by public officials and ask what really is of concern to the official. In other words, what are his true objectives related to the air pollution problem.

Preliminary Identification of Major Objectives
In almost every decision problem faced by the mayor of New York City, his most fundamental objective is to improve the well-being of his constituents. However, one must spell out in more detail what is meant by this objective as it pertains to air pollution. Precisely what would the mayor like to accomplish by his actions in

the air pollution area? After some serious thought, we divided the overall objective into four major objectives:

1. Decrease the adverse effects of air pollution on the health of New York City residents.
2. Decrease the adverse economic effects of air pollution on the residents.
3. Decrease the adverse effects of air pollution on the psychological well-being of the residents.
4. Decrease the net costs of air pollution to the city government.

These objectives require little justification. However, it should be noted that the second objective is meant to include costs of the air pollution control program in addition to the costs due to the pollution. Concerning the fourth objective, net costs include all the direct costs, such as the costs of an air pollution control program, as well as indirect costs such as those due to migration of businesses and industry from the city, less tourism, and tax revenue losses due to workers in the city who miss work, and so on, due to sickness caused by air pollution.

It was not too difficult to decide that the above four objectives are of major concern to the mayor of New York. However, the more difficult problem of whether these four include all the issues of importance to the mayor must be addressed. For instance, nothing has been said about political implications. No mention has been made of the economic consequences of the various alternatives on New York State, on the federal government, on businesses, or on nonresidents of New York City. Furthermore, nothing has been said about the benefits of improved air quality to nonresidents. Should these factors be included in a complete analysis of proposed air pollution control programs?

The next subsection examines the issue of how to decide whether a proposed objective should be included in the analysis of a decision problem. The results are then used to further specify the mayor's objectives.

Guidelines for Including an Objective in the Analysis
When should a proposed objective be included in a decision problem? Basically, this should be done if the decision maker feels that the different degrees to which that objective might be achieved by the alternative programs would be important when choosing among

them. To be more specific, we state what will be referred to as the test of importance: An objective is important to the decision maker if prior to any formal analysis, he feels that explicit introduction of that objective into the analysis of the decision problem could possibly alter the optimal strategy implied by a formal analysis not including that objective. If an objective is important in this sense, then it should be included in the analysis. It is worthwhile to mention that any objectives deemed unimportant by the criterion should be reconsidered, at least informally, after any subsequent analysis as a check on one's prior conclusions.

There are two levels on which one could use the test of importance. On a mathematical level, it is possible to ascertain whether an objective should be included in the analysis of alternatives by examining both the properties of the probability distributions describing the possible consequences for each alternative and the properties of the decision maker's preferences for those consequences. The details of this approach are found in Ellis [4] and will not be presented here.

The second level involves the informal use of the test of importance. The decision maker qualitatively considers the influence a particular objective might have on the ensuing analysis. If he feels it is likely to affect the outcome of the analysis, then the objective is included. When this approach is used, it is especially important to check the validity of the assumptions made after the results of the analysis are determined.

The Final Major Objectives

Now that we have a method for selecting objectives to be included in analyzing a decision problem, we can use it to help answer the questions raised in the preliminary identification of the major objectives.

Recall that one unresolved issue is whether an objective related to the political implications should be included in the analysis. The 1970 political campaign has shown that environmental protection is an important issue and that an elected official's choice of an air pollution control program may significantly influence his political career.

Thus, an informal use of the test of importance leads us to the definite conclusion that something like "achieve as desirable a political 'solution' as possible" should be included as an objective in choosing air pollution control programs in New York City.

The other issues raised earlier were whether objectives related to the economic consequences of the various potential air pollution programs on New York State, the federal government, businesses and nonresidents of New York City should be included in analyzing the problem. The mayor is certainly not indifferent about the varying extent to which each such objective might be satisfied. However, note that some aspects of these consequences, such as economic effects due to tourism and businesses moving to the city, are already included in the objective "decrease the net costs of air pollution to the city government." In view of this, it seems unlikely that explicit consideration of any of these in the analysis could possibly alter the optimal strategy. Therefore, based on an informal application of the test of importance, they are excluded from the list of objectives. Again we must mention that after a preliminary analysis, the reasonableness of such exclusions needs to be reexamined.

The same type of considerations lead us to exclude from the analysis an objective concerned with the benefits to nonresidents from any air pollution program. The case can also be made that since these benefits are probably highly correlated to the benefits to residents, in some sense the interests of nonresidents are implicitly taken into account via the benefits to residents.

To summarize our final conclusions regarding the major objectives of the mayor of New York City in choosing an air pollution control program, we only need to add

5. Achieve as desirable a political "solution" as possible to the four objectives listed earlier.

Assigning Measures of Effectiveness to Each Objective

In this subsection, we identify measures of effectiveness for each of our objectives. Each measure of effectiveness takes on values or amounts, often numerical, which should unambiguously indicate the degree to which the associated objective is achieved.

Health Effects on Residents

Several possible measures of effectiveness immediately come to mind for the objective "decrease the adverse effects of air pollution on the health of residents." These include the annual number of deaths attributable to air pollution, the annual number of mandays of morbidity attributable to air pollution, and some subjectively assessed health index that includes consideration of both morbidity and mortality.

Important objections can be raised against each of these. The annual number of deaths attributable to air pollution does not account at all for what is believed to be the more prevalent effect of air pollution on health, namely, its effect on morbidity. Similarly, the annual number of man-days of morbidity does not account at all for the extremely serious effect of air pollution on health in terms of mortality.

Thus, it seems clear that no single measure of effectiveness, aside from possibly a subjective health index, can be identified for this objective. However, because such an index does not refer to some physically measurable quantity, serious questions remain as to whether a probability distribution could be assessed over such an index and whether the mayor or his staff could indicate preferences for the various levels of effectiveness as indicated by the values of the index. Because of these difficulties, we'll avoid searching for such an index and try an alternative approach.

In many situations the difficulty in finding an adequate measure of effectiveness is that the associated objective encompasses several detailed objectives of basic concern to the decision maker. However, once the detailed objectives are identified, the decision maker can assign measures of effectiveness to these. This eliminates the necessity of assigning an effectiveness measure to the major objective. To identify these detailed objectives, the same idea used to specify the overall objective can be employed. The decision maker must ask what specifically he wants to accomplish with respect to this major objective. Alternatively, one can use measures of effectiveness suggested earlier in the process that were deemed inadequate, because they did not indicate all the relevant effects, as guides to further specification of the objectives.

The decision maker must safeguard against introducing a host of detailed objectives that are not required for his analysis. This can be achieved by applying the test of importance to each detailed objective. That is, the decision maker would decide whether explicit introduction of this detailed objective into his analysis could possibly alter the strategy that would be optimal without it.

This process of either assigning a measure of effectiveness to an objective or introducing a successive level of detailed objectives continues until a measure of effectiveness has been assigned to each objective for which one is sought. Throughout this process, the decision maker employs the test of importance to safeguard against introducing detailed objectives that only complicate his analysis. The end result is a hierarchy of objectives and measures of effectiveness for each lowest level objective in this hierarchy.

It should now be clear that a viable alternative to finding some subjective index for the objective "decrease the adverse effects of air pollution on the health of the residents" is to specify it in more detail. Based on the attempt to assign a measure of effectiveness earlier, it was clear that both mortality and morbidity effects were important. So we can specify the major health objective in terms of the two detailed objectives "decrease mortality" and "decrease morbidity."

For the first of these, two of the possible measures of effectiveness are the "annual number of deaths attributable to air pollution" and the "per capita increase in the number of days of remaining lifetime due to improved air quality." The first equally weighs the death of an old person and the death of a child, whereas the second measure weighs the death of a young person more heavily. Since we believe this latter more adequately describes the impact of a program alternative with respect to "decrease mortality," the latter measure was chosen.

For the objective "decrease morbidity," the "per capita decrease in the number of days of bed disability per year owing to improved air quality" was chosen as the measure of effectiveness. Obviously, this does not include such effects as sore eyes, which would not render one to a bed. Part of the consequences of sore eyes is psychological, which can be accounted for by the third major objective. However, the physical aspects of sore eyes intuitively seem important enough to be formally included in the analysis. To do this we would suggest calibrating a number of days of bed disability per year which one would feel is equivalent to having sore eyes for one day. Then for each program alternative, the effects due to sore eyes would be included in the analysis by either adding or subtracting an "equivalent number of bed-days disability" to our measure of the degree to which "decrease morbidity" is met.

Economic Effects on Residents

No single measure of effectiveness could be identified for the objective "decrease the adverse economic effects of air pollution on residents of New York City," because the mayor would likely differentiate between the economic impact on low-income residents and the economic impact on other residents.

But from the preceding discussion a solution to this problem should be evident. Clearly, a breakdown of the economic effects on low-income and other residents is required. This is done and "per capita annual net cost to residents" is used as the measure of effectiveness for each group.

Psychological Effects on Residents

There seems to be no direct measure of effectiveness for the objective "decrease the adverse effects of air pollution on the psychological well-being of the residents." One way to handle this problem would be to define some subjective index. It might be possible to interview residents and ascertain their feelings toward various levels of air quality. But a simpler approach, which seems reasonable, would be to use the daily concentration of sulfur dioxide as the measure of effectiveness for "psychological well-being."[2] Since this pollutant can easily be detected both visually and by breathing, it seems reasonable to assume "psychological well-being" is closely related to the concentration levels.

Economic Effects to the City

The fourth objective, "decrease the net costs of the air pollution control program to the city government," has the obvious measure of effectiveness "annual net costs." As mentioned previously, this includes both direct and indirect costs. Although, for some decisions, annual net costs may vary from year to year, these variations are not likely to be significant. If a large year-to-year variance is expected, the mayor or his staff might need to synthesize something like an equivalent net annual cost.

Political Implications

The fifth objective, "achieve the best political solution to the air pollution problem," has no nice objective index which indicates the degree to which this objective is met. In fact, the index for this objective will have to be a subjective index if it is to be at all realistic. Many considerations must be included in measuring the index, such as the possibility of court suits brought by landlords or home owners who are forced to pay higher fuel prices for heating, the mayor's relations with the city council and with Con Edison and with any of the political groups in the city, and the support of the general public for various program alternatives. These will all have

2. It is important to emphasize that this concentration level is to be viewed as a proxy for psychological well-being only and not for the other objectives.

a potential effect on the mayor's political future which also should be taken into account. Obviously, many political factors not mentioned here are also important.

The analyst can arbitrarily scale the subjective index in any convenient way. He could choose three levels of political implications such as good, bad, and in between. Then each program would be associated with one of these. Or he could arbitrarily scale the index from zero, representing the worst political solution, to ten, indicating the best political alternative. Each program alternative would then be assigned a number from zero to ten, the higher numbers indicating better political implications. A discussion of subjective indices and subjective scaling techniques can be found in Green [7].

The Final Set of Objectives and Measures of Effectiveness

As a result of the process spelled out in this section, a set of objectives and their associated measures of effectiveness for choosing an air pollution control program for New York City were identified. These are presented in Figure 18.2.

Of course, there may be important objectives of which we are unaware, and consequently omitting from the analysis. However, if one cannot identify such omissions before utilizing the implications of the analysis, it is safe to assume the same omissions would have occurred if any less formal procedure for guiding the decision-making process were followed. And thus, at least in this respect, we can conservatively conclude that we are no worse off using decision analysis than not. But, as we mentioned at the beginning of this paper, our intent is to provide a first step toward investigating the usefulness of decision analysis in governmental decision making. The results are meant to provide a basis for further discussion, modification, and improvement.

To be useful, in addition to meeting criteria implied by the definition, the measures of effectiveness as a group must be operational. That is, it must be possible for the analyst to ascertain the probability distribution that he and the decision maker feel describes the potential consequences of each alternative program and for the decision maker to express his utility function, which quantifies his preferences, for various amounts of the various measures of effectiveness. These issues are addressed in the following two sections.

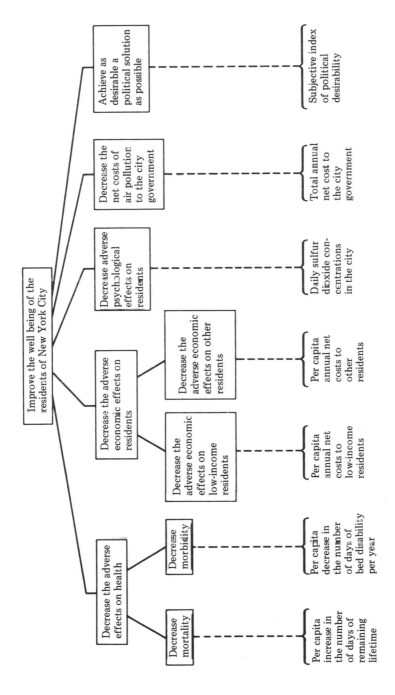

Figure 18.2 The complete set of objectives and measures of effectiveness for choosing an air pollution control program for New York City.

Actually, we would not expect the mayor of New York to spend his time working on details of the air pollution problem. It would be reasonable to expect members of the mayor's staff in the Environmental Protection Administration and the Department of Air Resources to work on this problem. These individuals and the mayor might then review the results and implications of such analyses in formulating and supporting air pollution control programs for New York City.

18.4 Describing the Consequences in Terms of a Probability Distribution Over the Effectiveness Measures

As we discussed at the beginning of this chapter, one cannot specify precisely the effects of any of the program alternatives. There are uncertainties about the degree to which each objective will be achieved by any particular program at the time the choice of an alternative must be made. Thus for each alternative strategy, one must assess a probability distribution over the seven measures of effectiveness which quantifies the decision maker's judgment about the extent to which the objectives will be met by that particular program. His final decision then involves choosing which probability distribution represents the preferred situation.

Since we will be discussing a probability distribution over seven effectiveness measures, we must define some notation. A small letter x_i will represent a specific amount of effectiveness measure X_i, which are defined as follows:

$X_1 \equiv$ per capita increase in the number of days of remaining lifetime,

$X_2 \equiv$ per capita decrease in the number of days of bed disability per year,

$X_3 \equiv$ per capita annual net costs to low-income residents,

$X_4 \equiv$ per capita annual net costs to other residents,

$X_5 \equiv$ daily sulfur dioxide concentrations in parts per million,

$X_6 \equiv$ total annual net cost to the city government,

$X_7 \equiv$ subjective index of political desirability.

The joint probability distribution which we wish to assess will be designated as $f_X(x) \equiv f_X(x_1, x_2, \ldots, x_7)$, where the X_i can be thought of as random variables.

The General Assessment Scheme

The basic strategy for assessing any probability distribution is to fully utilize all the relevant information available to the decision maker. In the case of air pollution control, a growing body of literature exists on the subjects of

1. The relationship between air pollution emissions and air pollution concentrations [12,13]; and
2. The relationship between air pollution concentrations over time and their adverse effects on the physical, economic, and psychological well-being of people [1,2,6,14,15].

Because this information is available and because the levels of air pollution emissions conditional on any program alternative can be predicted with almost complete certainty, the following steps are suggested as the assessment scheme:

1. Predict the certain level of air pollution emissions conditional on each particular program alternative.
2. Assess the probability distribution of air pollution concentrations Q conditional on the given level of emissions. Call this $f_Q(q)$.
3. Assess the probability distribution for X conditional on each level of air pollution concentrations. Label this $f_{X/Q}(x/q)$.
4. Calculate the joint probability distribution $f(x,q)$, from which you get the marginal distribution $f_X(x)$ conditional only on a particular program alternative.

Techniques to make this scheme operational are considered in the following subsection.

Simplifying the Assessment Procedure

It is a fact that the difficulty of assessing a probability distribution increases rapidly as the number of variables increase. And also, not surprisingly, the amount of work required in an assessment scheme is directly related to the number of separate assessments required.

With this in mind, there would appear to be three major obstacles in the general assessment scheme which was suggested. First of all, the quantity Q has not yet been specified and could involve several variables. Second, step 3 could possibly involve the assessment of an infinite number of conditional probability distributions since there may be an infinite number of Q levels. And finally, each function $f_{X/Q}$ is itself a seven-variable probability distribution. Let us consider these obstacles one at a time.

We have defined Q as air pollution concentrations. In the sulfur decision problem, the only pollutant whose concentrations depend on the program alternative is sulfur dioxide. Hence the quantity Q need only summarize sulfur dioxide concentrations, and Q can be defined as the daily concentration of sulfur dioxide. Recent research has indicated that the log normal family of probability distributions—a two-parameter family—provides an excellent fit to empirically observed cumulative frequency distributions for daily concentrations of sulfur dioxide [12,13].

Concerning the problem that there may be an infinite number of conditional distributions $f_{X/Q}$, it appears reasonable to organize the possible values of Q into approximately ten regions such that it is appropriate to assume $f_{X/Q}$ does not vary over any particular region. This was done in the sulfur decision problem, so conditional on each program alternative, one only needed to assess $f_{X/Q}$ for each of these regions.

To simplify the assessment of the seven-variable distribution $f_{X/Q}$, we would exploit the properties of probabilistic independence that exist among the effectiveness measures X conditional on any particular Q. Based on reasoning which is discussed in great detail in Ellis [4], it was concluded that the groups of effectiveness measures $\{X_1\}$, $\{X_5\}$, $\{X_7\}$, and $\{X_2, X_3, X_4, X_6\}$ would be conditionally mutually probabilistically independent. Thus, $f_{X/Q}$ can be evaluated using

$$f_{X/Q}(x/q) = f_1(x_1/q) \quad f_5(x_5/q) \quad f_7(x_7/q) \quad f_0(x_2, x_3, x_4, x_6/q)$$

where f_i, $i = 1, 5, 7$ are conditional probability distributions over X_i given q and where f_0 is a joint probability distribution over X_2, X_3, X_4, and X_6 given q. The single variable distributions can be assessed using techniques such as those described in Pratt, Raiffa, and Schlaifer [17]. In assessing f_0, we used

$$f_0(x_2, x_3, x_4, x_6/q) = f_2(x_2/q) \quad f_e(x_3, x_4, x_6/q, x_2).$$

Then to obtain f_e, which has three economic variables, the factors, such as fuel prices and sick days, which would influence these economic variables were first identified. Then the relationships between X_3, X_4, and X_6 and these influencing factors were specified. Finally, probability distributions over the influencing factors were assessed, and a Monte Carlo simulation was used to obtain f_e.

Table 18.3   Range of Possible Effects of Reducing the Legal Sulfur Content of Oil and Coal Used in New York City from the Present 1 Percent to 0.37 and 0.7 percent, Respectively

Effectiveness Measure	Upper Bound*	Lower Bound*	Unit of Measurement
X_1: per capita increase in the number of days of remaining lifetime	74.2	0.0	days
X_2: per capita decrease in the number of days of bed disability per year	0.224	0.0	days
X_3: per capita annual net cost to low-income residents	+$3.83	−$8.42	dollars
X_4: per capita annual net cost to other residents	+$3.83	−$9.57	dollars
X_5: daily sulfur dioxide concentrations in the city	0.33	0.01	parts per million parts of air
X_6: total annual net cost to the city government	+$4,499,000	−$2,000,000	dollars
X_7: subjective index of political desirability	10	0.0	—

*The upper bound was assessed as the 0.99 fractile and the lower bound as the 0.01 fractile.

Results of the Assessments

To briefly indicate one of the results of the assessment of f_X, we present an upper bound and lower bound for the possible effects on each effectiveness measure for the program alternative in the sulfur decision problem of lowering the legal limit on the sulfur content of all oil and coal burned in New York City to 0.37 and 0.7 percent, respectively. These effects are measured relative to the alternative of continuing the current situation which permits burning fuels with less than 1 percent sulfur content. The results are given in Table 18.3.

18.5 Assessing Preferences for the Program Alternatives

Once the consequences of each program alternative are described in terms of a probability distribution over X, the decision of choosing an air pollution control program consists of determining which of these probability distributions is preferred. With multiple effectiveness measures, there is little chance that the decision maker can make this choice directly with any degree of conviction. The problem is systematized using utility theory,[3] which requires the decision maker to quantify his preferences with a utility function assessed over the measures of effectiveness and then to use expected utility as the criterion for choosing among program alternatives. To simplify the assessment of the utility function over the seven effectiveness measures, the concept of utility independence, discussed in Keeney [9,10], was exploited. Based on the utility independence assumptions—made in the manner in which we would expect the mayor of New York to make them, based on discussions with staff members in the Department of Air Resources—the assessment of the complete utility function over X was reduced to the following:

1. Assessing seven one-attribute utility functions, one over each effectiveness measure, and
2. Assessing eighteen scaling constants to ensure that the seven utility functions are properly scaled.

Appropriate techniques for performing each of these tasks are found in Schlaifer [20].

No assessments of the utility function have yet been completed, although details of the assumptions made and the procedure to follow in these assessments are given in Ellis [4].

18.6 Impact of this Work
Because of the preliminary nature of this effort, we cannot report any dramatic impacts that are clearly consequences of this work. However, we believe the ideas and results expressed in this chapter have had some influence on the thinking of individuals responsible for air pollution control programs in New York City. The following events have occurred; however, no claim is made concerning causality.

The results of this work, including Table 18.3 concerning the range of possible effects of a program which lowered the legal

3. An introduction to multiattribute utility theory is found in Fishburn [5] and Raiffa [19].

limits of oil and coal used in the city from the present 1 percent
to 0.37 and 0.7 percent, respectively, were made available to the
New York City Environmental Protection Administration, which
was in the process of preparing a new air pollution control code
for the city. This group included, as one of the key provisions in
its recommended code to the city council, a program that is essentially the same program as the one we discussed.

These same results, as well as the methods of analysis upon
which these results are based, were presented in testimony before
the New York City Council in its legislative hearings on the proposed new air pollution control code.

Finally, the basic methods of analysis developed in this study—
especially those concerned with identifying objectives and effectiveness measures, and assessing probability distributions—were
discussed with program planners at the Environmental Protection
Administration, and it is believed these discussions will have some
impact on the way programs for environmental protection are
planned and evaluated.

18.7 Conclusions

Based on the above experiences with applying the methods of
analysis proposed in this study, we believe the following conclusions can be reached:

1. To determine which course of action he really prefers in decisions concerned with air pollution and other aspects of environmental quality, the public official requires a much better description than he now receives of the consequence of each course of
action in terms of the fundamental human benefits and costs of
real concern to him in these decisions.

2. Decision analysis is a potentially useful concept which would
likely improve aspects of the governmental decision-making process. It could be implemented in many areas, of which air pollution control is one example. One important contribution of decision analysis is that it often serves as a learning experience for
those attempting to utilize it. If the analysis is well documented,
one could expect that flagrant errors would be eliminated as critical experience is accumulated.

3. Because the decision analysis approach for choosing program
alternatives differs so much from traditional approaches, a great

amount of effort and positive results will be needed to convince public officials of the virtues of decision analysis. It is especially important to gain experience with using this approach.

As support for the first two conclusions, we can refer to Section 18.6. However, one should not erroneously think decision analysis is the panacea to our governmental decision problems; but the approach is promising and it could significantly contribute to improved decision making. It should go without saying that a poor analysis will lead to poor results. Therefore, the consumer of decision analysis must appropriately scrutinize the assumptions, the analysis, the results, and the implications of any such studies.

Concerning our third conclusion, the public official finds the decision analysis process foreign and is thus skeptical of its implications. There are many reasons for this. However, since these reasons apply to essentially all public decision making rather than specifically to decisions involving air pollution control, we shall not discuss them here. One point of view on the role of decision analysis in public decision making and problems inhibiting its use is given in Chapter 5 in this volume [11].

It remains that public officials need to be convinced of the validity of the decision analysis approach. The best way to accomplish this is likely to involve both an educational program on the foundations of decision analysis and participation in decision analytic projects where a program alternative must be chosen. But, at the same time, a serious attempt must be made by decision analysts to modify the procedures of decision analysis to conform more to the traditional methods of decision making now used. As one suggestive example to illustrate our point, rather than assess multiattribute utility functions directly, the decision maker may find it more intuitive to consider tradeoffs under certainty among effectiveness measures to reduce the dimensionality of the problem down to one. Then a utility function could be assessed over this one measure of effectiveness. This should not change any of the results of the subsequent analysis, but it may result in the decision maker feeling more comfortable with the approach.

Acknowledgment
We thank Professors Richard Meyer and Howard Raiffa of the Harvard Business School, who made substantial contributions to the dissertation [4] on which much of this work is based.

References

1. Brasser, L., P. Joosting, and D. von Zuilen, "Sulfur Dioxide-To What Level I, II Acceptable," Research Institute for Public Health Engineering, Report G-300, Delft, The Netherlands, July 1967.

2. Carnow, B. W., M. H. Lepper, R. B. Shekelle, and J. Stamler, "Chicago Air Pollution Study," *Archives of Environmental Health*, vol. 18, no. 5, May 1969.

3. Eisenbud, M., "Environmental Protection in the City of New York," *Science*, vol. 170, November 13, 1970, pp. 706-712.

4. Ellis, H. M., "The Application of Decision Analysis to the Problem of Choosing an Air Pollution Control Program for New York City," unpublished doctoral dissertation, Graduate School of Business Administration, Harvard University, Cambridge, Mass., 1970.

5. Fishburn, P. C., *Decision and Value Theory*, John Wiley & Sons, New York, 1964.

6. Glasser, M., L. Greenberg, and F. Field, "Mortality and Morbidity During a Period of High Levels of Air Pollution, New York, Nov. 23 to 25, 1966," *Archives of Environmental Health*, vol. 15, no. 12, December 1967.

7. Green, B. F., "Attitude Measurement," Chapter 9 in *Handbook of Social Psychology-Volume I: Theory and Method*, ed. by G. Lindzey, Addison-Wesley Publishing Co., Reading, Massachusetts, 1964.

8. Howard, R. A., "The Foundations of Decision Analysis," *IEEE Transactions on System Science and Cybernetics*, vol. SSC-4, September, 1968, pp. 211-219.

9. Keeney, R. L., "Utility Functions for Multiattributed Consequences," *Management Science*, vol. 18, no. 5, January 1972.

10. _____ , "Multidimensional Utility Functions: Theory, Assessment, and Application," Technical Report No. 43, Operations Research Center, M.I.T., October 1969.

11. _____ , and H. Raiffa, "A Critique of Formal Analysis for Public Decision Making," Chapter 5, this volume.

12. Larsen, R. I., "A New Mathematical Model of Air Pollutant Concentration Averaging Time and Frequency," *Journal of the Air Pollution Control Association*, vol. 19, no. 1, January 1969.

13. _____ , and C. E. Zimmer, "Calculating Air Quality and Its Control," *Journal of the Air Pollution Control Association*, vol. 15, no. 12, December 1965.

14 Lave, L. B., and E. P. Seskin, "Air Pollution and Human Health," *Science*, vol. 169, August 21, 1970, pp. 723-733.

15. Lawther, P. J., "Compliance with the Clean Air Act: Medical Aspects," *Journal of the Institute of Fuel*, vol. 36, no. 271, August 1963.

16. New York City Department of Air Resources, "Emissions Inventory," 1969.

17. Pratt, J., H. Raiffa, and R. O. Schlaifer, *Introduction to Statistical Decision Theory*, McGraw-Hill Book Co., New York, 1965.

18. Raiffa, H., *Decision Analysis: Introductory Lectures on Choices Under Uncertainty*, Addison-Wesley Publishing Co., Reading, Massachusetts, 1968.

19. _____ , "Preferences for Multiattributed Alternatives," RM-5868-DOT/RC, the Rand Corporation, April 1969.

20. Schlaifer, R. O., *Analysis of Decision Under Uncertainty*, McGraw-Hill Book Co., New York, 1969.

19

Analysis in Health Planning

Robert N. Grosse

19.1 Systems Analysis: From DOD to HEW

This chapter discusses the application of analytical approaches to budgetary and legislative decisions in health policy at the federal level. My personal experience included some years in analysis of national security problems followed by work on domestic social policies. The initiation of such activities in domestic agencies attempted to introduce approaches that had found some success in the Department of Defense (DOD). I thought it might be useful to begin with some points of contrast between the two settings. Discussions of health analyses in this chapter include allocations among disease programs, allocations within one disease problem area, and maternal and child health program comparisons. Rather than abstracting the technical structure of our methods and procedures, I shall go directly into the types of questions we considered and the nature of the results obtained. However oversimplified they may be, many of the studies discussed here constituted the first attempts at program analysis in their respective fields.

When the Secretary of Defense in 1961 desired to institutionalize the applications of operations research and systems analysis to decision making, a major problem identified was that planning and budgeting activities were being carried out independently of each other. They were independent in the sense of the people and of the time-frame in which they looked at the problems. The planners were usually spinning their dreams 5, 10, and 20 years into the future; the budgeteers were concerned with next year. They also dealt in different dimensions. Planners looked at the missions: tactical, strategic, logistical; areas such as the central plains of Germany, the Mediterranean, or the Far East; and weapon systems and organizations, such as bombers and missile systems, naval task forces, army divisions. The budget side of the process dealt in dimensions of input, purchases of equipment, construction of facilities, maintenance and operations activities, hiring and paying of personnel.

Decisions made in each area were weaker than they might have been had planning and budgeting been integrated. Planners rarely took into explicit consideration in their designs the financial and resource implications of alternative courses of action. They did, of course, screen the total plan for economic feasibility. But this was like designing your ideal house and discovering, after you have laid out the plans, that it will cost $350,000 but that you have only something in the order of $35,000. This usually led to a hasty cutting down of plans as though one looked at the plans of the $350,000 house and eliminated nine-tenths of the items, rather than redesigning the building to optimize what one could procure for $35,000. As a consequence, much of the midrange and long-range planning activity conducted by the Pentagon had little relevance when budget decisions were made with regard to research and development, procurement of equipment, and force structure.

The budget side of management, while in some sense more practical and obviously influencing the course of events, had little understanding of the military effects of budgetary decisions, as there was no mechanism available for determining what in the way of missions accomplishment or organization or force structure was implied by short-run purchases of inputs.

A major management objective of the early McNamara period became the construction of a link between planning and budget activities, permitting an understanding of the implications of the items and personnel procured in terms of military effectiveness and, in turn, an understanding of the resource considerations of alternative courses of actions for weapon systems and for organizational decisions made in the planning process. This bridging or translating device was given the name of "programming" or "program budgeting." Later, in nondefense applications, it was called the planning, programming and budgeting system (PPB). Four years later, President Johnson, searching for methods of improving management and decision making in the domestic side of government, ordered his cabinet to institute similar procedures and the planning, programming, budgeting system began to spread throughout the whole of the federal government.

In joining the Department of Health, Education, and Welfare (HEW), to help develop the system, I naïvely assumed that again the problem would be to link the planning and budgeting processes so that operations or systems analysis could be utilized in the planning process, and in turn affect the budgeting decisions. There were a number of significant differences, however, between the Defense Department and a department such as that of Health, Education, and Welfare.

One was that, while there were many people operating in the budget area, nobody at HEW engaged in any form of systematic planning. There were, of course, people scheming to get more money for particular programs. The problem was not one simply of linking a plan to a budgeting process but rather it also required the development almost from scratch of a planning capability and planning procedures.

A second difference was the extent of responsibility of the federal government in the areas to be studied. In defense or national security matters, the Department of Defense is responsible for most of the actions taken. There are, of course, the actions of the State Department, the Atomic Energy Commission, and, externally, those of our allies. But, by and large, what is recommended in the defense area is directed and controlled by one department. In matters such as health and education, this is not the case. The primary actors in health in the United States are private physicians, voluntary county and municipal hospitals, state and mental hospitals, state and local departments of health and welfare, and universities that train professionals and conduct research.

Further complicating the situation is the nature by which the federal government supports its activities. It does this largely through grants-in-aid. This means that the federal government transfers funds to state governments, local governments, universities, and hospitals which then organize the programs which use nonfederal funds as well. About 94 percent of the general funds of the Department of Health, Education, and Welfare is spent on grants-in-aid and an additional 1 percent or so on the administration of such grants. There are relatively few programs run directly by the federal government. There are some intramural research activities at the National Institutes of Health, and there are Public Health Service hospitals for the merchant mariners (soon to be eliminated) and health activities run on Indian reservations by the Division of Indian Health.

So we have a situation of only partial funding by the federal government, and essentially what is done is through nonfederal agencies. This complicates understanding the systems and how government programs affect them. Designing models and developing coefficients is indeed difficult.

I would add to the problems of model building the pervasive ignorance of social production functions. There has been very little work done on determining relationships between expenditures and results in social areas. We do not know the impact of different kinds of educational programs on people's capacities, nor the effects of social service on adjustment, nor health services on the status of health. Most social problems of any consequence are not rectified by any single program. The reduction of tuberculosis is related to housing conditions, diet, immunization, isolation of affected individuals, and therapy. Diet and housing are in turn related to income and employment levels. Income and employment levels are related to educational level, skill training, racial discrimination, health, the state of business, the labor market, income supplements, job training, job creation, job placement, fiscal policy, education, legal services, community power, and more can be added to this list.

The well-known weakness or absence of our social indicators makes it difficult to say what has happened, let alone why it happened. A summary of some difficulties in program evaluation would indicate that, with few exceptions:

—We lack agreement on the objectives of programs.
—We lack agreement on measures of achievement of objectives.
—We find it hard to estimate measures when we agree on them.
—We cannot sort out cause and effect relationships because of the multiplicity of inputs and the multidimensionality of outputs.
—We have little longitudinal information about programs whose effects come about over long periods of time.
—Usually we don't even know where we are.

A further problem was the philosophy and attitude of most of the program managers and bureau chiefs. They could hardly be described as sympathetic to the philosophy of analysis and operations research where one tries to define objectives, identify and price alternatives, trace the consequences of these alternatives, and through some test of preferredness relate costs and effectiveness to determine the preferred alternative. In most cases, program managers felt that there was a large gap between the needs of the society and what we were doing. Their preferred alternative was to spend money on expanding processes that they were already engaged in. "Desirable for what purpose," or "for what accomplishment," or "concerns about alternative methods of achievement of these accomplishments," were rare in the vocabulary or thinking processes. It was presumed that more hospitals, more nurses, more doctors, more research, and more services were what the society needed and that the only problem was to secure these on an ever increasing scale.

Finally, perhaps the most significant difference between military and domestic government is the much greater significance in the domestic area of political interests—those of the serving professions, such as medicine and education, and those of the communities and peoples to be served. The reconciling of such interests into a consensus or coalition and deciding whom you will fight and to whom you will make concessions is an important ingredient—perhaps the most important in the decision process.

Within the context described, we attempted in 1966 to develop an analytical process in the department of HEW. A small number of analysts, mostly economists, were formed into the office of the assistant secretary for Program Coordination (later called Planning and Evaluation). Despite pressure from the Bureau of the Budget to "analyze" all programs, it was obvious that only a few could be addressed. For these, program analysis teams were formed, consisting of staff from the secretary's office and the operating programs, and consultants. The time allotted to the studies was usually designed to bring results in about the time of budget formulation. This meant studies beginning in March or April were to have usable results by August or September. I shall try to sketch some examples of our initial efforts.

19.2 Disease Control Programs
One of the first applications of cost-benefit analysis was to disease control programs. Considerable work has been done during the last 10 years in estimating the economic costs of particular diseases. It was not surprising, then, that, when systematic quantitative analysis of government programs and policies began to spread from defense to civilian applications, one of the first analytical studies was a study of disease control programs.

The basic concept of the study was a simple one. The Department of Health, Education, and Welfare supports (or could support) a number of categorical disease control programs, whose objectives are to save lives or to prevent disability by controlling specific diseases. The study was an attempt to answer the question: If additional money were to be allocated to disease control programs, which programs would show the highest payoff in terms of lives saved and disability prevented per dollar spent?

I'm talking here not about research, but where a technology exists and the problem is whether to put the same or more or less federal funding behind these control programs to support activities in hospitals, states, and communities. We addressed the question of the allocation of available resources for disease control. The Department of Health, Education, and Welfare studied five programs: cancer, arthritis, tuberculosis, syphilis, and motor vehicle injury. After discussing some studies concerned with allocations among disease programs, I will describe a later study addressed to the proper mix of approaches within a single program (kidney disease).

Factors Influencing Control Programs

The effectiveness of the department's disease control programs is influenced by a number of factors. Of most significance are the abilities of medical technology to provide the scientific knowledge to prevent the disease, to diagnose disease early enough so that the impact on health can be minimized, and to treat the disease to cure the patient. In order to determine the relative emphasis on the department's disease control programs, we addressed such questions as:

—Does the knowledge exist for disease prevention?
—How can the knowledge be applied?
—Does the knowledge exist for disease diagnosis and treatment?
—What are the more productive methods for applying this knowledge?
—What are the costs involved in applying the knowledge?
—What benefits in terms of lives saved, disability prevented, and other economic and social losses averted can be achieved?

For each of the diseases discussed in this chapter, medical knowledge exists for some measure of disease control. However, for such diseases as head and neck cancer and colon-rectum cancer, techniques of diagnosis have not yet been developed to make it economical to screen a necessarily large number of people in order to identify even a relatively small number of these cancers. Although primitive technology exists, the cost of a control program may be too high measured by benefits forgone in programs with higher potential for saving of lives and decreasing the impact of illness.

The Federal Role

The particular federal interest in disease control programs stems from two concerns:

1. Those diseases that may be communicated across state boundaries.
2. Those diseases where people are not getting adequate medical care because either personnel, knowledge, or facilities may not be available, or because the people cannot afford health care.

Tuberculosis and syphilis control have been of concern to the Public Health Service for many years. The national spread of these communicable diseases through personal contact has been a key reason for the federal role in these programs. In addition, the technology (drugs and diagnostic procedures) for effective control of these diseases has been in existence for many years; penicillin and blood tests for syphilis, isoniazid and x ray for tuberculosis.

Technology for effective control of the selected cancer sites has only recently become available and in most cases is still under development. Although the Papanicolaou test for uterine cervix cancer disease dates back to 1928, its general acceptance dates to 1943; as late as 1960 fewer than 5 million tests were reported by national laboratories. With Public Health Service support for case finding and demonstration projects, including the training of technologists, utilization of this technique reached almost 15 million tests by 1965.

Arthritis includes a number of specific diseases where knowledge does not exist to permit prevention, control, or even effective amelioration of crippling and/or disabling symptoms in a large number of patients. The limited knowledge that is available is not widely disseminated, and only a small portion of the estimated 10 to 13 million people suffering from arthritis have access to good quality diagnosis and care. The federal concern here is to assure that more people receive better care. The method of approach is similar to that applied to the cancer programs—demonstration projects that have as a major component the training of physicians and technicians and developing and testing diagnostic and treatment methods.

Public Health Service programs in motor vehicle injury prevention are in their initial stages. The magnitude of this problem would indicate a major interest for all health agencies.

Selected Disease Alternative Analysis

The Department of Health, Education, and Welfare task groups were established to develop detailed analyses of the individual selected disease control programs. Each of these studied and analyzed a number of alternative programs. Program cost and anticipated benefits were compared for the alternatives within each of the programs.

Two principal criteria were used as a basis for recommending funding allocation among the programs within each disease category as well as among the different diseases analyzed. These criteria were the cost per death averted and the benefit cost ratio.

Cost per Death Averted

The "cost per death averted" is the 5-year program cost, divided by the deaths averted owing to the programs. These costs range from an estimated $87 per death averted for a seat belt use program to over $40,000 for such programs as head and neck cancer control, increasing driver skills, and emergency medical services.

The cost per death averted for each of the programs is an average cost figure. It would be expected that some of the costs would actually be many times the average cost. For example, a uterine cervix program recommended has an average cost per death averted of $3,470. However, of the 34,000 lives expected to be saved owing to the programs through 1972, 30,000 have an average cost of about $2,000; 2,300 have an average cost of over $3,500, and 400 have an average cost of over $7,000. While it may sometime be possible to add additional lives saved at the lower figure, any significant investment of funds in this program would probably be oriented toward the more expensive cases averaging over $7,000.

The Benefit Cost Ratio

There are at least two problems with cost per death averted as a sole criteria for evaluating program effectiveness.

1. There is no distinction made regarding the age at which the death is averted, and
2. There is no way to rank those diseases that are not primarily killers.

The benefit cost ratio includes both morbidity and mortality implications of the disease. The benefit cost ratio, simply stated, is the amount of dollars invested divided into the amount of dollars saved.

The economic savings for disease are composed of direct savings of dollars that would have been spent on medical care cost including physician's fees, hospital services, drugs, and so on, and indirect savings such as the earnings saved because the patient did not die or was not incapacitated due to illness or injury. The average lifetime earnings for different age groups is related to the age at which death occurs and a calculation of the present value of lost lifetime earnings. For example, if a 27-year-old man died this year of one of the diseases, his aggregate earnings would have been estimated at $245,000 had he lived a full life. However, discounting this at 4 percent to the current year, the economic loss is actually closer to $125,000. Included in this analysis are economic losses based on future earnings discounted to present value.

For the purposes of estimating benefits among diseases, it is recognized that economic loss or even death do not completely state the damage and harm caused by disease. Pain and the impact on family relationships are among the more obvious additional items. We do not know how to bring such items into this kind of analysis as yet, but it seems likely that these additional considerations argue in the same direction as the other benefits. We have no reason at this moment to believe that such considerations would have changed the relative preferences among programs.

Some of the programs are designed to have an effect beyond the directly supported federal operations. For example, the uterine cervix program and the proposed arthritis program have major demonstration and training objectives. The training of specialists who will take the newly learned or developed technology outside the public sector is a major benefit of these programs. This analysis does not credit these programs with such benefits since data are not currently available.

Costs Other Than Health, Education, and Welfare

The costs attributed to the programs are primarily the direct Health, Education, and Welfare program costs. In the syphilis and uterine cervix programs there are additional direct costs; serological screening costs for the syphilis program and early treatment cost of the uterine cervix program. These costs are directly related to the federal decision about the size and scope of the programs.

There are other expenses, costs, and benefits that may be indirectly attributed to the other programs, but since there is not a direct link between the federal decision and these costs, they have not been charged to the program. For example, the seat belt use educational program will probably cause an increased consumption of these devices. However, the program attempts to encourage people to use the belts that are already installed in the vehicle. The cost of the belts is not attributed to this program. The benefits of a successful injury prevention program could result in lower auto insurance rates; these are not credited to the programs in this analysis.

Examples of the Results

Table 19.1 illustrates the costs of various control programs for cancer. We estimated cost per examination and the number of examinations that would be required before a case would probably be found. From this was derived the number of cases that would be found, and estimates of the cost per case found. An estimate was made of the number of deaths that could be averted by the treatment following the detection of the cancers and then we calculated the cost per death averted which ranged from about $2,200 in the case of cervical cancer up to $40,000 to $45,000 in the case of head and neck and colon-rectum cancer.

On the vertical axis of Figure 19.1 we have plotted the program costs; including the cost of treatment in addition to the federal detection program. On the horizontal axis estimates of death averted are ordered by increase in cost per death averted in each program. Segments of the curve identified to each disease cover the extent

Table 19.1   Cancer Control Program: 1968–1972

	Uterine Cervix	Breast	Head and Neck	Colon-Rectum
Grant costs ($000)	97,750	17,750	13,250	13,300
Number of examinations (000)	9,363	2,280	609	662
Cost per examination	$10.44	$7.79	$21.76	$20.10
Examinations per case found	87.5	167.3	620.2	496.0
Cancer cases found	107,045	13,628	982	1,334
Cost per case found	$913	$1,302	$13,493	$9,970
Cancer deaths averted	44,084	2,936	303	288
Cost per death averted	$2,217	$6,046	$43,729	$46,181

Source: "Program Analysis: Cancer," Office of the Assistant Secretary for Program Coordination, U.S. Department of Health, Education, and Welfare, Washington, D. C., October 1966.

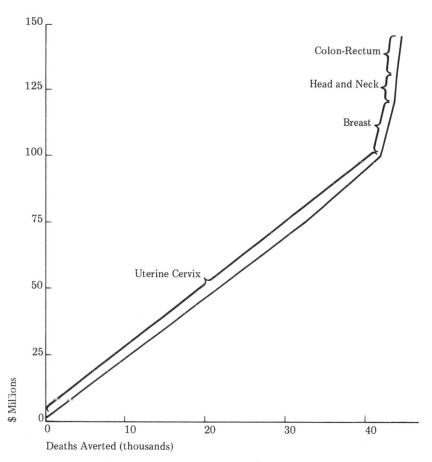

Figure 19.1   Programs for control of cancer. (Source: "Program Analysis: Cancer," Office of the Assistant Secretary for Program Coordination, U.S. Department of Health, Education, and Welfare, Washington, D.C., October 1966.)

of the program which it was estimated could be mounted in the years 1968–1972 before running into sharply increasing costs. In concept, the cervical cancer curve is cut off where costs become higher than the breast cancer program, and so on. From this analysis one might say that if there is only available $50 million, cervical cancer should get all the funds. If we have $115 million, then breast cancer control programs look quite competitive. Head and neck and colon-rectum cancer detection programs as major control programs did not look attractive when viewed in this context. The analysts recommended that they concentrate on research and development.

The same kind of analysis for each of the five programs studied is illustrated in Figure 19.2. There seemed to be a very high potential payoff for certain educational programs in motor vehicle injury prevention (that is, trying to persuade people that "the lump you're sitting on is a seat belt, use it; don't walk in front of a car," and so on). Again, as we move up this curve, ordered by cost of averting death, we begin adding other efforts. This particular criterion, deaths averted, was not completely satisfactory. The number of fatalities attributed to arthritis, for instance, is not very impres-

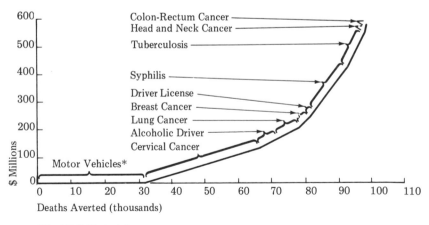

Figure 19.2   Analysis of programs for selected diseases: Cost of programs and deaths averted, 1968–1972. (Source: "Selected Disease Control Programs," Office of the Assistant Secretary for Program Coordination, U. S. Department of Health, Education, and Welfare, Washington, D.C., September 1966.)

sive. Secondly, we had returned to the question: Did it matter who died? Did it matter whether it was a 30-year-old mother or a 40-year-old father of a family or a 75-year-old grandfather? On Figure 19.3 I have used dollar savings, counting the avoidance of death, the use of lower cost treatment, and a crude estimate of the average (discounted) lifetime earnings saved, as a criterion in place of deaths averted. You will notice two changes in results: cervical cancer and syphilis change places in priority order, and we are able to justify arthritis programs.

The way we developed programs from such analyses was to use information such as this and the preceding charts as another insight to give us an additional feel for what were relatively high- and low-priority programs, and then to feed these insights into the decision-making process, which also considers other viewpoints, the existing commitments, political situation, rate of spending, and the ability to get people moving on programs, and so on.

Some Criticisms
These studies were not greeted with universal acclaim. Criticisms focused on a number of problems. First, with almost no excep-

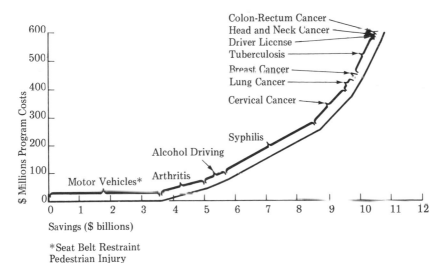

Figure 19.3   Cost of benefit: Selected Diseases, 1968–1972. (Source: "Selected Disease Control Programs," Office of the Assistant Secretary for Program Coordination, U. S. Department of Health, Education, and Welfare, Washington, D.C., September 1966.)

tion, the conclusions were based on average and approximate relationships. That is, the total benefits were divided by the total costs. There was little evidence of what the actual impact of increasing or decreasing programs by small amounts might be.

The lack of marginal data resulted from both a lack of such data for most programs together with a lack of economic sophistication on the part of the Public Health Service analysts who performed the studies. As in all modeling efforts, some common sense was required in applying the results.

Practical obstacles of existing commitments made it almost impossible to recommend *reductions* in any program. So the actual policy decisions dealt with the allocation of modest increments.

In the case of oral and colon-rectum cancers, the average cost per death averted seemed so high that the department recommended emphasis on research and development rather than a control program to demonstrate and extend current technology.

In cervical cancer, investigation indicated a sizable number of hospitals in low socioeconomic areas without detection programs that would establish these if supported by federal funds. The unit costs for increasing the number of hospitals seemed to be the same as for those already in the program. Shifting the approach to reach out for additional women in the community would increase costs per examination but not so high as to change the relative position of this program. At most, it raised costs to about those of the breast cancer control program.

Despite the seeming high potential payoff of some of the motor vehicle programs, there was far more uncertainty about success. As a consequence, recommendations were for small programs with a large emphasis on evaluation for use in future decisions. The same philosophy was applied to the arthritis program.

What resulted then was a setting of priorities for additional funding, based on the analytical results, judgment about their reliability, and other practical considerations.

A second type of criticism was concerned with the criteria, especially the calculation of benefits.[1] These were considered inadequate in that they paid attention to economic productivity alone and omitted other considerations. In particular, they were thought to discriminate against the old who might be past employment

1. For discussion of some of these issues see [11,13,14].

years and women whose earnings were relatively low. It was also feared that the logic, if vigorously pursued, would penalize not only health programs for the aged, such as the newly launched Medicare, but also programs aimed at assisting the poor whose relative earning power is low by definition.

In actual practice, for the particular programs studied, these concerns were not critical. The programs for cervical and breast cancer looked to be good despite their being for women. As for the poor, most of the programs considered, especially cervical cancer, syphilis, and tuberculosis, were aimed primarily at them, and projects were usually located to serve low-income residents.

Another type of objection was raised not against the technique of analysis but against its being done at all. Choices among diseases to be controlled and concern with costs of saving lives can be viewed as contrary to physicians' attitudes in the care of an individual patient. Prior decisions on allocations to various health problems (and such decisions are *always* made, with or without analysis) rested upon a combination of perception of the magnitude of the problem and the political strength organized to secure funding, for example the National Tuberculosis Association.

The disease control cost-benefit analyses suggest that additional considerations are very relevant. Given scarce resources (if they are not scarce, there is no allocation problem), one ought to estimate the costs of achieving improvements in health. If we can save more lives by applying resources to a small (in numbers affected) rather than a large problem, we ought to consider doing so.

A somewhat separate issue is that of the disease control approach to personal health. This is too large an issue to deal with here, but it may make more sense to develop programs of delivering comprehensive health care, including preventive services, than to maintain categorical disease programs. But that is another cost-benefit analysis.

19.3 Analysis of Kidney Disease Programs
The following year a number of additional disease control studies were performed. One of the most interesting and important was on kidney diseases [12]. This analysis was launched at a time when the public was becoming conscious of a new technique, the artificial kidney (chronic dialysis), which could preserve the life and productivity of individuals who would otherwise die of end-

stage kidney disease. About 50,000 persons a year do so die. It is estimated that about 7,500 of these were "suited" by criteria of age, temperament, and the absence of other damaging illnesses for dialysis treatment. The national capacity could handle only about 900, who would remain on intermittent dialysis the rest of their lives. About 90 percent would survive from one year to the next. The operating cost of dialysis treatment in hospitals was estimated at about $15,000 per patient per year. A home treatment approach might reduce this to about $5,000 per year.

The federal government was under great pressure to expand the national capacity, which was limited not only by the large money costs but also by shortages of trained personnel and supplies of blood. Indeed, at the same time as this analysis was being performed, an advisory group to the U.S. Bureau of the Budget was studying the problem of end-stage kidney disease. This group came in with recommendations for a massive national dialysis program.[2]

The HEW program analysis was somewhat more broadly charged and took a more systems-oriented approach. It concerned itself not only about the 7,500 annual candidates for dialysis but also about the other 40,000 or so who would suffer the end-stage disease but were unsuited to dialysis. If some way could be found to reduce the numbers falling into the pool of end-stage patients, perhaps a larger number of people could be helped. Figure 19.4 presents the classes of kidney diseases leading to end-stage disease. If these could be better prevented or treated we might keep down the number of patients requiring dialysis or transplantation.

The analysis group, therefore, examined a number of mechanisms or program components. Among these were:

1. Expanded use of existing preventive techniques.
2. Expanded use of existing diagnostic techniques.
3. Expanded use of existing treatments, including chronic dialysis, kidney transplantation and conservative management (drugs, diets, and so on).

2. The Bureau of the Budget convened an expert Committee on Chronic Kidney Disease. See [6]. Klarman, Francis, and Rosenthal [10] analyzed the committee's data to explore what is the best mix of center dialysis, home dialysis, and kidney transplantations. The authors restricted their beneficiaries to those in end-stage kidney disease and concluded that transplantation is economically the most effective way to increase life expectancy of persons with chronic kidney disease, although they recognize the factors that constrain the expansion of transplantation capability.

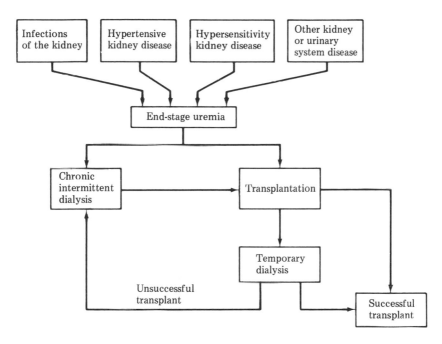

Figure 19.4   Schematic of transplant and dialysis patients. (Source: "Kidney Disease Program Analysis: A Report to the Surgeon General," Public Health Service, U. S. Department of Health, Education, and Welfare, Bethesda, Maryland, 1967.)

4. Laboratory and clinical research to produce new preventive, diagnostic, therapeutic, and rehabilitative methods.
5. Increased specialized scientific medical and paramedical training to provide the manpower needed for the research and treatment attack on the kidney disease problem. This also includes continued postgraduate education to train practicing physicians in the use of the latest diagnostic and treatment modalities.
6. Increased public education to alert potential victims of kidney disease to seek medical help at the earliest possible emergence of warning signs.
7. Provision of specialized facilities not currently in existence that are essential for the execution of any of the above programs.

It must be understood that in most cases these program components are interdependent. For example, preventive techniques exist that need further research to make them maximally effective

for broad application. New treatment methods are useless even if
existing diagnostic techniques are not being applied in medical
practice. Because of the present inadequacies of existing treatments, be they dialysis, transplantation, or conservative management, a considerable research effort is called for to increase their
efficacy and economy to make them more broadly useful.

A detailed description of the analysis cannot be presented here.
Costs were estimated for relevant public and private expenditures
for the nationwide treatment of kidney disease. The latter includes
cost of physician care, hospital care, nursing home care, and other
professional services for diagnosis and therapy of kidney diseases,
as well as the cost of drugs and net insurance costs. In addition,
the cost was estimated for ongoing research efforts, for demonstration, screening and detection programs, for education and training
efforts and for that portion of the cost of construction of hospital
and medical facilities which can be prorated to the use of patients
with kidney disease.

Based on the substantive information obtained and statistical
and economic data collected, estimates were made of the benefits
to be gained by different approaches to the solution or amelioration of the overall national kidney disease problem at different expenditure levels of HEW funds.

Several different funding levels were assumed, and estimates
were made assuming both the current state of the art and an expected advanced state of the art in 1975.

Each program consisted of a hypothetical situation where a specific level of HEW program funding was divided among a rational
mix of program components (screening, diagnosis and treatment,
research, training, and so on) based on the particular characteristics of the specific disease group involved, and was applied to specifically involved or particularly vulnerable groups or, as the case
may be, to the entire population. The benefits accruable from
these programs were then estimated and stated in terms of overall
reduction of mortality, prevalence, and morbidity due to kidney
disease.

Benefit indices were quantified in terms of the reduction in annual mortality, the reduction in annual morbidity (number of sick
days per year) and in terms of the disease prevalence in the total
population due to the specific type of kidney disorder analyzed,
which would accrue because of the impact of the various program

components—such as research advances, disease prevention, and improved treatment.

The analysis group originally chose to avoid estimates of the impact on economic productivity in their results, although such calculations have been made independently [7,8].

The HEW study concluded that concentration in future programs merely on the treatment of end-stage kidney disease is not likely to solve the problem of annual deaths due to irreversible uremia unless nearly unlimited funds are available for an indefinite continuation of such a program. Thus, steps must be taken to decrease the number of people who enter the irreversible fatal stage each year by a systematic prevention or treatment of the primary kidney diseases which initiate their progressive downhill course. It is obvious from the analyses in the three major kidney disease groups—infectious, hypersensitive, and hypertensive—that the otherwise inevitable annual reservoir of patients with irreversible kidney failure can be diminished considerably through vigorous programs activated to deal with each of these groups. The application of relatively minor funds in the group of infectious kidney diseases to stimulate systematic screening of high-risk groups followed by diagnosis and treatment, even within the current state of the art and without awaiting additional advances due to ongoing or future research, can bring about a significant future reduction in the number of end-stage patients. Continued and expanded research activities will be necessary to increase the percentage of patients ultimately benefited by this approach.

In the area of hypersensitivity diseases involving the kidney there appears to be no promising mode of attack in sight except for the launching of a systematic research effort intended to increase our knowledge of the disease mechanisms involved. The promise for benefits to be derived from this type of research effort is believed to be such that it should not be postponed—particularly since any new effective treatment or prevention modality would produce major benefits in the entire field of hypersensitivity diseases, such as rheumatic heart disease, rheumatoid arthritis, and others.

In the group of hypertensive diseases of the kidney an immediate start, within the current state of the art, of screening, diagnosis, and treatment can begin to diminish the number of patients who will eventually require end-stage treatment because of their progressive renal involvement. Simultaneous research efforts are likely to make this particular portion of the overall program more effective as time goes by, in the same fashion in which the new antihypertensive drugs developed during the last ten years have succeeded in decreasing by about 50 percent the mortality due to malignant hypertension.

Thus, a meaningful federal program to reduce the annual mortality due to kidney disease and aimed at a general reduction of the prevalence of the various kidney diseases must perforce be a multifactorial one that brings into play all of the program components— research, prevention, treatment, and education. An optimally proportioned mix of these program components should be present to yield maximum benefits in overall number of lives saved. This last concept includes not only deaths avoided today but deaths to be prevented in the years to come. Needless to say, such a total program, to be effective and productive, must be aimed at all three major primary kidney diseases, as well as at end-stage kidney failure.

Figure 19.5 shows a hypothetical program mix that might come from such conclusions. Note the early emphasis on research to offset the state of the art and the growth in allocations to the prevention and treatment of primary kidney diseases as relative allocations to dialysis are diminished.

To illustrate some of the cost and benefit calculations developed in the study, Table 19.2 summarizes the *federal HEW* costs. A similar tabulation was developed for all costs. As another illustration, Table 19.3 estimates the impacts of these programs on deaths, numbers of cases of each disease, and days of illness.

19.4 Maternal and Child Health Programs
HEW also did a rather different type of analysis in the field of health: a study of alternative ways of improving the health of children. The president had focused public attention on the problem of child health and expressed a desire to introduce new legislation in this field. The HEW study was an attempt to assess the state of health of the nation's children (to what extent the children have correctable health problems and in what groups in the population the problems were concentrated), and to estimate the cost and effectiveness of various kinds of programs to improve the health of children.

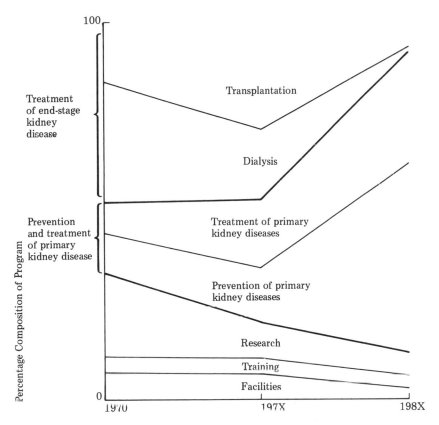

Figure 19.5   Effect of advancing state of the art on future program composition. (Percentages are wholly arbitrary and merely serve to illustrate shifting trends.) (Source: "Kidney Disease Program Analysis: A Report to the Surgeon General," Public Health Service, U. S. Department of Health, Education, and Welfare, Bethesda, Maryland, 1967.)

Table 19.2 HEW Cost Summary ($1,000)

| Program Level | Kidney Disease Categories | | | | Total | |
	Infectious	Hypersensitivity	Hypertensive§	End-Stage	Cost	Percent
Current Expending Level*						
Diagnosis, Prevention, Treatment Prevention (including education & administration)	3,803	1,500	4,000	—	9,303	19.92
Diagnosis and Treatment	—	—	—	7,240	7,240	15.50
Subtotal	3,803	1,500	4,000	7,240	16,543	35.42
Research	4,000	5,250	3,800	12,100	25,150	53.85
Training	400	560	380	1,000	2,340	5.01
Facilities	1,000	170	1,000	500	2,670	5.72
Total	9,203	7,480	9,180	20,840	46,703	100.00
Intermediate Expenditure Level*						
Diagnosis, Prevention, Treatment Prevention (including education & administration)	5,929	3,000	8,057	—	16,986	14.47
Diagnosis and Treatment	—	—	—	30,000	30,000	25.56
Subtotal	5,929	3,000	8,057	30,000	46,986	40.03
Research	5,500	8,250	4,650	18,000	36,400	31.01
Training	750	750	500	5,500	7,500	6.39
Facilities	8,000	8,000	8,000	2,500	26,500	22.57
Total	20,179	20,000	21,207	56,000	117,386	100.00
Accelerated Expenditure Level*						
Diagnosis, Prevention, Treatment Prevention (including education & administration)	9,919	3,000	10,114	—	23,033	7.94
Diagnosis and Treatment	—	—	—	171,000	171,000	58.98
Subtotal	9,919	3,000	10,114	171,000	194,033	66.92
Research	6,500	10,125	5,500	24,000	46,125	15.91
Training	975	750	1,425	10,000	13,150	4.54
Facilities	10,000	10,000	11,600	5,000	36,600	12.63
Total	27,394	23,875	28,639	210,000	289,908	100.00
Accelerated Expenditure Level— 1975†						
Diagnosis, Prevention, Treatment Prevention (including education & administration)	11,308	{ 43,000-Vaccine { 13,000	11,732	—	76,040	25.94
Diagnosis and Treatment	—	—	—	132,225	132,225	45.11
Subtotal	11,308	56,000	11,732	132,225	208,265	71.05
Research	7,410	12,450	9,500	1,500	30,860	10.53
Training	1,110	1,870	3,000	5,000	10,980	3.75
Facilities	11,400	10,000	11,600	10,000	43,000	14.67
Total	31,228	77,320	35,832	148,725	293,105	100.00

*Current state of the art
†Advanced state of the art
§ Attributable to renal disease associated with hypertension.
Source: "Kidney Disease Program Analysis: A Report to the Surgeon General," Public Health Service, U.S. Department of Health, Education, and Welfare, Bethesda, Maryland, 1967.

Table 19.3 Program Benefits

Program Level	Kidney Disease Categories				
	Infectious	Hypersensitivity	Hypertensive§	End-Stage	Total
Current Expenditure Level*					
Short-Term Benefit-Reductions:					
Mortality	70 Deaths	610 Deaths	2,190 Deaths	690 Deaths	3,560 Deaths
Prevalence	3,231,260 Cases		27,000 Cases	—	3,258,260 Cases
Morbid Days	15,962,420 Days		1,802,000 Days	—	17,764,420 Days
Long-Term Benefit-Reductions:					
Annual	1,750 Deaths	—	4,330 Deaths	—	6,080 Deaths
Cumulative	25,850 Deaths	—	86,560 Deaths	—	112,410 Deaths
Intermediate Expenditure Level*					
Short-Term Benefit-Reductions:					
Mortality	70 Deaths	610 Deaths	2,270 Deaths	1,560 Deaths	4,520 Deaths
Prevalence	3,243,860 Cases		34,880 Cases	—	3,278,740 Cases
Morbid Days	16,273,640 Days		2,056,820 Days	—	18,330,460 Days
Long-Term Benefit-Reductions:					
Annual	1,770 Deaths	—	4,820 Deaths	—	6,590 Deaths
Cumulative	26,190 Deaths	—	96,300 Deaths	—	122,490 Deaths
Accelerated Expenditure Level*					
Short-Term Benefit-Reductions:					
Mortality	70 Deaths	610 Deaths	2,380 Deaths	7,675 Deaths	10,735 Deaths
Prevalence	3,292,860 Cases		42,750 Cases	—	3,335,610 Cases
Morbid Days	17,483,880 Days		2,311,340 Days	—	19,795,220 Days
Long-Term Benefit-Reductions:					
Annual	1,870 Deaths	—	4,820 Deaths	—	6,690 Deaths
Cumulative	27,480 Deaths	—	96,300 Deaths	—	123,780 Deaths

Table 19.3 Program Benefits (*Continued*)

Program Level	Kidney Disease Categories				
	Infectious	Hypersensitivity	Hypertensive§	End-Stage	Total
Accelerated Expenditure Level—1975†					
Short-Term Benefit-Reductions:					
Mortality	80 Deaths	770 Deaths	9,300 Deaths	27,399 Deaths	37,549 Deaths
Prevalence	5,630,780 Cases	62,250 Cases	289,690 Cases	—	5,991,723 Cases
Morbid Days	26,064,430 Days	2,610,000 Days	5,578,860 Days	—	34,253,290 Days
Long-Term Benefit-Reductions:					
Annual	4,125 Deaths	8,610 Deaths	9,480 Deaths	—	21,090 Deaths
Cumulative	76,500 Deaths	320,000 Deaths	189,660 Deaths	—	586,160 Deaths

*Current state of the art
†Advanced state of the art
§Renal disease associated with hypertension.
Short-term benefits, reduction in *annual* mortality, and so on, when program is fully operative.
Long-term annual benefits, eventual *annual* reduction in number of cases reaching end-stage kidney disease.
Long-term cumulative benefits, sum total of long-term annual benefits.
Source: "Kidney Disease Program Analysis: A Report To the Surgeon General," Public Health Service, U.S. Department of Health, Education, and Welfare, Bethesda, Maryland, 1967.

This study proved more difficult than anticipated. Hard information on the state of health of children is hard to come by. Surprisingly, estimates of improvement in general health attributable to medical care are almost nonexistent. It is not easy to demonstrate statistically that children who see doctors regularly are healthier than children who do not.

In regard to maternal and child care programs the stated goal was to make needed maternal and child health services available and accessible to all, in particular to all expectant mothers and children in health depressed areas. Health depressed areas could be characterized as areas with excessive infant mortality rates. There is no universal index of good or bad health among children. Two measurable areas were selected—mortality and the prevalence of chronic handicapping conditions. Over a dozen possible programs aimed at reducing these were examined. In Table 19.4, three selected programs addressed to the problem of coverage of maternal and child health are illustrated, two of them comprehensive programs of care to expectant mothers and children. This table shows the estimated annual effects of spending the same amount of money, $10 million a year, in different ways. The analysts examined comprehensive care programs covering up to age 18 and up to age 5 with estimates based on the best assumptions derived from the literature and advisers on the probabilities of prevention of maternal deaths, premature deaths, infant deaths, and mental retar-

Table 19.4   Yearly Effects per $10,000,000 Expended in Health Depressed Areas

	Comprehensive programs to age		Case finding of treatment
	18	5	0, 1, 3, 5, 7, 9
Maternal deaths prevented	1.6	3	
Premature births prevented	100–250	200–485	
Infant deaths prevented	40–60	85–120	
Mental retardation prevented	5–7	7–14	
Handicaps prevented or corrected by age 18:			
Vision problems: all	350	195	3470
amblyopia	60	119	1140
Hearing loss: all	90	70	7290
binaural	7	5	60
Other physical handicaps	200	63	1470

Source: "Maternal Child Health Care Programs," Office of the Assistant Secretary for Program Coordination, U.S. Department of Health, Education, and Welfare, Washington, D.C., 1966.

dation, and handicapping conditions prevented or corrected by age 18. They also looked at a program of early case finding and assured treatment which focused on children at ages four days and again every other year until they were nine. Expending the same amounts, changing where one puts the money yields different results. With respect to reduction of infant mortality, several other programs had higher payoffs than these. For example, a program of intensive care units for high-risk newborns was estimated annually to eliminate 367 deaths if we put all our money in that basket —it would cost about $27,000 per infant death prevented. The programs shown cost about four times that, but they do other good things too.

The HEW analysts also looked at programs with a given amount of money (Table 19.5) aimed at reducing the number of children who will have decayed and unfilled teeth by age 18. Fluoridation programs in communities which do not possess this, will, for the same amount of money, give us close to 300,000 fewer children in this condition, compared to 18 or 44 thousand fewer in other programs noted. Fluoridation looks like a very attractive program. It was so attractive that one can assume that a program as cheap as this is not being inhibited by lack of financial support by the federal government; there are other factors at work.

One other program, additional funds on family planning, looked like a very good way not only to reduce the number of infant deaths but also the rate of infant mortality in high-risk communities.

Despite the information difficulties, several conclusions emerged clearly from the study. Two of these conclusions resulted in new legislation being requested from Congress. First, it seemed clear that a program of early case findings and treatment of handicapping conditions would have considerable payoff. It was also clear that if the large number of children who do not now have access

Table 19.5   Reduction in Number of 18-Year-Olds with Decayed and Unfilled Teeth per $10,000,000 Expended in Health Depressed Areas

Fluoridation	294,000
Comprehensive dental care without fluoridation	18,000
Comprehensive dental care with fluoridation	44,000

Source: "Maternal Child Health Care Programs," Office of the Assistant Secretary for Program Coordination, U.S. Department of Health, Education, and Welfare, Washington, D.C., October 1966.

to good medical care were to be provided with conventional pediatric services, an acute shortage of doctors would be precipitated. Ways have to be found to use medical manpower more efficiently. The Social Security Amendments of 1967 include provision for programs of early case finding and treatment of defects and chronic conditions in children and for research and demonstration programs in the training and use of physician assistants.

19.5 Afterword
The health analyses sampled here were done in 1966 and 1967. On what has taken place since that time, I have little evidence. The only analysis published since that time was the tardy release of a cost-effectiveness analysis of family planning program components.

1968 was a year of reorganizations in the Public Health Service, and many studies aborted because staffs were shifted, and because attention was given to organizational survival, elections, transition, and defense against budget cutting. Despite the Bureau of the Budget's zeal in promoting analytical activities, their own staff's approach was to hold to incremental budgeting and cut down any new programs in the interest of fighting inflation and the Vietnam War.

The Nixon administration in its first years placed little emphasis on systematic analysis, although the planning and evaluation office was much more a center of power than it had been. Little addition was made to the analytical staff, even to replace attrition. Thus far, little has been published. This phase appears to be changing. A new assistant secretary for planning and evaluation has been appointed who is a professor of business administration with experience in systems analysis in national security. His projected deputy for health planning and evaluation is an economist with analytical experience in defense and health. The shift back to economists from lawyers should bring new efforts to carry on analytical work in greater scale and depth.

References
1. Cheit, E. F., *Injury and Recovery in the Course of Employment*, John Wiley & Sons, New York, 1961.
2. Cohen, J., "Routine Morbidity Statistics as a Tool for Defining Public Health Priorities," *Israel Journal of Medical Sciences*, May 1965, pp. 457–460.

3. Conley, R., M. Cromwell, and M. Arrill, "An Approach to Measuring the Cost of Mental Illness," *American Journal of Psychiatry*, 12416, December 1967, pp. 63-70.

4. Dublin, L. I., and A. J. Latka, *The Money Value of a Man*, The Ronald Press Company, New York, 1930.

5. Fein, R., *Economics of Mental Illness*, Basic Books, Inc., Publishers, New York, 1958.

6. Gottschalk, C. W., *Report on the Committee on Chronic Kidney Disease*, Chairman, Bureau of the Budget, Washington, D.C., September 1967.

7. Hallan, J. B., and B. S. H. Harris, III, "The Economic Cost of End-Stage Uremia," *Inquiry*, Vol. V, No. 4, December 1968, pp. 20-25.

8. Hallan, J. B., B. S. H. Harris, III, and A. V. Alhadeff, *The Economic Costs of Kidney Disease*, Research Triangle Institute, North Carolina, 1967.

9. Klarman, H. E., "Syphilis Control Programs," *Measuring Benefits of Government Investments*, edited by Robert Dorfman, The Brookings Institution, Washington, D.C., 1956, pp. 367-410.

10. Klarman, H. E., J. O'S. Francis, and G. D. Rosenthal, "Cost Effectiveness Analysis Applied to the Treatment of Chronic Renal Disease," *Medical Care*, Vol. VI, No. 1, Jan.-Feb. 1968, pp. 48-54.

11. Pan American Health Organization, *Health Planning: Problems of Concept and Method*, Scientific Publication No. 111, April 1965, see especially pp. 4-5.

12. Rice, D. P., *Estimating the Cost of Illness*, Public Health Service Publication 947-6, Washington, D.C., May 1966.

13. Rice, D. P., "Measurement and Application of Illness Costs," *Public Health Reports*, February 1969, pp. 95-101.

14. Schelling, T. C., "The Life You Save May Be Your Own," *Problems in Public Expenditure Analysis*, edited by Samuel B. Chase, Jr., The Brookings Institution, Washington, D.C., 1968, pp. 127-176.

15. U.S. Department of Health, Education, and Welfare, Office of Assistant Secretary for Program Coordination, *Motor Vehicle Injury Prevention Program*, August 1966.

16. U.S. Department of Health, Education, and Welfare, Office of Assistant Secretary for Program Coordination, *Arthritis*, September 1966.

17. U.S. Department of Health, Education, and Welfare, Office of Assistant Secretary for Program Coordination, *Selected Disease Control Programs*, September 1966.

18. U.S. Department of Health, Education, and Welfare, Office of Assistant Secretary for Program Coordination, *Cancer*, October 1966.

19. U.S. Department of Health, Education, and Welfare, Office of the Assistant Secretary for Planning and Evaluation, *Kidney Disease*, December 1967.

20. U.S. Department of Health, Education, and Welfare, *Economic Costs of Cardiovascular Diseases and Cancer, 1962*, Public Health Service Publication 947-5, Washington, D.C., May 1965.

21. Weisbrod, B. A., *Economics of Public Health: Measuring the Economic Impact of Diseases*, University of Pennsylvania Press, Philadelphia, 1961.

22. Winslow, C. E. A., *The Cost of Sickness and the Price of Health*, World Health Organization, Geneva, Switzerland, 1951.

20

Puerto Rico's Citizen Feedback System

John D. C. Little
Chandler Stevens
Peter Tropp

20.1 Introduction

Compared to most chapters in this book, the present one deals with a much less structured problem, that of communication between citizen and government. The work is built around a concept from control theory, namely, that of feedback. A government or other public system that provides services, regulates activities, or otherwise affects the citizen must receive feedback of citizen reaction to ensure that the system is operating satisfactorily. With this concept in mind, one can ask: In what ways is feedback being transmitted? What new mechanisms can be created beneficially? In attempting to answer these questions, we have so far produced no sophisticated mathematical models. The questions, however, have led to some simple ideas that seem important and are being tested in a specific way in Puerto Rico. A start at representing such systems by analytic models has been made by Krendel [8].

Even a cursory examination of the operation of our society leads to the conclusion that democratic government requires more than elections to enable citizens to inform and affect government. Special efforts must be made to design two-way communications between government and the citizen, particularly in times like the present when substantial groups of people are estranged from the rest of society. Today's electronic media provide a powerful, virtually unobstructed channel from government to the citizen. Attention must be devoted to developing effective channels in the reverse direction—from the citizens to government.

Since taking office in 1969, Governor Luis A. Ferre has sought ways to develop a more responsive government in Puerto Rico. One outgrowth of this goal is the citizen feedback system to be discussed here. The system seeks to handle citizen complaints, requests, and opinions in a way that gives the individual citizen a more rapid and complete response, and, at the same time, gives government a more accurate and comprehensive view of citizen needs and government performance. The fundamental elements of the Puerto Rican citizen feedback system are applicable elsewhere, and similar but independent efforts are going on in other places.

These efforts include Rhode Island's Little State House Program, New York City's Service Monitoring System, and Wisconsin's Executive Normative Information Expediter System. In addition, the authors have recently started a program with Governor Francis Sargent to develop a citizen feedback system for the Commonwealth of Massachusetts.

Government Reform and Citizen Participation

In order to put citizen feedback in context, four major trends to improve the responsiveness of government to the citizen should be considered:

1. *Electoral reform.* "One man, one vote" redistricting is basic to any effort to improve the responsiveness of government.
2. *Administrative decentralization* of facilities and services. This includes, for example, the establishment of branch offices for tax collection, license issuance, or various public works activities. The decentralization of big city school systems and the creation of multiservice (social service) centers are increasing.
3. *Top-down* reform of government decision making. This encompasses the popular cabinet-style executive branch reorganization and consolidation, improving the planning and budget processes, upgrading of chief executive staff, the increasing use of computers and management information systems, and other administrative improvements. Recent developments have been reviewed by Botner [2]. The centralized ombudsman is, in a sense, a top-down reform that has been widely discussed but not much implemented.
4. *Bottom-up, ad hoc approaches to citizen participation.* The past decade has seen major moves in this area. Within government, citizen participation has been stimulated by federal antipoverty, urban renewal, and Model Cities programs. State and local governments are trying out new programs for handling citizen communications. Examples are little state houses and neighborhood city halls.

President Nixon has experimented with "listening post" programs in both the U. S. General Services Administration and in the Republican Party. The Republican Party has opened Republican Action Centers, primarily in black ghettos in large cities, while two Democratic candidates devised innovative campaign participation techniques: Eugene McCarthy's large-scale, house-to-house canvassing and Robert Kennedy's community organizing program.

Increasing numbers of other feedback innovations are being undertaken by social institutions outside of government—by churches, civic groups, and the mass media—particularly in the form of telephone "hotlines."

Media innovations include newspaper "Action-Line Columns," which handle complaints mailed in or phoned in by readers; regular reporting of topical opinion polls; radio talk shows, where listeners are encouraged to phone in and state their views on the air; and several experimental television programs with arrangements for viewers to dial one of two telephone numbers to indicate their "vote" for or against a specific proposal under discussion.

Citizen Alienation Still Exists

Considering the magnitude and seriousness of the problem of citizen alienation, these several trends to improve government responsiveness seem fragmented and insufficient. Administrative decentralization has often been done for administrative convenience. As Hallman [6] says, "Although administrative decentralization and community participation are often talked about together, they are not the same thing. It is possible to decentralize without providing for any citizen participation at the service area level. . . ."

The efforts of reformers concerned with top-down administrative improvements are not often connected to the efforts of bottom-up participatory reformers. The two groups may share ultimate objectives, but they do not always agree on the means or even have the same fundamental attitudes about "the system."

Most of the top-down reorganizations do little to affect the way the citizen interacts with the bureaucracy. Citizens generally "see" only two types of government officials: first, the people at the top (primarily the governor or mayor, some cabinet members, leaders of the legislative body or of the opposition parties, and relatively few others) who are visible to the public on a regular and timely basis through the electronic and other media; and, second, government personnel with whom the citizen has personal contact.

Much of the bureaucracy in between is invisible to the citizen and, for communications purposes, may be partially obsolete, since hierarchical channels have been short-circuited, at least in one direction. The electronic media are a more efficient communicator from government to the citizen than are long, bureaucratic channels. Without a corresponding increase in the speed of communications in the opposite direction, from the citizen to government, the increasingly aware citizen often becomes frustrated when he attempts to communicate with government.

The bottom-up citizen participation programs have generated tension and controversy. Nearly 1,000 Community Action Programs (CAPs) and 150 Model Cities programs are under way, but, according to Arnstein [1], these have often turned out to be cases of token participation in the form of consultation and placation, with few cases of real citizen power in the form of partnership, delegated power, or citizen control. As Moynihan [10] points out, the basic difficulty has been that the program was nominally designed to bring about institutional cooperation, while community leaders saw institutional change as the key objective. The CAPs most closely controlled by city hall were disappointing. The ones most antagonistic were destroyed.

The operations of little city hall programs are frequently the target of politically jealous city councils. Also, citizens seem to expect more follow-through than they have been able to get. Although neighborhood city halls process complaints and requests for services more rapidly than was possible before, Gusdorf [4] concludes that citizen participation in policy planning has been slow to increase.

At the same time, however, the financial crises and austerity programs in most state and local governments have meant that citizen feedback projects have been viewed as unaffordable. Austerity pressures have cut the budget of Boston's Little City Hall Program and eliminated New York's Urban Action Task Forces and other feedback channels of Mayor Lindsay's office; and the Little City Hall program in Somerville, Mass. operates without an appropriation by the city council. This means that many programs depend heavily on volunteers.

Citizen participation has thus been increasingly emphasized in federal, state, and local government programs in recent years, but usually in *ad hoc* ways. Both legislative and executive branches of government receive large quantities of communications from citizens. There is, however, a lack of systematic approaches, and the various efforts to handle these communications have suffered from (1) a lack of coordination among the various feedback mechanisms, (2) the absence of an overall reporting system, and (3) limited accessibility and comprehensiveness. In today's complex government, there is a need for a well-organized system for receiving, examining, and channeling citizens' complaints, requests for information and services, and opinions.

Ideally, the system should operate so that a single significant complaint or well-directed inquiry by a citizen could help trigger a change in government policy. The system described in this chapter and the further proposals growing out of the experience with it to date are intended to be first steps toward achieving some of these goals.

20.2 Service Feedback

Citizen feedback refers to the information transmitted from citizen to government and other institutions to improve their operation. Suitably collected citizen information can be used by government to modify policies, programs, and services. Two types of feedback can be distinguished: *service feedback*, which includes inquiries, requests, and complaints; and *involvement feedback*, which includes opinions, suggestions, and volunteering.

In a complementary way, citizen *feedforward* may be defined as information from the center out. Policy and program information can be projected forward to citizens who then provide feedback based on their values and judgments.

These, then, are two sides of a communication loop. A citizen feedback system concentrates on citizen to government communication, the weaker side. However, once this side is strengthened, the deficiencies on the other side will become more obvious. Quality feedforward is necessary for quality feedback.

The Puerto Rican system deals primarily with unsolicited and unstructured communications in the form of letters, phone calls, and personal visits. Ninety percent of these are service feedback; that is, they arise from a request for information, the lodging of a complaint, or the seeking of a service. Only ten percent of the communication is involvement feedback, such as an offer of an opinion, the making of a suggestion, or a desire to volunteer. The emphasis on service is to be expected from unsolicited communications and identifies the Puerto Rican prototype in its present stage as a service feedback system.

Involvement feedback is usually obtained by active, structured efforts, such as public hearings, special group meetings, and issue ballots. These require a certain amount of feedforward to which the citizens can then respond. Although plans for involvement feedback have been made in Puerto Rico, the system has not yet incorporated them.

The key to a successful service feedback system is information processing. To support the service function, the system must (1) receive citizen communications, (2) make referrals to appropriate problem solvers, and (3) trigger automatic follow-up for prompt, complete response. The feedback function requires procedures for classifying citizen problems and preferences so as to monitor (1) the level of activity of various government programs, (2) the delays involved in delivering public services, (3) the level of citizen satisfaction with government programs, and (4) preferences of citizens regarding issues faced by government.

System Components

In designing the Puerto Rican system six criteria were applied. It was felt that the system should be

1. *Strong* enough to curb buck-passing, cut unnecessary red tape, and redress legitimate grievances
2. *Independent* enough to give the citizen and elected officials a real check on the bureaucracy
3. *Informative for the citizen* as to what programs are available to serve him or to be influenced by him
4. *Accessible* enough to give all citizens an opportunity to communicate with their government
5. *Informative for government* as to what citizens need, what they are getting, and how they feel about various programs
6. *Comprehensive* enough to improve procedures, services, and programs throughout government

The Puerto Rican system has six components that correspond approximately to these six criteria:

1. *A feedback division* of the governor's office to coordinate the operation of the system
2. *Interagency citizen aides* who receive special training in non-buck-passing and case investigation
3. *A public service manual* which describes for each government service when, from whom, and how to obtain it
4. *An outreach network* of service stations, mobile units, and a special 24-hour phone service

5. *Feedback reports* which provide indications of volumes, delays, types, and examples of feedback on various services
6. *Personnel training* to develop both feedback analysis and citizen aide capabilities within government in general

Feedback Division

The most likely figure in government to oversee the operation of a citizen feedback system is the chief executive, since he is the center of citizen awareness of government. For example, in Puerto Rico the governor's office receives each day 200 to 300 letters, 50 to 100 visitors, and many phone calls. Some other elected official might conceivably be designated for the role, particularly if he runs for election with the chief executive as a team. In Illinois, for example, the lieutenant governor has been publicized as an ombudsman. However, a strong reason for associating the system with the chief executive himself is that he has the ultimate responsibility for seeing that government programs are carried out and services provided. He can also take the initiative to modify programs and set up new ones. For these purposes, he needs information. As Governor Ferre said at one point in the system development, "For a start, I would just like to know whether government is doing its job."

In the case of Puerto Rico, the coordination of the feedback system has been carried out within the governor's office. The development has gone through three phases: a design phase from June 1969 to January 1970, a testing phase from January 1970 to February 1971, an institutionalization phase from February 1971 to the present. Initially, the system was given limited publicity. At this time citizen aides were being trained, the public service manual was being compiled, and case handling procedures were being worked out. During this period the system treated about 250 communications (visits, letters, and phone calls) per month. When a special phone system was established and publicized, volume temporarily quadrupled and then stabilized at about 600 communications per month.

In February 1971 the feedback division became a formal entity through an executive order of the governor, which established a division of citizen services within the governor's office. The order states that the division will

1. Aid all citizens who write, phone, or visit La Fortaleza (the

governor's executive offices in San Juan), or other offices established throughout the island for the purpose of handling citizen inquiries, requests, complaints, opinions, and suggestions
2. Provide techniques by which these communications, along with social indicators and program costs, can be analyzed in order to evaluate government programs and to recommend improvements in government services and policies
3. Train agency personnel in the use of the feedback system so as to provide both better service to the citizen and better planning and management within government
4. Inform the public about various government programs so that they might have more direct access to the agencies that provide particular services or establish particular policies that may concern any particular citizen

Citizen Aides
Government civil servants are usually highly specialized. This inevitably leads to referrals from one government worker to another. Referrals often seem like buck-passing to a citizen and sometimes are undoubtedly just that. A citizen feedback system needs a group of knowledgeable, well-trained people who function as an information resource, switching center, and helping hand for any citizen. These people may be described as interagency citizen aides.

An important part of the job of a citizen aide is the following up of any referral he makes and, if necessary, conducting an independent investigation. Such investigations may be necessary for problems involving more than one agency.

In addition, the citizen aide represents a "court of appeal" for citizens who are not satisfied with their treatment at an agency. This investigating role is important and delicate. About four out of five citizen complaints are found not to be the fault of any civil servant but due rather to lack of information, which the citizen aide can provide the citizen. The cases where a civil servant is at fault are obviously important both to the citizen, whose grievance can be redressed, and to the government, which wishes to identify and correct shortcomings in its own operations.

The citizen aide, therefore, by virtue of his role and his location in the governor's office is able to influence, in a modest but persistent way, the way other civil servants treat citizens. The citizen aide sets an example, helps correct occasional grievances, and serves as a link in an information loop back to the governor; the very existence of the loop affects the behavior of the people that the aide deals with. This is the feedback concept at work.

During the 13-month testing phase of the Puerto Rican system, two groups of citizen aides were trained and joined the operation. There are now twenty aides working at the governor's office and the four remote feedback stations, handling citizen cases and working on various system components.

Public Service Manual

No matter how well trained a citizen aide is, he cannot rely exclusively on his own memory when helping citizens with the myriad of problems arising out of an increasingly complex society. He needs a public service manual.

The purpose of a public service manual is to provide a brief description of each governmental service and the requirements for obtaining it. How, where, and when the service may be obtained are presented, and any documents needed to receive the service are identified. In Puerto Rico the manual lists over 800 government programs spread over 85 agencies.

Listed along with each service is the name of an agency "problem solver" whom the citizen aide can call to straighten out any problems a citizen is having or to check on the status of a service request. This agency contact is crucial for short-circuiting the hierarchical communication flow usual in government. The aide can avoid delay and confusion by knowing the appropriate person in the agency and going directly to him. Procedures for doing this have to be set up in advance with the knowledge and help of the agency head.

In Puerto Rico the public service manual was prepared by the citizen aides themselves, starting from a draft developed by an outside firm. The aides visited the agencies to update, correct, and extend the listed information. The revised material was shown to agency heads for verification and then reproduced. During the testing phase of the project, further new ideas for indexing, format, glossaries, etc., were developed, and a variety of errors and omissions were uncovered. A new version of the manual was produced, and the feedback division now has the responsibility of keeping it updated. The public service manual has substantial value throughout government, and 20,000 copies of the new edition are being distributed.

The collection, maintenance, and dissemination of information on government programs is a massive undertaking to which modern technology can contribute. Microfilm retrieval offers the possibility of storing and retrieving large quantities of data cheaply. Computer terminals and time sharing could make possible rapid updating of frequently used information. This is an area where cost-benefit analyses and pilot programs would be very worthwhile.

Outreach Network

Once a feedback division with strong executive support has been established, once citizen aides have been trained to handle citizen communications, and once adequate service information has been put at their disposal, then a well-publicized outreach program should be undertaken.

The Puerto Rican outreach system is a flexible multimedia network consisting of a central location at the governor's office, four local feedback stations scattered in the densely populated areas of the island, a 24-hour call-in phone number, and a network of special phones that can be used for toll-free citizen service calls. The central location is at La Fortaleza, and local stations operate at San Jose, Ponce, Arecibo, and Mayaguez. In addition, a mobile unit that would serve smaller cities and isolated areas is planned.

In setting up local stations, cost, accessibility, and citizen familiarity favor the use of certain types of public buildings. The feedback station should be conveniently located, and the citizen should visualize it as politically and socially neutral. In Puerto Rico, fire stations meet these requirements (although schools might be an even better choice). Except for the control office at La Fortaleza and a government service center used in Arecibo, all the feedback locations are in fire stations.

A key part of the outreach network is the 24-hour phone system. A citizen can call in either of two ways. He can use his own phone to call a special, publicly advertised number at his own cost, or he can call toll-free from public pay phones located at all fire stations. An instruction card telling how to place the call and reverse the charges is affixed to the telephone. During working hours incoming calls from the network are handled directly by the feedback office. During off-duty hours, a caller can leave a message on a tape recorder. On the next working day, the message is transcribed and forwarded to a citizen aide.

Feedback Reports

A citizen feedback system is designed to provide better information not only for citizens but also for government policy makers. This goal requires a good information and reporting system. In effect, a government-wide service audit, which would be in some sense like the financial auditing process should eventually evolve. Feedback reports should be part of a system of social indicators to be used in government planning systems. Feedback is an indicator of the benefit side in cost-benefit analysis. Because this is the weaker side, better inputs are badly needed.

Many of the basic data for feedback reporting originate in "case accounting." In Puerto Rico individual case information is entered into an IBM 360/50 computer system that is then used to generate monthly statistics. Cases are classified by

1. Region
2. Agency
3. Service within agency
4. Mode of communication (letter, visit, phone)
5. Case type (request, complaint, etc.)
6. Manner of resolution
7. Age (open cases)
8. Length of time required to close (closed cases)
9. Name of citizen aide handling case

Plots of key data as time series help uncover trends and trouble spots by geographical area, agency, and service within agency. The age of the cases measures the promptness of the feedback division's response. Important feedback time series are included in the social and economic indicators which are displayed on a current basis in the Governor's Information Center.

Although some part of feedback reporting consists of numerical data, another portion is made up of qualitative information. Notable case histories, direct quotes, and interpretive analyses are included as relevant sources. A summary of opinion feedback on subjects currently of concern to citizens is extremely valuable to elected officials. Citizen views and problems have substantial human interest, and a feedback report, if skillfully written, makes good reading.

The recipients of feedback reports are the chief executive, his cabinet, and his policy advisors. Agencies receive material specifically relevant to them. Citizen aides receive reports detailing open cases and their ages. The authors advocate making summary information public. Distribution of feedback reports, however, raises certain privacy issues. Clearly, individual privacy must not be violated. Individual citizen names are not used without their consent. Institutional privacy also has to be protected to some degree so that agencies and civil servants have enough time to take corrective actions without public embarrassment.

Personnel Training
A well-trained staff of citizen aides is the heart of a citizen feedback system. Both formal and informal training programs are needed. The first group of citizen aides went through a one-month program. Since then, a combination of a two-week program plus on-the-job training has been developed.

The program includes a significant amount of sensitivity training focused on the individual's relations with others and their perceptions of him. The aide is encouraged to see himself as an intermediary between the citizen and the bureaucracy rather than as a representative of the bureaucracy. The citizen is viewed as intelligent but lacking information. In addition, the training introduces the citizen aide to the public service manual. Considerable time is spent working on sample cases drawn from real situations, and feedback analysis techniques are introduced.

The basic skills of the citizen aide are needed wherever government touches citizen in a service function. A feedback division can provide a valuable service to agencies by offering training programs to agency personnel.

20.3 System Evaluation
A variety of summary statistics on the system are given in the report of Gusdorf et al. [5]. Of general interest are the following breakdowns by type of feedback and mode of contact over the first nine months of system operation. Tables 20.1 and 20.2 show the preponderant service orientation of the system and bring out the importance of letter and telephone contact.

Three evaluative sets of interviews with people involved in the system were made in November 1970. One set was with citizens

Table 20.1   Summary of Types of Citizen Feedback (first nine months)

Type of feedback	Percentage of total
Service feedback	
Information	4.4
Request	61.6
Complaint	23.8
	89.8
Involvement feedback	
Opinion	6.2
Suggestion	3.8
Volunteer	.2
	10.2
Total	100.0

Table 20.2   Modes of Citizen Contact (first nine months)

Mode of contact	Percentage of total
Visits	23
Letters	40
Telephone	36
Other	1
	100

who used the system, another with agency problem solvers who were contacts for citizen aides, and the third was with the citizen aides themselves. The interviews provided much useful information. Some of the agency problem solvers saw conflicts between the feedback division's methods of handling cases and their own. Issues of priority came out. Some agency personnel were relatively uninformed about the feedback system. As a result of these interviews, several corrective actions were taken. The interviews with citizen aides uncovered areas for improvement and revision of procedures. Generally, the aides felt the system was meeting its goals.

The interviews with citizens probed their satisfaction with using the system. A sample of 24 citizens who had used the telephone network shortly after it was announced were interviewed. The following pertinent facts arose:

1. Twelve (50 percent) said they had learned of the phone system through publicity on the radio, TV, or newspaper. The other half heard of the system from friends or family.

2. Eighteen (75 percent) had tried to solve the problem by other means before using the feedback system. Most of these (12) had contacted a government agency, which they claimed had taken no action.

3. Two basic reasons were given for using the phone service: convenience and "I did not have anywhere else to go."

4. Twenty-one (87 percent) of the respondents did get an answer from the government, although the time varied from one week to two months. Three respondents (13 percent) did not receive any answer to the telephone message, although none was sure how long he had been waiting.

5. When asked "Would you have received a better response to your problem if you had gone directly to the agency involved, instead of using the 24-hour telephone system?" half of the respondents answered no; nine (38 percent) felt they would have received the same result; and three (12 percent) felt they would have got better response.

6. Twenty-one (87 percent) said they would use the telephone system again, while of the three (12 percent) who received no reply, one did not answer, and the two others said they would go directly to the appropriate agency.

The citizens who used the feedback system apparently feel they got a better response than they would have otherwise gotten from government. They liked the easy accessibility of the phone system. It is apparent that citizens would like the system better if delays could be reduced.

The citizen survey constituted feedback on the feedback system and was a valuable step that should become a standard part of the system operation.

20.4 System Evolution: Involvement Feedback

The Puerto Rican system is concerned primarily with service feedback. Yet ten percent of the citizen communications have fallen in the category of involvement feedback. These communications deserve special attention since they usually represent extra effort by the citizen to abstract from his experience and generalize about a problem or issue that concerns others.

In the long run, however, government should also develop methods to encourage citizen involvement and expression of opinion. Such feedforward has not yet been undertaken to any great extent in Puerto Rico. Certain pilot experiments have been proposed there and elsewhere. In particular, the authors are currently engaged in such efforts in Massachusetts. Several techniques are being investigated for structuring issue feedforward and opinion feedback. Among them are:

1. *Issue balloting*—a questionnaire containing a logical sequence of questions on one issue, interspersed with brief presentations of facts and pro and con arguments on the issue. The ballot is suitable for automatic tallying, for forwarding to a government official of the respondent's choice, and for other types of follow-up action.

2. *Technology-aided dialogue*—a more dynamic version of issue balloting, involving real time access of respondents. A tallying system immediately displays results of answers to questions formulated by a discussion leader or members of the discussion group. Issues and questions can be restated and modified, in interactive fashion, in order to move more rapidly to a resolution of the issue or at least to a better group understanding of differences in basic individual values and beliefs.

3. *Multiparticipant models*—an extension of the above to include not only a tallying of opinions, but also a working out of their implications in terms of possible policies and predicted consequences as represented by a computer model of the public system at issue.

It is hoped that these types of techniques coupled with a service feedback system will bring about significant progress toward a more responsive government.

References

1. Arnstein, S., "Ladder of Citizen Participation," *Journal of the American Institute of Planners*, vol. 35, no. 4, July 1969, pp. 216-224.

2. Botner, S., "Managing a State," *National Civic Review*, vol. 59, no. 6, June 1970, pp. 308-313.

3. Goudsmit, F., "The Impact of Boston Little City Halls on City Management," S. M. thesis, M.I.T., Cambridge, Massachusetts, June 1971.

4. Gusdorf, N., "Puerto Rico's Citizen Feedback System," S. B. thesis, M.I.T., Cambridge, Massachusetts, January 1971.

5. Gusdorf, N., J. D. C. Little, C. H. Stevens, and P. Tropp, "Puerto Rico's Citizen Feedback System," M.I.T. Operations Research Center Technical Report No. 59, April 1971.

6. Hallman, H., "Guidelines for Neighborhood Management," *Public Management*, ICMA, vol. 53, no. 1, January 1971, pp. 3-5.

7. Kaiser, J., "Citizen Feedback: An Analysis of Complaint Handling in New York City," Mayor Lindsay's Office of Administration, New York, April 1971.

8. Krendel, E. S., "Social Indicators and Urban Systems Dynamics," *Socio-Economic Planning Science*, vol. 5, no. 4, August 1971, pp. 387-393.

9. Little, J. D. C., C. H. Stevens, and P. Tropp, "Citizen Feedback System: The Puerto Rico Model," *National Civic Review*, vol. 60, no. 4, April 1971, pp. 191-198.

10. Moynihan, D. P., *Maximum Feasible Misunderstanding*, Free Press, New York, 1969.

11. Sheridan, T. B., "Citizen Feedback: New Technology for Social Choice," *Technology Review*, vol. 73, no. 3, January 1971, pp. 46-51.

12. Stevens, C. H., "Citizen Feedback: The Need and the Response," *Technology Review*, vol. 73, no. 3, January 1971, pp. 38-45.

13. Stevens, C. H., "Science, Government, and Citizen Feedback," *Operations Research*, vol. 18, no. 4, July-August 1970, pp. 577-591.

21

A Study of the Educational Process: The Structure of a Lesson

R. W. Revans

21.1 Preliminaries

We cannot define with confidence what we are trying to do in a classroom. It is not enough to say that we are providing education, for although there are theories of learning, there is no canonical definition of school education. Therefore, it may help us to understand what we are up to if we examine a few actual lessons and, in this way, develop methods for measuring the interactions, both physical and emotional, between teacher and class.

This study records the behavior of some children in classroom situations. It addresses questions such as: What do particular children do? What, if any, is the pattern of their activities? Is it possible to measure and classify them so as to identify the effectiveness of the classroom processes?

Observational Techniques and Field of Study

Ten teachers of mathematics, all from different modern secondary schools, met several times to discuss whether it would be possible to record the observable activities of their classrooms, and, if so, how this could be done. They agreed the lessons could be photographed by two undisguised motion picture cameras and that a continuous tape recording could be made of each lesson.

The 10 classes observed in this experiment contained about 35 13-year-olds each, whose 10 teachers each agreed to cover the same subject in approximately the same sequence, insofar as this could be defined among themselves before the observations were started. The subject chosen was the use of logarithms, including the the reading of tables. Each teacher dealt with this subject in the equivalent of five lessons of approximately 40 minutes. One teacher gave five distinct lessons on five different days; others gave three single lessons and one double lesson, and one two doubles and a single. Each camera took 1 shot every three seconds, approximately 800 frames in a single lesson, and twice as many in a double. After some experience with the cameras, the activities of a substantial number of children in each class could be quite clearly identified. Eight of the 10 series of lessons gave usable results, and our findings are based on samples totaling more than one-quarter of a million child photographs.

There were, of course, technical difficulties on which we need not dwell. But one difficulty that had been widely anticipated did not arise. Many people, including the teachers, had declared it impossible to make these recordings without seriously disturbing the work of the class. However, we could easily test this hypothesis by observing how many children persistently looked at the camera; the films give precisely this information. It was, in fact, very rare indeed for any child to look at the camera during the lesson. The children had been made thoroughly familiar with the instruments when they were first put into the room and were even allowed to photograph each other with them if they so wished; it seems that this introduction to the new equipment helped the children accept its presence in the classroom and allowed them to concentrate on the lesson.

Analysis of Observations

Our first attempts at interpretation consisted of showing the films to teachers, university lecturers, and other "experts" in the processes of education and inviting their suggestions about possible systems of classification. These exhibitions were an inexhaustible source of useless and sophisticated speculation, and at one stage more than 30 different criteria were postulated as necessary to catalog the activities of the pupils. Sorting so much data by so large a number of criteria is a completely unmanageable task. Furthermore, it is impossible by looking at a photograph of a child to guess whether he might be (1) performing a simple calculation in his head, (2) trying to recall some previously acquired piece of information, (3) trying to follow the argument of the teacher, (4) merely daydreaming, or (5) none of these. We can observe only the child's appearance; we cannot enter into his consciousness. We cannot even try to do so, as, for example, by cross-questioning, without unreasonably disturbing the lesson. It was thus impossible either to identify the conditions envisioned by the professionals or to discriminate among them.

The films were then shown to other schoolchildren of the same age. Their comments and suggestions were interesting and in many ways more acute and insightful than those of the "experts." Moreover, such was the interest displayed by the children that we encouraged them to work out their own systems of classification and to use these systems for analyzing what was on the films; one class of boys gave up a holiday to scan the films of another school. Another even devised a form of shorthand to speed the recording. With such help from the children, we eventually devised a list of seven categories, of which two are relatively unimportant; this list has been used throughout the analysis. We believe that the choice of our four major criteria is logically justified.

21.2 Criteria of Classification
These four major criteria are:

1. *Listening or appearing to listen* (*L*). If the child is seen to be watching the teacher and the teacher is heard to be speaking, we assume that the child is listening to what the teacher is saying; we make no comment upon the clarity of the teacher's output nor of the significance of the input to the child; we have, for example, already acknowledged that the child might well be daydreaming.

2. *Answering or asking a question* (*A*). It was apparent whether or not the child was either speaking to the teacher or attempting to speak to the teacher; the child's hand would be up or else the respective positions of teacher and pupil would suggest whether or not the child was responding. Dubious cases were usually resolved by the scanning children, who could quickly pick out which child might actually be speaking and which other children were attempting to speak.

3. *Writing or drawing* (*W*). It was generally clear when a child was writing something on a piece of paper or in his exercise book. No matter what the child might be writing on and no matter what aids he may have had, such as a ruler, the activity of writing could normally be identified; at times, however, it was hard to distinguish from the next activity.

4. *Referring or reading* (*R*). The reading of tables or textbooks could usually be unambiguously identified, but a child might also be referring to his own work, that is, reading what he had just written, with his pen still in hand. Although this was classified as referring rather than writing, the photographs often made no clear distinction between the two activities. At times the child was seen to be copying from the blackboard; the reading associated with this was classified as referring, but often reading from the blackboard went with listening to the teacher. This total activity (listening and referring) was then classed as listening.

Secondary Criteria of Classification
The other three criteria of classification are:

5. *Not attending.* It was fairly clear when the child was no longer participating in the lesson. He might be searching under his desk, talking to the child next to him, looking out of the window, etc.; there is no need to name these manifold diversions.
6. *Entering or leaving the classroom.* These child movements are quite ambiguous. Some double lessons are broken in the middle for a short period, but the majority of observations of this kind come at the start and finish of the lesson.
7. *Child not observable.* As the teacher walks about the classroom a particular child may be hidden from the camera, or another child may stand up in front of him. The number of lost observations of this kind is small; the grand average is just over 1 percent, though it varies between classes and between lessons.

Consistency of Observed Lesson Structures
Our main source of confidence in the validity of our measurements is found in the consistent differences between lessons recorded by independent observers. Each teacher inevitably imposes a serial structure upon every lesson merely because he determines, from minute to minute, whether the children ought to be listening, asking or answering questions, reading and referring, or writing. Thus, at any given moment, the children sampled are all supposed to be listening, or reading, or whatever it may be. Although some individuals will occasionally deviate from the pattern of activity, there is on the whole a simultaneity in the responses of the whole class that should be captured in the simultaneous records of the observers, providing they all judge by the same criteria. A statistical measure of this unanimity is the ratio of the variance between lessons to the residual variance; this residue will include, among other influences, the errors of the observers. In all sets of our four positive activities (that is, excluding inattentiveness, which is personal to the child), these variance ratios are highly significant; the common patterns of the individual lessons of any teacher stand out in independent records of different observers. Only if all observers systematically made the same misinterpretations of the behavior of a particular child could this agreement be wrongly written into the records.

21.3 Four Examples of Lesson Structure

We illustrate the argument with a set of observations from the five lessons of equal length observed in School 3; because they are of equal length, the variance between lessons cannot be influenced by the total of all activities differing between one lesson and another. The results are given in Table 21.1. The relative magnitudes of the variances between lessons (which indicate not only the different structures of the lessons, but also the consistency of the eight observers in recording the activities of the particular children) are impressive. The variances between lessons in all four cases are too great to have occurred by chance; the eight children observed are following a significantly common pattern of behavior. Note that only in A, answering or asking questions, do the *children* show significant differences among themselves; at least for this series of lessons the class was closely disciplined, and all eight children observed were held significantly to the class average.

Table 21.1a   Distribution by Lesson and by Child of Frames of Listening

Lesson	Child								Lesson Totals
	A	B	C	D	E	F	G	H	
1	440	391	369	444	352	375	339	439	3149
2	166	226	233	207	188	212	262	300	1794
3	294	264	191	257	209	300	281	255	2051
4	216	224	186	212	194	194	220	202	1648
5	39	21	18	39	100	39	52	76	384
Child Totals	1155	1126	997	1159	1043	1120	1154	1272	9026

Table 21.1b   Distribution by Lesson and by Child of Frames of Referring

Lesson	Child								Lesson Totals
	A	B	C	D	E	F	G	H	
1	258	233	258	290	260	262	325	226	2112
2	321	411	326	346	366	287	365	321	2743
3	258	267	243	323	278	223	207	211	2010
4	228	228	266	255	170	256	229	156	1788
5	329	346	325	370	149	151	278	316	2264
Child Totals	1344	1485	1418	1584	1223	1179	1404	1230	10917

Table 21.1c   Distribution by Lesson and by Child of Frames of Asking or
Answering a Question

Lesson	Child A	B	C	D	E	F	G	H	Lesson Totals
1	71	141	136	43	119	116	110	97	833
2	47	79	97	33	81	71	64	47	519
3	64	138	152	72	99	94	130	153	902
4	37	87	48	23	72	49	67	56	439
5	1	32	4	8	11	0	0	0	56
Child Totals	220	477	437	179	382	330	371	353	2749

Table 21.1d   Distribution by Lesson and by Child of Frames of Writing

Lesson	Child A	B	C	D	E	F	G	H	Lesson Totals
1	25	2	14	16	15	20	17	22	131
2	231	54	102	195	82	174	91	83	1012
3	94	35	88	51	55	57	58	73	511
4	192	126	191	194	190	153	176	170	1392
5	320	266	300	290	328	425	322	255	2506
Child Totals	862	483	695	746	670	829	664	603	5552

The Duration of Inattentiveness

It is not uncommon for a child to be inattentive for, say, ten seconds at a stretch; this, at one shot every three seconds, would show on the film as three (or four) successive frames each registering the child's inattentiveness. About two percent of spells of inattentiveness exceed half a minute in the lessons observed. We may thus determine, for samples of child lessons with different teachers, the average numbers of frames per spell. We should expect these averages to vary from one child to another within any particular class. And we should be very surprised, knowing the distracting influences available to the child of thirteen, if the time distribution of spells in one class was the same as that in another. If they appeared to be so, we might have to conclude that our discovered averages were some constant artifact of our observations, such as arbitrary interpretations by our observers of the state of inattentiveness.

We give in Table 21.2 the average length of spells of inattentiveness during 46 child lessons in School 3 and 32 lessons in School 6. (Since 10 of the School 6 sample were double periods, the equivalent, in total time duration, of the School 6 sample is 42 single periods. A single child lesson is one child observed for 40 minutes.)

It is clear from Table 21.2 that the patterns of the 2 samples are significantly different; the average duration of inattentiveness in School 3 is about 4.7 seconds and in School 6 about 7.8 seconds. So great a statistical difference must be real; it could not possibly be explained by sampling or observer error. Further analysis of the data shows it not to be related to longer average length of lesson in School 6.

21.4 The Classification of Transitions

Our concern is now not so much that the observer can accurately recognize inattentiveness, nor even that he can discriminate between referring and writing, or between listening and answering, but that *he can recognize a change* from any one activity to any other, including inattentiveness. We want to know how far the stream of activity of any one child is continually diverted from one occupation to another; on purely general grounds we should expect some children to "concentrate" less than others, irrespec

Table 21.2 Distribution of Child Lessons by Average Length of Spells of Inattentiveness

Average Length of Spell in Frames*	No. of Child Lessons	
	School 3	School 6
Less than 1.00	0	0
1.00–1.50	27	3
1.50–2.00	14	12
2.00–2.50	2	5
2.50–3.00	1	2
3.00–3.50	2	4
3.50–4.00	—	3
4.00–4.50	—	—
4.50–5.00	—	1
5.00–5.50	—	2
Totals	46	32

*Separated by intervals of 3 seconds

tive of the activity temporarily imposed by the teacher upon the class as a whole. We thus observe a sample of children over a series of lessons and record the duration of each spell of activity. For this purpose inattentiveness is classed as the fifth activity. This gives the distribution of the total of observed spells with respect to their duration, but irrespective of their content; the observer is now asked to record not *what* the child appears to be doing, but *when* he appears to change to something different.

From this distribution we may, for any given class, then prepare a table showing, by children and by lessons, the numbers of single frame activities, including any inattentiveness; these entries are a measure of restlessness, since a single frame occasion suggests at least three consecutive spells within six seconds or less, that is, in the period of three seconds before that frame was shot and of three seconds thereafter. The analysis of the variance of this table should show a child effect, since each child may be expected, independently of the lesson content, to exhibit his own characteristic mobility of interest sufficiently clearly for observers to discriminate between the records of any one child and another. In the same way we may prepare a second table, of the number of spells during which the attention of the child is held on any activity for longer than some given period, chosen here as 15 seconds. Tables 21.3 and 21.4 give the results of this classification for the same

Table 21.3   Number of Single Frame Spells of Inattentiveness by Children

Lesson	Child								
	1	2	3	4	5	6	7	8	9
1	64	81	54	65	62	74	64	79	75
2, 3	94	178	58	91	78	100	103	157	129
4	73	108	27	45	52	43	72	140	94
5	85	111	62	39	76	64	59	84	99

Table 21.4   Number of Spells of Inattentiveness of 5 Frames* or More by

Lesson	Child								
	1	2	3	4	5	6	7	8	9
1	32	35	37	34	31	40	39	30	37
2, 3	63	66	68	67	64	65	67	52	58
4	50	44	52	61	58	54	55	41	55
5	31	40	43	63	40	45	43	36	40

*5 frames = 15 seconds

nine children in School 4 over four periods—three single and one double.

The analyses of variance of short spells between children indicated that, in these conditions, the probability of finding a value of F as high as was found is completely negligible. In simple English, some children (as all of us know) consistently find it harder than others to hold their attention upon any activity for more than a few seconds.

The analysis of variance of the longer spells is no less interesting. The F-ratio is significant at about 1 percent, so that our observations again reveal real differences among the inherent capacities of the children to hold their attention upon any activity for longer than 15 seconds. We should expect this quality to be related to that displayed in Table 21.3 although there is no a priori reason for favoring any particular degree of association.

The Mean Duration of Listening

We may now compare the averages of more positive activities such as, for example, listening to the teacher. The distribution of spells of listening by duration for all children sampled in Schools 3 and 6 is shown graphically in Figure 21.1, where the logarithm of the number of spells recorded throughout 30 child hours in the classroom is plotted against the length of spell, taken in multiples of 15 seconds. We note that beyond spells lasting about half a minute the probability distribution of the length is logarithmic. The length in seconds of the average is characteristic of the class observed; we do not know, however, whether it is also characteristic of the school, of the class teacher, of the subject of the lesson, or whether it depends upon any of these at all; it may even be an environmental factor depending upon local noise as a cause of interruption or distraction. It is clear from Table 21.5 that the tempo of the lessons in School 3 is much brisker than that of School 6, except for A-intervals. The teacher here was able to hold the attention of the children during those parts of the lessons devoted to answering or asking questions a great deal longer than was the teacher at School 6.

We may also show the distribution by children and by lessons of average duration of other main activities. Comparing Schools 3 and 6 once more, we obtain the data of Table 21.5. We see that the structures of the two sets of lessons are quite different. Similar differences can be traced throughout our sample of 50 lessons.

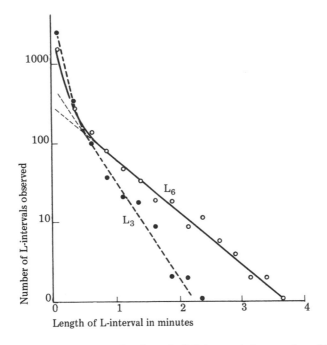

Figure 21.1   Distribution of all L-intervals in samples of lessons from School 3 and School 6.

21.5 Teacher and Child

The Frequency of Feedback

Any series of lessons demands for its success a system of two-way communication. How far does the teacher know what impact, if any, his output is making on the children? How far can the children verify their newly-ordered impressions by testing them in exchanges with the teacher? We begin with a numerical estimate of the frequencies of such contacts, here confined to the short-term verbal exchanges A rather than the slower written outputs, W. The analysis of time spent on A-activities by the children randomly observed in a sample of eight schools is given in Table 21.6.

Significant Differences between Classes

It is clear from Table 21.6 that the opportunities both of the chil-

Table 21.5 Distribution by School of Average Duration of Spells of Activity per Lesson

Average in Seconds	School 3*				School 6**			
	L	R	A	W	L	R	A	W
0-6	4	0	9	1	1	0	14	0
6-9	11	12	8	9	1	0	12	2
9-12	17	21	16	14	9	9	10	4
12-15	8	13	7	7	3	11	4	9
15-18	6	1	1	9	3	3		8
18-21	1		3	4	5	9		6
21-24			1	0	3	3		3
24-27			2	1	5	3		2
27-30				1	3	0		4
30-33				0	0	1		0
33-36				1	1	0		0
36-39					4	0		0
39-42					1	1		2
42-45					1			
Means (Secs)	10.2	10.2	10.0	12.7	20.5	16.6	6.6	18.0

*N = 47 child lessons
**N = 40 child lessons

Table 21.6 A Spells Observed during 336 Child Lessons in 8 Schools

School	No. of child lessons	No. of A spells in all	Average A spells per child lesson	A as percentage of all activities
1	19	323	17.0	5.8
2	41	456	11.1	3.8
3	47	986	21.0	9.6
4	58	2090	36.0	11.4
5	34	837	20.4	4.0
6	50	281	5.6	2.5
7	41	387	9.4	3.6
8	46	590	12.8	4.2
Totals	336	5950	17.71	5.63

*N = 242,912 activity frames

dren to test their inputs and of the teacher to test his outputs vary greatly from class to class. There is a range of averages (for all 7 or 8 children sampled from any particular class) between 5.6 and 36.0 in the average number of attempts per single lesson of 40 minutes to answer or ask a question; the average percentage of class time these attempts occupy varies between 2.5 and 11.4 percent. In the absence of more detailed information about learning processes, we are unable to interpret this result. We can only emphasize that a child needs to reveal both his discoveries and his misunderstandings; he will normally do this on trying to give a reply to a question from the teacher, or by asking a question if he is clear about his difficulty and on friendly terms with the teacher. He may also rearrange his pattern of misunderstanding if he hears the teacher correct another child who gave a wrong response similar to that he himself was about to give, had he been picked by the teacher.

Proposed Classroom Monitor

More insight into individual differences in capabilities among children could be secured by having on the desk of every child a (say) five-position switch connected to a monitor in front of the teacher, and by inviting *every* child in the class to select, on critical responses, that position of the switch indicating his answer. This system would demand both preparation by the teacher of the five alternatives and an unambiguous agreement with the class over the allocation of the five switching positions to the five possible answers. A specially ruled blackboard could be used for entering and exhibiting up to any five alternatives in any critical response. No child would readily be able to copy his answer from another, and by a suitable choice of critical questions and possible responses to them, the teacher could get an instant record of the progress of all the children. We can design a monitor that both accumulates and prints out at the end of the lesson the responses of each member of the class. By matching this against the expected sequence of responses, an experienced teacher can see at once the success and errors of every pupil; the nature of the errors recorded against each child throw light upon his particular difficulties. Such a device was developed during this study and seems to hold possibilities for enriching the learning process that is the focus of our attention; it has also been used to examine the achievement of children previously judged both illiterate and unintelligent. With its help these children were able to demonstrate that, although they might have been illiterate, they were certainly not unintelligent. Such a system of key questions and monitored responses may also have promise for the developing countries, where problems of mass teaching need special attention.

21.6 Learning Theory

Our main classification of L, R, A and W was not made for ease of observation alone; it was also guided by learning theory. The important element in this is feedback, or supplying the organism with early knowledge of the results of its own specific actions; even a mechanical control without learning properties must be aware of its deviations from set standards before it can correct them. The need for the learning loop is universal: the system, whether Plato's academician, Köhler's ape, or a B-stream child in a Lancashire secondary school, must have intelligent information about its performance before it can hope to improve upon it. This feedback loop, relating inputs and outputs, is a necessary but not sufficient element in a learning system; other elements are memory, transfer, logical process, and, above all, in human subjects, a source of motivation.

Inputs from Teacher to Pupil

In a school classroom it is one function of a teacher to provide the children with a program of inputs. In a lesson on logarithm tables much of these inputs will consist either in what the teacher says or in what he writes on the board, although a good teacher provides many inputs other than words and figures. Our observations classified as L are thus a rough indication of the relative amount of input directly from the teacher, but without regard for its quality. Yet it is at least interesting to know what percentage of any lesson or set of lessons given by a teacher is devoted to such input into the children from the teacher; and it may be of still further interest to know whether that input is delivered in one unbroken stream or in several smaller bursts.

Inputs Read by Pupil

The other major input is R, the activity of reading or referring; some of L, insofar as this includes paying attention to what the teacher may be doing as well as to what he may be saying, will serve the same purpose as R, for the children will also be reading both what the teacher has written on the board and the expressions that pass across his face. Our distinction is not, however, between what is written and what is spoken; it is the distinction between inputs from the teacher and inputs drawn by the child from any documents in front of him. That is, given the opportunity to do so, the L-input source is capable of becoming the receptor of a child's unprogrammed or irrelevant output and an immediate source of fresh input for the child about such output; this cycle can then be indefinitely repeated. R-inputs, on the other hand, are the products of two-way communication systems *only if they are specially designed to this end*; they are then assimilated to teaching machines, but are nevertheless still capable of limited responses only, and *these must first be deliberately built in after having been anticipated.*

Sensitivity of Inputs to Response

Yet R-inputs have their essential qualities; a table of logarithms or a book of examples have a permanence and accessibility denied to L-inputs; R-inputs, insofar as they refer to the child's own written work (such as notes of previous classes or corrected exercises), are both a form of feedback and a powerful access to past experience; they also help in searching the memory. But they must remain supplementary to the teacher's input, because this alone can give information not only about subject matter, but also about the child's performance. The child must know whether his responses are those expected of him before he can start to modify them if they are wrong. A busy or indifferent teacher may see the child to be wrong and yet do nothing, of course; L-input sources are not part of a two-way communication system *unless the teacher chooses to make them so.* The extent to which the teacher achieves this feedback is, in our series of observations, suggested by A, the occasions on which the children can ask or answer questions. So far we do not pretend to assess the relevance of these questions, nor the intelligibility of the replies; we merely discover that many children can go through a series of five lessons on the teaching of logarithms without a single opportunity to test their understanding at any stage by an exchange with the teacher. A child cannot begin to rearrange a confused set of ideas, that is, a program of error, until he is aware of what that error may be. In general, only contact with other persons in a learning situation will effectively give the pupil that awareness, although the teaching machine may act as the monitor in *specific and contrived cases.*

Written Exercises as a Form of Feedback

The activity denoted by W is fairly precise in definition, although in observation not always easy to distinguish from R. Then W must include the child's copying material from the blackboard or writing notes dictated by the teacher, but it consists mainly in the records of exercises worked by the child on paper. Some W may be scrutinized by the teacher, either during the lesson or afterwards in the staff room. If the child is working through exercises to which he will be told the correct answers after the teacher has examined them, then W may form another essential feedback link of the cybernetic process that we know as learning. Some teachers arranged their series of five lectures so that in the fourth or fifth the major part of the time was given to written exercises. An illustration is in Table 21.1d.

21.7 Models of the Classroom Lesson

We may now integrate these four classes of activity into a simple model. The work of the child can first be partitioned into inputs and outputs; it can then be partitioned into activities that directly and immediately involve the teacher and activities that do not. Let the irregular shape in Figure 21.2 represent the total lesson, which

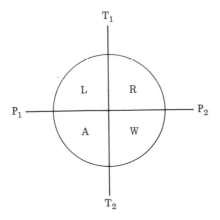

Figure 21.2   Total lesson divided into input/output and teacher-involved/ non-teacher-involved activities.

we divide twice by intersecting lines. $T_1 T_2$ represents the boundary between activities that involve the teacher and activities that do not; $P_1 P_2$ represents the boundary between input activities and outputs. The areas into which the total lesson is quartered are readily identified under our system of classification as

L = input/teacher-involved
A = output/teacher-involved
R = input/teacher-not-involved
W = output/teacher-not-involved.

Our observations suggest that, for any particular child, a lesson of about 40 minutes on the use of logarithms will generally be a sequence of about 200 spells of activity, some finished in three seconds or less, others lasting a minute or more. A useful representation of the child lesson can readily be visualized in terms of a simple model such as that of Figure 21.2. The total area represents a lesson; and the teacher, by his design of the lesson, cuts it into a particular set of quadrants. Each child then, by the pressures of his individual preferences, squashes or stretches the same quadrants to roughly the same degree, whatever the teacher's original scheme.

Socratic Discourse and the Teaching Machine

However this may be, there is a useful way of recording the transitions among the 200 or so spells of activity. Figure 21.2, divided by the line $T_1 T_2$, may now be taken to suggest two archetypical teaching systems: LA, the Socratic discourse; RW, the teaching machine. In system LA the teacher and pupil converse, presumably ranging, in this social process, over a wide field, seeking to explore by question and answer the misperceptions of both; in system RW the pupil is, as it were, granted time at the console and instructed to press the keys, either until he learns the steps by which he can extract the square root by logarithms (within the limitations of the particular program in the machine) or until his time runs out. It is true that with an actual machine the inputs R, which the pupil receives, have a highly specific structure, and that his W-outputs or responses must be related, by a one-to-one correspondence, to these R-inputs as a condition of his progress. In the classroom the ordinary operations of referring (recognition) and writing (rearrangement) often have no such closely programmed relationship, but it might be the mark of a good teacher to attempt to create such a relationship.

Transitions as Feedback Loops

The transitions L to A and A to L are thus strongly anticipated in any learning system; so also are the transitions R to W and W to R. We may simplify the notation and, as shown in Table 21.7, set out the possible transitions as a matrix. The elements on the diagonal are measures of how far the existing state of affairs continues unchanged. For the present we do not need to discuss these and will go on to examine the meaning of the others, apart from LA, AL, RW and WR, which have been discussed above.

The transition LR may be expected whenever the teacher is explaining a document to the class at large and when each child in the class has a copy of that document to refer to. For example, if each child has a set of logarithm tables and the teacher is explaining their structure, or how to enter them, or how to compute the fourth figure from the columns of differences, the children are bound to mix spells of listening to the teacher with spells of referring to the tables. Some children will, of course, not look up when the teacher makes a further remark, but will continue to search the printed tables with their eyes (and perhaps a finger) while the teacher is still talking. Hence many child instants that are recorded as R will also be loaded with L, although no note can be taken of this. It may well be that this type of search will also be broken by A; the teacher, while encouraging the whole class to refer to the table, may nevertheless ask questions of particular children. At times during the search the children may be asked to make notes, so that the LR and RL transitions will be broken by short spells of A or W. Our photographic records, since they are also sequential, will easily throw out such patterns of transition if asked for.

The transitions AR or RA show the occasions on which the children are answering the teacher while referring to documents on their desks, rather than while the teacher is addressing them as a

Table 21.7   Transitions between Activities of a Particular Child during a 90-Minute Lesson

	L	R	A	W	N
L	458	50	17	2	42
R	45	466	3	31	14
A	16	3	87	0	3
W	4	22	1	225	6
N	47	18	1	0	177

class with their attention largely upon him. Even while the teacher is the main source of input to the children (during his usual delivery), however, they might still have documents before them from which they attempt to extract the answer to any question that the teacher might ask. Such an occasion would show the double transition LRA. Transitions AR would be observed when, having given the teacher a reply, the child at once returns to consulting the document before him.

The transitions WA and AW occur whenever the child breaks off writing in order to ask or answer a question of the teacher or proceeds at once to write after such a question. On purely a priori grounds one might judge such transitions to be powerful episodes in the learning cycle: on the one hand, verbal output toward the teacher at once reinforced by manual output on the desk, or, on the other, manual output followed at once by evaluation through feedback from the teacher.

Finally, the positive transitions LW and WL suggest the frequency of any dictation or note-taking with which the child is occupied; combined with information about what, if anything, is done with such notes, either by the child for immediate use, or by the teacher as feedback (to establish by marking them how far the child has grasped what the teacher has been saying), these transitions suggest a somewhat roundabout learning loop. Although the child is giving a response to the input from the teacher, it is not of a kind that lends itself to a rapid comparison either with what the child expected the teacher to say or with what the teacher expected the child to write. The delay in relating what the child wrote with what the teacher said may prove a bar to effective learning, and we should know more than we do about these interactions of listening and writing.

The Incidence of Inattentiveness

We have, until now, in this display of abstraction, ignored the incidence of inattentiveness. It is, nevertheless, important to know not only the extent of this, but during which spells of positive activity it descends. The positive activity that is followed by inattentiveness should be debited with the record of it. Does the child wander most while the teacher is talking? Or is it the more direct activities of referring and writing that tend not to hold his interest? Such questions lend themselves to approximate replies.

21.8 Transition Analysis

The distribution of all frames (other than those showing the children entering or leaving their desks and those in which a particular child could not be seen) for one child in a double lesson of 90 minutes is shown in Table 21.7.

Several conclusions are possible from Table 21.7. They refer, of course, only to this given child during this given lesson. Thus, inattentiveness is significantly more probable during the discourses of the teacher than during any other positive part of the lesson. Of 570 instants recorded as listening, 42 were followed by spells of inattentiveness, whereas 926 other instants in which the child is either referring, answering, or writing are followed by only 23 spells of inattentiveness. This gives a value of X^2 which could not possibly have occurred by chance. *This particular child has greater difficulty in giving attention to the teacher than to other positive activities.*

A Null Hypothesis: The Unstructured Lesson

We may omit the diagonal of the matrix (since this suggests nontransition) and proceed to compute Table 21.8. We assume that there is no structure to the lesson in the sense that, given the total number of transitions actually observed (in this example, 325) they occurred with equal probability between any two activities. This null hypothesis states that the chance of activity X following activity Y depends only upon the number of spells of X that occur and the total time devoted to activity Y.

It is, however, clear that there are great differences between the corresponding elements of the two tables. It is interesting to discuss some of them in terms of the pairs of transitions set out above.

1. LA/AL. The expected total of these is 18.03, and the observed

Table 21.8   Distribution of Transitions between Activities of a Particular Child

	L	R	A	W	N
L		53.08	10.35	24.50	23.07
R	44.88		8.60	20.35	19.17
A	7.68	7.55		3.48	3.28
W	12.69	12.47	2.43		5.42
N	25.12	24.68	4.81	11.39	

Note: We assume that these activities follow in random sequence.

33. There is thus significantly more listening and answering than would be expected by pure chance. This is evidence of design; the Socratic discourse can be sighted in this particular classroom. Our conclusion is perhaps no more than a statement of the obvious, but one that helps to build confidence in our approach.

2. RW/WR. The contrast here is between an expectation of 32.82 and an observed total of 53. This also shows a significant emphasis on the feedback loop associated with desk work; it is thus a sight of the principle of the teaching machine, using this analogy for the RW/WR couplet.

Having traced these firm outlines of both discourse and machine, it follows that the other transitions must be significantly feeble. Our results show this clearly.

3. AR/RA has an expected total of 16.15 and an observed value of 6; the corresponding figures for AW/WA are 5.91 and 1. The overall totals are thus 22.06 expected and 7 observed.

4. For WL/LW the expected and observed totals are, respectively, 37.19 and 6, and for AW/WA again, 5.91 and 1. The overall totals are thus 43.10 expected and 7 observed.

Evidence of Transition Structure

These four sets of conclusions show that the two distinct outputs of this particular child, namely, answering (or asking) and writing, are respectively associated with the two distinct inputs of listening and referring and respectively disassociated from, on the one hand, referring and writing, and on the other, listening and answering (or asking). The child does not write much following what the teacher has to say or to ask; nor does the child ask or answer much while he is referring or writing. This particular child lesson is thus significantly characterized both by enduring verbal exchanges and by uninterrupted desk exercises. This may well be a statement of the apparently obvious, and most teachers might suggest that no study is needed to confirm it. It may, however, prove important to know whether and, if so, to what extent, the balance between the principle of the Socratic discourse or social process, on the one hand, and, on the other, of the teaching machine, or individual exercise, influences the learning processes of different children in different subjects. It may be that the clarity with which they appear (that is, the extent to which the transition matrix does not suggest sequential randomness) is an index of importance.

The only pair of transitions in Table 21.8 that does not suggest a significant difference between our expectation from the null hypothesis and our result is LR/RL, 97.96 against 95. This implies that transitions from listening to referring depend only upon how frequently the child was listening, and from referring back to listening merely upon how often he was referring. Since the total periods of these were, in this child lesson, practically the same (569 against 559), we also find this close correspondence between the two expectations and the two actualities as well. Our conclusion is that the references made by this particular child were strongly guided by the instructions of the teacher.

Transitions at Random
We give in Table 21.9 two further transition matrices; they are for two children throughout the same single period. It is clear that there are marked differences between the behaviors of the pair; one has 166 frames of inattentiveness, the other but 12. It is clear that the inattentive child has difficulty in listening to the teacher and is not very diligent at referring. But whichever child we take, we find no evidence of structure in the lesson; there are no significant differences between Table 21.9 and the corresponding tables derived on the null hypothesis of random transitions.

21.9 Comparison of Schools by Summary Totals
We conclude this chapter with a summary of the distribution of main activities among eight of the classes in the schools sampled in this first survey; it is confined to the eight whose records we succeeded in analyzing well enough to exhibit with confidence. We have not examined our two earliest films in the same detail as our eight later; we were obliged to experiment with such variables as

Table 21.9   Distribution of Transitions between Major Activities for 2 Pupils of School 7 throughout Lesson 5

Pupil	L		R		A		W		N	
	1	2	1	2	1	2	1	2	1	2
L	237	352	31	64	2	3	2	4	13	3
R	28	56	449	316	1	2	4	25	20	2
A	3	2	0	3	3	6	0	0	0	0
W	3	13	5	16	0	0	35	110	2	1
N	13	2	18	3	0	0	4	1	131	6

lens, exposure, film, interval between exposures, and so forth, and this experience cost us the records of two classes. The results for the other eight follow, however, in Table 21.10.

21.10 General Conclusions

It can be seen that we have classified about one-quarter of a million observations. This is on the average a 25 percent sample of the total observations made on the 8 classes altogether, although the percentage varies from class to class. Some films were clearer than others, simply because the lighting of the room differed. But even in the school that was given our least attention we still scanned 13,000 child frames. Recorded differences between class performance are thus suitable for highly discriminating statistical evaluation, and we find substantial differences persisting among the structures of lessons; these may be traced in all the lessons of the different classes. For example, in the discussion on feedback we have already shown that the opportunities for children to ask or to ignore questions differ significantly among schools. So also does the percentage of time lost by inattentiveness; averaged over all children observed throughout 5 lessons, this may be as low as 1.5 percent and as high as 10.6 percent. It is true that the children

Table 21.10a   Numerical Distribution of Frames by Activity and School

Activity	School							
	1	2	3	4	5	6	7	8
L	3956	8016	10908	17639	12503	14947	23473	12351
R	4713	8814	12789	8209	10787	13370	13893	12678
A	753	1075	3272	3891	1173	964	1677	1379
W	2218	8754	6270	3720	3324	8435	6361	5215
N	1377	1959	734	529	1257	981	1387	1488

Table 21.10b   Percent Distribution of Frames by Activity and School

Activity	School							
	1	2	3	4	5	6	7	8
L	30.4	28.0	32.1	51.8	43.0	38.6	50.2	37.3
R	36.2	30.8	37.6	24.1	37.1	34.6	29.7	38.3
A	5.8	3.8	4.6	11.4	4.0	2.5	3.6	4.2
W	17.0	30.6	18.4	10.9	11.4	21.8	13.6	15.8
N	10.6	6.5	2.2	1.5	4.3	2.5	3.0	4.5

were sampled in conditions that some who saw little of the experiment have described as artificial and that those who saw nothing at all hold as immoral. But the teachers who took part, while sometimes admitting to considerable anxiety under the unusual experience, felt that there was no way in which these 5 lessons might have differed significantly from those they normally gave. Certainly there was no evidence from the films and the tapes themselves that the researchers distracted either teacher or class. We therefore feel entitled to speculate upon the performances of the 8 classes as they are recorded in Table 21.10. We admit that later comparison between them is of low value beside what might have been done had we had the results already available for discussion with the teachers as the films were being taken. We see no reason why this, and many other instructive things, such as relating speculation to measurable child learning, should not be done at some future time by a research team wiser and more capable than mere beginners like ourselves.

22

Operations Research in University Planning

Robert M. Oliver

22.1 Introduction

The American college (or university) must operate more economically and with greater understanding than it has in the past. A number of important books and pamphlets (Dobbins [9], Cheit [7], Bowen [4], Bowen [3], Tickton [28], Dunlop et al. [10], Carnegie Commission [6], and Hitch [12]) and a number of articles in newspapers and popular journals (Holsendolph [13]) attest to the increasing importance of defining objectives, predicting and understanding the financial impacts of new operating policies at private and public educational institutions, and proposing alternative ways of offering higher education to young people and to adults.

At least four of our major charitable foundations devote a substantial part of their annual income to studies on the economics of private and public universities and on the gathering of data and the measurement of historical indices, to the evaluation of trends in the financing of higher education, and, in a few cases, to the development of better managerial techniques and improved planning procedures.

Two nonprofit institutions, the Western Interstate Commission for Higher Education (WICHE) and the Organization for Economic Cooperation and Development (OECD), support major programs in the analysis of data information and retrieval systems and the development of management and planning models for institutions of higher education. Through its Center for Educational Research and Innovation, OECD supports research programs on institutional management at several universities in Europe, collects documents, and makes reviews of related projects. The Center has recently published a long list of European and American studies and reports relevant to such projects [21]. The WICHE project, on the other hand, is more specifically concerned with the development and implementation of data storage, management, and retrieval systems that not only allow interinstitutional comparisons, but also "promote efficient reporting to state and federal government [17]."

The disturbing fact is that there have been far more articles and papers pointing to the economic woes of the higher education industry than there have been publications resolving some of the difficult institutional problems. Even the bibliography by Rath [26] cites few actual applications. In an article for the Ford and Carnegie Foundations, Bell [2] points out that the application of operations research and management science techniques has probably had less impact on the management of this industry than on most others in the country. ERIC Abstracts [11] list approximately a dozen references under these headings; of these only two or three address specific operational problems; the others are largely a collection of papers describing philosophical difficulties one gets into by misusing these techniques. In brief, there has been much talk and little action.

Looking at the Educational Institution as a Firm

Economists have made it tempting to think of an educational institution in terms that are familiar to a businessman operating a firm; raw inputs (students) arrive at a plant (the educational institution) and are processed (taught), converted (educated), and eventually give rise to a finished product (a degree recipient).

To carry their analogy a bit further, there are by-products (dropouts without formal degree status), a technology (student-faculty ratios), and in-process inventories (student enrollments) that depend upon operating policies constrained by certain given operating and capital budgets. Many of the analogies cease to apply, however, when one considers the nature of educational objectives and the way in which educational services are budgeted.

Whereas a firm usually seeks out and pays money for a raw product, the student requests acceptance by the educational institution and in most cases is willing to pay money to gain admission. Upon graduation, the degree recipient seeks employment, but the salary that he commands is seldom related to the cost of the product, nor is the educational institution directly rewarded for profit based on the type and quality of his education. The quality of the degree or the value of the education to the individual may not have any significant connection with the economist's usual concept of market price or the laws of supply and demand for a commercially manufactured product. If, on the other hand, the student is viewed as the consumer of the service offered by the university, only a small part of the revenue for the university is generated by the consumer.

Magnitude of the Problem Area

In the United States there were approximately 8 million students enrolled in universities and colleges during the 1970–1971 period, and an increase of about 20 percent is forecast during the next decade. A crude estimate of the composition of this student force is that approximately 8 million will be enrolled in undergraduate schools, and less than 2 million will be enrolled in graduate and professional schools. Approximately 2 million of these undergraduates will be in community or junior colleges. At many public institutions, less than half of the entering students will actually obtain a degree. Part of this attrition is due to the inherent mobility of the student population, but part also is due to the fact that many students who enroll do so not knowing why they should pursue an advanced education.

The annual budget for a large institution such as the University of California can run anywhere from 30 million dollars to 400 million dollars, of which anywhere from 25 percent to 60 percent may be derived from federal sources. The 1970 edition of the *U.S. Statistical Abstracts* cites total federal and local government support of university research and teaching programs as being approximately 8 billion dollars per annum. This represents about 50 percent of the national allocation for the higher education industry. These numbers are almost double the corresponding figures of 4.3 billion and 7.8 billion dollars in 1963–1964 [3].

The Problems

Planning problems at the national level differ in scope, purpose, and size from those at the university or college level. While this paper is concerned with problems of the latter type, it may be helpful to place them in the context of the broader problems that include such important questions as the amount of federal budgets that should be allocated to support research programs at universities and restrictions on them, budgets allocated for special minority or economic opportunity programs, the support of community or junior colleges whose graduates may then enter state colleges or private universities, the impact of open-door admission policies at state and federally supported institutions, the support of adult education and educational programs that stress education during the lifetime of an individual rather than during his late teens and early twenties, research and development in new technologies such as computer-aided instruction, and so on.

At the institutional level, the typical questions one might pose are slightly narrower in scope, but they overlap substantially with those just mentioned. They include questions on the specific effects of adopting new enrollment ceilings, developing a new curricular program in the undergraduate or graduate school, adding a new campus or expanding the capacity of an old one, modifying admission policies for students with special educational or economic backgrounds, adopting new fellowship or teaching programs, as well as questions of cost and student flow patterns that will result from year-round operations. Under severe budgetary constraints, administrators will consider such plans as dissolving an individual department, abandoning educational programs, modifying the length and content of a lower division education, or restructuring the benefits and costs of a faculty retirement system.

To consider the merits of such proposals, several types of questions must be answered: How will the new policy affect the number, type, and quality of degrees produced over a given planning horizon? How will student flow patterns and enrollments be altered? What are the underlying costs of the new proposals, and what will be the form of new constraints that must be imposed on faculty and staff resources to implement the new policies?

Since unit and marginal costs are sensitive to student and faculty flow patterns throughout the institution, it is important first of all to obtain satisfactory models to describe these flow patterns, admission rates, graduation rates, dropouts, student enrollments, and other relevant flows and stock levels. This is not a simple task as both the internal institutional restrictions and the external flow rates into and out of the system contribute to its complexity. In such models it appears to me that the emphasis in forecasting movements of student flows and budgets should be on relative magnitudes, not precision, for the latter is a task more appropriately related to that of preparing detailed accounting and budgetary information once a particular plan or policy is judged desirable and feasible.

A major difficulty in formulating, testing, and implementing models of the flow and budgetary process is the lack of good data. I emphasize the word *good* as there are certainly ample data; what are lacking are institutional data relevant to the planning models and to the policy questions that administrators ask. A good example is the matter of student dropouts. While almost every institution processes vast amounts of historical data on the number who leave without a degree during a given semester or term, few distinguish between those students who drop out permanently and those who only take temporary leaves of absence but eventually return. In forecasting future enrollments and planning for future admissions, it is absolutely essential to distinguish between these two groups. But to the best of my knowledge, that data analysis problem remains largely unresolved. Even so important a study on student entrants and dropouts as that undertaken by the Office of Education [16] is more concerned with the motivational reasons for dropping out, the reactions dropout students have to their educational experience, and the plans these students have about reenrollment than with determining the actual flows and attendance patterns from a longitudinal examination of student cohorts.

A good example of an institutional problem that is amenable to operations research techniques is the matter of year-round operations. Since the late 1950s and the early 1960s many economists and educational administrators have seen some salvation in the proposal that universities operate on year-round rather than nine-month schedules in their undergraduate schools. The arguments ran that by using the facilities during the summer, it was theoretically possible to increase the productivity of the institution. By enrolling in the summer, undergraduate students could graduate in three rather than four years, which, after the new procedures and systems had settled down, would mean that the number of students graduating per unit time would increase by a factor of one-third. It is interesting to note that all the arguments were based on the assumptions that (1) the institution's peak capacity for enrollments would always be used, (2) students would voluntarily substitute continuous attendance patterns for their historical ones, and (3) institutions would, in fact, offer the appropriate sequence of prerequisite courses to satisfy degree requirements.

Tickton, in a 1963 study for the Ford Foundation [28], made it clear that the soundness of year-round operations was no longer in question. Although he does not give any quantitative estimates of the increases in productivity, there does not appear to be the slightest question as to its eventual success. Events changed rapidly in the next few years. By 1968 there were rumblings that year-round operations were not working well at some of our larger universities. To gain more insight into the problem, we undertook a study during that year to estimate the maximum increase in productivity of degrees that could be expected; the major findings showed that under a broad set of assumptions (based on real data) about the attendance patterns of student cohorts attending the institution in question, a maximum increase in the admission rates would be of the order of 10 percent, and the maximum number of students enrolled during the summer period would be of the order of one-third the enrollment capacity of the institution [14]. The simple, deterministic queuing model that was developed to answer these order-of-magnitude questions was straightforward and easy to obtain; no extensive data collection or computational programs were required. The data showed that only a small fraction of entering students chose continuous attendance patterns. By far the majority of students either had interrupted attendance patterns or attended consecutive quarters in order to enrich their education by enrolling in more courses. In neither of these cases would the overall objective of graduating students earlier or increasing the graduation rate be realized.

It is interesting to note that by 1969 the University of California made formal plans to cancel its year-round operations on the grounds that summer enrollments were too low, a conclusion that could and should have been obtained long before the earlier adoption of the system. By 1971, there was an almost complete reversal on the nationwide assessment of the value, cost, and productivity of year-round operations. The reversal of opinion is not due to the analytical studies that have been undertaken to support this conclusion, but rather to the results of many costly full-scale implementations made during 1965–1970. The tragedy of such costly, nationwide experiments lies not only in the many millions of dollars that have been spent with little apparent return on the investment, but also in the fact that it will be exceedingly difficult to reawaken interest in year-round operations even when well-designed plans are proposed.

22.2 Educational Planning Models
In this section we attempt to give a brief survey of some of the more important educational planning models that have been proposed by various authors. In Section 22.3 we shall discuss a small-scale planning model for a hypothetical university.

The simplest mathematical formulation of an educational planning model assumes that for a given demand for educated students (a vector **x**) there exists a statement of input-output requirements (a matrix **M**), an unknown input of resources (a vector **y**), and a linear transformation

$$y = Mx, \tag{22.1}$$

relating demand for educated students to the resources required. Such models can be interpreted broadly in the sense that the elements of x may correspond to student degrees of various types and levels, and the elements of y may include capital equipment, instructional staff, and even the input stream of uneducated students. The coefficients of the matrix M may include technological requirements, such as teacher-student ratios, and the important feature that a certain fraction of the instructional staff is directly derived from the students being educated. Thus, the input-output or production model can explicitly recognize a feedback effect of the educational sector consuming the very product it manufactures. Depending upon the specific formulation in mind, the dimensions of x and y may change, but these should be expressed as flows, that is, outputs and inputs per unit time—students per year, dollars per year, etc.

How does one go about developing, testing, and implementing a model such as that described in Equation 22.1? Many institutions have found it tempting to look at large amounts of historical cross-sectional data and assume that the coefficients of M observed in past periods will remain constant in future periods. Unfortunately, the coefficients of M are themselves functions of the decisions and policy variables being studied. Thus, the purpose of the model in Equation 22.1, which is to predict the effect of new plans and policies, is frequently defeated by the fact that historical policies are already built into the coefficients of M. The availability of large computers notwithstanding, the experience with large-scale, fixed coefficient models has been expensive, time-consuming, and largely disappointing in terms of the accuracy of their forecasts, the large amount of numerical output they generate, the cost of implementation, and, more fundamentally, the questionable validity of the assumptions upon which they are based.

One of the first published works of a planning model that attempted to reveal the structure of student and faculty flows through an educational system (including components outside higher education) was done by Thonstad [27]. His models were motivated by educational planning at the national levels with specific application to the economy of Norway. The primary problem that he addressed was: How can one analyze and predict the flow rates and stocks of people with a given level of education (teachers and nonteachers)? Since teachers are required to educate nonteachers, their influence may be substantial, even though the fraction of the total population represented by teachers may be small. Thonstad did not specifically include dropouts or changes of majors; nor did he include capacity constraints on enrollment levels. He required that the educational systems have a Leontief structure in order to estimate the educational expansion required to meet the growth in demand for educated students.

Consider the following vector quantities with physical dimensions indicated in parentheses:

h: a vector of student arrivals into the educational system (number per unit time)
g: a vector of internal demand for educated students (number per unit time)
f: a vector of external demand for educated students (number per unit time)
L: a vector of student inventories or enrollment levels (number)
N: a vector of stocks of teaching staff (number)
A: a technological requirement matrix of teacher-student ratios (dimensionless)
W: a diagonal matrix of lifetimes for the teaching staff (time)
V: a diagonal matrix of lifetimes required for students to obtain their education in the system (time).

With this notation, it is possible to write conservation equations for student flows and stock levels of teachers and students as a function of the technology and the time to earn a degree. To simplify the discussion in this paper, we assume that students in each cohort are potential candidates for at most one category of teaching staff and that at most, one cohort can supply a teaching category. Thus, there is a one-to-one correspondence between the set of student cohorts and the set of teaching categories. This is a sufficient (but by no means necessary) condition for the matrices A, V, and W to have well-defined matrix products and inverses.

We first write an inventory equation that states that the enrollment level of students in each category is the product of the arrival rate in that cohort and the time spent in the educational system,

$$L = Vh. \tag{22.2}$$

The second inventory equation states that the instructional levels equal the input rate of teachers times the lifetime in the educational system,

$$N = Wg. \tag{22.3}$$

If flow rates of students split into two parts, that meeting external demand and that returning to the educational system,

$$h = f + g, \tag{22.4}$$

and if we assume that a constant level of students generates a known requirement for various categories of faculty and teaching staff, we can also write,

$$N = AL. \tag{22.5}$$

A straightforward solution of these inventory and flow equations expresses the instructional staffing levels in terms of final output or demand for trained students. Since V and W have inverses, one obtains the teaching levels,

$$N = A[I - VW^{-1}A]^{-1}Vf, \tag{22.6}$$

and the admission flow rates,

$$h = V^{-1}[I - VW^{-1}A]^{-1}Vf, \tag{22.7}$$

in terms of the final demand f. It is not difficult to obtain similar expressions for student enrollments and the internal flows of student cohorts. Basically, this model tells us how inputs are related to outputs under the simplest assumptions about student and faculty lifetimes and technological requirements of student-teacher ratios. The coefficients of $A[I - VW^{-1}A]^{-1}V$ in Equation 22.6 and $V^{-1}[I - VW^{-1}A]^{-1}V$ in Equation 22.7 (analogous to the coefficients of M in Equation 22.1) reveal a structure that is not, a priori, completely obvious. Consider, for example, the case where all variables in Equations 22.6 and 22.7 are scalars. We then obtain

$$N = \frac{AWVf}{W - VA}; \quad h = \frac{Wf}{W - VA}, \tag{22.8}$$

where the first quantity has the dimension of a stock level and the second the dimension of a flow rate. The denominators of both expressions point up the fact that for positive stock levels of faculty and positive admission rates one must have $W/V > A$, that is, the ratio of teacher to student lifetimes must be greater than the teacher-student ratio. For very large student lifetimes the institution or industry may not be able to generate sufficient teachers to educate the required stream flows of educated students.

This model has substantial overlap with one developed independently by Radner and Miller [25]. If their inventory and flow problem is specialized by removing time dependent variables, one obtains (in their notation)

$$x = A[I - (I - M)A]^{-1}f, \tag{22.9}$$

where x is the vector of faculty stocks or inventory levels. In their notation (not ours) M is called the faculty persistence matrix and $M = I - W^{-1}$; inventory levels and flows are defined so that $V = I$. Thus, there are similarities between the model in Equations 22.2–22.7 and the model in Equation 22.9. The former specifically includes parameters that quantify the time to get a degree while the latter does not. On the other hand, the latter is primarily concerned with nonequilibrium growth. A major difference in terms of application is that Radner and Miller are concerned with a nationwide system of junior colleges, rather than the entire educational system or a single institution.

A book by Armitage, Smith, and Alper [1] formulates and solves problems of more modest scope than those addressed by Thonstad but at the same time achieves much more insight into the planning process and even into some of the important institutional decision variables that affect student flows and enrollment levels. The authors provide a computational model that can be used to project flows through an educational system. They are particularly careful to include the effects of institutional capacities and to show that the normal assumptions about constant transition proportions between grades is not generally valid when institutional constraints are operative.

An article by Clough and McReynolds [8] provides a sound basis for a computer simulation of the Ontario, Canada, educational system. Although the details are different from the models of Armitage, Smith, and Alper, the Ontario model also describes the growth of an educational system over time in the presence of inequality constraints on supplies and demands of students. In both cases, stocks in one period are related to stocks in earlier periods through the use of "Markov-like" transition proportions denoting the fraction of a given population that moves between grades or states of the educational system. What is important in both of these papers is that the transition proportions depend upon the supply of educational resources and the demand for places to be occupied in various employment categories (including educational institutions themselves). As a result of the analysis the authors show how the transition proportions must themselves satisfy certain inequalities, an idea that is quite foreign to the traditional input-output models in which the transition proportions are fixed coefficients derived from historical data. One might summarize both of these papers by noting that the authors view the transition proportions as the key policy variables that can be influenced by administrative policies.

22.3 University Planning Models

In this section I would like to give a brief summary of some additional studies we made and the reasons for undertaking them at the University of California during the 1968–1970 period. These studies were funded partially by a Ford Foundation grant to the University of California and partially by the Chancellor's Office on the Berkeley campus.

It might be useful to point out that for planning purposes, university operations and resources are usually classified into five major categories: students, faculty, facilities, equipment, and items that might be called supporting services. University budgets are often separated into two parts: operating and capital. Typically, the operating budget is estimated, requested, and used on a periodic (annual) basis, while the capital budget is often sought and expended on an aperiodic and item-by-item basis. An operating budget is further subdivided into instructional and noninstructional categories, where salaries in the instructional component generally represent the major portion of the total annual figure.

Enrollment Forecasting Models

In many educational institutions it is an unfortunate fact that the size of student enrollments rather than the quality of the education or the quantity of degree outputs forms the basis for budgetary planning and resource allocation. In my opinion, this fact, more than any other, has been largely responsible for the inefficiencies and high costs of many state-supported universities, as they derive large budgets from large enrollments rather than from large output rates or high academic standards. Thus, large numbers of dropouts or students with long lifetimes in degree programs are more useful sources of large budgets than are shorter academic programs or lower dropout rates. As long as this bad practice is continued it will probably be necessary to forecast student enrollments in great detail and then, by means of a set of intermediate calculations, transform these estimates to equivalent full-time budgeted faculty positions, space, and other needs. The underlying calculations presuppose that one has available (1) either an actual headcount of enrolled students or some estimate of what it will be in future time periods and (2) norms or standard weighting factors to convert these enrollments to budgets.

Generally speaking, the shorter the planning horizon, the greater is the need for accurate estimates of enrollments. In this context, accuracy does not refer so much to the ability to make precise numerical calculations as it does to the ability both to understand the mechanisms whereby students decide to attend or not and to predict the impact of new policies on attendance and dropout patterns. In the short run, forecasting enrollments is largely a problem of predicting the number of returning students, whereas in the long run the problem is predominantly one of predicting demands from demographic data.

There are at least two ways of describing the admission, enrollment, and attrition of students. One of these methods, and by far the most popular, is to base the forecast of future enrollments on head counts observed in time periods immediately preceding the period under consideration. For short-term forecasts where administrative policies are not likely to undergo changes, such methods are acceptable. On the other hand, they lead to quite erroneous results when admission policies change with time or when we are dealing with long planning horizons. An alternative way to predict enrollments is to examine the behavioral patterns of groups of students having identifiable attrition characteristics that are stable over time. Such stabilities almost always exist; when they can be properly identified and quantified, one can predict future enrollments by superimposing cohorts with different attrition characteristics.

The enrollment forecasting models we studied were basically

"Markov-like" models that estimated enrollments in the next period in terms of enrollments during past periods, fixed transition probabilities appropriate to the particular period (term or semester), and the admission policies for new entrants. As a special case, and because we were motivated by the desire to find a simple model with minimal data requirements, we developed a specially structured Markov model based on the assumption that each student had to satisfy a certain "work" requirement in order to obtain a degree [19]. In addition, we became involved in large-scale experimental tests of a number of such models to fit our theoretical calculations with independent observations on student attendance patterns [20].

Models for Appointment, Promotion, and Retirement of Faculty

It soon became obvious that we should undertake studies of the flows of manpower and budgets associated with nontenure and tenure faculty appointments, promotions, resignations, and retirements. An earlier study by Dunlop [10] at Harvard University suggested that resignation rates for tenure and nontenure faculty differed by substantial amounts. Berkeley data showed that in some faculty ranks the fraction promoted or remaining in grade was stable over reasonably long time periods [5]. The data had been based on a period of time when there was virtually unrestricted growth in student enrollments and in the number of staff positions. As student enrollments approached their prescribed limits, it seemed reasonable to assume that the number of budgeted faculty positions would also reach limiting values. Several questions that we wanted to answer were: Could we predict limiting values of tenure and nontenure faculty positions? With budgetary constraints, would it be possible to continue the high nontenure to tenure promotion rates? Were fractional promotion rates, lifetimes in nontenure, and the rates of new appointments to tenure positions being planned at that time consistent with one another and, in fact, achievable as a long-range goal?

We analyzed some of these policy questions by formulating a simple deterministic model of the flow through three major faculty categories: nontenure, tenure, and retired members. With subscripts 1, 2, 3 denoting these three categories, let λ_i denote new appointment rates, θ_1, θ_2 the promotion rate from nontenure to tenure and the retirement flow rate, N_i the number of faculty, and μ_i the resignation or death rates from each category. We can then write

$$\lambda_1 = \mu_1 N_1 + \theta_1$$
$$\lambda_2 + \theta_1 = \mu_2 N_2 + \theta_2 \qquad (22.10)$$
$$\theta_2 = \mu_3 N_3$$

for the conservation of faculty flows in the three categories. In most cases of interest to us at that time feasible flow patterns would have to satisfy Equation 22.10 and the added constraints,

$$N_1 + N_2 = \text{a constant}$$
$$0 \leqslant \theta_1 \leqslant \lambda_1 \qquad (22.11)$$
$$0 \leqslant \theta_2 \leqslant \theta_1 + \lambda_2$$
$$N_1 \geqslant 0, \ N_2 \geqslant 0, \ N_3 \geqslant 0.$$

The first *equation* imposes a ceiling on budgeted faculty positions, the second requires that promotions from nontenure not exceed the steady state nontenure appointment rate, and the third *inequality* requires that retirements be less than or equal to promotions plus new appointments into tenure. Nonnegativity of flows and stock levels are also required. We found that many policy questions were simply answered by finding whether the predicted flows were or were not feasible solutions of Equations 22.10 and 22.11. For example, it was found that there did not exist a feasible equilibrium for promotion rates and desired nontenure staffing levels if the new appointment rates being planned at that time continued. Details of the analysis and a summary of promotion and resignation data for the period 1955–1967 are included in a report by Oliver [22].

Equilibrium Flow and Budget Models

Another group of models we developed were concerned with predicting budgets and flow patterns of students and staff in a network where nodes represent educational or instructional programs, and a path in the network (a sequence of nodes and arcs) represents the set of programs undertaken by a cohort of students pursuing a particular degree.

One of the reasons we became deeply involved in an attempt to describe and predict flow patterns and enrollment levels for the institution as a whole is that operating budgets were estimated and then allocated on the basis of particular departmental and college needs, which were almost always expressed in terms of student enrollments, credit hours, and number of graduates. In the overall planning of the university it was not clear how budgetary constraints, enrollment ceiling, restrictions on admissions, or the modification of teaching ratios might affect these flow patterns, the enrollments, and the consequent budgetary allocations. A particularly difficult set of unanswered questions surrounded the resources required to employ teaching assistants while they were enrolled as students pursuing a graduate degree.

A second reason for our interest in these models was that, to the best of our knowledge, no university planning models had ever before explicitly included the costs of dropouts. Experimental data that we had obtained from our earlier studies of student attendance patterns suggested that dropout flow rates were much higher than any numbers we had seen published in the literature. Since the lifetimes of dropouts are significantly smaller than those of students who continue at the institution, and since total costs of instructing students are roughly proportional to their lifetimes, it seemed essential to obtain a better understanding of the way in which admission policies, teacher-student ratios, enrollment ceilings, and other administrative policies affect the number and composition of dropouts.

A third reason such models were formulated was to try to understand and predict a number of productivity indices that were computed during the preparation of each budget plan. These included such ratios as degrees per faculty member, degree graduates per students admitted, faculty members per number of students enrolled, and many others. We made an attempt to point out to budgetary analysts that these ratios and indices are not independent of one another and that it is possible, given certain operating conditions, to have increases in some productivity measures while observing decreases in others. Identifying the magnitude and direction of movement of these productivity indices was an important result of our analysis.

For the purpose of illustration, consider the network and flow patterns of Figure 22.1. Nodes or educational programs are identified as follows: node 1 for dropouts, node 2 for undergraduate degree recipients, node 3 for graduate degrees, and node 4 for teaching assistants. In other words, every student who passes through

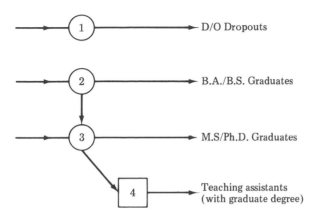

Figure 22.1   A planning model with three instructional programs and one teaching category.

node 2 obtains an undergraduate degree, every student who passes through node 1 is a dropout, and so on.

To keep the problem small enough to describe in this paper, we restrict our attention to the six cohorts defined in Table 22.1; a more realistic model of a large college or university would probably include several types of teachers and a much larger number of student cohorts entering and leaving the university. Notice that in our example, one cohort drops out and never receives a degree, three cohorts receive undergraduate degrees, while four receive graduate degrees. Of these, two provide a supply of teaching assistants who are used to educate the undergraduates. Thus, there is included in the model the important feedback among undergraduate students, graduate enrollments, and teachers who are produced by the institution from these enrollments.

The six different student cohorts associated with Figure 22.1 are defined and listed in Table 22.1. In the second column each cohort is defined by the type of students who are members of the cohort; in column 3 we list the nodes or programs through which each student in a given cohort passes. In columns 4, 5, and 6, we give the notation used for cohort flows $h_j^{(k)}$, unit costs $C_j^{(k)}$ of these flows, and the total lifetime $V_j^{(k)}$ that each cohort spends in the educational institution. In the last three columns the numbering convention is as follows: the superscript of h, C, or V refers to the node where the cohort originates, that is, enters the educa-

Table 22.1 Cohorts, Flows, Costs, and Lifetimes for the Network of Figure 22.1

Cohort Number	Cohort Definition	Nodes in Cohort	Cohort Flow	Unit Cost	Cohort Lifetime
1.	Students who enter as either undergraduates or graduates and drop out before they receive a degree	{1}	$h_1^{(1)}$	$C_1^{(1)} = c_1$	$V_1^{(1)} = v_1$
2.	Students who enter as undergraduates and leave upon receiving a bachelor's degree	{2}	$h_1^{(2)}$	$C_1^{(2)} = c_2$	$V_1^{(2)} = v_2$
3.	Students who enter as undergraduates, receive a bachelor's degree, and then continue until they receive a graduate degree.	{2,3}	$h_2^{(2)}$	$C_2^{(2)} = c_2 + c_3$	$V_2^{(2)} = v_2 + v_3$
4.	Students who enter as undergraduates, receive a bachelor's degree, and then continue in a graduate program in which they serve as teaching assistants before receiving a graduate degree.	{2,3,4}	$h_3^{(2)}$	$C_3^{(2)} = c_2 + c_3$	$V_3^{(2)} = v_2 + v_3 + v_4$
5.	Students who enter as graduates and receive a degree without serving as teaching assistants.	{3}	$h_1^{(3)}$	$C_1^{(3)} = c_3$	$V_1^{(3)} = v_3$
6.	Students who enter as graduates and receive a degree after serving as teaching assistants	{3,4}	$h_2^{(3)}$	$C_2^{(3)} = c_3$	$V_2^{(3)} = v_3 + v_4$

tional institution. The subscript is simply a sequential enumeration of cohorts with a common origin. The unit costs and lifetimes are obtained by adding program costs and lifetimes over the appropriate nodes listed in column 3 of the table, with the following exception: the cost of a cohort that passes through node 4 (teaching assistant) incurs costs only in nodes 1, 2, or 3.

It is known from historical data that a fraction α of all admissions drop out, that average lifetimes of each program are v_1, v_2, v_3, v_4, that the teaching ratios for each program are μ_1, μ_2, μ_3, and that the salary level of teaching assistants is s per year. The administration of this hypothetical university imposes a ceiling on total enrollments (including teaching assistants) and requires that the number of undergraduate and graduate degrees be fixed. In other words, constraints are imposed on flow rates as well as stock levels. The accounting office assumes that the unit cost of educating a single student in a given program is proportional to his lifetime in the program, the teaching assistant-student ratio, and the salary of the teaching assistant. In other words, for the program costs of Table 22.1 we have

$$c_1 = \mu_1 v_1 s; \quad c_2 = \mu_2 v_2 s; \quad c_3 = \mu_3 v_3 s \qquad (22.12)$$

in terms of the data for μ_i, v_j, and s. Using these costs and the notation for cohort flows in Table 22.1, we consider the case where final external demands for undergraduates,

$$h_1^{(2)} = b^{(2)}, \qquad (22.13)$$

and the final demand for graduates without teaching assistant experience,

$$h_2^{(2)} + h_1^{(3)} = b^{(3)}, \qquad (22.14)$$

are given and fixed by some choice of $b^{(2)}$ and $b^{(3)}$.
Since dropout flows (cohort 1) are a constant fraction α of all entering students, we write

$$h_1^{(1)} = \alpha \sum_k \sum_j h_j^{(k)} \qquad (22.15)$$

or, alternatively, the homogeneous equation,

$$h_1^{(1)} - \frac{\alpha}{1 - \alpha} h_1^{(2)} - \frac{\alpha}{1 - \alpha} h_2^{(2)} - \frac{\alpha}{1 - \alpha} h_3^{(2)} - \frac{\alpha}{1 - \alpha} h_1^{(3)}$$

$$- \frac{\alpha}{1 - \alpha} h_2^{(3)} = 0.$$

An enrollment ceiling can be taken into account by writing

$$\sum_{i,k} V_i^{(k)} h_i^{(k)} = \text{a constant},$$ (22.16)

where $V_i^{(k)}$ is obtained from v_i in Table 22.1.

The policy that the number of teachers teaching a given program be proportional to the number of students enrolled in that program is easy to state in equation form. Suppose that dropouts (node 1) require μ_1 teaching assistants, undergraduates (node 2) require μ_2 teaching assistants, and graduates (node 3) require μ_3 teaching assistants. Then the technological equation simply requires that the number of teaching assistants at node 4 be

$$L_4 = \mu_1 L_1 + \mu_2 L_2 + \mu_3 L_3,$$ (22.17)

where L_j is the inventory or enrollment level in program j.

Since each inventory level can be written as the product of total flow entering the program with the lifetime of the program, we obtain

$$v_4(h_3^{(2)} + h_2^{(3)}) = \mu_1 v_1 h_1^{(1)} + \mu_2 v_2 (h_1^{(2)} + h_2^{(2)} + h_3^{(2)})$$
$$+ \mu_3 v_3 (h_2^{(2)} + h_3^{(2)} + h_1^{(3)} + h_2^{(3)})$$

or,

$$\mu_1 v_1 h_1^{(1)} + \mu_2 v_2 h_1^{(2)} + (\mu_2 v_2 + \mu_3 v_3) h_2^{(2)}$$
$$+ (\mu_2 v_2 + \mu_3 v_3 - v_4) h_3^{(2)} + \mu_3 v_3 h_1^{(3)}$$ (22.18)
$$+ (\mu_3 v_3 - v_4) h_2^{(3)} = 0.$$

The technological requirements, enrollment ceilings, and dropout equations can be summarized as the set of linear equations and inequalities

$$\mathbf{Mh} = \mathbf{b}, \quad \mathbf{h} \geqslant 0,$$ (22.19)

where

$$\mathbf{M} = \begin{bmatrix} V_1^{(1)} & V_1^{(2)} & V_2^{(2)} & V_3^{(2)} & V_1^{(3)} & V_2^{(3)} \\ 0 & 1 & 0 & 0 & 0 & 0 \\ 0 & 0 & 1 & 0 & 1 & 0 \\ \mu_1 v_1 & \mu_2 v_2 & \mu_2 v_2 + \mu_3 v_3 & \mu_2 v_2 + \mu_3 v_3 - v_4 & \mu_3 v_3 & \mu_3 v_3 - v_4 \\ 1 & \dfrac{-\alpha}{1-\alpha} & \dfrac{-\alpha}{1-\alpha} & \dfrac{-\alpha}{1-\alpha} & \dfrac{-\alpha}{1-\alpha} & \dfrac{-\alpha}{1-\alpha} \end{bmatrix},$$

is the matrix of coefficients derived from Equations 22.13–22.16 and Equation 22.18, the flow vector is

$$\mathbf{h} = (h_1^{(1)}, h_1^{(2)}, h_2^{(2)}, h_3^{(2)}, h_1^{(3)}, h_2^{(3)}),$$

and the right-hand side of Equation 22.19 is

$$\mathbf{b} = (b^{(1)}, b^{(2)}, b^{(3)}, 0, 0).$$

The total enrollment restriction including teaching assistants is $b^{(1)}$. A feasible student flow pattern is any vector of cohort flows $\mathbf{h}$ that satisfies these constraints.

The number and type of restrictions or alternative policies one might want to study is by no means restricted to the ones we have selected. For example, one might want to constrain undergraduate admissions rather than external flows of undergraduate degrees. One might want to substitute a budget restriction for an enroll-ment ceiling or drop the enrollment ceiling altogether. Numerous possibilities exist, and before concluding this section it might be interesting to use the model to forecast the effects of the specific proposal of the Carnegie Commission that lower division programs be reduced from two years to one year in the presence of the re-strictions we have formulated [6].

Use of the Planning Model

How does one go about analyzing such a proposal in the context of the model we have just formulated? First of all, v_2, the lifetime of the undergraduate program (node 2), must be reduced; sec-ondly, a reasonable assumption is that the lifetime of dropouts (node 1) will also decrease. Notice that by altering the lifetimes of undergraduate programs, costs $C_j^{(k)}$ and lifetimes $V_j^{(k)}$ of 4 out of 6 student cohorts will be reduced. As a result, 8 out of 21 nonzero coefficients in the matrix of Equation 22.19 will be changed!

Without getting into the details of the mathematical solutions of Equation 22.19, it is interesting to see what they predict for the composition of student enrollments, admissions, graduating flows, and operating budgets both before and after we introduce the shorter undergraduate programs. It may be helpful to point out that Equation 22.19 has one degree of freedom, as there are five equations in six unknowns. Of the many solutions of the equation that are available to us, we shall consider only two of them, which satisfy the further condition that the chain flows are nonnegative.

The first column of Table 22.2 corresponds to a feasible student flow pattern of Equation 22.19, when the enrollment ceiling $b^{(1)}$

Table 22.2   A Comparison of the Flows and Costs Following a Reduction in Undergraduate Lifetimes

Flows and Costs	Pre-Carnegie	Post-Carnegie Minimum Cost Budget	Post-Carnegie Maximum Degree Output Rate
Admissions			
Undergraduate	2,358	3,446	2,714
Graduate	2,767	1,670	3,144
Dropouts	3,434	3,428	3,924
Total admissions	8,559	8,544	9,782
Enrollments			
Undergraduate	9,432	10,338	9,432
Graduate	8,625	8,598	8,626
Teaching assistant	1,075	1,066	1,074
Dropouts	6,868	5,998	6,868
Total enrollments	26,000	26,000	26,000
Degrees			
Undergraduate	2,250	2,250	2,982
Graduate	1,800	1,800	1,800
Graduate (with TA)	1,075	1,066	1,075
Total Degrees	5,125	5,116	5,857
Dropouts	3,434	3,428	3,925
Total output	8,559	8,544	9,782
Cohort Costs			
Dropouts	1,375,552	1,199,688	1,373,551
Undergraduate	1,350,000	1,012,500	1,341,972
Graduate	2,652,393	3,117,516	2,660,421
Total budget	5,375,944	5,329,704	5,375,944

equals 26,000 students, the salary of teaching assistants is $5000 per year, teacher-student ratios are $\mu_1 = .04$, $\mu_2 = .03$, $\mu_3 = .06$, the fractional dropout rate α equals .40, final demands for undergraduates and graduates are $b^{(2)} = 2250$ and $b^{(3)} = 1800$, respectively, and program lifetimes are $v_1 = 2$, $v_2 = 4$, $v_3 = 3$, and $v_4 = 1$. These values are representative of the institutions we have studied.

Not only does the nonnegative flow pattern reported in the first column satisfy the constraints of Equations 22.13–22.18, it also has two other interesting features. First of all, it is a flow pattern that minimizes the total operating budget

$$C = \sum_{j,k} C_j^{(k)} h_j^{(k)}. \tag{22.20}$$

Secondly, it is a flow pattern that maximizes the total number of undergraduate and graduate degrees supplied by the university to meet external demand when Equation 22.20 is used as a budget constraint in place of the final demand constraint for undergraduates in Equation 22.13. We emphasize the fact that the flows and enrollments in column 1 of Table 22.2 correspond to a feasible solution of Equation 22.19 before the lifetimes of the undergraduate programs are reduced in accordance with the Carnegie recommendation. Columns 2 and 3 of Table 22.2 correspond to feasible flow patterns and student enrollments after the undergraduate program lifetimes are reduced to $v_1 = 1.75$, $v_2 = 3$. The second column is a minimum-cost solution, while the third column corresponds to a flow pattern that maximizes the total number of graduates supplied to meet external demands. It is interesting to compare these costs and flow patterns with those reported in the first column.

It appears, first of all, that the reduction of lifetimes in the undergraduate programs will either reduce the number of enrolled students that eventually drop out or increase the number who eventually receive an undergraduate degree. If the number of graduates meeting external demands is held constant, the total operating budget is reduced and the cost per degree remains constant. If the number of degrees meeting external demands (and admissions) is increased to the fullest extent possible, subject to a total operating budget of $5,376,000, we obtain an increase of approximately 15 percent in total degrees awarded and a reduction in the cost per degree of approximately $130. In summary, it appears that degree production can be influenced substantially by the adoption of shorter undergraduate program lifetimes.

Extensive applications of models of this type were made during 1969 and 1970, using data from the Berkeley campus for the 1965–1966 and 1969–1970 academic years. Fractional dropout rates, teacher-student ratios, graduation rates, and other parameters related to the flow process eventually yielded good fits with actual operating characteristics observed during 1967, 1968, and 1970. Many of the data and predicted flows, enrollments, and budgets are summarized in papers by Oliver and Hopkins [24].

22.4 Conclusion

In university planning, what little model-building has been done has overemphasized the descriptive role. Many policy makers have been content with finding an empirical set of relations that approximate historical operations and then using these models to extrapolate into the future. This is, at best, naïve planning and, at worst, no planning at all, for it is equivalent to predicting for a future in which there are no new administrative decisions and no new courses of action.

In general, every statistical, economic, or financial analysis of an operating institution presupposes a model. A good model abstracts key interrelationships that exist in the real world—by no means all the variables that can be observed, but only those that are significant to the purpose of the analysis. So it is with planning in an educational institution. The wealth of detail that can be incorporated in a university planning model is unlimited, and there are potentially as many models as there are different details and different degrees of detail. If the real point of formulating these models is to gain understanding, reduce costs, select better plans, and improve university education, then the quality of university planning models must improve. There must be much less attention to collecting, storing, retrieving, and manipulating large volumes of data, and more attention to the analysis of data within a sound conceptual framework; there must be less attention to purely descriptive models and more to models that reveal how outcomes of plans depend on policies and decision variables; there must be less fascination with computers per se and more with the substance of their computations; there must be less time spent in dreaming of "the all-embracing model" and more energy devoted to finding quantitative answers to specific problems; less emphasis on trying to make outcomes fit the model and more concern with experimental verification of theoretical analyses. For the time being there should be less concern with developing sophisticated economic indices of productivity and mathematical objective functions, and more concern with the down-to-earth task of sorting out student and faculty flows, enrollments, dropout rates, and the unit and marginal costs of operating an educational institution in different ways.

Finally, university administrators should recognize that uncertainties exist and that a number of outcomes are possible in most real situations. Planning, in this context, is not simply the process of picking a single course of action that achieves some unique mathematical objective. It involves, rather, selecting a set of alternatives which, in the final analysis, may do no more than avoid costly, inefficient, or undesirable programs. In the long run, university planning models should be highly useful to help us grasp explicit relationships among decisions, actions, plans, and outcomes. They are no substitute for good judgment, but they should reveal the structure of institutional problems, that, historically, have been obscured by data and have not received the analytical attention they deserve.

Acknowledgment

Much of the research discussed in this chapter has been supported by the Esso Education Foundation.

Annotated References

1. Armitage, P., C. Smith, and P. Alper, *Decision Models for Educational Planning*, The Penguin Press, London, England, 1969.

This professional piece of work answers such questions as: How many places should be provided in universities in future years? What are the effects of raising the school leaving age? How can the demand and supply of teachers be evaluated and predicted? The authors are critical of traditional forecasting methods and formulate models to illustrate how rational plans can be evaluated and selected. This book should be on the reading list of anyone seriously interested in the use of mathematical models for university planning.

2. Bell, C., "Can Mathematical Models Contribute to Efficiency in Higher Education," Chapter 22 of *More Scholars Per Dollar*, A Report Prepared for the Ford Foundation and Carnegie Commission on Higher Education, PPRO, University of California, Irvine, California, 1971.

This paper is a review of mathematical models that may be helpful to university administrators. The role and scope of large-scale simulation models are discussed.

3. Bowen, H. R., "The Finance of Higher Education," Carnegie Commission on The Future of Higher Education, Berkeley, California, 1968.

This report addresses the two interrelated questions: "How should students be financed?" and "How should institutions be financed?" under the assumptions that the United States should maintain an excellent system of higher education, that higher education should be open to all independently of race, creed, or socioeconomic background, and that sources of funds for higher education should be diversified so that no special interest group dominates. Bowen's conclusions are that (1) students should be financed partly by grants on the basis of financial need, (2) students should have access to loans for "extras," (3) institutions should receive unrestricted grants, (4) tuitions in public institutions should be kept low, and (5) direct power of the federal government over institutions should be held in check by ensuring that its support is divided between the institutions and the students themselves. Although many data for costs, student tuitions, and incomes are cited, no quantitative models are provided to support the conclusions.

4. Bowen, W. G., "The Economics of the Major Private Universities," Carnegie Commission on the Future of Higher Education, Berkeley, California, 1968.

This paper provides a discussion of the financial problems facing the major private universities. The trends in expenditures, the labor-intensive nature of the higher education technology, and the high degree of specialization in graduate programs are offered as reasons for the annual 7.5 percent increases in costs and expenditures. While the sources of revenues for these universities are analyzed and projections of the increasing gap between revenues and costs are made, the author does not present any specific institutional policies to reduce costs or provide new forms of support for the private institutions.

5. Branchflower, N. H., Jr., "A Case Study of the Distribution of Faculty within the College of Engineering at the University of California, Berkeley, for the Period 1960-1968," Administrative Studies Project in Higher Education, University of California, Berkeley, California, 1969.

The movement of faculty within the College of Engineering at the University of California, Berkeley, is analyzed for the nine-year period 1960-1968. Movements within the system and between the system and the outside world are assumed to be homogeneous over time. Faculty promotions and departures from various ranks are determined by aggregating yearly totals. These aggregates are then used to estimate the transition matrix of a Markov chain model that predicts future faculty distributions based upon present distributions and known appointment policies. Predicted distributions for the years 1966-1968 are compared with actual data.

6. The Carnegie Commission on The Future of Higher Education, *Less Time, More Options, Education Beyond the High School*, Berkeley, California, 1971.

This report by the Carnegie Commission staff makes recommendations regarding degree options available to students and the lifetimes of their academic programs. If adopted, these recommendations would force numerous changes in the student flow patterns and the composition of undergraduate and graduate enrollments. Promised future reports giving quantitative analyses and background material for these recommendations are awaited with keen interest.

7. Cheit, E., "The New Depression in Higher Education," Carnegie Commission on the Future of Higher Education, Berkeley, California, 1971.

This report points out that approximately two-thirds of the nation's colleges and universities are headed for financial difficulty. The report is based on detailed interviews on forty-one campuses. The difficulties stem from a decline in the rate of income growth, an increase in the number of costly options being made available to students, and the increasing costs of high quality academic programs.

8. Clough, D. J., and W. P. McReynolds, "State Transition Model of an Educational System Incorporating a Constraint Theory of Supply and Demand," *Ont. Jour. Ed. Res.* vol. 9, 1966.

The paper proposes a model for the Ontario, Canada, educational system and provides the basis of a computer simulation for the flows of people through various phases of the educational and employment system. As a result of the formulation that includes inequality constraints on flows and enrollment levels, the authors show how to derive feasible regions for the transitions and movements of people in successive time periods.

9. Dobbins, C. G., "Higher Education and the Federal Government: Programs and Problems," American Council on Education, 1963.

This volume is a collection of papers presented at the 45th annual meeting of the American Council on Education, October, 1962. Authors address both the federal and the university sides of federally supported research contracts and other grants. Various papers deal with the relationship between federal agencies and the university (J. C. Weaver, N. M. Pusey), student aid through federal fellowship programs (R. G. Moon), federal dollars, institutional freedom and faculty productivity (McG. Bundy).

10. Dunlop, J. T., et al., *Report of the Committee on Recruitment and Retention of Faculty*, Faculty of Arts and Sciences, Harvard University, 1968.

A faculty committee at Harvard University, chaired by J. T. Dunlop, considered problems involved in the recruitment and retention of faculty and the need to review terms, titles, and conditions of academic appointment. The major parts of the study were given to I: Titles, Salaries, and Benefits; II: The Recruitment Process Itself; III: Research Appointments; IV: Housing and Schooling; and V: Educational Policy and Financial Constraints.

As a result of this study a number of recommendations were made to rename certain academic titles and increase salary levels in order to make positions more competitive with the outside market. It was also suggested that the members retiring from active professional status be able to choose benefits from several options, specifically, that a variable annuity rather than the usual fixed annuity plan be made available. Particular attention was given to morale issues and dissatisfaction voiced by many of the younger, nontenure faculty with respect to their chances of internal promotion.

11. *ERIC Abstracts*, Educational Resources Information Center, U. S. Department of Health, Education, and Welfare, 1970.

These abstracts provide a monthly journal of recently completed research and reports in the field of education. An index for searching related titles is included.

12. Hitch, C. J., "The Systems Approach to Decision Making in the Department of Defense and the University of California," *Operations Research Quarterly*, Symposium Issue, vol. 19, 1968, pp. 19–45.

This paper comments on the application of program-budgeting methods, developed for the U.S. Department of Defense, to university operations and plans. Unfortunately, the operating budget is still calculated in terms of the number of students enrolled at one particular time during the year. It is not obvious how the marginal costs of alternative degree programs, libraries, and other services can be properly analyzed in the context of budgets that are based on enrollment levels rather than degree outputs. It will be interesting to see whether PPBS techniques will achieve the desired economies and efficiencies.

13. Holsendolph, E., "A Tale of Two Universities," *Fortune*, February 1971.

This interesting and timely article compares the fiscal problems of Yale University and the University of Southern California; the former of the two universities has been operating at a sizable deficit for several years, while the latter has not yet encountered a deficit. There is a brief description of the internal auditing system used by the University of Southern California to monitor departmental expenses and budgets. The paper concludes by noting that administrations of both universities forsee a relentless cost consciousness in the forthcoming decade!

14. Hopkins, D. S. P., "An Analysis of University Year-Round Operation,"

Administrative Studies Project in Higher Education, University of California, Berkeley, California, 1969.

By breaking down the student population into cohorts with recognizable attendance patterns and workload requirements, the author is able to predict the admission and graduation flows of students at an institution offering year-round instruction. Flows and enrollments are compared with the same institution offering a normal nine-month program.

15. ———, "On the Use of Large-Scale Simulation Models for University Planning," *Review of Educational Research*, vol. 41, no. 5, 1971, pp. 467–478.

This report examines the mathematical structure of a number of cost simulation models and discusses some of their uses and misuses in the context of university planning. The author shows how the cost of collecting and analyzing data for such models can be estimated.

16. Iffert, R. E., and B. S. Clarke, "College Applicants, Entrants, and Dropouts," Office of Education Bulletin No. 29, OE-54034, U. S. Department of Health, Education, and Welfare, 1965.

This document reports the findings from a study of undergraduates entering twenty cooperating institutions in the fall terms of 1956 and 1957. Data include the number of applicants to these institutions, the number of admissions, no-shows, registrations, dropouts, and actively enrolled students. Unfortunately, the section on dropouts is probably not useful as there is no careful distinction in definition and classification between those individuals who drop out and never return and those who drop out but in fact return to some institution. It appears that most of the information on "permanent" versus "temporary" dropouts is obtained by asking individual dropouts what their future plans are, a source that has proved most unreliable in the past. What reason is there to believe the well-intentioned plans of those students who have already indicated (by their dropout status) an inability to forecast their own attendance patterns? Had they been asked the same question on registration day, it is unlikely they would have answered by classifying themselves as dropouts.

17. Johnson, C. B., and W. G. Katzenmeyer, *Management Information Systems in Higher Education: The State of the Art*, Duke University Press, Durham, North Carolina, 1969.

This volume is a collection of papers given at Duke University under a seminar of the same name. The emphasis is on the development of management information systems (Part I), special characteristics associated with large national and regional data collection programs (Part II), and modeling (Part III).

The article by B. Lawrence ("The Western Interstate Commission for Higher Education Management Information Systems Program") describes the questionable goals of that program. The first of four papers in Part III by R. A. Wallhaus ("Modeling for Higher Education Administration and Management") describes various types of models, how to gather data, how to make model validations, etc. These ideas are discussed in abstract; no specific models are formulated or analysed.

The paper by Arcuri, Mason, and Meredith ("The Impact of Academic Program on the Utilization of Space and Time Resources of Colleges and Universities") formulates a model of the effect of academic programs upon the utilization of instructional time and space; the authors accurately point out how the usual space standards are in error. They also provide the reader with several measures for making quantitative appraisals of the scheduling capability of a given institution.

The last two papers are "A Simulation Modeling Approach to a Scheduling Problem" and "The Use of a Scheduling Algorithm in a Gaming Environment for Administrative Planning." As is often the case with descriptions of large-scale simulations, it is difficult to gain understanding of the problem or to see what guidelines or better policies are suggested by the analysis. Much is obscured by the uninteresting details of the steps required to program such computer models.

Sorely lacking from most of the papers in this volume are answers to the fundamental questions: What specific planning and policy questions should a management information system support? What models will use the data and in what form? How will operating and planning problems influence the data collection and analysis?

18. Koenig, H. E., M. G. Keeney, and R. Zemach, "A Systems Model for Management, Planning, and Resource Allocation in Institutions of Higher Education," NSF Project C-518, Final Report, Division of Engineering Research, Michigan State University, 1968.

This report describes the models developed by the authors to predict the flow of resources and manpower over time at an educational institution. The purpose of the models is to provide a technique for evaluating changes in the types of resources or the allocations of these resources.

19. Marshall, K. T., and R. M. Oliver, "A Constant Work Model for Student Attendance and Enrollment," *Operations Research* vol. 18, 1970, pp. 193-206.

Under the assumptions of the model, the probability of graduation is shown to be a power of the conditional probability of successful completion of a unit of work, where a unit of work is defined along with four other parameters in the model.

20. Marshall, K. T., R. M. Oliver, and S. Suslow, "Undergraduate Enrollments and Attendance Patterns," Administrative Studies Project in Higher Education, University of California, Berkeley, California, 1970. Also available as "Statistical Models for Education and Training," NATO Science Committee, Proceedings of Conference on Manpower and Planning, August 31–September 11, 1970.

Several Markov enrollment models proposed in the scientific literature are used to predict student attendance patterns and undergraduate enrollments during the period 1955-1966. Theoretical results are compared with data gathered at the Berkeley Campus of the University of California during that period.

21. *OECD Bibliography and List of Documents*, Center for Educational Research and Innovation, OECD, Document CERI/IM/70-14, Paris, France, 1970.

This preliminary list of documents includes reports, papers, and a selected number of abstracts under the headings of Higher Educational Planning, Institutional Management Techniques, and Other Reference Documents. See also the earlier book entitled *Systems Analysis for Educational Planning, Selected Annotated Bibliography*, OECD, Paris, France, 1969, for items not included in the 1970 list.

22. Oliver, R. M., "An Equilibrium Model of Faculty Appointments, Promo-

tions, and Quota Restrictions," Report No. 10, Ford Foundation Research Project in University Administration, University of California, Berkeley, California, 1969.

The author develops an equilibrium flow model for the appointments, promotions, resignations, and retirements of tenure and nontenure faculty in a university of fixed size.

23. Oliver, R. M., and D. S. P. Hopkins, "An Equilibrium Flow Model for a University Campus," *Operations Research*, vol. 20, no. 3, 1972.

This paper develops a simple deterministic model that relates admissions and enrollments to the graduation and dropout rates of students. Specific administrative policies are examined, and comparisons are made between the numbers predicted by the model and independent data gathered during 1965–1968 at the Berkeley campus of the University of California.

24. _____, and _____, "Instructional Costs of University Outputs," *Proceedings of the National Bureau of Economic Research*, to appear 1972.

The authors develop a planning and budget model based on flows, enrollments, and unit costs of educating student cohorts that is used to analyze the costs and flows of a proposed Carnegie Commission recommendation that Lower Division programs be reduced by one year.

25. Radner, R., and L. S. Miller, "Resource Requirements for a Universal Two-Year College Program," *Demand and Supply in U. S. Higher Education*, Carnegie Commission on the Future of Higher Education, Berkeley, California, 1971.

By means of a dynamic input-output model, this report predicts the student flows and costs that would result by increasing the nationwide enrollments in the first two college years to a level consistent with numbers recorded in 1963 for the State of California. Specifically, enrollments in each age group were to be equal to the California percentage.

26. Rath, G. S., "Management Science in University Operations," *Management Science*, vol. 14, no. 6, 1968, pp. B373-384.

The author gives brief summaries of the status of several university projects in scheduling, semiautomated registration systems, facility location, and campus planning.

27. Thonstad, T., *Education and Manpower*, Oliver and Boyd, London, England, 1968.

This interesting book is divided into four parts: An Introduction, The Consequences of Given Educational Propensities, Educational Requirements Under Stationary Conditions, and Elementary Dynamics of Education and Manpower. As mentioned earlier, the data he uses are relevant to the Norwegian educational system, although the models should have much wider applicability.

The author is to be complimented for his attention and care in the use of real data and his frequent comparisons of model predictions with actual performance of the educational system over a number of years.

28. Tickton, S. G., "The Year-Round Campus Catches On," New York Fund for the Advancement of Education, New York, 1963.

This report is a survey of forty educational institutions, in terms of their plans for the use of year-round operations.

23

Use of Decision Analysis
in Airport Development
for Mexico City

Richard de Neufville and
Ralph L. Keeney

23.1 Introduction

This chapter describes the application of decision analysis to a
large-scale public decision problem—selecting a strategy for developing the major airport facilities of the Mexico City metropolitan area. The case involves multiple conflicting objectives, uncertainties about future events, and a long-range planning horizon.
We first indicate the environment in which the analysis was carried
out and our orientation as analysts. Next, a static analysis used to
identify "effective" strategies is presented. This work provides
part of the information for a dynamic analysis to evaluate airport
developmental strategies that could be taken by the government of
Mexico in the fall of 1971. Finally, we discuss the effects of this
work on the overall decision process.

Many people contributed significantly to the study. It was done
for the government of Mexico under the auspices of the Secretaria
de Obras Publicas (SOP, Ministry of Public Works) and directed by
F. J. Jauffred, Director of the Center for Computation and Statistics, and F. Dovali, Head of the Department of Airports. Howard
Raiffa of Harvard University and the two of us were consultants
assisting SOP on the project. The total time spent by the consultants on the project was 50 man-days.

23.2 The Problem

Rapid growth in the volume of air travelers, combined with increasingly difficult operating conditions at the existing airport
facilities, compelled the Mexican government to address the question: How should the airport facilities of Mexico City be developed to assure adequate service for the region during the period
from now to the year 2000? This was the essential question put to
the study team.

As with practically all decisions about the development of public
facilities, the overall question of what to do can be redefined into
questions of where, how, and when to implement the services.
Specifically, one needs to be concerned about

1. The location and/or the configuration of the elements of the
system;

2. The operational policy that defines how the services are to be performed and where they will be located; and
3. The timing of the several stages in the development.

In this case, because of severe environmental constraints, there are only two different sites adequate for a large, international airport in the Mexico City metropolitan area. One of these is the existing site at Texcoco, which is fairly close to the center of the city. The other is at Zumpango, located approximately 25 miles north of Mexico City. The kinds of configurations possible at either site, with respect to the runways, for example, are not really significant in this particular program.

Many different ways of operating the airports—with significant differences in the quality of service provided—are possible, however. In particular, it is necessary to decide what kinds of aircraft activity (international, domestic, military, or general), should be operating at each of the two sites.

Finally, the question of timing can be most important. Failure to act at a given time may preclude important options, such as the ability even to acquire a site. Premature action can, on the other hand, significantly increase total costs to the nation. Timing and the question of operational control are the most important aspects of this decision problem.

23.3 The Situation

Physical Conditions
The existing airport is located about 5 miles east of the central part of Mexico City, on the edge of the remains of Lake Texcoco, a very shallow, marshy body of water. The other site is about 25 miles north of the city in an undeveloped farming area, near the village of Zumpango. The relative location of the two feasible sites is indicated in Figure 23.1—T for Texcoco, Z for Zumpango.

Mexico City itself is situated at an altitude of about 7,400 feet in a valley closely ringed with high mountains ranging to over 17,000 feet above sea level. The mountains remain very high in all directions except the northeast. In this direction the range lowers to around 10,000 feet, but is still some 3,000 feet above Mexico City. Essentially, all the flights entering or leaving the Mexico City area fly over the lower mountains to the northeast although some do proceed through a smaller and higher pass to the south.

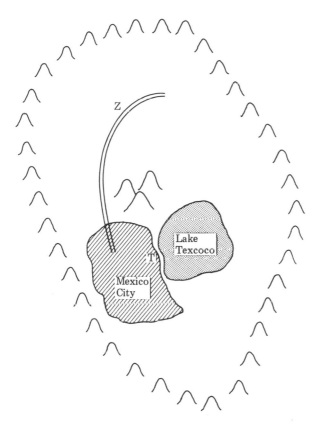

Figure 23.1   Geography of the Mexico City metropolitan area.

The maneuverability of the aircraft themselves at this high altitude is low, especially in hot climates. This limitation requires that
the flight patterns be broader than usual and prevents planes from
threading their way safely through mountainous regions. There
are thus considerable restrictions on the usable airspace around
Mexico City. This constraint, which principally affects the capacity of the Texcoco site, is serious since Mexico City already handles over 2 million enplaned passengers a year and ranks among
the busiest airports on the continent.

Access to the airport by ground transportation appears to be
reasonable for both sites. The Texcoco site is near the main peripheral highway, which can distribute traffic around the suburbs.

It is not, however, especially well connected to the center of the city, to which one has to proceed through congested city streets. The Zumpango site has the clear disadvantage of being farther away, but it can be linked directly to the tourist and business areas via an existing north-south expressway.

The location of Mexico City on a former lake bed makes construction very expensive, especially at Texcoco. Heavy facilities such as runways sink not only rapidly, but at different rates in different locations, depending on their loads. The existing runways at Texcoco have to be both leveled and resurfaced every two years. These repairs closed down half the airport for four months when they were done in 1971. Because the Zumpango site is on much higher and firmer ground, it is not expected to have the same kind of difficulties.

When the Texcoco airport was organized in the 1930s, it was out in the country. But the population of the metropolitan area has grown at the rate of about 5 percent a year, passing from about 5 million in 1960 to about 8 million in 1971. During this time, Texcoco has been surrounded on three sides by mixed residential and commercial sections. This has created problems of noise, social disruption, and safety: a large school is located under the flight path some 500 feet from the end of a major runway.

Should a major accident occur on landing or takeoff toward the city it would almost certainly cause numerous casualties. Using current worldwide accident rates, such an accident could be expected once every 10 years or so [3]. Since the approach pattern passes directly over the central parts of the city, noise levels of 90 CNR or more now affect hundreds of thousands of people. (The Composite Noise Rating, CNR, is one of many standard indices of noise that combine decibel level and frequency of occurrence.) These noise levels are bound to persist until all the more noisy engines are replaced, which necessarily will be many years after the development of quieter engines. Finally, the construction of any new runways at Texcoco would require either particularly expensive construction in the shallow lake bed or the displacement of up to 200,000 people. The compensating advantage for the Texcoco site is that major facilities already exist.

Institutional Conditions

Political power in Mexico tends to be concentrated in the federal government and, for major decisions such as the location of the capital's airport, toward the President. The government has been in the hands of a single party, the Partido Revolucionario Institucional, for almost forty years. Dissent with governmental policies, once they have been enunciated, is dampened by a strong tradition of authority.

Ultimately, any decision about a new airport will be ratified by the President, specifically by Lic. Luis Echeverria during 1970–1976. The debate about this decision has been carried on by three major governmental bodies:

1. The Ministry of Public Works, that is, the Secretaria de Obras Publicas (SOP)
2. The Ministry of Communication and Transport, that is, the Secretaria de Comunicaciones y Transportes (SCT)
3. The Secretaria de la Presidencia, a body with functions similar to those of the Office of Management and Budget in the United States.

Significant rivalries exist between the SOP and the SCT. The goals of these ministries almost inevitably conflict since the SOP is responsible for building and maintaining essentially all transportation facilities, in particular the airports, and the SCT has the responsibility for operating these facilities. The study discussed here was conducted under the auspices of the SOP for use by the Secretary and the government of Mexico.

Previous Studies

Both the SOP and the SCT had commissioned large-scale studies of the airport problem within the past few years. The SOP study, done for its Department of Airports between 1965 and 1967, had recommended that a new airport be built at Zumpango and that all commercial flights be shifted to this facility [10,12]. The master plan then proposed was not adopted at that time.

The study commissioned by the SCT in 1970 [4] resulted in a master plan for expanding the airport at Texcoco by adding new runway and terminal facilities. Interestingly, this report assumed that aircraft could take off away from the city toward the east and land coming to the city from the east in opposing streams of traffic aimed at adjacent parallel runways. While this proposal "solves" the noise and capacity problems, its implications for safety are extremely serious at any significant level of traffic and are unlikely to be acceptable for the expected volumes. This re-

port also assumed that "quiet" engines would completely eliminate any noise problems outside the airport boundaries by 1990.
The SCT study was prepared and submitted during the closing
months of the 1964–1970 administration of the previous president
and appears to have been part of an eleventh-hour attempt to
obtain a decision before the administration of President Echeverria.
The SCT study was not accepted in 1970.

The government of Mexico did, however, wish to resolve the issue. In early 1971 the new administration committed itself to a
restudy. As stated by the president in his State of the Union Message of September 1, 1971, "Construction of a new international
airport in the metropolitan area [of Mexico City] is also under
study at this time." The study referred to is the one presented
here.

23.4 The Analytic Approach

Choosing the best strategy for developing the airport facilities of
Mexico City is an extremely complex problem. It is on such problems that a formal analysis can potentially be most worthwhile in
providing important insights and indicating what might be the best
decision to make. For the airport problem, such an analysis—
which purports to help the decision maker choose a course of action—must recognize the multiple conflicting objectives, the uncertainties about future events and the impact of possible actions,
and the effects of policy decisions on the future as well as on the
present. And it is clear that the airport development problem requires the consideration of subjective values and tradeoffs.

The decision analytic approach—as distinguished from the more
traditional analytical techniques—takes these multiple objectives,
probabilistic uncertainties, and time effects into account. Furthermore, it formally encodes the subjective attitudes of the decision
makers into the analysis of the problem. Decision analysis requires
the analyst to consider these complexities explicitly, and it provides a framework for integrating them into an efficient structure
for prescriptive decision making.

At the risk of greatly oversimplifying, let us try to explain the
basic ideas of decision analysis for readers who are unfamiliar with
this approach. More complete discussions are found in Howard [2]
or Raiffa [8].

First the alternatives, objectives, and measures of effectiveness need to be identified. The measures of effectiveness must be useful for indicating both present and future impacts of the various alternatives. For each alternative, a joint probability density function is assessed over the measures of effectiveness. This formally encodes the judgment of the decision maker as to the possible impacts of the alternative and how likely they are. Separately, the preferences of the decision maker for all the possible levels of achievement as indicated by the measures of effectiveness are assessed. These preferences, obtained by questioning the decision maker, are expressed by a utility function. Finally, to evaluate the alternatives, the probabilities and the preferences are systematically combined using the "axioms of rational behavior," which are specified in von Neumann and Morgenstern [11]. These axioms are acceptable to most decision makers, and they do not introduce any oversimplifications of the problem. The major difficulties of the approach, aside from the ever-present ones of identifying alternatives and objectives, are obtaining the requisite probability densities and the decision makers' utilities.

It should be mentioned that the use of decision analysis in public problems is in its embryonic stage. Many of the reasons for this —both technical and nontechnical—are discussed in Chapter 5. This study represents one of the first attempts to apply decision analysis to a major strategic problem involving multiple objectives.

Our Orientation

This study measured and incorporated the best professional judgments of the SOP Director of Airports and his staff in the attempt to analyze the problem from the point of view of the government of Mexico. The purpose of this effort was to choose the best strategy according to their expert assessments.

Since it may be expected that impartial experts might disagree with the overall structure of the problem as well as on the details of the analysis, the framework used provides a systematic procedure for examining differences in opinion. This capability was especially important since the analysis was to provide the basis for an orderly advocacy proceeding. Indeed, once the SOP was convinced of what was the best strategy for the country, they had to convince others of its merit. It was also necessary to explain the analysis and its implications to the other major agencies involved, the SCT and the Presidencia. With enough time for a critical review of the study and a serious probing of the differences of opinion between interested parties, the quality of the final decision should be improved.

23.5 The Static Model
The first analysis effort was directed toward finding the best developmental strategies for the next thirty years. The alternatives for this analysis were essentially defined as the sequences of decisions that could be taken at three specified decision points, 1975, 1985, and 1995. These alternatives were master plans since no provision was made at this stage for adapting the strategies to account for possible further events.

The results of this phase of the decision analysis indicated general types of developmental plans that seemed attractive. These were included, along with a range of important political factors, in the dynamic analysis of the options open to President Echeverria in the fall of 1971. The dynamic analysis is discussed in Section 23.6.

Objectives and Measures of Effectiveness
The overall objective of the analysis was to determine how to provide adequate air service for Mexico City for the remainder of the century. To evaluate how different alternatives measure up to this objective, one needs to specify some indices, that is, measures of effectiveness. These should explicitly consider the effects of each alternative on the various important groups that will be affected. In this case, the various groups are the government as operator, the users of the air facilities, and the nonusers.

The objective for almost every system design has several dimensions. To get any realistic feeling for the impact of the various alternatives, it is therefore necessary to define relevant subobjectives for the problem. The partial objectives chosen for this study were:

1. Minimize total construction and maintenance *costs*
2. Provide adequate *capacity* to meet the air traffic demands
3. Minimize the *access time* to the airport
4. Maximize the *safety* of the system
5. Minimize *social disruption* caused by the provision of new airport facilities
6. Minimize the effects of *noise* pollution due to air traffic.

Although there is obviously much overlap, the first two objectives account for the government's stake as operator, the third for the users', and the last three for that of the nonusers.

The measures of effectiveness, X_i, associated with each of these six objectives are reasonably standard in airport planning. They are:

$X_1 \equiv$ Total cost in millions of pesos

$X_2 \equiv$ The practical hourly capacity in terms of the number of aircraft operations per hour

$X_3 \equiv$ Average access time in minutes, weighted by the number of travelers from each zone of Mexico City

$X_4 \equiv$ Expected number of people seriously injured or killed per aircraft accident

$X_5 \equiv$ Number of people displaced by airport expansion

$X_6 \equiv$ Number of people subjected to a high noise level, in this case, 90 CNR or more.

The Alternatives

The alternative strategies for the static analysis were defined as the feasible set of all combinations of designs that might be established by different decisions about location, operational configuration, and timing. Two different sites were considered, Texcoco (T) and Zumpango (Z). Operations were classed into four categories: domestic (D), international (I), general (G), and military (M). And three decision points, 1975, 1985, and 1995, defined the time dimension.

The total number of combinations to be considered was thus of the order of $(4^2)^3$. In fact, somewhat less than 4000 alternatives were considered since some initial (1975) choices precluded, in practice, some subsequent choices. One was not likely, for example, to move all operations to Zumpango in 1975 only to switch them all back to Texcoco in 1985. Especially since we were dealing with a six-dimensional set of attributes for each alternative, a computer model was necessary to execute the analysis.

Specifying the Possible Impacts of Each Alternative

To identify the possible impact of each alternative, it is necessary to assess joint probability distributions over the six measures of effectiveness conditional on each alternative. Thus for each alternative a_j, we wish to assess the joint probability distribution, which we will denote by $P^j (x_1, x_2, x_3, x_4, x_5, x_6)$.

A number of important assumptions were made to simplify the probability assessments. Most importantly, it was assumed that, conditional on a_j, the X_i were mutually probabilistically independent, such that

$$P^j(x_1, x_2 \ldots x_6) = P_1^j (x_1) P_2^j (x_2) \ldots P_6^j (x_6), \tag{23.1}$$

where $P_i^j(x_i)$ is the marginal probability density for X_i conditional on alternative a_j. The reasonableness of the assumption was qualitatively checked by identifying underlying factors contributing to the amounts of each X_i and then examining the degree of overlap. For instance, the size of the airport and quality of facilities would obviously affect both construction costs and capacity. Based on this, it was decided that the probabilistic independence assumption was not "correct," but that it was probably appropriate given the use we had in mind—trying to gather some insights into what were effective developments.

The actual assessments of the marginal probability distributions were done by the leaders of the study in the SOP and the directors of the Department of Airports and of the Center for Computation and Statistics and their staffs. The fractile technique discussed in Raiffa [8] was used for this purpose. Thus all the probabilities represented the quantified judgment of a group of people very familiar with the impact of different alternatives. In most cases, they had much informative data to back up their judgment, and which, indeed, had formed their judgment.

As an example of the types of data collected, consider the probability distribution for access time, given that all the airport facilities would remain at Texcoco. First, the Mexico City area was divided into relatively homogeneous districts and the population characteristics of each identified. The airport usage characteristics of these groups were also identified. A central node was designated for each district, and experiments were conducted under many conditions (time of day and week, weather, etc.) to see how long it would take to get to the airport.

Information used for any particular alternative could also be used for evaluating other possibilities. In this case, for example, if an alternative had domestic aircraft landing at Texcoco, one could generate the contribution to the access time distribution from domestic travelers by knowing the percent of domestic travelers from each district.

Using such information, joint probability distributions were generated for each of the sixteen alternatives in each of the three years: 1975, 1985, and 1995. The assessments were conducted in group sessions meeting two to three hours at a time over a period of a month. Consistency checks were performed to indicate any "unreasonable" assessments that needed to be altered.

The probability distribution for access time for the "all Texcoco" alternative in 1975 is illustrated in Figure 23.2. The dots represent the fractiles on the curve that were empirically assessed.

Preferences for the Various Possible Impacts

Choosing a "best" alternative requires consideration of both the possible impact of each alternative and the relative preferences of the decision maker for each of these impacts. The probability density functions quantify the possible impacts, and the preferences are quantified by assessing a utility function over the six measures of effectiveness. This utility function $u(x_1, x_2, \ldots, x_6) \equiv u(\mathbf{x})$ will assign a number to each vector of impacts x such that

1 The higher of two numbers indicates the preferred set of impacts, and

2. In situations involving uncertainty, the alternative with the highest expected utility is preferred.

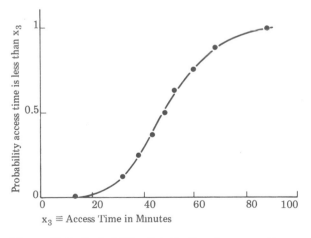

Figure 23.2   Probability distribution for access time.

Given the probabilities for any impact and the utility for every set of impacts, it is a straightforward operation to calculate the expected utility, which is a measure of relative desirability of (or preference for) each alternative. This follows from the axioms of rational behavior mentioned earlier.

The assessment of a multiattribute utility function is a complex task. It involves interaction with the decision maker to quantify his subjective preferences. Details of the assessment are given elsewhere [5], but here we shall try to indicate the general idea. In structuring the discussion, we shall try to identify assumptions such that

$$u(\mathbf{x}) = f[u_1(x_1), u_2(x_2), \ldots, u_6(x_6)], \tag{23.2}$$

where f is some function and $u_i(x_i)$ is a one-attribute utility function over X_i. It is much easier to assess these $u_i(x_i)$ separately and then appropriately scale them than it is to assess $u(\mathbf{x})$. If it is possible to verify these assumptions in discussions with the decision maker, it is then appropriate to use Equation 23.2. Such was the case in the Mexico City airport problem. The specific assumptions used involved the concepts discussed in Keeney [6].

Once we had ascertained the particular form of the utility function we needed to assess the six $u_i(x_i)$ and then consistently scale them. Let us illustrate the types of information needed to do each.

The $u_i(x_i)$ were assessed by asking the proxy decision makers, that is, the directors of the SOP, a number of questions about their preferences for each measure of effectiveness. First we identified the minimum and maximum possible amounts as indicated from the probability assessments. Considering access time, for example, the range was from 12 to 90 minutes. Since utilities are constant up to a positive linear transformation, it was possible to scale the utilities from 0 to 1. In this case we set

$$u_3(12) = 1 \tag{23.3}$$

and

$$u_3(90) = 0, \tag{23.4}$$

since 12 is preferred to 90. By questioning the group and obtaining a consensus, we found the utility function illustrated in Figure 23.3 by using the techniques discussed in Schlaifer [9].

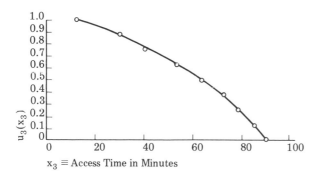

Figure 23.3   Utility function for access time.

To scale the $u_i(x_i)$ consistently, we asked the proxy decision makers to trade off amounts of different attributes. The questions were of the form: For what probability P_i are you indifferent between

1. A sure consequence with all attributes but X_i at the least preferred level and X_i at the most preferred level; and
2. An alternative with two possible consequences, all attributes either at their most preferred level with probability P_i, or at their least preferred level with probability $1 - P_i$?

To evaluate the impacts that might occur at each of the different points in time considered—1975, 1985, and 1995—it was necessary to determine a means for placing these impacts on a common basis of comparison. For the cost impacts, this was done in the usual way by using discounted present values [1]. For all but one of the other impacts, "average" values over years seemed appropriate. Specifically, we used

1. The average access time weighted by the number of passengers
2. The expected number of casualties per accident in the thirty-year period
3. The total number of people displaced
4. The average number of people subjected to high noise levels.

There was no reasonable way to average capacity over time since the desirability for capacity is highly dependent on the volume of traffic, which is presumed to grow significantly with time. To

assess the utility function for the six attributes over the three decision periods, it was necessary to evaluate an eight-dimensional
function in terms of the five average or discounted attributes and
three attributes representing capacity at the different times, denoted by $(x_2)_{75}$, $(x_2)_{85}$, and $(x_2)_{95}$. The function to be assessed
was then

$$u(\overline{x}_1, \overline{x}_2, \ldots, \overline{x}_6) = u\{\overline{x}_1, [(x_2)_{75}, (x_2)_{85}, (x_2)_{95}], \overline{x}_3, \ldots, \overline{x}_6\},$$

(23.5)

where the $\overline{x}_i$ represent the "averaged" amounts of X_i as defined
above. The procedure for doing this using a decomposition as indicated in Equation 23.2 is described in detail by Keeney [5].
Once the assessment of the $u_i(\overline{x}_i)$ and the scaling were completed,
it was a straightforward operation to synthesize $u(\mathbf{x})$.

This function u not only allows one to determine the relative
preference for different alternatives but also specifies the value
tradeoffs between specific design features: it is possible to specify
how much of attribute X_i is worth a specified amount of X_j given
specific levels of each.

The Computer Model

An interactive graphical input-output program was developed to
assist in evaluating the alternatives. Computationally, the program
was quite simple: given any set of probability distributions and
utility functions, it calculated the expected utility for specified
alternatives.

The interactive capability offered a very flexible and efficient
way to do sensitivity analysis of the results. Appropriate graphical
terminals for doing this were installed both at the offices of the
analytic study team, and in the office of the Secretary and Under-
Secretary of the SOP, in the Presidencia, and in the President's
own offices. This capability was used daily by the SOP and could
also be used by the other interested parties to examine the relative
merits of alternative developmental policies.

In practice, the probability and utility functions which had been
assessed in this study were stored in the computer. Alternative
ones could be input by changing the ranges of possible values on
the probability function or by altering the scaling between attributes for the utility function. The more subtle changes in shapes
of the single variable probability distribution and the single attri-

bute utility functions could not be done with the interactive program.

A particularly useful feature of this program was a routine that calculated certainty equivalents. For a given alternative, the decision maker's certainty equivalent for a particular attribute is the amount of that attribute that is indifferent to its probabilistic distribution. Using this routine, the overall possible impact of any alternative could be reduced to an equivalent impact described by a vector of certainty equivalents. This permits an analysis of dominance and gives insight into how much of attribute X_i it would be necessary to trade off for a specified amount of attribute X_j for any alternative to be preferred to another.

Results
The static analysis indicated that two general types of developmental strategies appeared better than all others. These were:

1. "Phased Development at Zumpango," that is, a gradual development of this site over the next 30 years, with some activities remaining at Texcoco
2. "All Zumpango," implying that all airport activities should be moved to Zumpango by at least 1985.

This conclusion appeared to be fairly insensitive to the specific utilities and probabilities used.

It should be noted that the optimum plans determined by the formal decision analysis do not translate directly into decisions. Indeed, the decision maker does not have to define what he will do for the next 30 years right at the beginning. On the contrary, he would be foolish to adopt such a fixed master plan since the future is so uncertain. His better course is probably to make some initial decisions, partially based upon the static analysis, and then, based upon the results of these actions, to revise his strategies as necessary.

Any action taken now can be ambiguous insofar as it is the first step of several strategies. The wise decision maker can adapt his decisions to account for significant shifts in political preferences and community priorities. To advise him properly, it is necessary to examine the specific actions that are immediately available to the decision maker, taking into account both the utilities that have been formally estimated for the alternatives implied by these actions and the other considerations that may be or become significant. This was the task undertaken in the dynamic analysis.

23.6 The Dynamic Model

The purpose of the dynamic model was to help decide what action should be taken in 1971 to best serve the overall objective of providing quality air service to Mexico City for the remainder of the century. This model assumed that the second step in the decision process could be taken in 1975 or 1976, at the end of the current president's six-year term. The action taken then would depend on both the action taken now and critical events that might occur in the interim. This model was less formal than the static model.

Alternatives for 1971

A very important aspect of the problem involved identifying the alternatives open to the government in 1971. It was decided that the essential differences in 1971 among the many alternatives concerned the degrees of commitment to immediate construction at the two sites. To categorize these into a manageable number, we roughly divided the "alternative space" into the sixteen nominal cases indicated in Figure 23.4. Thus, an alternative might be moderate commitment at Zumpango and low commitment at Texcoco. Actually, each nominal case in the figure represents a class of specific alternatives. The idea was to do a first-cut analysis to decide which alternatives were sufficiently viable to be examined in more detail. It should be noted that the two strategies defined by the static analysis could be compatible with all the nominal options except 11, 12, 15, and 16.

The next step involved defining what was meant by the alternatives. Briefly summarized, the alternatives at Texcoco (for the period 1971–1975) were defined as follows:

—Minimum: Maintain existing facilities and introduce safety equipment only

—Low: Extend the runways, upgrade support facilities, such as terminals, do all routine maintenance, and introduce new safety equipment

—Moderate: In addition to low strategy improvements, buy and prepare land for building a new runway, expand passenger facilities, and so on

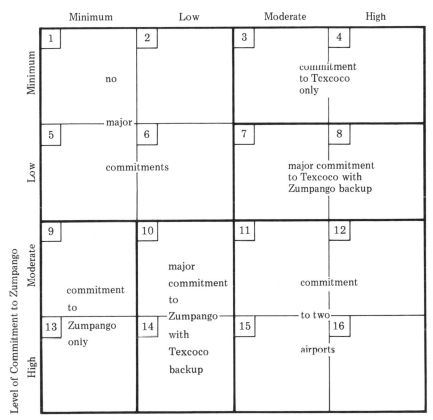

Figure 23.4   The 16 nominal alternatives for 1971.

—High: Build a new runway and passenger facilities, improve the airport access, in short, build a totally new airport at Texcoco.

Similarly, for Zumpango, we defined the commitment levels:

—Minimum: At most, buy land at Zumpango
—Low: Buy land, build one jet runway and very modest passenger facilities
—Moderate: Buy land, build a first jet runway and plan others, build major passenger facilities and an access road connection to the main Mexico City highway
—High: Build multiple jet runways, major passenger facilities and access roads, that is, a complete new airport at Zumpango.

Critical events that could occur in the period 1971–1975 that would be likely to affect the best strategy in 1975 were identified. These involved safety factors and air disasters, shifts in demand in terms of both passengers and aircraft, technological innovations, changes in citizen attitudes toward the environment, and changes in priorities concerning, for example, national willingness to have government funds used for major airport construction.

For each of the 1971 options, the manner in which the strategy should be altered by 1975 in light of each of the events just named was identified. The purpose of this exercise was to indicate better what the overall impact of a 1971 decision might be. Certain options in 1971 eliminate the possibility of other options in 1975, regardless of the events that occur in the interim.

Objectives
We identified four major objectives that were important in choosing a strategy for airport development. These involved the effectiveness, political consequences, externalities, and flexibility of the various alternatives. The components of the effectiveness are indicated by the six measures of effectiveness covered in the static model. The political consequences of concern were those important to the President, including the political effects that would be felt by the SOP, the SCT, and the Presidencia. Flexibility meant the range of options that would remain open to the government by the second stage of the decision-making process, with whatever alterations he could make contingent on events that might occur. Finally, all other considerations that would be important were lumped together as "externalities." These included the amount of

access roads needed, the distribution of federal expenditures between the Mexico City region and the rest of the country, the distribution of expenditures for airports and other uses, regional development away from central Mexico City, and the national pres-
tige associated with new airport facilities.

First Evaluation of Nominal Alternatives
The sixteen alternatives defined in Figure 23.4 were evaluated in a
series of extensive discussions between the directors of the Department of Airports and of the Center for Computation and Statistics, other staff members in the SOP, and ourselves. A preliminary
evaluation indicated that seven of the sixteen alternatives could be
discarded. Alternative 1 did not provide for maintaining the present service levels due to anticipated increases in demand. Alternatives 7, 8, 11, 12, 15, and 16 were undesirable because a high level
of commitment to Texcoco in 1971 would make it the major airport for the near future and remove the need for simultaneous
construction at Zumpango. Finally, since the location of the new
runway specified by the moderate Texcoco commitment would
require new passenger facilities, there was not much difference
between options 3 and 4, so they were coalesced into alternative
3-4.
    The next stage of the analysis involved having the members of
the SOP rank the remaining broadly defined alternatives on the
attributes of flexibility, political effects, externalities, and effectiveness, as described before. The particular rankings were arrived
at by open discussions, and as such, they represent the consensus
judgment. When some alternatives were "indistinguishable" on a
particular attribute, they were assigned the same ranking. For the
political considerations and externalities, the assessments on the
components were first carried out, and then the overall ranking
for these attributes was established. The ranking of the alternatives
according to effectiveness was provided directly by the results of
the static model.
    The results of the first ranking effort are shown in Table 23.1,
where the smaller numbers represent the better rankings. From
this table it can be seen that alternatives 3-4, 9, 13, and 14 are
each dominated by others on the basis of their overall rankings for
the four measures of effectiveness. Alternative 6, for instance, is
better than alternative 14 in terms of all four measures. Hence

Table 23.1 Preliminary Evaluation of Plausible Presidential Options for 1971 by Rank Order

| Attributes | | Political Effects on | | | | Externalities due to | | | | | |
Alternative	Flexibility	Presidencia	SOP	SCT	Overall	Prestige	Reg. Dev.	Fed. Exp.	Roads	Overall	Effectiveness
2	1	1	8	2	3	4	4	1	1	3	7
3–4*	7	4	5	1	4	1	4	6	3	7	8
5	2	3	6	4	3	3	3	2	1	1	3
6	3	2	7	3	2	3	3	3	1	3	1
9*	4	6	3	6	5	2	2	4	2	2	4
10	5	5	4	5	1	2	2	5	2	4	5
13*	6	8	1	8	7	1	1	6	4	5	2
14*	8	7	2	7	6	1	1	7	4	6	6

*Dominated on overall ranking of four attributes.

Table 23.2 Final Evaluation of Options for 1971

| Attributes | | | | |
Alternative	Flexibility	Political Effects	Externalities	Effectiveness
2	1	4	4	3
5A	2	3	3	2
5B*	4	5	5	4
6	3	1	1	1
10*	5	2	2	1

*Dominated on overall ranking of four attributes

517   23.6 THE DYNAMIC MODEL

alternative 14—and likewise alternatives 3-4, 9, and 13—can be dropped from further consideration. The contending alternatives are those represented by the nominal cases 2, 5, 6, and 10.

Final Analysis of Options

To complete the analysis of the dynamic options it was necessary to define the dominant alternatives more precisely. This was done as follows:

—Alt. 2: At Zumpango, do no more than buy land for an airport. At Texcoco, extend the two main runways and the aircraft apron, construct freight and parking facilities and a new control tower. Do not build any new passenger terminals.
—Alt. 5A: At Zumpango, build one jet runway, some terminal facilities, and a minor access road connection. Buy enough land for a major international airport. At Texcoco, perform only routine maintenance and make safety improvements.
—Alt. 5B: Same as alternative 5A, only buy just enough land for the current Zumpango construction.
—Alt. 6: At Texcoco, extend one runway and make other improvements enumerated in alternative 2. At Zumpango, buy land for a major international airport and construct one runway with some passenger and access facilities.
—Alt. 10: Same implications for Texcoco as alternative 6. At Zumpango, build two jet runways with major passenger facilities and access roads.

These five alternatives were ranked in the manner previously described. The results are given in Table 23.2. Proceeding as before, we can quickly see that alternative 6 dominated 10, and alternatives 2, 5A, and 6 all dominate 5B. Thus the three remaining viable alternatives are 2, 5A, and 6.

The relative advantages of these governmental options were, finally, subjectively weighed by the SOP personnel as follows. Alternative 6 ranks better on effectiveness, externalities, and political considerations than either 2 or 5A. Although it is worse in terms of relative flexibility, it does allow the President to react effectively to all the critical events that might occur between 1971 and 1975, when the second stage of the airport decision could be made. Hence, in the opinion of the members of the SOP working on this problem, alternative 6 was chosen as the best strategy.

23.7 Overall Results

The final recommendation developed from both the static and dynamic analyses was that a phased development should begin at Zumpango, but that no final commitment should be made as to the final size or ultimate impact of this program. Specifically, it was suggested that land be acquired at Zumpango and that a major runway and modest terminal facilities be planned for construction during President Echeverria's term. It was also proposed that he reserve until 1975 or 1976 a more detailed decision on how the airport facilities for Mexico City should be developed.

In a major sense, the process for arriving at this final result was as important as the recommendation itself. Indeed, the analysis revealed many important issues to the staff of the SOP—for example, the importance of flexibility—and changed their original intuitions as to the nature of the optimal solution. Whatever the final decision that will be evolved by the government of Mexico, it can be done with greater awareness of the relative importance of the different attributes and of the dynamic issues.

The formal analysis described in this report was completed in early September 1971. The staff of the SOP then began a planned series of discussions with the Secretary of the SOP, the Secretaries of the SCT and the Presidencia, and the President himself. In November, the study was presented by the SOP to the President. As of January 1972, no decision had been announced.

Acknowledgment

We thank R. Felix, F. J. Jauffred, and F. Dovali R., and the members of their staffs in the Secretaria de Obras Publicas, Howard Raiffa of Harvard University, and Leonard Blackman of M.I.T.— all of whom we had the pleasure of working with on this study.

References

1. de Neufville, R., and J. H. Stafford, *Systems Analysis for Engineers and Managers*, McGraw-Hill Book Co., 1971.

2. Howard, R. A., "The Foundations of Decision Analysis," *IEEE Transaction Systems Science and Cybernetics*, vol. SSC-7, September 1968.

3. ICAO Bulletin, "Safety on Scheduled Traffic," May 1971, pp. 42-44.

4. Ipesa Consultores and the Secretaria de Comunicaciones y Transportes, "Estudio de Amplicacion del Aeropuerto Internacional de la Ciudad de Mexico," Mexico, D.F., October 1970.

5. Keeney, R. L., "A Decision Analysis with Multiple Objectives: the Mexico City Airport," to be published.

6. Keeney, R. L., "Multiplicative Utility Functions," Technical Report 70, Operations Research Center, M.I.T., Cambridge, Mass., 1972.

7. Keeney, R. L., and H. Raiffa, "A Critique of Formal Analysis in Public Decision Making," Chapter 5, this volume.

8. Raiffa, H., *Decision Analysis: Introductory Lectures on Choices Under Uncertainty*, Addison-Wesley Publishing Co., 1968.

9. Schlaifer, R. O., *Analysis of Decisions Under Uncertainty*, McGraw-Hill Book Co., 1969.

10. Secretaria de Obras Publicas, "Aeropuerto Internacional de la Ciudad de Mexico," Mexico, D.F., September 1967.

11. von Neumann, J., and O. Morgenstern, *Theory of Games and Economic Behavior*, 3rd edition, Princeton University Press, Princeton, N. J., 1953. (1st edition, 1944).

12. Wilsey y Ham de Mexico, S.A. de C.V., "Aeropuerto Internacional de la Ciudad de Mexico," Mexico, D.F., July 1967.

List of Contributors

Edward H. Blum is Coordinator of Research and Leader of the Fire Project, New York City–Rand Institute. He also has more general responsibilities at the Institute, including the development of research and staffing priorities and new project development. He assisted in the establishment of the Urban Science and Engineering Program at the State University of New York at Stony Brook, where he holds a part-time appointment as Adjunct Professor of Engineering. He has the B.S. degree in chemical engineering from Carnegie-Mellon University and a doctorate in the same field from Princeton University.

Alfred Blumstein is Professor, School of Public and Urban Affairs and Director, Urban Systems Institute, Carnegie–Mellon University. He became involved in the work reported in Chapter 16 during his employment at the Institute for Defense Analyses, where one of his assignments was Director of the Science and Technology Task Force of the President's Commission on Law Enforcement and the Administration of Justice. Mr. Blumstein has an undergraduate degree in engineering physics from Cornell University, an M.A. in statistics from the University of Buffalo, and a doctorate in operations research from Cornell University.

Jan M. Chaiken is Police Studies Leader at the New York City–Rand Institute. As a researcher in a study sponsored by the U. S. Department of Housing and Urban Development, he has become particularly interested in the common features and differences in the deployment of various municipal services. He has an undergraduate degree in physics from Carnegie–Mellon University and a doctorate in mathematics from the Massachusetts Institute of Technology.

Edward W. Cushen is chief, Technical Analysis Division, Institute for Applied Technology, National Bureau of Standards. His group has displayed initiative in developing working relationships with local and regional public agencies. Before joining the National Bureau of Standards in 1964, Mr. Cushen worked at the Institute for Defense Analyses and served on the operations research faculty of Case Institute of Technology. He has a B.A. in mathematics from Western Maryland College and a doctorate in logic and metaphysics from the University of Edinburgh.

Richard de Neufville is Associate Professor of Civil Engineering and Director, Civil Engineering Systems Laboratory, Massachusetts Institute of Technology. He is interested in the systems analysis of transportation problems, especially in the area of airport planning and design. The work reported in Chapter 23 was performed as a consultant to the Ministry of Public Works (Secretaria de Obras Publicas) of Mexico. Mr. de Neufville served as a White House Fellow assigned to Robert McNamara in 1965 and 1966. He has S.B., S.M., and Ph.D. degrees in civil engineering from M.I.T.

Alvin W. Drake is Associate Director of the Operations Research Center and Associate Professor of Electrical Engineering at the Massachusetts Institute of Technology. His professional interests include public administration and probabilistic models. As thesis supervisor, he assisted with work reported in several chapters of this volume. Mr. Drake is the author of *Fundamentals of Applied Probability Theory* (McGraw-Hill Publishing Co.). He did his undergraduate and graduate work in electrical engineering at M.I.T.

Howard M. Ellis is President, Ellis and Company, a firm that provides consulting services in the area of environmental management. He also is an Adjunct Assistant Professor and teaches decision analysis at Baruch College of the City University of New York. He has testified before several air pollution regulatory agencies on the development of sane pollution emission standards. Mr. Ellis has an undergraduate degree in electrical engineering from the Massachusetts Institute of Technology and M.B.A. and doctoral degrees from the Harvard Business School.

Martin L. Ernst is Vice-President of Arthur D. Little, Inc., a consulting firm in Cambridge, Massachusetts, where he directs the Management Sciences Division. He is responsible for professional activities in the areas of operations research, systems analysis, and computer systems design in consulting assignments for private industry and for federal, state, and local government agencies. Mr. Ernst obtained his B.S. degree in physics from the Massachusetts Institute of Technology.

Joseph Ferreira, Jr., is a staff member of the Operations Research Center and an Assistant Professor of Operations Research and Urban Studies at the Massachusetts Institute of Technology. He served as a staff member of the U. S. Department of Transportation's Federal Automobile Insurance and Compensation Study. His teaching work at M.I.T. is in the areas of probability theory, data analysis, and the analysis of public systems. He did his S.B. and S.M. work in electrical engineering and his doctoral work in operations research, all at M.I.T.

Robert N. Grosse is Professor of Health Planning and Director, Interdepartmental Program in Health Planning, at the University of Michigan. From 1966 to 1968, he was Deputy Assistant Secretary for Program Systems, U. S. Department of Health, Education, and Welfare. He has been a consultant to health programs in many nations. Mr. Grosse has an A.B. degree from Columbia College and M.A. and Ph.D. degrees in economics from Harvard University.

Frederick O'R. Hayes is Visiting Lecturer in Political Science and Study of the City, Yale University. He was Director of the Budget, City of New York, from 1966 to 1970. During his tenure in that position, New York City formed its initial relationships with the Rand Corporation and established the New York City–Rand Institute. Mr. Hayes has also served in the U. S. Bureau of the Budget and in the Office of Economic Opportunity. During 1970–1971, he was Occupant, Chair of Urban Management, at the Urban Institute. He has an undergraduate degree from Hamilton College and an M.B.A. and an M.A. (Political Economy and Government) from Harvard University.

John B. Jennings is the Project Leader for Court Studies and an operations research specialist at the New York City–Rand Institute. He is also interested in operational analysis relating to possibilities for decentralized municipal services integrated at the neighborhood level. The blood bank work he reports in this volume was performed as his doctoral dissertation work in operations research at the Massachusetts Institute of Technology. He also has a B.E. degree in electrical engineering from Yale Univeristy and S.M. and E.E. degrees in the same field from M.I.T.

Ralph L. Keeney is a staff member of the Operations Research Center and an Assistant Professor of Civil Engineering at the Mas-

sachusetts Institute of Technology. He recently developed the
M.I.T. graduate subject Analysis of Public Systems, and he is interested in the theory and practice of decision analysis, a field in
which he has consulting experience with public agencies. After an
undergraduate program in engineering at the University of California at Los Angeles, he received the S.M. and E.E. degrees in
electrical engineering and the doctorate in operations research at
M.I.T.

Richard C. Larson is an Assistant Professor at the Massachusetts
Institute of Technology with a joint appointment in the Department of Electrical Engineering and the Department of Urban Studies and Planning. He has served as a consultant to many agencies,
including the Institute for Defense Analyses and the New York
City-Rand Institute, in matters related to the analysis of the criminal justice system. His book *Urban Police Patrol Analysis* was
published by the M.I.T. Press in 1972. IIis undergraduate and doctoral work were in the Department of Electrical Engineering at
M.I.T.

John D.C. Little is Professor of Operations Research and Management and Director, Operations Research Center, at the Massachusetts'Institute of Technology. He is the author of many fundamental works in the field of operations research. In the area of
citizen feedback, he served as a consultant to the Governor of
Puerto Rico and he was involved in a service feedback system
study for the state of Massachusetts. Mr. Little has S.B. and Ph.D.
degrees in physics from M.I.T.

David H. Marks is an Assistant Professor in the Water Resources
Division, Department of Civil Engineering, Massachusetts Institute
of Technology. He is also associated with the Operations Research
Center, the Civil Engineering Systems Laboratory, and the Urban
Systems Laboratory. He was formerly employed with the U. S.
Public Health Service study of water quality management for the
Delaware Estuary. He has S.B. and S.M. degrees in civil engineering
from Cornell University and a doctorate in environmental engi-
neering from Johns Hopkins University.

Charles C. McBride is a staff member at the Institute for Defense
Analyses. His projects there have included work with a postal sys-

tems study concerning the development of evaluation criteria for capital investment and with the Science and Technology Task Force of the President's Commission on Law Enforcement and the Administration of Justice. He has the S.B. and S.M. degrees in electrical engineering from M.I.T.

Philip M. Morse is Professor Emeritus in the Department of Physics at the Massachusetts Institute of Technology. He was the founder of both the Operations Research Center and the Computation Center at M.I.T. and served as director of both centers. He is the author of books in several fields including acoustics, library analysis, operations research, theoretical physics, and thermodynamics. He did his undergraduate work in physics at Case Institute of Technology and received his doctorate in physics from Princeton University.

Amedeo R. Odoni is an Assistant Professor in the Department of Aeronautics and Astronautics at the Massachusetts Institute of Technology. He works with the Flight Transportation Laboratory and has general interests in applications of operations research to public systems. He is one of the faculty members who recently developed an M.I.T. graduate subject Analysis of Urban Service Systems. Mr. Odoni has B.S., M.S., and Ph.D. degrees, all in electrical engineering, from M.I.T.

Robert M. Oliver is Professor of Operations Research and Engineering Science at the University of California, Berkeley. He has a continuing interest in university planning, and he has worked closely with the Berkeley administration for several years. He teaches subjects in operations research, applied mathematics, and computer science. He has an S.B. degree in physics and a doctorate in physics and operations research from the Massachusetts Institute of Technology. He has also studied mathematics and economics as a Fulbright Scholar at the University of London.

Howard Raiffa is a member of the teaching faculties of the Harvard Business School, Department of Economics, and the Kennedy Program in Public Policy. He holds the Frank P. Ramsey Chair in Managerial Economics. Some of his publications are the books *Games and Decisions* (with Luce), *Applied Statistical Decision*

Theory (with Schlaifer), *Introduction to Statistical Decision Theory* (with Pratt and Schlaifer), and *Decision Analysis*. He obtained his doctorate in mathematics at the University of Michigan.

Reginald W. Revans is Scientific Advisor at the Fondation Industrie-Université in Brussels. His interest in operational research developed from his responsibilities for certain civilian emergency services in London during the Second World War. The work described in Chapter 21 was performed with three graduate students while Mr. Revans was Professor of Industrial Management at the University of Manchester. He studied at the Universities of London and Michigan and at Cambridge University and received the doctorate in astrophysics from the latter.

Chandler H. Stevens is Professor of Urban Environmental Studies, Rensselaer Polytechnic Institute. He has been an independent member of the Massachusetts House of Representatives, Visiting Social Scientist at the Massachusetts Institute of Technology's Center for International Studies, and Science Advisor to the Governor of Puerto Rico. He is interested in the interface between citizens and their governments. Mr. Stevens has an undergraduate degree in electrical engineering from the Georgia Institute of Technology and a doctorate in economics from M.I.T.

Keith A. Stevenson is a doctoral candidate in operations research at the Massachusetts Institute of Technology and a consultant to the New York City–Rand Institute. He is interested in urban emergency services. He has degrees in engineering from the University of Cape Town, South Africa, in economics from Trinity College, Oxford, and an S.M. degree in electrical engineering from M.I.T.

Peter L. Szanton directed the Rand Corporation team during its initial work with the government of New York City and became the first president of the New York City–Rand Institute, a position he left in 1970. He is presently a Fellow of the Institute of Politics at Harvard University. Mr. Szanton previously worked in the U. S. Bureau of the Budget and with the President's Task Force on Government Reorganization (1967). After an undergraduate program at Harvard, he continued at the same institution and received an M.A. and an LL.B in history.

Peter F. Tropp is employed in the Office of Administration in the New York City Mayor's Office. He has held positions in Puerto Rico with the Planning Board and the Office of the Governor. For the work reported in Chapter 20, Mr. Tropp was a Research Associate at the Operations Research Center at the Massachusetts Institute of Technology. He has an undergraduate degree in government from Dartmouth College and an M.G.A. degree from the Fels Institute of Local and State Government, University of Pennsylvania.

Index

DATE DUE